BRITISH NOTES
Specialists in Banknotes of the British Isles
Pam West

Top prices paid for single items and collections

British Notes • PO Box 257 • Sutton • Surrey • SM3 9WW
Tel: 020 8641 3224
www.britishnotes.co.uk
Email: pam@britishnotes.co.uk

Life Member IBNS No. 79

PAPER MONEY OF SCOTLAND

Including Polymer

Volume I

Jonathan Callaway
and
David Murphy

Bank of Scotland £100 composite essay for the 1995 Tercentenary issue

This book is dedicated to the memory of the late Professor Iain Stevenson

Pam West
Editor / Publisher

First Edition Published 2018

British Library Cataloguing in Publication Data
Callaway, Jonathan and Murphy, David
Paper Money of Scotland Volume I
Scottish Banknotes / Paper Money - Collector's Guide

ISBN   978-0-9543457-6-1

Front Cover Illustration:
   Union Bank of Scotland £10 1935

Back Cover Illustrations:
   Bank of Scotland £20 1969
   Clydesdale Bank £100 1947

Royal Arms on British Linen notes

© Jonathan Callaway and David Murphy

Edited / Published by Pam West, PO Box 257, Sutton, Surrey SM3 9WW

Printed by Melita Press Malta

PAPER MONEY OF SCOTLAND

CONTENTS

	Page
Contents	3 & 595
Foreword	9
Preface	11
Acknowledgements	12
Introduction	
Historical Background	14
Guidance for Collectors	27

Volume I
BANK OF SCOTLAND GROUP

	Catalogue Reference	
Bank of Scotland 1695 *to date*	BA	38

Leading Constituent Banks

British Linen Bank 1746 *to* 1970	BL	235
Caledonian Bank, Inverness 1838 *to* 1907	CA	322
Union Bank of Scotland 1843 *to* 1956	UB	339
Bank of Scotland - Other Constituent Banks		407
Banking Company **in** Aberdeen (in) 1767 *to* 1849 (to Union Bank)	BC	407
Central Bank of Scotland, Perth 1834 *to* 1868 (to Bank of Scotland)	CE	414
Sir William Forbes, James Hunter & Company, Edinburgh 1773 *to* 1838 (to Union Bank)	FH	419
Glasgow Bank Company 1809 *to* 1836 (to Union Bank)	GB	428
Glasgow & Ship Bank 1836 *to* 1843 (to Union Bank)	GS	431
Glasgow Union Banking Company 1830 *to* 1843 (to Union Bank)	GU	432
Hunters & Company, Ayr 1773 *to* 1843 (to Union Bank)	HU	434
Kilmarnock Bank 1802 *to* 1821 (to Union Bank)	KB	437
Paisley Banking Company 1783 *to* 1837 (to British Linen)	PA	439
Paisley Union Banking Company 1788 *to* 1838 (to Union Bank)	PU	443
Perth Banking Company 1787 *to* 1857 (to Union Bank)	PB	446
Perth United Company 1766 *to* 1787 (to Union Bank)	PE	455
Ship Bank, Glasgow 1750 *to* 1836 (to Union Bank)	SH	457
Thistle Bank, Glasgow 1761 *to* 1836 (to Union Bank)	TH	463

Contents

CLYDESDALE BANK GROUP

	Catalogue Reference	Page
Clydesdale Bank 1838 *to date* *(including* Clydesdale & North of Scotland Bank 506*)*	CL	467
Index		586 & 1137

Volume II

Contents		595 & 3
Leading Constituent Banks		
North of Scotland Bank, Aberdeen 1836 *to* 1950 *(including* North of Scotland & Town & County Bank 623*)*	NS	601
Town & County Bank, Aberdeen 1825 *to* 1908	TC	655
Clydesdale Bank - Other Constituent Banks		672
Dundee Commercial Bank (2) 1825 *to* 1838 (to Eastern Bank)	DC	672
Eastern Bank of Scotland, Dundee 1838 *to* 1863 (to Clydesdale Bank)	EB	675
Edinburgh & Glasgow Bank 1844 *to* 1858 (to Clydesdale Bank)	EG	681
Edinburgh & Leith Bank 1839 *to* 1844 (to Clydesdale Bank)	EL	684
Glasgow Joint Stock Banking Company 1840 *to* 1844 (to Clydesdale Bank)	GJ	687
Greenock Union Bank 1840 *to* 1844 (to Clydesdale Bank)	GR	688
Southern Bank of Scotland, Dumfries 1838 *to* 1840 (to Edinburgh & Leith Bank)	SO	689

ROYAL BANK OF SCOTLAND GROUP

Royal Bank of Scotland 1727 *to date*	RB	691
Leading Constituent Banks		
Commercial Bank of Scotland 1810 *to* 1959	CO	826
National Bank of Scotland 1825 *to* 1959	NA	899
National Commercial Bank of Scotland 1959 *to* 1969	NC	949
Royal Bank of Scotland - Other Constituent Banks		958
Aberdeen Commercial Banking Company 1778 *to* 1833 (to National Bank)	AC	958
Arbroath Banking Company 1825 *to* 1844 (to Commercial Bank)	AR	959
Caithness Banking Company, Wick 1812 *to* 1825 (to Commercial Bank)	CN	962
Dundee Banking Company 1763 *to* 1864 (to Royal Bank)	DB	963
Dundee New Bank 1802 *to* 1838 (to Dundee Banking Company)	DN	973
Perth Union Bank 1810 *to* 1836 (to National Bank)	PH	975

Contents

THE LOST BANKS OF SCOTLAND

	Catalogue Reference	Page
The Lost Banks of Scotland		976
Aberdeen Banking **of** Company (of) 1749 *to* 1753	AB	976
Ayrshire Banking Company, Ayr 1830 *to* 1845 (to Western Bank)	AY	978
John Belch & Company, Stirling 1804 *to* 1806	JB	980
Berwick Bank (1): Surtees, Burdon & Company 1788 *to* 1803	BS	980
Berwick Bank (2): Mowbray, Hollingworth, & Company 1803 *to* 1820	BB	983
Berwick & Kelso Bank: Mowbray, Hollingworth, & Company 1808 *to* c.1815	BK	984
Campbell Thomson & Company, Stirling 1786 *to* 1793	CT	985
City Banking Company of Glasgow 1836	CB	985
City of Glasgow Bank 1839 *to* 1878	CG	987
Bank of Mona, Isle of Man 1849 *to* 1878 (branch of City of Glasgow Bank)	BM	998
Cupar Banking Company 1802 *to* 1811	CU	1001
Douglas Heron & Company, Ayr 1769 *to* 1773	DH	1001
Dumfries Bank 1766 *to* 1772 (to Douglas Heron & Company)	DM	1003
Dumfries Banking Company c.1800 *to* 1802	DS	1003
Dumfries Commercial Bank 1804 *to* 1808	DF	1004
Dundee Commercial Bank (1): 1792 *to* 1802	DD	1007
Dundee Union Bank 1809 *to* 1844 (to Western Bank)	DU	1008
East Lothian Banking Company, Dunbar 1810 *to* 1822	EA	1011
Falkirk Banking Company 1782 *to* 1825	FB	1014
Falkirk Union Banking Company 1803 *to* 1816	FU	1015
Farming Banking Company at Kincardine 1782	FA	1017
Fife Banking Company, Cupar 1802 *to* 1825	FI	1018
Galloway Banking Company, Castle Douglas 1806 *to* 1821	GL	1020
Gartmore Banking Company 1791	GM	1022
Gibson, Balfour, Aitken & Company, Bannockburn 1772	GI	1023
Glasgow Arms Bank 1750 *to* 1793	GA	1024
Glasgow Banking Company (Glasgow Bank/Bank of Glasgow) 1843	GC	1027
Greenock Bank Company 1785 *to* 1843 (to Western Bank)	GN	1028
Greenock Commercial Banking Company 1825	GK	1033

Vignette of Perth on CE 3c

Contents

	Catalogue Reference	Page
James Inglis & Company 1805 *to* 1834	IB	1034
Leith Banking Company 1793 *to* 1842	LB	1035
John McAdam & Company, Ayr 1763 *to* 1771 (to Douglas Heron & Company)	JM	1049
Merchant Banking Company of Glasgow 1769 *to* 1793	MB	1050
Metropolitan Bank of Scotland, Edinburgh 1834	ME	1051
Middlemass, Hay & Company, Dunbar 1789	MH	1051
Montrose Banking Company 1814 *to* 1829 (to Western Bank)	MO	1052
North British Bank, Edinburgh 1844	NB	1055
Northumberland Bank, Berwick 1804 *to* 1821	NO	1056
Paisley Commercial Banking Company 1838 *to* 1844 (to Western Bank)	PC	1057
Perth General Bank 1767 *to* c.1772	PG	1058
Ramsays, Bonars & Company, Edinburgh 1738 *to* 1837	RA	1059
Renfrewshire Banking Company, Greenock 1802 *to* 1842	RE	1061
Shetland Bank, Lerwick 1821 *to* 1842	SL	1064
Stirling Banking Company 1777 *to* 1826	ST	1065
Stirling Merchant Banking Company 1784 *to* 1805	SM	1067
Stirlingshire Banking Company 1831	SB	1069
Andrew, George & Andrew Thomson, Glasgow 1785 *to* 1793	AT	1070
Tweed Bank, Berwick 1813 *to* 1841	TW	1071
Western Bank of Scotland, Glasgow 1832 *to* 1857	WE	1075

Non-Issuers (pre 1844 only)   1079

Vignette of Victoria and scenes of Dundee and Edinburgh on EB 5 Colour Trial

Contents

PRIVATE NON-BANK ISSUES

	Catalogue Reference	Page
Private Non-Bank Issues		**1082**
Abbey Bank of Industry, Paisley 1871	PR	1083
William Alexander of Menstrie (Alexander Humphrys) 1840s	PR	1084
Alloa Glass Works Company 1817	PR	1085
David Bain, Glasgow 1884	PR	1085
Balgonie Iron Works 1807	PR	1086
Ballindalloch Works, Balfron 1829 *to* 1830	PR	1087
Bank of Dundreary, Glasgow 1863	PR	1088
Bank of Economy, Edinburgh	PR	1088
Bank of Elegance, Edinburgh 1823	PR	1089
Bank of Poyais 1823	PR	1090
Campbell, Richmond & Company, Glasgow 1845	PR	1090
Cargill MacDuff & Company, Dunkeld 1764	PR	1091
Carron Company 1797	PR	1091
Catrine Works 1815	PR	1093
Chapel Hill Bank	PR	1093
Clackmannan Colliery 1797	PR	1094
Commercial Bank of New Mill Moor, Edinburgh	PR	1095
Company of the Bank of Aberdeen 1796 *to* 1798	PR	1096
Craig & Simpson, Glasgow 1827 *to* 1829	PR	1096
John, James & George Lindsay Craufurd 1835	PR	1098
John Craw & Company, Edinburgh 1760	PR	1099
Darien Company 1696 *to* 1699	PR	1099
Deanston Cotton Mill 1803	PR	1100
William Duncan, Dumfries 1770	PR	1101
Ekopia Resource Exchange Limited, Findhorn 2002 *to* date	PR	1101
Falkirk 1761	PR	1105
Alexander Fleming & Company, Kirkliston 1764	PR	1106
Glasgow Union Bank 1824 *to* 1826	PR	1106
Hawick Pound 2010	PR	1107
George Keller & Company, Glasgow 1764 *to* 1765	PR	1108
William Kirkwood & Company, Glasgow 1829	PR	1109
Lipton's, Glasgow 1877	PR	1110

Contents

	Catalogue Reference	Page
John Maberly & Company, Aberdeen 1818 *to* 1832	P R	1111
Stephen Maberly, Aberdeen c.1817	P R	1114
J Stewart Mackenzie, Stornoway 1823 *to* 1826	P R	1114
Malachi Malagrowther, Edinburgh 1846	P R	1115
Daniel M'Funn, Duncan Buchanan & Company, Glasgow 1765	P R	1116
Mason Barrowman Company, Glasgow 1764	P R	1117
Montrose 1832	P R	1118
Morris & Company, Glasgow 1828	P R	1118
Morris, Kirkwood, Bland & Company, Glasgow	P R	1119
Mutual Exchange Deposit, Discount & Loan Company, Paisley	P R	1119
New Lanark Mills 1815 *to* 1821	P R	1120
John Richmond & Sons, Glasgow 1834	P R	1120
Douglas Robertson & Company, Perth 1764	P R	1121
R Robertson Junior & Company, Perth 1765 *to* 1766	P R	1122
Royal Bank of Fashion, Dundee 1820s	P R	1123
Scottish Banking Company 1873	P R	1123
Shortbridge, Scot & Company, Leith 1812	P R	1125
James Smiton, Edinburgh 1764	PR	1125
Prince Charles Edward Stuart 1746	P R	1126
War Department / Prisoners of War camps 1943 *to* 1947	P R	1127
Andrew Whitecock, Duncan Dick & Company, Glasgow 1765	P R	1129

Banking Ephemera 1130

Bibliography 1132

Index 1137 & 586

British Linen Composite Essay reverse of 1937

PAPER MONEY OF SCOTLAND

Foreword

I first encountered Scottish currency notes when, at the age of eight, I accompanied my father, a circuit manager, on his daily rounds during the school holidays. A glimpse in his wallet revealed alongside the rather dull Bank of England notes, a fascinating collection of printed money which caught my youthful imagination. Most were the blue and acid yellow issues of the Royal Bank of Scotland where my father banked featuring a bewigged gentleman (whom I later learned to be King George II), but these were leavened by the shipbuilding scenes from the Clydesdale Bank, the iconic view of the Forth Bridge from the National Commercial, and the strangely crude but compelling imagery of the Bank of Scotland. Even more interesting were the austere yet impressive blue and pink emissions of the British Linen Bank. What did money have to do with textiles? Even more rarely did notes appear from other banks, the vivid portraits, street scenes and industrial views from the National, Commercial and Union banks.

My father explained that while England only had one note issue, Scotland had several and this should be a source of pride. Most of the notes I saw were one pound denominations and I suspect few Scots saw any higher values. Nevertheless, once a year, I would accompany my uncle, a skilled motor mechanic, as he visited his bank to withdraw four or five crisp £100 notes which he allowed me to study and hold as we made our way to the local motor dealers where they would be exchanged for his annual new car. The sight of a "hunnerd" of the 1950s still gives me a Proustian jolt of the smell of fresh paint, leather, metal and rubber that conjures up the products of Ford and Austin.

Later still, when I was earning a modest salary working in the local mental hospital during the summer holidays, my father took me to the long defunct Wishaw West Cross branch of the RBS. This was a solidly stone built typically Scottish "Bank House" with obscured window glass (a feature shared with pubs interestingly enough), a long polished mahogany counter surmounted by a fearsome metal grille and an air of Presbyterian gloom. There I was ushered into the presence of the Manager, a formidable yet kindly figure, who took my details, graciously accepted my proffered £15 and exchanged the notes for a receipt and a book containing three cheques for which I was charged an additional sixpence. He shook my hand, addressing me as "Sir" (the first time I had ever been so called) and reminded me that I must never EVER write a cheque against funds which I did not have.

Since then I have developed an abiding interest in Scottish bank notes. These oblongs of printed paper are both tangible links with home for an exiled Scot and for an academic with interest in printing and communication history represent a body of study material unequalled anywhere in the world. Many Scottish banknotes are beautiful works of art: they are often innovative (the first multicolour printing or electronic sorting marks, for example) while their iconic imagery of thistles, city and country views and portraits conjure up a rich and diverse history.

When I first seriously started to collect Scottish banknotes over forty years ago I used James Douglas's Scottish Banknotes as a guide. For its time it was a remarkable achievement and remains a very useful handbook. Other books have been published since and there have been many new discoveries and interpretations. The numbers of collectors have increased not least due to the energetic activities of the Banknote Society of Scotland. The time had come for a thorough new look at the entire Scottish series based on intensive study in the archives, published literature and the notes themselves, not only in their issued form but from the essays, trials, artwork and proofs many of which have only recently turned up. Jonathan Callaway and David Murphy have risen superbly to this challenge. They have gained unprecedented access to bank archives to solve many questions about how the notes were issued and used. They have indefatigably sifted note registers, board minutes and memoranda to reconstruct numbering and issue dates. They have made important and resonant discoveries, not least the "lady signatories" who signed National Bank notes at the close of World War One. They have scoured auction catalogues and dealers' stocks to document what exists for collectors to find. While new discoveries will continue to be made it is hard to imagine that their careful and exhaustive work will be superceded for many years. This is now the standard work of reference for the entire field of Scottish paper (and polymer) currency, not only a worthy successor to Douglas but a model of research and presentation that sets a new level for notaphilic scholarship. Jonathan and Dave, along with their estimable publishers Pam and Pete West, are owed a great debt of gratitude from collectors of Scottish notes as well as economic historians for making the fruits of their research so clearly and attractively accessible in this fine book.

The late Professor Iain Stevenson FRGS FRPSL
Emeritus Professor of Publishing
UCL Centre for Publishing
University College London

A De La Rue essay featuring the portrait of a rather too fearsome bank manager

PAPER MONEY OF SCOTLAND

Jonathan Callaway and Dave Murphy

Preface

This book has had a long gestation. The authors have both been researching aspects of Scottish banknotes for many years and Dave in particular has spent many years wading through the archives of the Bank of Scotland and the Royal Bank – he has recorded several hundred visits to both over a ten year period during which he read some 125,000 pages of minute books and other records! Jonathan merely concentrated on the writing – an easy task in comparison. Together we managed to access the remaining archive material held by the Clydesdale Bank. That yielded another 40+ minute books of the North of Scotland Bank, a discovery which seemed to come as a surprise to the bank itself.

Our researches have been driven by our joint interest in the long and fascinating history of Scottish banking and the many forms of paper money issued in Scotland since 1695. Gradually we came to the conclusion that a comprehensive successor was needed to James Douglas's pioneering work, first published over forty years ago. We very much hope our readers will agree this has been a worthwhile enterprise.

We have worked hard to pull together all the information in this catalogue, relying firstly on the archives of the major banks and secondly on the evidence provided by surviving notes in private and institutional collections. Records we have studied include ancient handwritten ledgers, mutilated note registers, board minutes, actual note registers where these have survived, and much more. Too often, however, these records do not go beyond the mechanics of note issuance and we have had to turn to the notes themselves and the proofs and essays left behind by the printers and engravers who produced them, to learn more about how the designs evolved. The banks' records were clearly kept for their own benefit, not collectors'.

The research effort has however brought much pleasure to both of us but we did create a problem by unearthing so much new information that by far the most difficult decision became what we had to leave out. If everything had been included this would have become far more than the two volumes now before you. The hardest work was organising and presenting everything in a consistent and accessible way. After all, we wanted to cover the histories and note issues of over eighty banks and more than fifty private non-bank issuers. A final challenge was to agree pricing in constantly changing market conditions.

We can also be sure there is yet more out there still to be discovered and we leave it to our readers to inform us of the inevitable omissions and inaccuracies in the hope that one day a Second Edition can incorporate any necessary changes to bring our work closer to completion.

Putney / Dalkeith, January 2018

Acknowledgements

Many individuals and organisations have contributed to our research effort and helped us to bring this project to a successful conclusion. First and foremost we would like to thank those who have given us material assistance including, in strict alphabetic order:

Keith Austin	Richie Fraser	Claire Lobel (Coincraft)
Andrew Balsillie	Garry/Numismondo.net	Andrew Macmillan
William Barratt	Alistair Gibb	John McBeath
Barry Boswell	Ian Gibson	Billy McCreath
Jim Boyd	Ian Gradon	Andy McLoughlin
Ronnie Breingan	Robert Hafenbradl	John Martin
Michael Brill	Iain Harrison	Colin Meikle
Andrew Carmichael	John Harvey	James Morton (Morton & Eden)
Les Chapman	Martin Hepworth	Nathan Nelson
The late Robert Cormack	Eric Hodge	Chris Nield
Mike Crouch	Bob Hudson	Dave Pointon
Walter Elliot	Fergus Hutchison	Roy Robertson
Harm van Essen	Andrew Jamieson	The late Prof Iain Stevenson
Geoff Ewing	Tim Lawes	Peter Symes
Ian Fraser	Robert Letham	David Twynholm

Plus many members of the Banknote Society of Scotland and those who prefer to remain anonymous.

A number of institutions have assisted us including:

- Aberdeen Art Gallery & Museum (Judith Stones)
- British Library (Paul Skinner & Richard Morel)
- British Museum (Katie Eagleton, Tom Hockenhull & Helen Wang)
- De La Rue plc (Arthur Gearing)
- Dundee City Council (The McManus, Dundee's Art Gallery & Museum)
            (Sally McIntosh & Carly Cooper)
- Dumfries Museum (Joanne Turner)
- The Hunterian, University of Glasgow (Dr Donal Bateson)
- National Museum of Scotland (George Dalgleish, Lyndsay McGill & Margaret Wilson)
- Royal Philatelic Society London (Mark Copley, Archivist)
- Smith Art Gallery & Museum, Stirling (Michael McGinnis)
- West Highland Museum (Fiona Marwick)

We thank in particular all the fantastic and ever helpful staff in the archives of the Royal Bank of Scotland (Alison Turton, Ruth Reed, Susan Patterson, Laura Yeoman, Lynn Crawford and also Mary McConnachie, Patricia Wilson and Jennifer Jack); the Bank of Scotland/Lloyds Banking Group (Alan Cameron, Helen Redmond-Cooper, Seonaid McDonald, Reto Tschan, Sian Yates, Amanda Noble, Hania Smerecka, Rosemary Moodie and David Lauder); and the Clydesdale Bank (Derek Walker and Irene Swankie) who have all given us unstinting support during the years of research behind this catalogue and permision to use many images of notes in their archives.

Special mention is due to the auction teams at Spink (Barnaby Faull, Andrew Pattison, Monica Kruber and Thomasina Smith) and DNW (Chris Webb and Mike O'Grady) who have both been so helpful to us in our quest for scans and information.

We acknowledge the pioneering work by James Douglas whose 1975 catalogue *Scottish Banknotes* encouraged so many to turn to collecting and studying Scottish paper money. The follow-up catalogues overseen and published by Trevor Jones, and his own ever helpful input, are also gratefully acknowledged.

A special debt of thanks is due to Colin and Simon Narbeth who arranged for the digitisation of the extensive archive of photographic negatives accumulated by James Douglas and bequeathed to Colin. In many cases these images are the only record some notes ever existed.

We must of course also thank our editor/publisher Pam West (British Notes), whose drive and commitment has kept us (mostly) on the straight and narrow! Pam's husband Pete has done a fantastic job of type setting, layout and proof reading the manuscripts and correcting the many errors which crept in. All remaining errors and omissions are very definitely the authors' responsibility.

And finally, both authors would like to acknowledge the support and infinite patience of their better halves, Hilary (Callaway) and Joyce (Murphy).

PR 271 Pull of intended issue by Bonnie Prince Charlie (enlarged)

Introduction

Historical Background

The Origins of Scottish Banking

Before 1695 and the creation of the Bank of Scotland by an Act of the Scottish Parliament no formal banking system existed in Scotland. Commercial transactions between merchants and the sale and purchase of land were evidenced by bills of exchange or legal agreements known as 'bonds'. Smaller transactions required only coin of the realm, in the form of gold, silver and copper. Given the small size of the economy many of these coins were foreign, having entered circulation as a result of trade with England or the Continent. Due to trade imbalances there was a constant shortage of coin of any sort.

Borrowing and lending was uncommon as such capital as existed was usually in the form of land and property rather than cash. Any lenders were likely to be wealthy merchants or landowners though there was a small band of goldsmiths active in Edinburgh in the mid-17th century. These also acted as money changers and lenders while on a much smaller scale than in London or other Continental centres such as Amsterdam or Hamburg. The Scottish economy was weak and poorly developed and things only gradually began to change with some modest growth in trade with the Baltic. The dramatic growth of the Virginia tobacco trade began only after the Act of Union in 1707.

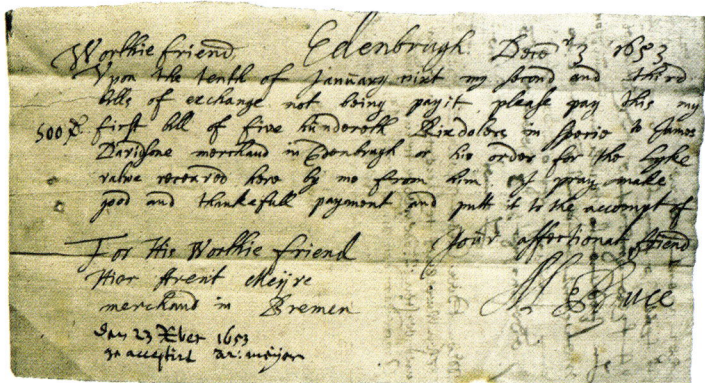

Bill 1653 Edinburgh
This bill of exchange is believed to be the oldest surviving Scottish bill although its current whereabouts are unknown. It was drawn by S L Bruce on the Bremen merchant Arendt Meijre requesting him to pay the Edinburgh merchant James Davidsone or his order 500 Rixdolors in specie for like value received.

Gradually the need grew for a better system of exchanging and remitting money as the usual bills on London were costing too much in commissions and discounts to leave sufficient profit in the Scottish merchants' hands. The decisive moves were made in London by a small group of expatriate Scottish businessmen who had moved there in the final years of the 17th century. As a result of their efforts two enterprises were established in 1695 under Acts of the Scottish Parliament, the Bank of Scotland and the Company of Scotland Trading to Africa and the Indies, known as the Darien Company. The leading campaigner behind the Darien Company was William Paterson, a Scot who had also been a prime force in establishing the Bank of England in 1694, while the creation of the Bank of Scotland was led mainly by the Englishman John Holland who became the Bank's first Governor. The Bank was intended from the outset to be a trading bank and it took on no state funding role in contrast to the Bank of England.

The 'Scotch System of Banking' & the three 'Chartered Banks'

Despite opposition from the Darien Company which also briefly started a banking business, the Bank of Scotland was able to establish itself and overcome some precarious moments in its early years. The Bank watched the decline and catastrophic fall of the Darien Company in the early years of the new century and the subsequent Act of Union in 1707 when the Scots and English parliaments were combined. The Bank had been granted a monopoly which expired in 1717 but did not seek its renewal. Ten years later the Royal Bank of Scotland was established by Royal Charter. The capital used to set up the Royal Bank came in part from the Equivalent Company, created to administer the compensation monies paid to Scotland for taking on a share of England's national debt following the union of the two parliaments.

A fierce rivalry developed between the two banks and continued for many years. This included the use of tactics such as 'note picking', the gathering and presenting of large quantities of the rival bank's notes in the hope that they were unable to honour them on demand. This led to the introduction of 'Option Notes' where payment could be delayed for up to six months, a device used not only by the two dominant banks but also some of the smaller ones which had been set up in their shadow. Option notes were banned in 1765. Eventually it became clear that the market was sufficient in size to accommodate both major banks. Indeed, a third one joined them in 1746 in the unlikely guise of the British Linen Company. This firm had also been incorporated by Royal Charter and had started life as a linen trader and manufacturer. The proprietors found banking more lucrative and within twenty years had given up their other activities. The name was not changed to include the word 'bank' (on the notes, at least) until 1906.

These three institutions, known as the 'Chartered Banks' (or 'Public Banks'), came to dominate Scottish banking in the 18th century. All three were based in Edinburgh and as Glasgow developed as a commercial centre on the back of extensive trading links with the British Empire merchants in that city tried to counter this by setting up their own banks. The most famous of these was the Ship Bank of Dunlop, Houston & Company, later to be absorbed into the Union Bank of Scotland. The three Chartered Banks, meanwhile, established a network of branches and agents across Scotland and these soundly established banks with their cautious and prudent business approach soon set Scotland's banking history very noticeably apart from that of England and the rest of the United Kingdom.

Competition to the three Chartered Banks did exist. Initially this was limited to a few provincial banks in towns where they did not operate, but gradually more appeared. They were all private partnerships where each partner had unlimited joint and several legal liability for all the firm's obligations. Unlike in England where six was the limit, there was no restriction on the number of partners. In most cases a partnership agreement (or 'contract of co-partnery') was drawn up setting out the responsibilities of the managing partners ('directors') and senior officials and the terms on which partnership shares could be bought and sold.

An early example of the strength and influence of the three Chartered Banks was seen in 1772 following a serious commercial crisis when Douglas, Heron & Company (the Ayr Bank) collapsed triggering further failures of private banks in Edinburgh and much economic distress across Scotland. The crisis might have been even more serious had the three banks not acted effectively as lenders of last resort by supporting some of the smaller banks who had suffered short term liquidity problems. The willingness of the Edinburgh bankers to act in this way generated much confidence in the stability of the 'Scotch System of Banking' as it came to be called.

Their note issues were accepted without question across the country and while the smaller local banks also issued notes for circulation mainly in their own localities, and indeed occasionally failed, the existence of a strong nationwide network of bank offices enabled Scottish banking to achieve a reputation without rival in the world and underpinned the growth of Scotland's industrial economy in the 18th and 19th centuries. Paper money became preferred to gold or silver coin due to its reliability and convenience. This hard-won reputation was further protected by honouring the notes of the Western Bank of Scotland in 1857 and the City of Glasgow Bank in 1878 after these banks' catastrophic failures. This ensured noteholders and depositors of both banks emerged unscathed. The shareholders carried the full burden of the losses.

The Scottish banking system became a widely admired and copied model and remains an exemplar for some economists who argue for a return to those days of minimal regulation and maximum market-driven self-discipline. Indeed the very lack of a central bank or formal lender of last resort was held to be an essential part of the model's success. This does, however, overlook the occasional interventions by the Bank of England (when so requested) and the concerted support provided by the three Chartered Banks at times of acute stress (albeit acting in self-interest).

The contrast with the state of affairs in England was highlighted by the crisis of 1825 when a large number of small local English banking partnerships failed and the government decided to control their note-issuing activities by banning £1 notes across the whole UK. There was an outcry in Scotland where the £1 note was widely used and popular. Opposition was led by Sir Walter Scott, writing as Malachi Malagrowther, who successfully persuaded the British Government not to ban £1 notes in Scotland. The denomination also survived in Ireland but the episode served to underline the systemic differences, and the relative standing of both banks and bankers, in Scotland and England.

Propaganda note for use in the campaign against the 1845 Scottish Banking Act

Minimal regulation had been imposed prior to 1825. The main example was the 1765 Act banning option notes as well as 'small notes' due to concerns about inflation (though that term was not used or properly understood at that time) and apparent threats to trade and the economy. The Act was entitled '*Act to prevent the inconveniences arising from the present method of issuing notes and bills by banks, banking companies and bankers in that part of Great Britain called Scotland*'. Largely prompted by the chronic shortage of silver coin there had been a proliferation of small notes, often for sums as little as 1 Shilling (1s), issued by shopkeepers, traders and other opportunists with only slender resources. Such notes had evidently been stoking inflation and had certainly threatened to undermine the standing of paper money in general, even that issued by the Chartered Banks.

A formal note exchange between the three Chartered Banks was established in Edinburgh in 1771. The banks had agreed that they would not issue each other's notes and participation by other banks was by invitation only so banks deemed to be unwisely run were excluded. Some smaller banks were initially reluctant to join as their principal source of finance was their note circulation and the note exchange would potentially have curtailed that by returning notes to them for redemption more quickly than they hoped for. This effect served to maintain confidence in the system, a confidence underlined by the concept of unlimited shareholder liability plus the comfort gained from the wide shareholder bases of the Chartered Banks (where by contrast limited shareholder liability had been enshrined from the outset; these companies had been accorded their own legal persona unlike the partnership structure of all other firms). In time, local note exchanges appeared in several other Scottish towns.

A very apt description of the status of Scottish banking in Victorian Britain came courtesy of a parliamentary Commission report prior to the 1844 Banking Act:

'*A system admirably calculated to economise the use of Capital to excite and cherish a spirit of useful Enterprise, and even to promote the moral habits of the people, by the direct inducements which it holds out to the maintenance of a character for industry, integrity and prudence*'.

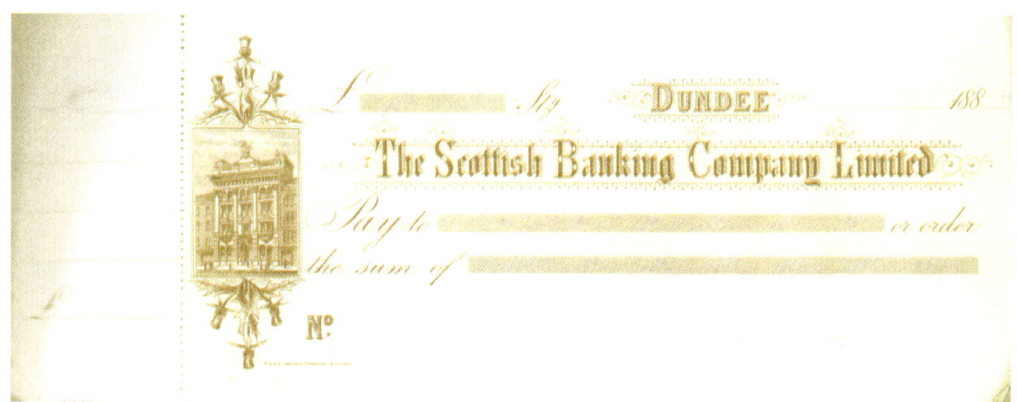

Unissued cheque of the short-lived The Scottish Banking Company Limited

The Napoleonic Wars and the Bank Restriction Act

The Bank Restriction Act, passed in 1797 and renewed annually until 1821 (known as the Suspension Period) prohibited all banks including the Bank of England from meeting their obligations by payment in specie (i.e. gold and silver coins). This combined with wartime exigencies resulted in a shortage of coin and a sharp rise in the price of wheat. Producers sought to grow more and sought credit to achieve this, resulting in at least a dozen new banks being set up in Scotland by 1810. Several more followed by 1825. All were note issuers and even though there were a few failures confidence in the system was not damaged. Further growth of these private banking partnerships was however curtailed by the arrival of a new form of banking company, the joint stock bank.

The Joint Stock Bank Era

The first bank which might properly be described as a joint stock bank was the Commercial Banking Company of Scotland, founded in 1810 with several hundred jointly and severally liable partners, or shareholders, subscribing its £3,000,000 of capital. The bank was granted a Royal Charter in 1831 but by then it had expanded rapidly and established deep roots. The bank was a precursor of the new, well-capitalised banks which would sweep away the older private banks and challenge the three dominant banks. Its sheer scale marked it out from the private banking partnerships hitherto the Chartered Banks' only competitors, although its legal structure was the same. One key difference was that the bank's shares were freely transferable. Such a construction would have been impossible in England at that time due to the limitation of six partners per bank imposed as part of the Bank of England's monopoly.

The Commercial Bank was followed in 1825 by the National Bank of Scotland and the Aberdeen Town & County Bank. That year legislation had made it possible for joint stock companies to assume their own legal identity and thus they could sue and be sued. Another sixteen joint stock banks were established between then and the coming into force of the 1845 Scottish Banking Act, enacted a year after its English forerunner. Many of these new banks were in Glasgow and ranged in longevity from the Clydesdale Bank, still in operation today, through to the Glasgow Joint Stock Bank which merged with the Edinburgh & Glasgow Bank after just four years of operation.

A few proposed new schemes failed to get off the ground as they came too late to enjoy the right to issue their own notes. Note issuance was still seen as a vital part of a successful banking business even if its relative importance as a source of funding was declining compared to customer deposits. In any event no new joint stock bank of any significance was formed after 1844 other than as a result of amalgamations.

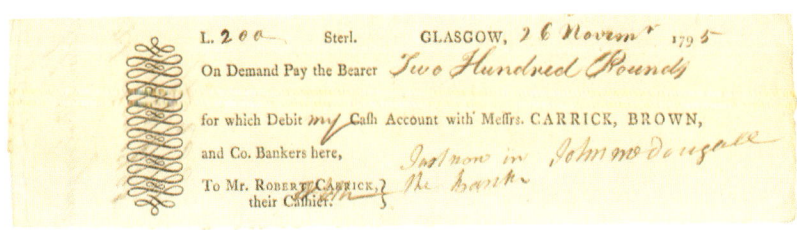

Very early printed cheque of Carrick Brown & Co (Ship Bank)

The 1845 Scottish Banking Act

This key piece of legislation introduced the principle of the Authorised Circulation (also known as the Fiduciary Issue or Fixed Issue). The Act defined the basis on which banks could continue their note issue backed only by the strength of their own balance sheet. Simply put, existing issuers were allocated a limit based on the average of their outstanding issue in the year to 1st May 1845 while no new bank would be permitted to issue notes. Should two issuers merge then the Authorised Circulation limits could be combined, but should a bank fail then that issue would lapse, as happened in the cases of the Western Bank and the City of Glasgow Bank. The existing issuing banks in Scotland were effectively being shielded from any future competition, allowing, in some historians' view, a complacency and uniformity to develop. Issuance beyond the prescribed limit was permissible but only if covered by holdings of gold and silver coin (or, after 1928 when the UK abandoned the gold standard, Bank of England notes).

The regulations as applied to English banks in the corresponding Act of 1844 differed considerably; in their case if two banks merged or one was taken over by a non-issuer then their right to issue either lapsed or was passed to the Bank of England. Also, no excess over their authorised circulation limit was permitted. The clear intention was to ensure that over time the Bank of England gained a monopoly over note issuance in England. It was however accepted that a separate solution was appropriate in Scotland for political reasons as well as in acknowledgement of established tradition. The two Acts came to emphasise not only the difference between the Scottish and English systems but also acted as a deterrent to banks venturing into each other's territory.

Nineteen Scottish banks were granted an Authorised Circulation in 1845, of which three issues later lapsed due to the bank's failure (the Ayrshire Bank's limit also lapsed as it had merged with the Western Bank). Most of the nineteen were joint stock banks with just three survivors of the smaller private banking partnerships. The total Authorised Circulation for the Scottish banks was £3,087,209, a sum which contrasts starkly with the Bank of England's own Authorised Circulation of £14,000,000 and represented just 9·8% of the total for the UK as a whole.

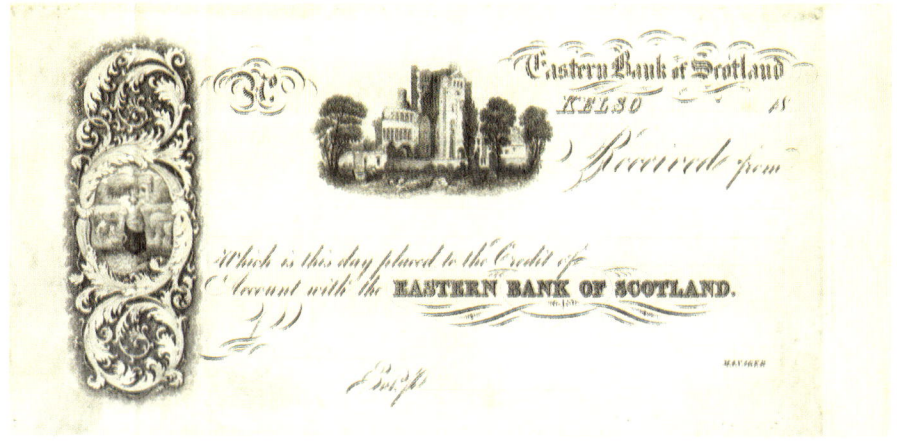

Eastern Bank of Scotland proof receipt for their Kelso branch

Authorised Circulation limits set in 1845:

Bank	Amount	Comment
Aberdeen Town & County Bank	£70,133	To North of Scotland Bank 1908
Ayrshire Banking Co **	£53,656	To Western Bank 1845
Bank of Scotland	£300,485	
Banking Co in Aberdeen *	£88,467	To Union Bank 1849
British Linen Co	£438,024	To Bank of Scotland 1970
Caledonian Banking Co	£53,434	To Bank of Scotland 1907
Central Bank of Scotland	£42,933	To Bank of Scotland 1868
City of Glasgow Bank **	£72,921	Failed 1878
Clydesdale Banking Co	£104,028	
Commercial Bank of Scotland	£374,880	To National Commercial 1959
Dundee Banking Co *	£33,451	To Royal Bank 1864
Eastern Bank of Scotland	£33,636	To Clydesdale Bank 1863
Edinburgh & Glasgow Bank	£136,657	To Clydesdale Bank 1858
National Bank of Scotland	£297,024	To National Commercial 1959
North of Scotland Banking Co	£154,319	To Clydesdale Bank 1950
Perth Banking Co *	£38,656	To Union Bank 1857
Royal Bank of Scotland	£183,000	
Union Bank of Scotland	£327,223	To Bank of Scotland 1955
Western Bank of Scotland **	£284,282	Failed 1857
TOTAL for the 19 banks	£3,087,209	

* Private partnerships
** Issue lapsed

The total after the City of Glasgow collapse in 1878 had fallen to £2,676,350, a figure unchanged until the Act of 2009. By then the Authorised Circulation limits had become meaningless as over 99% of issuance was subject to backing in the form of coin or Bank of England notes. The 1845 Act did have an interesting proviso in that the level of backing was tested only once a week. As a result the banks deposited cash at the Bank of England on a Friday and withdrew it again on Monday, thus maximising their profits from note issuance. These transactions were made easier by the creation of the Bank of England's internal Giant and Titan notes for £1,000,000 and £100,000,000 respectively.

The 2009 Act made fundamental changes to this. The Authorised Circulation was abolished, banks were required to deposit their now 100% backing on a permanent basis and these sums were ring-fenced, while regulatory responsibility moved from the Stamp Office to the Bank of England. This was intended to reassure the public that Scottish (and Northern Irish) notes were as secure as Bank of England ones. To enable the banks to continue to make some profit from note issuance 40% of the backing could be in the form of interest-bearing securities rather than interest-free cash. The banks also benefit from not having to provide backing for notes still in their own possession, thus saving considerable sums compared to those having to hold Bank of England notes.

Amalgamation and Consolidation

After 1845 Scottish banking continued much as before with further growth in line with the expansion of the industrial economy, though arguably there was a slowdown in the rate of innovation. A slow process of consolidation also began, ending ultimately with the three issuing banks we see today. The inability of new banks to issue their own notes was one reason for the absence of serious new competitors, though the savings bank movement proved to be a successful gatherer of deposits from thrifty Scots.

New banks were still founded after 1845, such as the 'Exchange Banks', vehicles for speculation in railway company shares, an activity which had been shunned by the commercial banks. These were all short-lived and all had collapsed or ceased to trade by 1849. Other small banks, such as the Scotish (sic) Border Bank and the London & Scottish Bank also appeared, albeit briefly. These were examples of the few London-based finance houses which were started in the mid-19th century specifically to do business in Scotland. Another small bank was the rather dubious Dundee-based Scottish Banking Company Limited which operated for a short period in the 1880s. Cheques issued by all these banks can be found today. There were others too, such as the Peoples Bank, the Mercantile Bank of Scotland, the Mutual Credit Bank and the Provident Bank of Scotland. None of course could issue notes, having been founded after the 1845 Act.

The banking industry continued to develop and prosper, but progress was, however, interrupted by the dramatic failures of first the Western Bank of Scotland in 1857 and then the City of Glasgow Bank in 1878. This latter collapse resulted in some changes to the law. Limited shareholder liability was introduced and eventually adopted by the seven surviving joint stock banks in 1882. There had been some reluctance to do this as it had been a major source of comfort to depositors and noteholders that they enjoyed full recourse to each and every one of the banks' shareholders. The limitation on shareholder liability did not, however, extend to the note issue and the notes of most banks were amended to make reference to the relevant Act of Parliament. The adoption of limited liability was carefully co-ordinated by the seven joint stocks as this extract from the minutes of the North of Scotland Bank records:

Limited Liability: '… *It was unanimously agreed on 19th July 1881 to recommend to their shareholders to adopt the principle of Limited Liability, and that all necessary steps be taken by each Bank for registering under the Companies Acts 1862 and 1879, as a Limited Bank: and in order to perfect the necessary arrangements, and that all the Banks may enter on business as Limited Banks on the same day, or as nearly as may be possible…*'.

The shareholders of the three Chartered Banks continued to enjoy limited liability and these banks therefore had no need to re-register as limited companies.

Apart from a brief incursion by the Leith Bank in 1830 when a branch was opened in Carlisle (and registered as an English bank, only to close in 1837) the only expansion of Scottish banks into England started in the 1860s when they began to open branches in London, overcoming strong protests from the English banks along the way. There were one or two minor exceptions: a few Clydesdale branches in Cumbria and the arrival of three Scottish banks in Berwick-on-Tweed. Of course, issuing their own notes outside Scotland was out of the question.

In 1900 ten issuing banks were left out of the nineteen in 1845; by 1907 this had fallen to eight and thereafter only Aberdeen was home to a Scottish bank outside Edinburgh and Glasgow. That, too, ceased in 1950.

The amalgamation process was more dramatic in England when dozens of provincial and joint stock banks started merging, to result by the 1920s in the emergence of the 'Big Five' clearing banks. These banks, by now much larger than their Scottish equivalents, looked to acquire controlling interests in banks north of the border. The first to move was Lloyds Bank who acquired the National Bank in 1918. Barclays was next when they bought up the British Linen in November 1919, then the Midland moved to acquire first the Clydesdale and later the North of Scotland Bank. The first noticeable effect of these moves occurred only in 1950 when the Midland brought about the merger of their two Scottish subsidiaries.

One Scottish bank moved in the opposite direction: the Royal acquired the prestigious London private bank Drummonds in 1924 and the Bank of England's West End branch in 1930. They then went on to acquire the long established English bank Williams Deacon's and the even longer established London private bank, Glyn, Mills & Co, which importantly was a member of the London Clearing House.

More Recent Developments

By 1970 only three major banks were left, one of which was in English hands. At its peak in 1825 there were over thirty issuing banks operating in Scotland and our catalogue lists some 85 in total. Also listed are over fifty non-bank paper money issuers mostly from the 18th and 19th centuries. Many of the banks were swept up in the amalgamation movement leaving a dense network of branches operated by the three dominant players reaching into the furthest corners of the country.

This over-banking had in part driven the merger process but Scotland was a relatively small economy and the two independent Scottish banks felt increasing pressure to expand outside their home market. Branches were opened in England and the Royal built on its existing English subsidiaries. The most eye-catching move was the Royal's take-over in 2000 of the much larger but stagnating National Westminster Bank. In 2001, six years after its Tercentenary, the Bank of Scotland retaliated by seeking a merger with the recently demutualized Halifax Building Society to create HBOS.

Rapid, indeed reckless, growth by both Scottish banks followed – the days of the prudent, cautious and conservative Scottish banker were clearly over. The inevitable crunch came in October 2008 when they both had to be rescued by the UK Government. Supported by some £20·5bn of UK Government aid HBOS was acquired by Lloyds Banking Group while the Royal required new capital of £45bn to escape oblivion. Allegedly the cash machines were within two hours of being switched off. The Royal had badly over-extended itself by acquiring the Dutch giant ABN Amro at the height of the market, making itself, if briefly, the world's largest bank by assets. The UK Government remains (in late 2017) 72% owners of the Royal (down from a peak of 84%) while their stake in Lloyds was finally sold off in May 2017 after peaking at 43%. In 1987 the Midland had sold its stake in the Clydesdale to National Australia Bank who in February 2016 demerged and floated it (together with what is now its subsidiary, the Yorkshire Bank) as part of the London-listed CYBG PLC group.

Circulation Statistics

To the surprise of some, the three major banks are not the only paper money issuers in Scotland today; there is also the Ekopia Resource Exchange in Findhorn, whose average circulation of 'trading vouchers' stands at just £20,000 (see chapter on Private Non-Bank Issues). The following chart tracks the growth in circulation and changes in the relative positions of the three majors. Very noticeable is the growth of the Clydesdale who have now become the largest issuer by some distance.

	Authorised Circulation		March 1975		Average for 2015	
Bank of Scotland	£1,289,222	48·2%	£93·8mn	37·0%	£1,000mn	22·2%
Clydesdale	£498,773	18·6%	£39·9mn	15·8%	£2,000mn	44·5%
Royal Bank	£888,355	33·2%	£119·6mn	47·2%	£1,500mn	33·3%
TOTAL	£2,676,350	100%	£253·3mn	100%	£4,500mn	100%

Scotland's fourth paper money issuer

The Future – Independence and the Currency Question

What next for the banks? Centuries of proud history and the banks' unblemished standing is now badly tarnished. The Bank of Scotland is little more than a brand; the Royal remains in intensive care and 90% of its business is conducted outside Scotland; and the Clydesdale, while once again independent, remains vulnerable to being swallowed up by a larger predator. For now, however, their position as note issuers remains secure.

Scotland's future as a country will determine what ultimately happens to the distinctive note issues of the three banks, whose status now looks anomalous in an era of monopoly control by central banks in virtually every country of the world. Should Scotland become independent the Scottish government's decision on the country's currency will be crucial. If Sterling remains the de facto currency the Bank of England will have the final word on whether the Scottish banks can continue their note issues. Should a new currency be established then quite possibly a new Central Bank of Scotland will have to take over the note issue. Finally, should Scotland join (or remain) a member of the European Union, then adoption of the euro may become inevitable, a process first requiring the creation of a new Scottish currency. Having to adopt the euro would definitively spell the end of Scotland's long and fascinating banknote story.

Stamp Duty & Key Legislation

Stamp Duty

Stamp Duty was first levied in 1783 on banknotes of 1 Guinea and over. To the annoyance of the Scottish banks the Bank of England was exempted from having to stamp each note individually and they lobbied hard over many years to change that. From the outset different regulations applied in England, Scotland and Ireland and these were subject to frequent revision. Stamps had to be embossed on each note by hand in the Stamp Office in London, a major inconvenience for the Scottish banks relieved only when the Stamp Office in Edinburgh was authorised to carry out the task. This seems to have happened in 1822 (though some banks continued to have their notes stamped in London as their notes were being printed there). The main changes in stamp duty legislation are outlined below.

(Note: much of this section is drawn from a series of articles by Marcus Samuel in *The Essay-Proof Journal* between 1964 and 1966).

1783 – 3d duty payable on new notes of over 1 Guinea from 1st August 1783 and an embossed stamp applied to each note. Notes with earlier dates but not issued until after that date also had to be stamped. 6d duty payable on notes over 5 Guineas.

1797 – Distinction made between notes re-issuable at the first place of issue only and those re-issuable anywhere. The rate for the latter doubled to 6d on notes of less than 5 Guineas and 1s on notes of higher value. The newly permitted 5s notes incurred either ½d or 1d duty on the same basis. An increase in duty rates the same year required notes to be returned and a second stamp added.

1799 – From July £1 notes had to be stamped at the same rate as 1 Guinea notes, i.e. 2d or 4d if re-issuable anywhere. The paper had to be stamped before each note was printed. Some notes with earlier dates were re-dated to ensure the duty stamp remained valid. The Bank of Scotland and the Royal Bank were given permission to compound duty payments on notes, i.e. they could pay a lump sum and avoid having to have individual notes stamped, but only on notes for less than £5 and dated 2nd December 1799 or later. Again, some earlier notes were re-dated.

1801 – The rates are again increased on notes over 1 Guinea. 5s notes could no longer be issued after 31st December 1800.

1804 – Regulations are simplified and the lower rates are now applicable on all notes, although subject to a three year validity period after which the note had to be withdrawn and replaced. Rates are set at 3d on notes up to 1 Guinea, 6d on notes up to 2 Guineas, 9d on notes up to 5 Guineas, 1s on notes up to £20 and 5s on notes of £100. All notes are dated by hand due to the new three year rule.

1808 – Rates are increased to 4d on notes up to 1 Guinea, 8d on notes up to 2 Guineas, 1s on notes up to 5 Guineas, 1s 6d on notes up to £20 and 7s 6d on £100 notes. Bank licences are introduced at a cost of £20 per annum per issuing bank. Specimens of new notes had to be lodged at the Stamp Office in order to obtain the licence.

1813 – Further minor changes to exempt partnerships who reissue notes not reflecting any subsequent change of partner. The three year validity limit on re-issuable notes is confirmed but now applies only in England.

1815 – Rates increased to 5d on notes up to 1 Guinea, 10d on notes up to 2 Guineas, 1s 3d on notes up to 5 Guineas, 1s 9d on notes up to £20 and 8s 6d on £100 notes. Notes dated prior to 31st August 1815 could no longer be re-issued and no notes with printed dates were permissible after that date. Notes dated 1st September 1815 or later could now circulate indefinitely. The bankers' licence fee increases to £30 p.a. with Scottish banks required to take out no more than four licences to cover their branch networks (as a result of lobbying by the three majors).

Congreve Stamps

1821 – The embossed revenue stamps on the £1, 1 Guinea and £5 notes are replaced by red and black revenue stamps for 5d and 1s 3d designed by Sir William Congreve using his compound plate printing technique patented in 1820. These were printed on the reverse of the notes.

The initial Congreve stamps were large complex oval designs first issued in March 1821. There were no fewer than eight minor varieties of the oval 5d stamp and four varieties of the 1s 3d stamp. In 1825 both stamps were replaced by smaller circular ones and again minor varieties are known. Six varieties are known of the circular 5d stamp and three of the 1s 3d stamp. Congreve stamps stayed in use in Scotland until about 1850. 10d stamps for use on 30s and £2 notes were also prepared but were never used in Scotland.

After the banning of £1 notes in England in 1826 the use of Congreve stamps declined on English notes. It is not known if a Congreve stamping machine was ever installed at the Edinburgh Stamp Office, so if not then all the notes with these stamps must have been despatched to London, as before. It should be noted that many forgeries of Congreve stamps have been seen, some of high quality but most are easily identifiable. The compound plate process was not seen as a success despite being in use for almost thirty years. There were too many stories of slow operation, defective machines and ill-functioning plates. The machines were also very expensive to operate requiring up to seven men full time.

Proof Congreve stamp for 1s 3d

Congreve 5d Stamp on issued Ramsays Bonars £1 note 1822

1854 – Act 16 & 17 Vic Cap 63 was passed on 4th August 1853 and finally permitted all Scottish banks to compound stamp duty on their notes. Individual stamping was discontinued. The new law took effect on 1st April 1854 and many banks made reference to this law on their notes. Compounded duty was payable at the rate of 8s 4d p.a. for every £100 of notes issued.

Stamp duty on Scottish banknotes was abolished in 1972 and payment of bank licenses ceased in 1971.

Key Legislation

1695 – Act of the Scottish Parliament 'for erecting a Publick Bank' brought the Bank of Scotland into existence.

1765 – Option notes and 'small notes' for less than £1 abolished.

1797 – Notes for values under £1 permitted (but banned again at the end of 1800).

1826 – Act 7 Geo IV Cap 6 prohibits the issue of notes under £5 in England.

1826 – Act 7 Geo IV Cap 46 permits the creation of note issuing joint stock banks in England outside a 65 mile radius of London.

1844 – Act 7 & 8 Vic Cap 32 is the Bank Charter Act regulating banknote issuance in England.

1845 – Act 8 & 9 Vic Cap 38 is the Scottish Banking Act.

1853 – Act 16 & 17 Vic Cap 63 – see above.

1856 – Act 19 & 20 Vic Cap 47 confirmed the ability of companies to limit shareholder liability, though this is not adopted by any Scottish banks at this stage. Referenced on certain notes of the Clydesdale Bank.

1862 – Act 25 & 26 Vic Cap 89 is referred to on the notes of the Aberdeen Town & County Banking Company which incorporated with limited shareholder liability under the terms of this Act.

1879 – Act 42 & 43 Vic Cap 76 is referred to on North of Scotland Bank notes and again relates to shareholder liability. Scottish banks finally adopted limited shareholder liability in 1882 (apart from liability for the note issue) under the terms of this Act.

1914 – Scottish notes are made legal tender, but only until 1st January 1920. They were again made legal tender from 1939 to 1945.

1928 – Bank of England starts to issue 10s and £1 notes. These were made legal tender in Scotland as well as England but notes of £5 and upwards were not included. Scottish banks can now hold Bank of England notes in preference to gold coin as part backing for their own note issues.

2009 – The new Banking Act imposed new backing requirements on the Scottish note issuers.

Legal Tender and Legal Currency

These definitions occasionally lead to confusion. The definition of 'legal tender' is quite narrow and means that the notes or coins concerned, up to any limit specified, can be used to pay a legal debt and if offered for the exact amount cannot be refused. 'Legal currency' means only that the notes or coins concerned have been legally issued and may be accepted if offered although there is no compulsion to do so. All Scottish notes are legal currency but none are legal tender, while Bank of England notes are legal tender in England but not, at least since the withdrawal of their 10s and £1 notes, in Scotland or Northern Ireland. In practice, Scottish notes are almost always accepted for payment across the whole UK (with the exception of the occasional London cabby!).

Some Guidance Notes for Collectors

Evolution of Scottish Banknote Design

Scottish banknotes are widely admired and collected for their attractive and colourful designs and the sheer variety available to collectors. For historians there is the rare chance to obtain examples of 18th century notes and track the evolution of engraving techniques. Scottish banking history shows how valued they are by the public – and consequently how rare the older notes have become – as nearly all notes, even those issued by banks which went on to fail, were redeemed by the issuer itself or one of the major banks in a support operation.

Early notes were simple in design with perhaps one small vignette, maybe a coat of arms or the issuer's emblem, but gradually more technically able engravers such as Robert Kirkwood and his sons came on to the scene. Their talents helped banks to combat the ever-present forgery threat. Until the 1820s all notes were printed from copper plates but then steel plate engraving was introduced and quickly replaced the older method. A step change in engraving quality was immediately apparent and in the hands of artistically gifted Scottish engravers such as William Home Lizars, Joseph Swan and William and Alexander Keith Johnson, some of the most beautiful of Scottish banknotes were created. Many were truly works of art.

The imagery on Scots notes became ever more elaborate and distinctive. Royalty was a feature of the Royal Bank's notes from 1727 to 1966 but began to appear on the notes of other banks, for example on the commemorative notes of the Leith Bank, the notes of the Eastern Bank, the City of Glasgow Bank and the Glasgow Union Bank, while the top Scottish engravers seemed ever more devoted to the Victorian fashion of classical allegory. Well known views and street scenes, bank buildings and historic monuments were used and banks also started to consider portraits of famous Scots. One of the earliest recorded occasions was in 1871 when the Clydesdale mulled putting Adam Smith on their new £1 note (though he did not appear on their notes until 1981). Thoughts also often turned to both Sir Walter Scott and Robert Burns, as some photographic essays of Bradbury Wilkinson from the 1920s suggest. They had to wait until 1962 and 1971 respectively. It must be recorded that every non-royal historical figure on the front of a Scottish note has so far been a native Scot while the Bank of England has felt able (if not compelled) to include not only Englishmen but also Scots and at least one Anglo-Irishman.

Note printing on an industrial scale was pioneered by London-based Perkins & Heath, later Perkins Bacon, who developed hardened steel plate engraving and whose extensive archives have yielded much of value to our research efforts. Perkins Bacon were followed by leading firms such as Waterlow & Sons, Bradbury Wilkinson and of course Thomas De La Rue who ultimately acquired both of their main competitors and are now the UK's sole manufacturer of banknotes. Their high quality work during the 20th century illustrates the further advances in colour printing and improved security features essential to modern note designs.

Beautiful example of steel plate engraving by Perkins & Heath

Bradbury Wilkinson essay with marked similarities to their
essay prepared for the Union Bank in 1904

Scottish Note Sizes

The original size letters were an invention of James Douglas, the author of the first catalogue of Scottish banknotes in 1975, but are only used in part in this catalogue. Notes of all denominations reduced steadily in size from the 1940s onwards but not all banks issued notes conforming to Douglas's definitions of Size D, X, Y or Z so these are not used and exact dimensions given instead. Also, further size reductions have occurred since Douglas published his book. Sizes referred to in the text include:

Size	Dimensions	Description	
Size A	155/165 x 120/130mm	Squares	all £1 & 1gn notes until the 1920s
Size B	150 x 80mm	£1 from 1920s	same size as the Bank of England £1 of 1928
Size C	150 x 72mm	£1 from c.1960	same size as Bank of England 'Portrait' £1 of 1960
Size W	195/220 x 125/135mm	Horse Blankets	all notes of £5 and above, issued until the 1940s

Size dimensions vary due to the extent of paper margins on some notes, especially earlier ones issued before machine-cut edges became the norm.

Illustrations

All illustrations are in colour and are approximately 50% of true size unless otherwise stated.

Pricing

The value of a note is no more and no less than what two parties agree it to be. But for the purposes of providing useful pricing guidance in this catalogue we have drawn heavily on our publisher Pam West's many years of experience and extensive knowledge of the Scottish market to supplement what we have gleaned from dealers' lists and auction results. All prices are in £ Sterling. The value of an issued Scottish note (but not a specimen or trial note) will include its face value if the bank is a constituent of one of the three current issuing banks.

Pricing will not reflect the popularity of those modern notes with low or 'special' serials which often attract a significant premium. The few number one notes (e.g. A/1 000001) and million notes (A/1 1000000) that have come on to the market are particularly sought after. In most cases we have not separately priced first and last dates of an individual issue, or first and last prefixes, though these can also attract a premium.

Million serial

In the catalogue no value is given if no surviving example of the note is known. If a note has only been seen in an archive, or where few if any have ever come on to the market, the word 'RARE' has been used. Otherwise what we believe to be current market prices are provided although if there has been no recent transaction we have made an estimate.

Million serial

Grading

Like pricing, grading is a matter of judgement. However, the following guide might be helpful to readers:

Uncirculated	UNC	As new, pristine, no defects of any kind
Extremely Fine	EF	Still in excellent condition, one crease or minor folds but little wear
Very Fine	VF	Still clean overall but showing signs of circulation and folding
Fine	F	Shows considerable circulation, may be grubby especially in the folds
Very Good	VG	Well used but intact, may have stains, small holes, ragged edges etc

For a more detailed explanation of note grading see:
The International Bank Note Society (IBNS) website www.theibns.org

A current phenomenon is the 'slabbing' of notes by professional grading companies using a scale from 1 (worst) to 70 (perfect, unblemished). Opinion is split on the value of slabbing, with sellers insisting they get better prices while some collectors avoid them or even remove the note from its sometimes air-tight plastic holder. Time will no doubt tell if slabbing is here to stay.

Early Scottish notes have often survived in VG or worse condition. Due to their relative scarcity this should not be a deterrent to acquiring them: both authors have made the mistake of turning down a poor quality note and then never seeing the note type again!

A term occasionally heard is 'Scottish UNC'. This is an attempt to describe a note which has not been circulated but has been handled by a Scottish bank teller. Scottish tellers have long had the habit of folding their notes when they put them in their till and older Size W notes, for example, frequently display two clear vertical folds, whether they have actually circulated or not. If these are missing it is possible the note has been cleaned or flattened. More modern notes may well have a single vertical fold but those coming from cash machines should not.

Cleaned notes are the bane of banknote collecting. They can be difficult to spot and should be avoided if at all possible. A cleaned note will lose its original sheen and strength of colour and often feels limp and lifeless. If chemicals have been used a telltale smell may linger. Unfortunately, too many surviving Scottish notes seem to have been cleaned or pressed. But this does not make them uncollectable as you may never get a better one! However, where un-doctored notes are available, they are to be preferred.

Attractive Caledonian Bank cheque

Forgeries

Forgeries were a serious problem for the banks during the 18th and 19th centuries, and it will be observed that many survivors from this time are indeed forgeries. Some of these are of excellent quality (in fact a note marked 'Forgery' could be a genuine note where only the signature has been forged). It can therefore be difficult to differentiate between a forged note and the genuine original on which it is based. Clues may be found in minor details such as an illegible printers' imprint, the engraving of the vignette, the quality of the paper, the absence of a watermark or sometimes just the 'feel' of the note. If the note has a Congreve stamp on the back then that might provide a further clue as to whether it is genuine. Congreves were often forged.

Forgeries, whatever their quality, should be taken as being generally faithful to the originals and given the rarity of genuine survivors they can be regarded as just as collectable, if cheaper to acquire. They have proved valuable for research purposes and often provide information not available elsewhere.

As the 19th century progressed forgeries reduced in number. The banks ascribed this to two main factors; firstly constant improvements in the quality of the engraving and printing, as well as of the paper and watermarks deployed; and secondly the regular note exchanges where any forgery attempts were usually picked up very quickly. Notorious forgeries did however afflict the Union Bank in 1866 (Greatrex) and the Bank of Scotland in 1888 (Mitchell) and these are described in more detail in the relevant chapters.

Specimens - Colour Trials - Essays/Trials - Printers' Proofs - Remainders

Specimens come from two sources – the banks and the printers. Banks had specimen notes prepared both for internal purposes and to provide to other banks, while printers' specimens, usually identified by a printers' stamp or the printers' name in perforated form, are samples produced for internal archival purposes as well as for advertising or display. Specimens will normally have 000000 serials and carry SPECIMEN stamps on both sides, often but not always applied diagonally. Some will have the signature or prefix/serial area punch hole cancelled as additional protection against illicit use.

Bradbury Wilkinson specimen from 1896 showing first and last serials of print run

Our listings attempt to cover all specimen notes including the many released in recent years from the De La Rue archives. These also include many printers' archival specimens prepared by Bradbury Wilkinson as a record of the first and last prefix and serials of each print run. Some print runs were clearly very small indeed and as a result there may be more than one such specimen bearing the same date.

Colour Trial is a misnomer in some cases, though there are genuine trial notes prepared to test different inks and allow the issuing bank to compare the colours before deciding which to use on the issued notes. Most colour trials are however commercial specimens printed from the same plate but using different inks. De La Rue, Bradbury Wilkinson and Waterlow are the main sources of such notes and the choice of a non-standard colour was often deliberate to protect against illicit use. Again, these are covered here wherever we have information on them.

Purple colour trial otherwise identical to issued note in green

Essays or **Trials** are unadopted designs, often containing original artwork by the note designer or engraver, and can be found in many forms including stage proofs. The latter often comprise printed elements pasted on to an earlier design and provide important evidence of how the design of an issued note evolved. Many such essays will be unique and not all will be individually listed, especially the more recent material from the De La Rue archives.

Printers' Proofs have been the source of much useful knowledge on otherwise rare 19th century issues. The appearance on the market in the 1990s of notes from the extensive Perkins Bacon archives was of great importance to our research effort. These were nearly all printed from the primary plate using black ink (or sometimes blue ink where the notes were issued using this colour). Proofs from other printers, especially William Home Lizars and Joseph Swan, are often the only record of the notes they prepared. Proofs are generally found printed on card but sometimes plain paper was used. Notes printed on the watermarked paper used on issued notes will most likely be specimens, even if not stamped 'SPECIMEN'. Confusingly, some proofs are stamped 'SPECIMEN' but this will be noted in the listings. Coloured proofs will attract a premium. **Stage Proofs** are partially printed notes or notes with certain colour elements missing, printed to test the quality.

Remainders are notes emanating from the printers representing unused material. Some of this material, cast aside due to errors made during the printing process, or imperfections noticed at the quality control stage, is referred to as **Spoilage** or **Printers' Waste**. Sometimes this is seen with annotations to indicate the errors or areas on the note in need of correction or amendment.

Waterlow Positional Plate Letters

Most Waterlow notes carry tiny positional plate letters on them. These have not been fully researched and are not detailed in the catalogue. Their plates were all made up of multiple engravings of the note, with impressions per plate ranging from four to twenty depending on the note's dimensions and possibly also the anticipated print runs. Sheets of banknote paper would be sized accordingly. Taking a plate of eight notes with the impressions arranged to two columns of four, the top left hand impression would be letter A and the bottom right one plate H. The reverse plate would follow the same pattern but once the sheet had been printed on both sides the combination would result in the following schematic:

Front A	Front E
Reverse E	Reverse A
Front B	Front F
Reverse F	Reverse B
Front C	Front G
Reverse G	Reverse C
Front D	Front H
Reverse H	Reverse D

With long print runs the alphabet would quickly be used up and subsequent lettering would see dots, dashes and other tiny symbols appearing alongside the plate letter to differentiate plates using later sequences. For the true specialist a huge field of research lies in wait. Some philatelists try to recreate complete sheets of stamps. Maybe now is the time for banknote collectors to follow suit?

Close up of British Linen note showing positional plate letter J

Secret Marks

Many printing firms used secret marks to enable them to spot potential forgeries. Occasionally stage proofs or similar are seen annotated to highlight where these marks are but generally they are not easy to find. They tend to be found on notes printed by De La Rue, Bradbury Wilkinson and Waterlow, though other printers may well have used them.

Electronic Sorting Codes

From 1967 to 1983 Scottish £1 and £5 notes carried CMC7 magnetic ink sorting codes on the reverse in the form of seven small bars. They are found on the notes of five banks and ten different combinations have been recorded. Their role was to enable the Crosfield sorting machines used in the note exchange to process the increasing numbers of notes in circulation. The codes allowed notes to be sorted by bank and denomination but were discontinued when newer technology was deployed using bars printed in ultra-violet ink. Trial notes exist with experimental sorting codes. It is believed that the use of electronic sorting codes on banknotes was unique to Scotland.

Summary of CMC7 Codes on Issued Notes:

Bank	Denomination	Code	First date	Last date
Bank of Scotland	£1	3 1 3	3 Mar 1967	30 Jul 1981
Bank of Scotland	£5	2 1 4	1 Nov 1967	25 Jun 1982
British Linen *	£1	2 3 2	13 Jun 1967	20 Jul 1970
British Linen *	£5	4 2 1	17 Jul 1964 **	23 Apr 1968
Clydesdale	£1	2 2 3	3 Apr 1967	5 Jan 1983
Clydesdale	£5	2 4 1	1 May 1967	5 Jan 1983
National Commercial ***	£1	5 1 1	4 Jan 1967	4 Jan 1968
National Commercial ***	£5	4 1 2	4 Jan 1968	4 Jan 1968
Royal Bank	£1	3 2 2	1 Sep 1967	3 May 1982
Royal Bank	£5	3 3 1	19 Mar 1969	5 Jan 1983

*   Taken over by Bank of Scotland in 1970
**   These notes were not delivered until Sept 1967. The first 'regular' issued £5 notes with sorting codes were dated 23 Apr 1968
***   Merged into Royal Bank of Scotland in 1969

Reverse of Clydesdale Bank £5 showing how the
design allowed space for the codes

Replacement Notes

There have probably always been replacement notes, i.e. notes specially prepared to replace those damaged during the production process. In the past these were probably numbered by hand to replace the machine-numbered original. But from around 1970 Thomas De La Rue introduced a system of special prefixes for their replacement notes, with packs of new notes carrying an identifying mark on the wrapper to assist tellers when they were taken to cash and issued to the public.

Not all banks accepted the system straight away so it cannot be assumed that all De La Rue issues featured identifiable replacement notes after 1970. The first replacements to be recorded in the Scottish series were Bank of Scotland notes from 1970. These can be identified by use of De La Rue's preferred prefix letter Z. Clydesdale replacements first appeared in 1985 and they are seen for the first time on Royal Bank's notes in 1986 after De La Rue acquired Bradbury Wilkinson. As far as we are aware, the only other printer of Scottish notes to use replacement note identifiers was B A Banknotes, on Royal Bank £1 notes in 1994.

Analysis of De La Rue issues indicates that replacements comprised between 0·1% and 0·4% of regular issue volumes (but closer to 1·5% of the first Clydesdale polymer £5 note). The catalogue attempts to set out the serial number ranges of all replacement notes based on firm sightings where official print run information is not available. It is probable that more replacements were printed than were absolutely needed which might explain gaps in the serial number ranges.

The first Scottish replacement notes were issued in 1970

Polymer Notes

While our book is entitled *Paper Money of Scotland* it is now apparent that paper money is on its way out in Scotland and we are in danger of having to find a new title. All three banks have started to issue polymer notes ending a tradition of paper money going back over three hundred years. The old paper notes are being withdrawn and only collectors, museums and archives (or hoarders) will continue to hold these reminders of Scotland's paper money history.

Why polymer? Polymer has been chosen by the Bank of England for its own notes and the Scottish banks decided to follow suit. Indeed the Clydesdale beat the Bank of England to the title of the first bank in Great Britain to issue a polymer note when their new £5 note came out on 23rd March 2015. In fact the UK winner was the Northern Bank in Northern Ireland who issued a polymer £5 note as early as 1999, but no further polymer issues have been seen in Ulster, although we understand the Ulster Bank plans to issue polymer £5 and £10 notes. Polymer has become the material of choice because it is, according to the Bank of England, cleaner, safer, stronger and longer lasting. Over fifty countries around the world have issued polymer notes and more are expected to follow.

Error Notes

Error notes from before the 1970s are not often seen in the Scottish series. It was during the 1970s that issue volumes started to rise steeply and printing errors, which previously would have been removed at the quality control stage started to get into circulation. Error types fall into three main categories:

> **Paper Errors**, such as mis-cuts, folded paper resulting in additional paper ('shark fin' / 'boat rudder'), concertina folds, notes badly centred, etc
>
> **Printing Errors**, such as missing colours, printing offset on front or reverse, ink smudges, design elements out of register, missing signatures, etc
>
> **Numbering Errors**, prefix/serials missing, mis-matched numbers, same numbers on two or more notes, missing digits, etc

Many collectors like to add error notes to their collection and they can attract a considerable premium over regular notes of the same type.

Mismatched serials on RB 75

Spectacular extra paper error on BA 116d

Collecting Hints

The Scottish series is complex, fascinating and often beautiful. We hope this catalogue will help attract new collectors to the series. A new collector will probably seek to commence with more modern issues. An initial target might be to attempt to complete a type collection of current Scottish issues. Those on a budget might start with £1 notes – these alone will form an excellent type collection though £1 notes have more or less died out in circulation today. Add to this even a representative selection of earlier notes, especially the delightful 'squares' and you should gain a good impression of just how varied and colourful Scottish notes can be.

Many enthusiasts collect modern notes by signature variety, by date, by prefix or a combination of these. This catalogue seeks to cater for all these approaches.

A greater collecting challenge might be to build up a type collection of all post-1900 notes but do not expect to complete this very quickly – few collections are complete on this basis. More collectors are venturing into the world of pre-1900 Scottish issues, where most notes are scarce if not rare. We hope we have managed to throw much needed light on the early issues which should enable collectors to acquire these rare notes with confidence when they appear on the market.

Perhaps the ultimate collecting challenge would be to try and find a note dated before the earliest known surviving Scottish banknote, a £1 note issued by the Bank of Scotland in 1716. The earliest note currently available to collectors is the 1723 £1 (£12 Scots) note issued by the same bank. All 18th century issues are rare but new discoveries do appear from time to time.

Many Scottish collectors look beyond banknotes to include cheques, bills of exchange, letters of credit, traveller's cheques, banking-related letters and other ephemera. These can add breadth and interest to collections but they remain under-researched and incompletely catalogued to date. Such instruments are beyond the scope of this book.

Traveller's cheques were often engraved to the same
high standard as banknotes themselves

Further Study

Our Bibliography covers the wide range of Scottish banking history books available. Most have been drawn on by us to a greater or lesser extent. For those seeking to study Scottish banknotes old and new there are major collections in the National Museum of Scotland, the British Museum and in the archives of the leading banks (available by appointment). The Museum on the Mound in Edinburgh, the Bank of Scotland's former head office, is also highly recommended.

Bank of Scotland

Bank of Scotland 1695 *to* 2007
Bank of Scotland plc 2007 *to* date

The Bank of Scotland was established by an Act of the Scottish Parliament passed on 17th July 1695, thus making it not only Scotland's oldest bank by some distance but also the only one to be created by the old parliament. The Bank's first Governor was John Holland, an Englishman, who served only a single year in that position while staying on the Court of Directors until his death in 1722. A total of twelve Scottish and English directors were appointed under the Act, the Scottish directors being William Erskine, (son of the 3rd Lord Cardross), Sir John Swinton, Sir Robert Dickson of Sornbeg, George Clerk Jnr and John Watson, while the English directors were named as James Foulis, John Holland himself, David Nairn, Walter Stewart, Hugh Frazer, Thomas Coutts (uncle of the founder of that family's private bank) and Thomas Deans.

While authorised capital was set at £1,200,000 Scots or £100,000 Sterling, the initial paid-up amount was a much more modest £120,000 Scottish or £10,000 Sterling. This was subscribed by 136 proprietors and shareholders (or 'Adventurers') in Scotland and another 36 in England. The Bank was granted a 21 year monopoly which inexplicably was not renewed once it expired, thus making it possible for the Royal Bank to be established in 1727. So began the rivalry, intense for many years, between the 'Old Bank' and the 'New Bank', one said to have Jacobite leanings and the other supporters of the House of Hanover. Certainly, the Old Bank never put a royal portrait on its notes while the Royal Bank featured one member of the House of Hanover after another.

The Bank was always intended to be a trading bank rather than becoming bankers to the government and so when it finally opened for business in April 1696 it focused initially on financing trade and exports. Its first home was in Mylne Square, in Edinburgh's Old Town. Growth was however slow due to the considerable caution exercised by the directors. It did oversee the Scottish mint and the coinage changeover after the Act of Union, and of course issued its own notes. Currency union at the rate of £12 Scots to £1 Sterling followed political union in 1707 but notes were still being denominated in Scots Pounds as late as 1731. Branches were opened in 1696 in Dundee, Montrose, Aberdeen and Glasgow but had all been closed by 1699. An attempt in 1696 by the Darien Company to set up a banking business to compete with the Bank was seen off. An office in London was established from the outset but could not be described as an operating branch. Eventually full branches were opened, the first being in the market towns of Dumfries and Kelso in 1774. The London office did not become a full branch until 1867. By 1793 there were eighteen branches and expansion was steady thereafter. The Bank survived the 'war' with the Royal and continued to grow and prosper. It did not however come to dominate Scottish banking the way its English counterpart the Bank of England did south of the border.

Authorised Circulation under the 1845 Act was £300,485 rising to £1,289,222 following the British Linen acquisition. Actual average circulation in 1975 was £93·8mn and by 2015 had risen to about £1bn. This makes the Bank now the smallest of the three Scottish issuers.

Acquisitions were few and far between until the 1950s. The Central Bank of Scotland was absorbed in 1868 and the Caledonian Bank in 1907. The Bank's first big move was to acquire the Union Bank in 1955. This combination briefly created Scotland's largest bank and was followed by the absorption of the British Linen Bank in 1970. Meanwhile expansion started into new activities such as consumer credit and international lending on the back of the oil boom of the 1960s. Ever more rapid growth took place in the 1990s culminating in the merger with the former Halifax Building Society in 2001 to create HBOS. A subsequent reorganisation in September 2007 resulted in the creation of a new company, Bank of Scotland plc, which took over the banking and note issue licence in Scotland. The direct connection with the Bank founded by Act of the original Scottish Parliament before the Act of Union of 1707 had been lost. HBOS embarked on a massive push for growth but collapsed in the credit crisis of October 2008 and had to be rescued by the Lloyds Banking Group, with the support of some £20·5bn of government aid.

The history of the Bank's note issues is as long as that of the Bank itself. No notes prior to the £12 Scots (£1 Sterling) issue of 1716 are known to have survived so the appearance of the earliest issues is a matter of conjecture. They are likely to have been relatively simple unadorned designs like the 1716 notes and indeed those of subsequent 18th century issues. During the 18th century notes were produced from copper plates with a simple promissory clause in black using various styles of lettering and with the Bank's seal embossed. There were no vignettes, emblems or value panels and the notes were all uniface.

For many years the Bank referred to the different issues as '*Setts*'. On issues after 1700, (and possibly also the 1st Sett of 1696), the notes had an ornate, vertical panel of interwoven letters, (known as the 'cheque') about one third of the way along from the left, dividing the stub (counterfoil) from the note, in the same way the modern cheque book works. These notes were also bound into books, usually 500 for the Twenty Shillings (£1 Sterling) notes and 200 for the 'large' higher value notes. The reference to 'books' continued well into the 20th century long after the binding process had ceased. The Bank's Teller detached the note from the stub by cutting through the ornate panel with scissors. When the note was returned it would be matched against the panel to provide a check of its authenticity. Nevertheless, forgery was a problem almost from the beginning, the first attempt being recorded as early as 1700.

PULLS: A feature of the early Bank of Scotland notes is the number of plate pulls available to collectors. These have all been taken from the original copper and steel plates in four separate undertakings:

- In 1883 when thick hand-moulded paper was used, with the watermark 'GREVILLE & SON / 1883'. Perhaps no more than three pulls were taken from each plate, some from the full double plate used on many early notes, hence the plate numbers 1 and 2 to identify the specific engraving
- In the 1970s when plain paper was used
- In 1995 at the time of the Tercentenary when possibly just 150 pulls were drawn from the 1768 1 Guinea plate. All were numbered by hand and dated 31st May 1995. A small circular impressed seal of Bacon & Bacon will identify these pulls
- In the early 2000s when pulls were prepared in limited numbers, on plain paper, for sale in the Bank's Museum on the Mound. These are all numbered by hand in pencil

Only in the early 19th century was more elaborate engraving introduced as the Bank tried to meet the challenge of the forgers. A step change came in the 1820s when engraving on steel plate was first deployed. The technical and artistic standard of engraving by the renowned **W H Lizars** was impressive indeed though the Bank subsequently turned to **Perkins Bacon** whose work fell short of his high artistic standards but whose industrial production techniques enabled them to produce notes more quickly and in far higher quantities. Forgeries still occurred and the new series introduced in 1885 was the result of extensive experiments to combat new forging techniques such as the use of photography. The Bank's claims that these notes were '*forgery-proof by any known photographic process*' prompted a disgruntled and impoverished Edinburgh engraver to prove the Bank and its printers **Waterstons** wrong. He successfully reproduced a number of the newly issued £1 notes. The Bank made changes to the design but remarkably it remained in issue, through size reductions and the introduction of printed reverses, until 1969.

A 'modern' design was then brought in but lasted only a short time thanks to the absorption of the British Linen Bank in 1970, whose printers **Thomas De La Rue** won the contract to prepare new designs for the Bank. These featured a portrait of Sir Walter Scott who had first been seen on the £1 and £5 notes of British Linen. These attractive designs lasted 25 years until 1995 when a new series of notes was prepared for the Bank's Tercentenary. These too featured Scott's portrait. The current series was introduced in 2007 and while Sir Walter remained on the obverse of the notes, each reverse was devoted to images of a major Scottish bridge. The £50 note, featuring the Falkirk Wheel, a technically advanced canal lift reopening a canal link between the east and west coasts, won the International Bank Note Society (IBNS) Banknote of the Year Award for 2007. Along with the other two Scottish note issuers, the Bank introduced polymer £5 notes in October 2016 and £10 notes in October 2017. £20 polymer notes are expected by 2020.

FIRST ISSUE – 1696 *to* 1699

1st Sett Large Notes

This issue was referred to by the Bank of Scotland as the '*1st Sett Large Notes*' and comprised five denominations: £5, £10, £20, £50 and £100 Sterling. The notes were produced from copper plates with a simple promissory clause in black using various styles of lettering and with the Bank's seal embossed. The notes were printed on unwatermarked paper in black on one side only, (uniface) and bound in books of 200 in London. They were numbered and dated by hand and payable to David Spence (Secretary), whose name was inserted by hand. The first notes were dated 25th March 1696 and signed by James Majoribanks (Treasurer) and George Watson (Accomptant); 12th February 1699 signed by James Majoribanks (Treasurer) and James Cuming (Accomptant) and 12th April 1699 signed by James Cockburn (Treasurer) and James Cuming (Accomptant). No issued notes from the 1st Issue are known to have survived and the only clue as to their design comes from a sheet of paper (~ 255 x 166 mm) containing the promissory text for two notes, one for £120 Scots (£10 Sterling) and one for £20 Sterling. It cannot however be confirmed that these were 1st Issue designs. This was found in the Bank's archives in 2005.

BA 2 Unissued note for £120Sc (£10 Sterling) with part of text of note for £20 Sterling

BA 1	£5	**Black**	uniface
BA 2	£10	**Black**	uniface
BA 3	£20	**Black**	uniface
BA 4	£50	**Black**	uniface
BA 5	£100	**Black**	uniface

The First Forgery

In February 1700 seven £5 notes were altered to read £50 and passed by Thomas MackGhie (McGee) of Prestonpans near Edinburgh. This unexpected crime prompted a fresh look at the design of the Bank's notes by the Committee. It was decided that new notes '*With many plain and evident Cheques obvious to the weakest capacity for preventing the like abuse and villany of vitiation* (i.e. forgery)...' be produced. A sub-committee was formed to oversee the production and printing of banknotes at Yester Mill near Gifford, East Lothian. The copper plates were engraved by James Clark, the Engraver at the Scottish Mint. McGee, having been questioned by officials of the Bank and asked to return the next day, hurriedly departed Scotland. As 'Thomas Jones' he was arrested in Newcastle and brought before the bench, however he was released by the Mayor for lack of evidence and was never heard of again.

SECOND ISSUE – 1700

2nd Sett Large Notes

As a result of the McGee forgeries this issue of £5, £10, £20, £50 and £100 Sterling notes had the denomination added in numerical form. Notes dated 1st April 1700 were signed by James Cockburn (Treasurer) and James Cuming (Accomptant) while those dated 20th November 1700 were signed by David Drummond (Treasurer), and James Cuming (Accomptant). Again a simple design in black, embossed with the Bank's seal and uniface, payable to David Spence, Secretary. No notes of this issue are known to have survived.

BA 6	£5	**Black**	uniface
BA 7	£10	**Black**	uniface
BA 8	£20	**Black**	uniface
BA 9	£50	**Black**	uniface
BA 10	£100	**Black**	uniface

THIRD ISSUE – 1704

1st Sett £12 Scots or 20s Sterling Notes

The printing of notes for Twenty Shillings was first discussed in Committee in January 1699. All notes of this denomination were referred to as 20s (£1) Sterling in the Bank's records. Copper plates were to be engraved by James Clark of the Scottish Mint and the notes to be produced in Scotland, but at the Annual General Meeting on 24th March 1699 the Committee decided not to proceed with this denomination. However by March 1704 the Board had changed its mind and the printing of 20s notes was authorised. The two plates for 20s Sterling notes were engraved by James Clark and the paper produced at Yester Mill, East Lothian. It is not clear if the denomination of the notes was expressed as 20s Sterling or £12 Scots, as on the later 20s notes of 1716 and 1723. They were dated 25th March 1704, signed by David Drummond (Treasurer) and James Cuming (Accomptant) and made payable to David Spence, Secretary. As the Bank's first notes of this denomination they were referred to as the 1st Sett. No notes from this issue are known to have survived.

BA 11 £12 Scots **Black** uniface
or 20s

Cash Payments Stopped: Rumours spread around Edinburgh in December 1704 that the Privy Council were about to raise the value of money, i.e. declare coins in circulation to be worth more than their face value. This caused a mild panic resulting in the burghers of the city rushing to the Bank to change banknotes into coin. Payments of cash were stopped on the 18th December and the Committee gave notice on the 20th that banknotes '*presently running shall and ought to bear annualrent*' (interest). The idea was that when the crisis was over the notes could be cashed for the face value plus interest. Problems continued into the spring when the Committee recommended to the Court of Directors '*to cause make and prepare new notes with such alterations as they shall Judge necessary to distinguish them from the old Ones*'. Notes dating 18th December 1704 or earlier were called in from May 1705.

FOURTH ISSUE – 1705 *to* 1713

2nd Sett £12 Scots or 20s Sterling
3rd Sett Large Notes

All these notes were dated 1st May 1705 and signed by David Drummond (Treasurer) and James Cuming (Accomptant). Large notes issued later are believed to have been of the same design. They were dated 1st May 1713 and signed by David Drummond (Treasurer) and James's brother William Cuming (Accomptant). All notes were made payable to David Spence, Secretary. None of these notes are known to have survived.

BA 12 £12 Scots **Black** uniface

BA 13 £5 **Black** uniface

BA 14 £10 **Black** uniface

BA 15 £20 **Black** uniface

BA 16 £50 **Black** uniface

BA 17 £100 **Black** uniface

The Act and Treaty of Union became effective on 1st May 1707 and one of its twenty-five articles called for a single coinage. The Bank's part in this re-coinage was to collect all the foreign and Scots coins circulating in Scotland and transport them to the mint in Edinburgh for re-minting. This task lasted until 1709 and brought a small profit to benefit the Bank's shareholders.

Another financial crisis loomed in March 1708 when a run on the Bank's reserves was caused when a French fleet was sighted entering the Firth of Forth. A storm dispersed the fleet and, in turn, the panic, thereby allowing the Bank to get on with its daily business.

The Jacobite rebellion of 1715 caused the Bank to close its doors on 19th September 1715 *'occasioned by extraordinary demands these six or seven weeks past. The Court of Directors are unanimously of opinion That all Bank Notes presently running shall and ought to bear annualrent from this day and untill payment thereof or calling in of the same in order to payment'*. This was passed by the General Court of Directors on 22nd September and payment was held back until the notes were called in between May and July 1716. In the meantime James and William Cuming left the Bank and George Falconar was elected Accomptant on 2nd April 1716.

1716 ISSUE

3rd Sett £12 Scots or 20s Sterling
4th Sett Large Notes

A new issue of notes was proposed on 5th April 1716 as a result of the 1715 rebellion. They were all dated 16th April 1716 and signed by David Drummond (Treasurer) & George Falconar (Accomptant). The 20s note is expressed as £12 Scots. It is not known if the higher denomination notes were expressed in £ Scots or £ Sterling. One genuine example of the £12 Scots note is known to have survived in the Bank's archives. It is notable for 'Edinburgh' being spelt 'Edenburgh'. The promissory text reads *'The GOVERNOUR & COMPANY of the BANK of SCOTLAND constituted by Act of Parliament Do hereby oblige themselves to pay to ... or the Bearer Twelve pounds Scots on demand'*. The note is printed using several different typefaces in an attempt (unsuccessful as it turned out) to deter forgers. Dimensions ~ 118 x 126mm.

Two forged £12 Scots notes, now in the Bank's archives, were found on 12th January 1723 when the tellers tried unsuccessfully to match the 'cheques' on the notes with the corresponding panels on the stubs bound in the book. An advertisement was put in the Edinburgh Courant asking anyone owning a 20s note to bring it to the Bank for checking. On the same day William Jeffery, an employee of the Bank, was sent *'over the water'* to get a warrant from a Justice of the Peace and to apprehend William Caldwall, a gardener at Abbotshall near Kirkcaldy in Fife. All 3rd Sett £12 Scots notes were withdrawn from 4th April 1723 because of this forgery.

BA 18 £12 Scots Black printed date uniface
16 Apr 1716

RARE

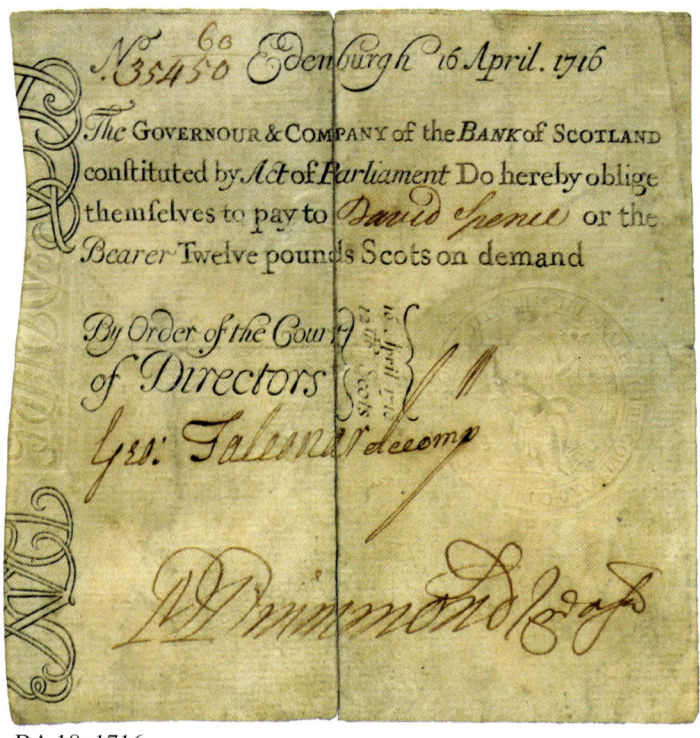

BA 18 1716

Forgery

RARE

BA 19	£5	**Black** printed date uniface 16 Apr 1716
BA 20	£10	**Black** printed date uniface 16 Apr 1716
BA 21	£20	**Black** printed date uniface 16 Apr 1716
BA 22	£50	**Black** printed date uniface 16 Apr 1716
BA 23	£100	**Black** printed date uniface 16 Apr 1716

End of the Bank's Monopoly in 1717

The twenty-one years monopoly enjoyed by the Bank of Scotland expired on 27th March 1717 and although this was referred to in the minutes of 28th November 1716, no further action was taken. This may have been an act of complacency, it may just have slipped the Court's mind, or perhaps they took the view the monopoly might not have been renewed anyway. In any event this opened the way for the 'New Bank', better known as the Royal Bank of Scotland, to be established in 1727.

1723 20s ISSUE

4th Sett £12 Scots or 20s Sterling Notes

There is no specific mention of this issue in the minutes but reference is made on 24th April 1723 to '... *the making of New Paper for Bank Notes at Yester*'. This 'new paper' was the first banknote paper to have a watermark. Notes were signed by David Drummond (Treasurer) and George Falconar (Accomptant). These notes are the earliest notes likely to be available to collectors. Some will, however, be forgeries but it can be difficult to distinguish genuine and forged notes by the quality of the printing. The lack of a watermark should be decisive and all genuine notes will carry an impression of the Bank's seal. The Bank issued 55,400 notes numbered from 1/1 to 93/55400 in books of 600 notes each, i.e. the 600th note was numbered 1/600, the next in sequence 2/601 and so on. It seems many of the survivors have numbers which do not fit this pattern and these are likely to be forgeries, though not necessarily the only ones. The Bank's records are incomplete but indicate that at least 46 genuine notes are still outstanding. Dimensions ~ 118 x 126mm.

In November 1726 a total of 48 forged notes of the 1723 issue were discovered. The minutes show the lengths the Bank was willing to go to in a search for the forgers: '*The Directors are of the opinion that the same is done by the same hand or hands by which the counterfeitts of these notes were made three years ago. And considering that such a forgery cannot be done without the art and concurrence of an engraver and the help and use of a Rolling or hand squeeze Press. And the Court having considered a list of the engravers known to be in Town & Suburbs and of such as keep Rolling presses or Squize Presses have unanimously resolved and agreed that application be made to My Lord Justice Clerk for searching the Houses and Work houses of the persons now thought on as most lyable to Suspicion*'. This search was fruitless despite a reward of £100 being offered in 1726. However, in 1728 John Currie, a bookbinder, was tried and convicted as the forger of these notes. Currie had his 'lug' (ear) nailed to the door of the Tron Kirk in Edinburgh, then he was whipped and banished from the city (magnanimous treatment by the standards of the day; many forgers were executed). The costs of his prosecution were borne by the Bank and came to £192 Sterling.

Of 16 surviving notes examined just five were judged to be genuine and the balance felt to be forgeries. Several more survivors exist but it has not been possible to examine them.

BA 24 £12 Scots Black printed date uniface
24 Jun 1723

From 2500 F

Forgery

From 1500 F

BA 24 Possible forgery 1723

1727 20s ISSUE

5th Sett £12 Scots or 20s Sterling Notes

This issue was brought about by the discovery of forgeries of the previous issue. The new notes were to be '*very conspicuously different from former .... of different character & letter*' with a new, smaller seal and different 'cheques' or ornate panel to the left. The copper plates were engraved by Joseph Cave, Engraver at the Mint. 26,400 notes numbered from 1/1 to 44/26400 were issued. The notes 1/1 to 11/6001 were paid with interest on 27th June 1728. All notes were signed by David Drummond (Treasurer) and George Falconar (Acomptant). Dimensions ~ 118 x 126mm. Very few have survived.

BA 25 £12 Scots Black printed date uniface
2 Feb 1727

RARE

1728 to 1731 ISSUES

6th & 7th Sett £12 Scots or 20s Sterling
5th Sett Large Notes

The 1728 issue of £12 Scots (20s Sterling) notes is believed to be similar in design to the preceding issue. They were also engraved by Joseph Cave. It was not long before these too were being forged. On the morning of 28th August 1730 a counterfeit 20s note bearing the date 17th April 1728 was presented to a Teller. The bearer had been given the note in the town of Stirling and suspicion immediately fell on Glasgow and the southwest. By 3rd September 1730 one John Campbell, a goldsmith from Glasgow, and his brother Archibald were in custody for forging and passing respectively. All notes were signed by David Drummond (Treasurer) and George Falconar (Accomptant) and made payable to David Spence (Secretary). 33,000 20s notes were issued in books of 600 each, as before. The Bank's records indicate there are twenty outstanding, of which only one has been recorded as surviving.

In 1731 a revised £12 Scots note was prepared in yet another attempt to defeat the forgers. 28,200 notes were issued, numbered from 1/1 to 47/28200 with only a revised 'cheque' panel differing, this now comprising the elaborately interwoven letters reading 'EDINBURGH' and 'SCOTS BANK'. The signatories were unchanged. Proofs are known as well as a modern pull, one hundred of which were printed in 2006 using the original plate. Only one issued note dated 1731 (BA 27) is positively known to have survived.

BA 26 £12 Scots Black printed date uniface
  17 Apr 1728 & 17 Apr 1730   **RARE**

  Forgery   **RARE**

BA 26 Forgery 1728

BA 27 **£12 Scots** **Black** revised 'cheque' panel printed date uniface
 4 Feb 1731

RARE

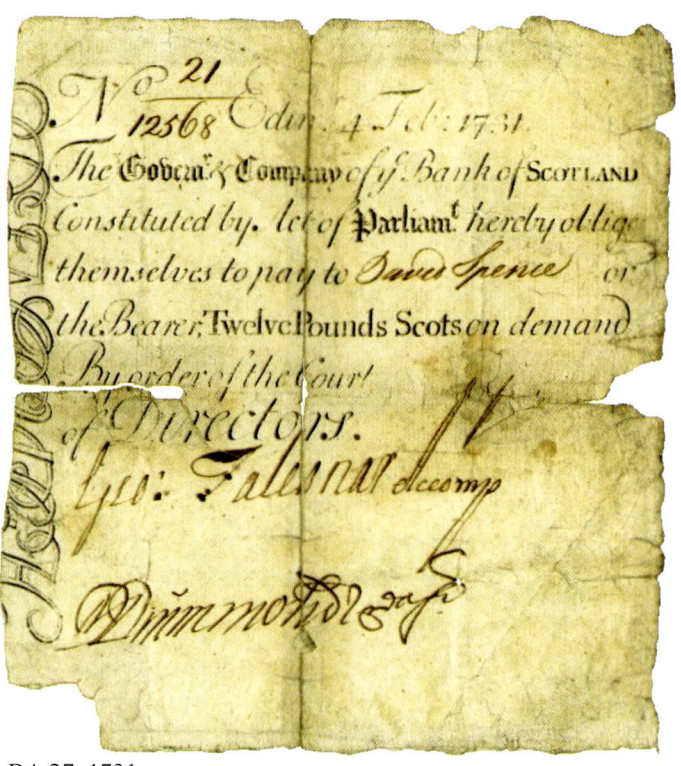

BA 27 1731

Proof (possible pull) On double plate From 150 EF

Modern Pull From 20 EF

BA 28 £5 **Black** printed date uniface
 17 Apr 1728

BA 29 £10 **Black** printed date uniface
 17 Apr 1728

BA 30 £20 **Black** printed date uniface
 17 Apr 1728

BA 31 £50 **Black** printed date uniface
 17 Apr 1728

BA 32 £100 **Black** printed date uniface
 17 Feb 1728

OPTION CLAUSE ISSUES – 1730 *to* 1766

The Bank of Scotland was the first to issue notes with the notorious option clause which on the £5 note ran: '*The Governours and Company of the Bank of Scotland constituted by Act of Parliament do hereby Oblige Themselves to pay to ... or the Bearer Five Pounds sterling on Demand or in the Option of the Directors Five Pounds Two shillings and Sixpence sterling at the End of Six Months after the Day of the Demand And for ascertaining the Demand And the Option of the Directors the Accomptant and one of the Tellers of the Bank are hereby ordered to mark and sign the Day of presenting this Note on the Back of the same*'. The interest rate on all denominations was set at 5% per annum. The Bank felt compelled to issue such notes due to the risk of its aggressive new competitor gathering its notes and presenting them en masse for immediate payment. In the Bank's records they are referred to as 'Conditional Notes'.

The 1st Sett of notes to be issued with the option clause were the large notes, from £5 to £100 Sterling, all hand dated 9th November 1730 and signed by David Drummond (Treasurer) and George Falconar (Accomptant). The 2nd Sett, signed by David Scott (Treasurer) and George Falconar (Accountant), were dated 25th March 1741, the 3rd Sett, signed by David Scott (Treasurer) and Robert Dundas (Accountant) were dated 25th May 1745 and the 4th Sett, also signed by Scott and Dundas, 2nd June 1748. In total there were four Setts of large Conditional Notes and five Setts of £1 notes. The £1 notes were the first of this value to be denominated solely in Sterling. Total issuance of £1 notes with the option clause was a considerable 607,200, all in books of 600 notes each. The records indicate only around 70 remain outstanding but as few as four issued notes have actually survived in museums and archives. Forgeries are known but are also rare.

The £1 note designs remained simple with little adornment beyond the 'cheque' panel down the left hand side. Additional proofs or pulls exist with variant 'cheque' panels and promissory text styles. Dimensions ~ 118 x 126mm as before.

BA 33a £1 **Denomination £1 Sterling** printed date
12 Dec 1732   **RARE**

Forgery   **RARE**

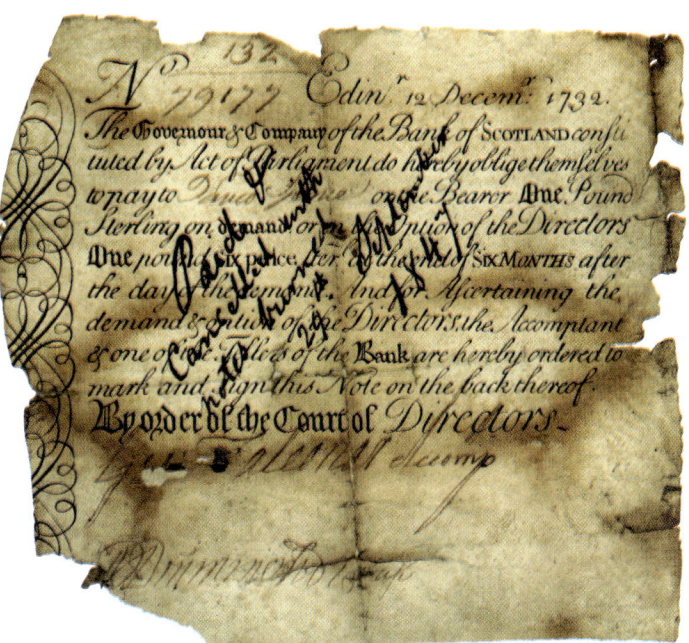

BA 33a Option note issued 1732, redeemed 1847

BA 33b   £1   **Unchanged 'cheque' panel** Dated by hand
                25 Mar 1741
                25 May 1743
                 2 Jun 1748   **RARE**

              Proof/Pull undated   From 150 EF

BA 33b 1741

BA 33c   £1   **Revised 'cheque' panel** Dated by hand
                14 Sep 1752   **RARE**

BA 33c 1752

Proof/Pull undated   **From 150 EF**

Two designs of the large notes have survived as proofs or pulls, the first a simple design featuring just the promissory text and a 'cheque' panel of elaborately interwoven letters reading 'EDINBURGH' and 'SCOTS BANK'. One issued £5 note is known to have survived in an archive. Dimensions of all issues of the large notes ~ 255 x 116mm.

BA 34   **£5**   **Cheque panel EDINBURGH and SCOTS BANK** Dated by hand
                        1 Sep 1751   **RARE**

Proof/Pull undated   **From 150 EF**

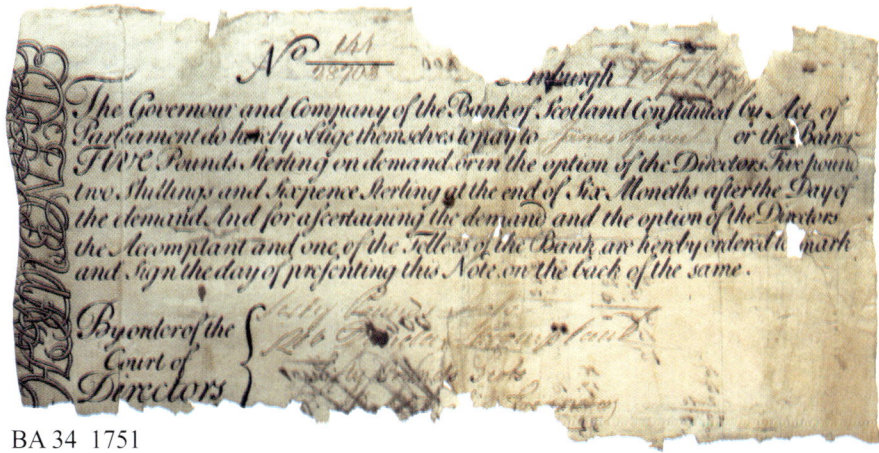

BA 34 1751

BA 35	£10	Similar to BA 34	
		Proof/Pull undated	From 150 EF
BA 36	£20	Similar to BA 34	
		Proof/Pull undated	From 150 EF
BA 37	£50	Similar to BA 34	
		Proof/Pull undated	From 150 EF
BA 38	£100	Similar to BA 34	
		Proof/Pull undated	From 150 EF

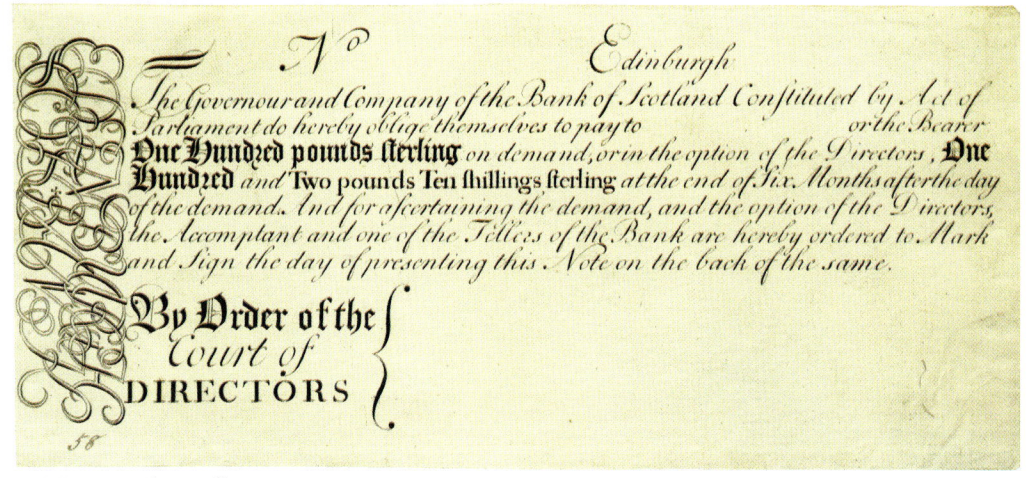

BA 38 Proof or Pull

The second design of the large notes features a scrollwork panel and a small oval value panel upper left.

BA 39	£5	Scrollwork panel Small oval value panel upper left	
		Proof/Pull undated	From 150 EF
BA 40	£10	Similar to BA 39	
		Proof/Pull undated	From 150 EF

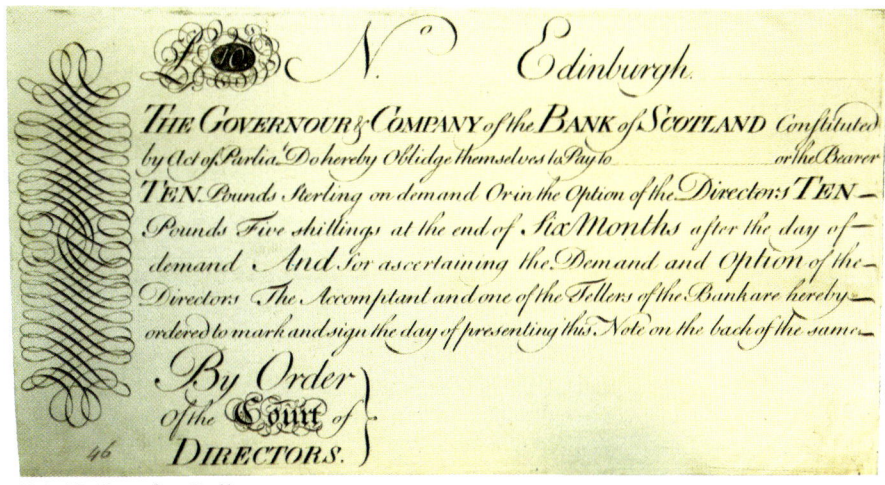

BA 40 Proof or Pull

BA 41   £20   Similar to BA 39

             Proof/Pull undated   From 150 EF

BA 42   £50   Similar to BA 39

             Proof/Pull undated   From 150 EF

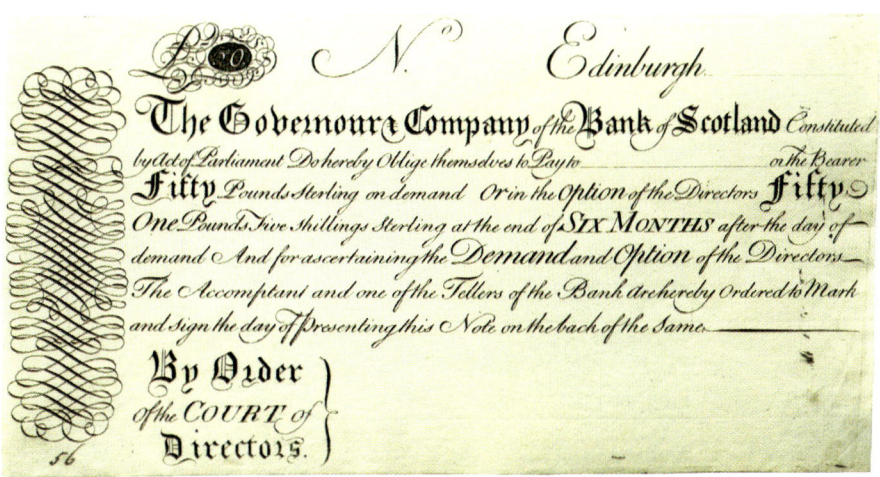

BA 42 Proof or Pull

BA 43   £100   Similar to BA 39

             Proof/Pull undated   From 150 EF

The issue of Option Clause notes finally ended on 14th May 1766.

POST BILL ISSUES

Post bills were intended to provide security for money in transit and were normally made payable to a named person or order (not bearer), seven days after sight, thus allowing the holder to alert the Bank if the bill was lost or stolen. The Bank's promissory text carried the additional words '*for value received*'. The decision was taken on 1st December 1757 to issue post bills to satisfy complaints of '*moneys being lost by miscarriage of letters*'. Three plates were ordered and engraved in early 1758, one for £10, one for £20 and one with the sum left blank to meet any other sum required. From 24th July 1771 no post bills under £20 were issued and the payment date was fixed at seven days after sight. 8,400 post bills were issued between 1758 and 1784 and only one is known to have survived, a £20 note with the words '*this to be paid in the Company's notes*' added by hand. Pulls exist of both the £10 and £20 post bills.

BA 44   £10   Post Bill Promissory text ends '… for value received'

  Proof/Pull undated   From 150 EF

BA 45   £20   Post Bill Promissory text ends '… for value received'
              1764   RARE

BA 45 Post Bill for £20 issued 1764

  Proof/Pull undated   From 150 EF

TEN SHILLINGS NOTES

To accommodate merchants and other traders who complained that payments under 20s were frequently made and required coin to complete the transaction, the Bank considered issuing 10s notes in the summer of 1760. Plans were drawn up and specimen notes dated 15th May 1760 were prepared from plates engraved in London. The issue did not however go ahead. Proofs and pulls have survived in small numbers.

BA 46   10s   **Simple design Ten Shillings or £6 Scots** printed date 15 May 1760

        Proof/Pull   **From 150 EF**

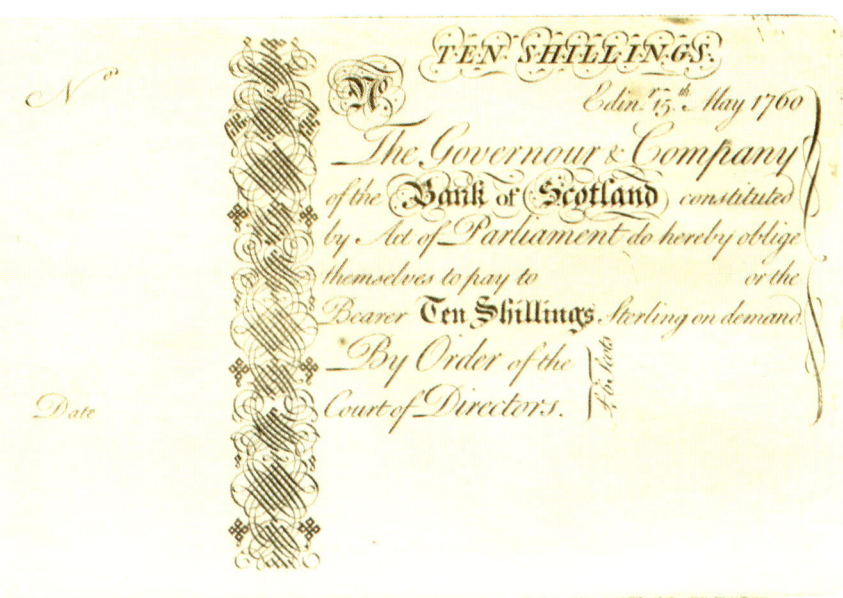

BA 46 Proof or Pull

1765 to 1780 ISSUES

11th Sett £1 notes
9th Sett, 12th Sett 1 Guinea Notes
10th & 11th Setts Large Notes

Option clause notes were abolished with effect from 15th May 1766 but it was already clear that new notes would be needed to replace them. New plates were ordered in June 1765 for all denominations including £1 notes. In June 1774 Parliament permitted the Bank to increase its capital stock to £200,000 and an increase in note issuance volumes followed. This period of expansion also saw branches being opened in Kelso and Dumfries in 1774, Kilmarnock, Inverness and Ayr in 1775, Stirling in 1776 and Aberdeen in 1780. Agents were established in Paisley and Dunfermline in 1781.

£1 notes carried the printed date 1st August 1765. Designs remained very similar to the pre-option clause notes. 90,000 £1 notes were issued, the first 48,000 of which were hand signed by Alexander Falconar (Accomptant) and John Spence (Teller). All notes are payable to James Spence (Secretary 1746 to 1792). Issued £1 notes were numbered from 1/1 to 150/90000.

BA 47	£1	**Scrollwork panel** printed date 1 Aug 1765	**RARE**

BA 47 1765

    Proof/Pull   From 150 EF

    Tercentenary Pull (1995)   From 150 EF

In July 1765 it was decided to issue a 1 Guinea note for the first time. Plates were ready by 31st July and engraved with the date 1st August 1765. There is no evidence these were issued and it is possible that pressure from the Royal Bank (whose own 1 Guinea issue had first appeared in 1758) caused the Bank to decide to hold off. No notes of this date have been seen and the first 1 Guinea issue did not appear until 1768, referred to in the Bank's records as the 9th Sett. With the issue of these notes the minutes of 17th February 1768 recorded ' ... *that no more twenty shilling Notes be filled up*'. 144,000 notes were issued in books of 600 notes numbered from 1/1 to 240/144000. All notes handsigned by the Accomptant and the Teller.

BA 48   1gn   Scrollwork panel Black value panel printed date
2 May 1768   **RARE**

Proof/Pull   From 150 EF

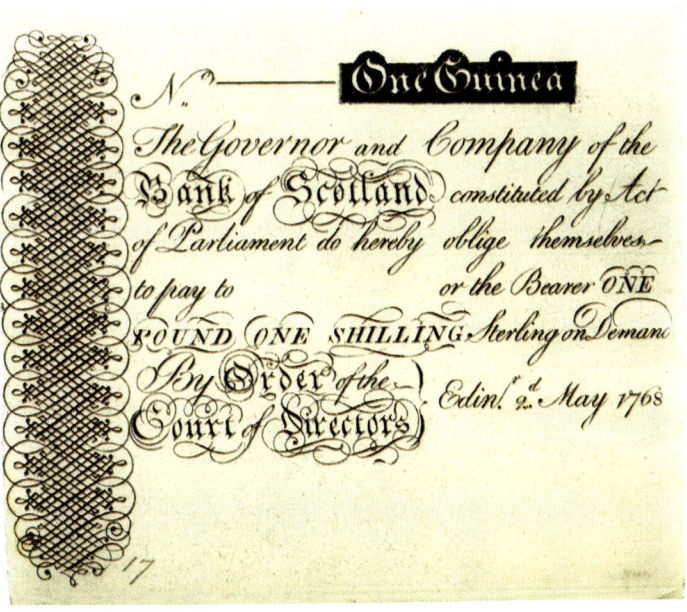

BA 48 Proof or Pull

A forgery of the 1768 1 Guinea notes was discovered on 21st January 1774. New plates were ordered to be engraved by Andrew Bell and were approved after minor alteration on 24th January. These are referred to as the 12th Sett. They were printed in two colours in an attempt to deter future forgers, the value panel upper centre and the ornate lettering of the Bank's name in the left hand panel now being printed in blue. This is the Bank's first dual-coloured note. In 1775 the tellers were instructed that when paying coin in exchange for Guinea notes '*one half ... shall be given in silver, unless it be suspected that a bad use is to be made of it*'. Guinea notes of this issue were engraved with plate letters from A to I, each series being numbered 1/1 to 100/60000, i.e. a total issue of 540,000 notes. All notes hand signed by the Accomptant and the Teller.

BA 49   1gn   **Promissory text in black Blue value panel upper centre**
Blue 'cheque' panel printed date
2 Feb 1774   plate A to I   **From 2500 F**

BA 49 1774 Blue panels

Proof/Pull (Black)   **From 150 EF**

Proof No value panel or cheque panel   **From 100 EF**

Apart from the change to the promissory text the large notes were mostly unchanged from the second option note issue. They remained dated by hand. 10th Sett notes were dated 2nd January 1766 and were signed by David Inglis (Treasurer) and Alexander Falconar (Accountant). Notes were issued in books of 200 and the single run of book numbers was shared across all five denominations. In total 24,200 large notes of this Sett were issued. 11th Sett notes were dated 6th July 1768 and are believed to be the same design. A total of 58,000 notes of the 11th Sett were issued. No higher value issued notes are known to have survived.

BA 50	£5	Scrollwork panel Small oval value pane	
		Proof/Pull	From 150 EF
BA 51	£10	Similar BA 50	
		Proof/Pull	From 150 EF
BA 52	£20	Similar BA 50	
		Proof/Pull	From 150 EF

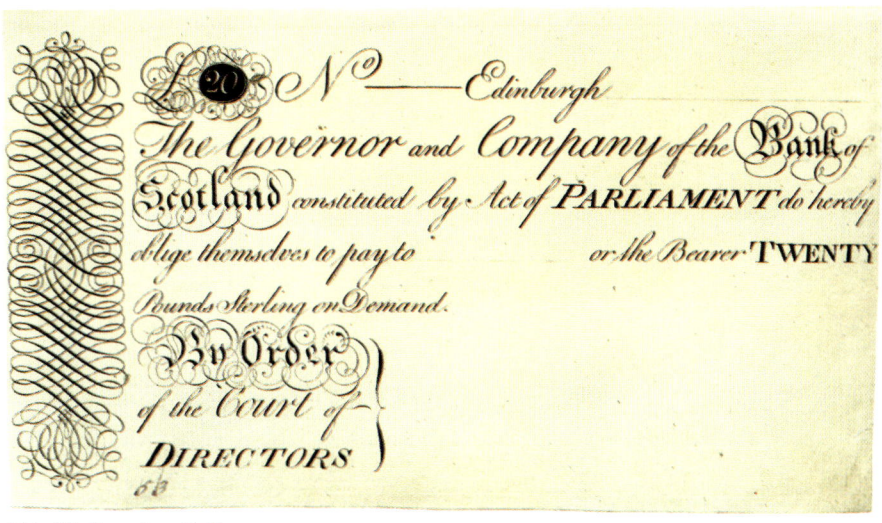

BA 52 Proof or Pull

BA 53	£50	Similar BA 50	
		Proof/Pull	From 150 EF
BA 54	£100	Similar BA 50	
		Proof/Pull	From 150 EF

1780 *to* c.1827 ISSUES

New notes of all denominations were engraved in 1780 according to Douglas though it appears that no new £1 notes were issued until 1795 despite the Bank considering the idea in 1792 and even ordering new plates to be prepared. The £1 and 1 Guinea notes were replaced in 1810 but the large notes continued essentially unchanged in design until at least 1827. In 1810 notes for the short-lived denominations of £2 and 2 Guineas were issued. Note issuance records are incomplete for this period but with the Bank's capital increasing to £1,000,000 in September 1793 the Bank clearly expected business to expand at a greater rate than hitherto and note issuance no doubt kept pace. Notes issued on or after 2nd December 1799 bear an embossed revenue stamp.

All notes are payable to the Secretary or bearer and except where stated the Secretary's name was inserted by hand. During this period the position was held in part jointly by James Spence (1746-1786) and Thomas Steuart (1767-1786), then James Fraser (1786-1809), William Wardrop (1792-1802), George Neilson (1792-1824) and George Sandy (1805-1837).

BA 55a   **£1**   **ONE POUND upper centre**   **Payee added by hand**
                       BANK OF SCOTLAND EDIN^R in vertical panel left
                       Imprint: **Paton and Kirkwood**   Dated by hand
                       1795 to 1808   plate A to E   **From 2000 F**

BA 55b   **£1**   **Similar to BA 55a**   printed dates
                       1 Jan 1795
                       2 Dec 1799   plate K   **From 2000 F**

In 1808 and starting with plate E the letters 'N.D.' were added upper left to indicate 'no duty'. This was done to distinguish notes issued under the 1808 Stamp Act, prior to which notes could circulate for only three years from the date of issue. Some of the forged notes were produced by French prisoners of war housed in the Valleyfield paper factory at Penicuik and in Edinburgh Castle.

BA 55c   **£1**   **Similar to BA 55b**   **N.D. upper left**   Dated by hand
                       1808 to 1821   plate E to I   K   **From 2000 F**

                       Unissued (pull) plate F G H K   **From 150 EF**

                       Forgery 1810 to 1821   plate H I K   **From 150 F**

BA 55c Forgery 1812

A new 1 Guinea note was issued in 1780. The design was similar to the £1 note with 'One Guinea' across the top of the note in bold Gothic script and the Bank's name in a vertical panel to the left. It was on a note of this type that Robert Burns wrote his famous poem '*Wae worth thy power, thou cursed leaf!*' The note can be seen in the Robert Burns Birthplace Museum in Alloway, Ayrshire.

BA 56a	1gn	One Guinea in Gothic top centre printed date Bank of Scotland in vertical panel to left Signed & numbered by hand Payee inserted by hand *Imprint:* **Butterworth & Ashby**		
		1 Mar 1780	plate B C D E G K	**From 2000 F**
		Forgery plate C G		**From 150 F**

Some notes with the printed date 1st March 1780 carry an additional stamp dated either 2nd December 1799 or 11th October 1808, applied to ensure the note could be reissued following changes in the Stamp Acts.

BA 56b	1gn	Similar to BA 56a By Order … now lower left printed date		
		1 Mar 1780 No date stamp	plate A to G	
		1799 date stamp	plate Q S U V	
		1808 date stamp	plate A D	
		1 Mar 1798		
		2 Dec 1799	plate S	**From 2000 F**

BA 56b 1780 with date stamp 1799

		Forgery		**From 150 F**
BA 56c	1gn	Similar to BA 56a Dated by hand		
		1802 to 1806	plate A C D E F	**From 2000 F**
		Unissued (pull) plate C E		**From 150 EF**
		Forgery plate F V		**From 150 F**
BA 56d	1gn	Similar to BA 56a N.D. upper left Dated by hand		
		1808 to 1812	plate F G H I K to N P R S	**From 2000 F**
		Unissued (pull) plate F H		**From 150 EF**
		Forgery		**From 150 F**

In 1810 the Bank decided it needed notes of £2 and 2 Guineas, possibly in response to other banks issuing notes of the same denominations. The designs of both values featured a vignette of the Bank's Arms for the first time, probably as an anti-forgery device. Two issued survivors exist in the Bank's archives but pulls have been prepared from the original plates.

BA 57	£2	Bank Arms top centre with TWO & POUNDS either side		
		Imprint: **Butterworth & Menzies**		
		1810	plate A	**RARE**
		Pull plate A		**From 150 EF**

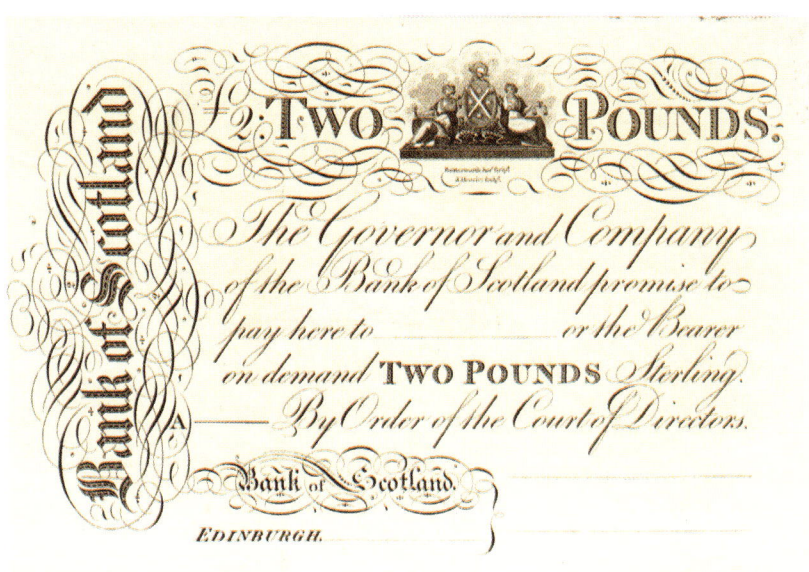

BA 57 Pull

Modern Pull plate A   From 20 EF

BA 58   2gn   Bank Arms top centre with **TWO GUINEAS** curved above
                  Imprint: **Butterworth & Menzies**
                  1810   plate A   **RARE**

            Pull plate A   From 150 EF

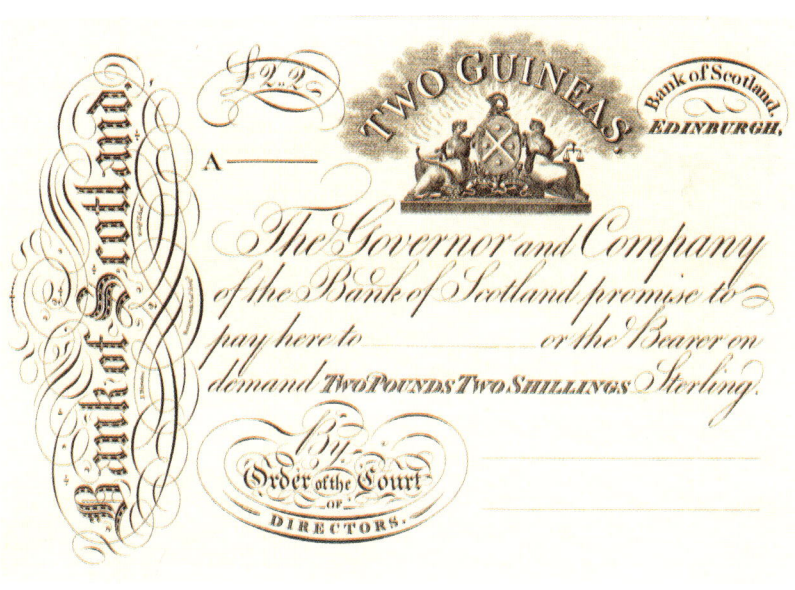

BA 58 Pull

From 1780 to at least 1827 a very simple design was used on all the higher denomination notes. £50 and £100 notes were discontinued from June 1780 but issuance of £100 notes was resumed in 1791 using an unchanged plate.

BA 59a	**£5**	**Edinburgh top centre in Gothic script Payee by hand** **No printers' imprint** year printed as 1779 & 1780 1779 1780		
		Pull plate 1		**From 150 EF**
BA 59b	**£5**	**Similar to BA 59a Payee by hand** year printed as 18 *Imprint:* **Butterworth, Dumfries & Ashby, London** 1809 to 1812 plate 2		**RARE**
BA 59c	**£5**	**Similar to BA 59a Pay George Sandy** year printed as 18 1824 plate 2		**RARE**
		Pull plate 2		**From 150 EF**
		Forgery		**From 300 F**

BA 59c 1824 Possible forgery

BA 60a	**£10**	**Similar to BA 59a Payee by hand** year printed as 17		
		Proof/Pull		From 150 EF
BA 60b	**£10**	**Similar to BA 59a Pay George Sandy** year printed as 18 1808 to 1816		**RARE**
		Proof/Pull		From 150 EF
BA 61a	**£20**	**Similar to BA 59a Payee by hand** year printed as 1780		
		Proof/Pull		From 150 EF
BA 61b	**£20**	**Similar to BA 59a Payee by hand** year printed as 18 1808 to 1813		**RARE**
BA 61c	**£20**	**Similar to BA 59a Pay George Sandy** year printed as 18		
		Proof/Pull		From 150 EF

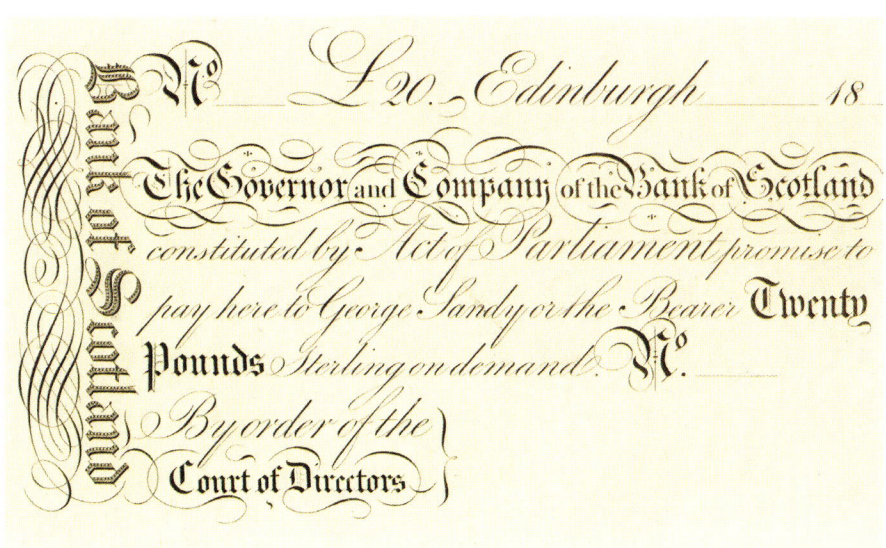

BA 61c Proof or Pull

BA 62   £100   Similar to BA 59a   Pay George Sandy

          Proof/Pull   **From 150 EF**

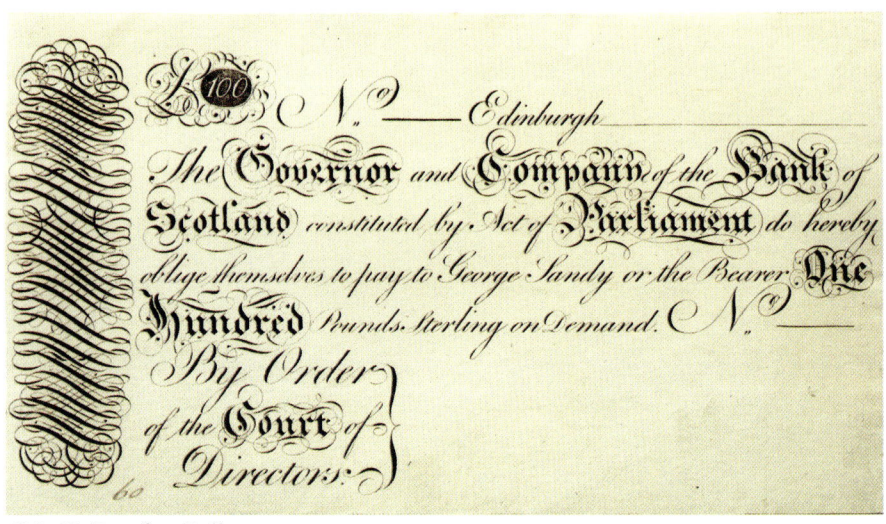

BA 62   Proof or Pull

1812 *to* 1827 ISSUES

Bank Arms design - £1 & 1 Guinea

Once again as a result of the activities of the forgers, including French prisoners of war housed in camps at Penicuik and Edinburgh Castle, it was decided in January 1812 to have new £1 and 1 Guinea notes prepared. The elaborate designs represent a marked and quite deliberate departure from earlier issues while also featuring the Bank's Arms. Although still engraved on copper plate they foreshadow the introduction of steel plate engraving in the 1820s. **John Menzies** engraved the first plates but his contract was taken over first by **W & D Lizars** (William and Daniel, his brother), then by **W H Lizars** (William Home). Only very minor differences can be detected in the plates despite the change of engravers.

An unusual essay with a large central oval design, prepared in 1820 by Sir George S MacKenzie, can be found in the Bank's archives.

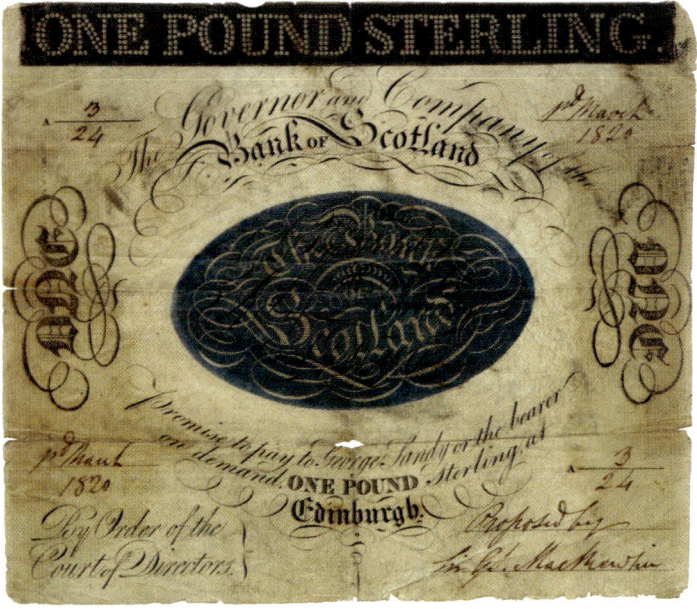

Essay by MacKenzie 1820

BA 63a	£1	**Oval vignette of Scotia top centre flanked by ONE & POUND** **Bank name & Arms in vertical panel to left,** **with full stop after Scotland Payee George Sandy** *Imprint:* **J Menzies** Dated & numbered by hand

1813 to 1819   plate A to G   From 2000 F

           Pull plate A   From 150 EF

BA 63b £1 **Similar to BA 63a** *Imprint:* **W & D Lizars** Congreve after 1821
1819 to 1821   plate G H I K L M   **From 2000 F**

Pull plate M with full stop after Scotland in side panel
plate M without full stop   **From 150 EF**

BA 63c £1 **Similar to BA 63a No stop after Scotland in side panel**
Imprint: **W H Lizars**
1824 to 1825   plate I K L M   **From 2000 F**

Pull plate M   **From 150 EF**

BA 63c Pull

The 1 Guinea design is very similar to the £1 note. There are two varieties with different printers' imprints.

BA 64a 1gn Similar to BA 63a **Pay George Sandy Full stop after Scotland**
Imprint: **J Menzies**
1813 to 1817   plate A to F   **From 2000 F**

              Pull plate A D   **From 150 EF**

              Forgery 1818 to 1826 (some with forged Congreve)   **From 150 F**

BA 64b 1gn Similar to BA 63a *Imprint:* **W & D Lizars**
1818 & 1819   plate F G   **From 2000 F**

BA 64b 1818

              Pull plate G   **From 150 EF**

              Forgery 1818 to 1826 (some with forged Congreve)   **From 150 F**

Records have survived of the total issuance and numbers outstanding of large notes for the period from 1801 to 1827. These are summarised below:

Set 15: 1801

Denomination	£100	£20	£10	£5	Totals £
Numbers issued	1000	2800	6000	7600	£254,000
Retired/Burnt	1000	2798	5993	7586	£253,820
Outstanding in 1832	-	2	7	14	£180

Set 16: 1805 *to* 1808

Denomination	£100	£20	£10	£5	Totals £
Numbers issued	1200	8000	7000	7400	£387,000
Retired/Burnt	1200	7987	6984	7381	£386,485
Outstanding in 1832	-	13	16	19	£515

Set 17: 1808 *to* 1811

Denomination	£100	£20	£10	£5	Totals £
Numbers issued	1000	7400	4000	7400	£325,000
Retired/Burnt	1000	7367	3984	7373	£324,045
Outstanding in 1832	-	33	16	27	£955

Set 18: 1811 *to* 1813

Denomination	£100	£20	£10	£5	Totals £
Numbers issued	1000	6000	5800	7200	£314,000
Retired/Burnt	1000	5976	5782	7174	£313,200
Outstanding in 1832	-	24	18	26	£790

Set 19: 1813 *to* 1815

Denomination	£100	£20	£10	£5	Totals £
Numbers issued	800	4000	3600	3600	£214,000
Retired/Burnt	800	3973	3572	3561	£212,985
Outstanding in 1832	-	27	28	39	£1,015

Set 20: 1815 *to* 1818

Denomination	£100	£20	£10	£5	Totals £
Numbers issued	1400	5200	5400	8000	£338,000
Retired/Burnt	1400	5149	5343	7935	£336,085
Outstanding in 1849	-	51	57	65	£1,915

New Series: 1818 *to* 1827 (design unchanged)

Denomination	£100	£20	£10	£5	Totals £
Numbers issued	2400	11400	15400	35000	£797,000
Retired/Burnt	2400	10880	15349	34981	£785,995
Outstanding in 1867	-	520	51	19	£11,005

LIZARS STEEL PLATE ISSUES – 1827 *to* 1858

In 1827 new £1, 1 Guinea and £5 notes were prepared by **W H Lizars**. The quality of the steel plate engravings is exceptional. There is nothing in the Bank's minutes to suggest the £1 notes were ever issued but the plates have survived so both printers' proofs and modern pulls are available to collectors. The Bank's archives contain a series of £1 colour trials based on the original plate but adding a coloured border or other coloured elements to the design. Few of these interesting experimental designs have been seen on the market. They may not have been prepared until the 1830s or later. All issued notes up to 1855 were made payable to George Sandy (even though he retired as Secretary in 1837).

BA 65   £1   **Bank Arms above Vertical machinework panels left & right
                    Central machinework panel**

        Proof Black   **From 500 EF**

        Colour Trials Blue - Green - Yellow - Pink   **RARE**

BA 65 Colour Trial with pink border

        Modern Pull Blue   **From 20 EF**

BA 65 Modern Pull in blue

A £1 essay or trial, probably by Lizars, was also prepared in the 1850s, payable to Archibald Bennet. The essay's features are similar to the £5 note engraved by Lizars in 1855.

BA 66   **£1**   Pay Arch Bennet Bank Arms Allegorical females left & right

Essay   **From 600 EF**

BA 66 Essay

Later colour trials, probably prepared in the 1850s, combine features of Lizars' £1 notes for the Perth Banking Company with a vignette of the Bank of Scotland's Arms and a promissory text payable to bearer. Several varieties exist, many in the Bank's archives.

BA 67 £1 **Pay bearer Vignettes of Queen Victoria & Prince Albert**

   Colour Trials Blue with Red panel - Red with Blue panel   **From 750 EF**

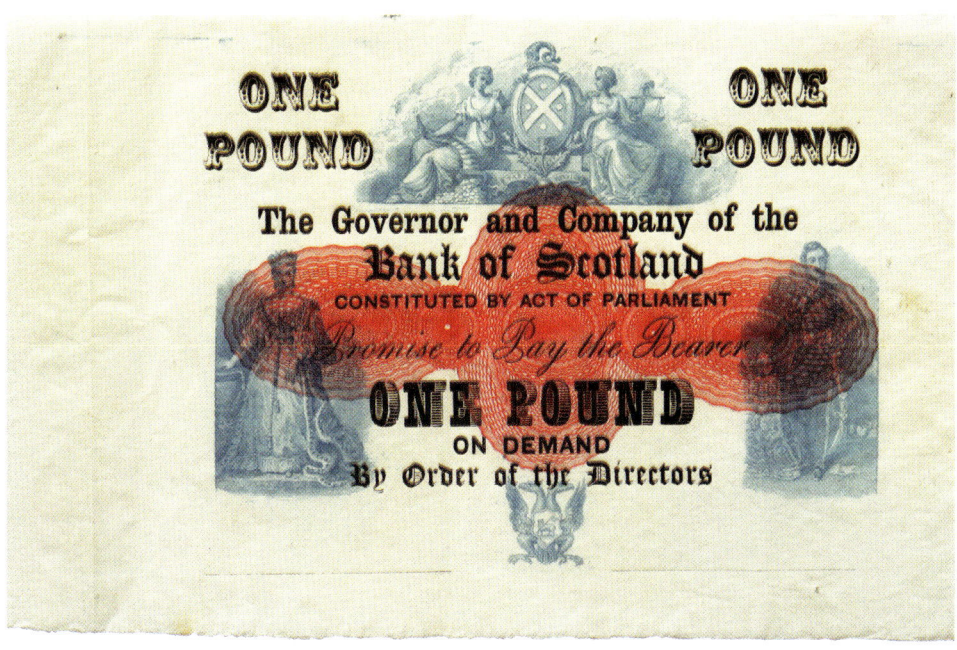

BA 67 Colour Trial in blue with red panel, elements of Perth Banking Co design

The Bank's final 1 Guinea issue appeared between 1827 and 1830. 50,000 notes in total were issued, all made payable to George Sandy (Secretary to 1837). One issued note is known to have survived in the Bank's mutilated notes register.

BA 68 1gn **Bank Arms top centre**
   Vertical panels with vignettes of allegorical females
   Central machinework panel Dated, numbered & signed by hand
      2 May 1827   **RARE**

   Proof black (also with GEOEGE SANDY mis-spelt)   **From 500 EF**

BA 68 Proof with printers' instructions George Sandy mis-spelt

Modern Pull Black   **From 20 EF**

Lizars produced three designs of the £5 note. The first was similar in design to the other denominations and has only been seen in proof form.

BA 69   £5   **Bank Arms top centre Vertical panels with vignettes of allegorical females Central machinework panel Pay George Sandy**

                Proof (no issued notes)   **From 600 EF**

BA 69 Proof

A second design was then created with a distinctive ornamental border and this was issued from 1827 to 1855. A total of 99,000 notes were issued in 495 books of 200 notes each.

BA 70a £5 **Heavy ornamental border containing Bank name above**
Bank Arms upper centre Pay George Sandy
Machinework central panel with promissory text
Dated & numbered by hand
1827 to 1838   **RARE**

Proof Black   **From 500 EF**

BA 70 Proof

BA 70b £5 **Similar to BA 70a** printed serials
1838 to 1849   **RARE**

BA 70c £5 **Similar to BA 70a Additional text in Red:**
Pursuant to Act / 16 & 17 Victoria Cap. 63
1854   **RARE**

A third design was prepared in 1855 made payable to Archibald Bennet (Joint, then sole, Secretary from 1824-1868). Between 1855 and 1858 30,000 notes were issued in 150 books of 200 notes each. The last batch of these notes was delivered by W & A K Johnston who took over Lizars's business after his death in 1859, but there is no evidence that the printers' imprint was changed. Notes of this type have only been seen on the market as proofs. An essay is known payable to James Simpson rather than Archibald Bennet. It is not known why this name was chosen as there is no record of an official at the Bank by this name.

BA 71 £5 **Bank Arms top centre No border Pay Archibald Bennet**
Two allegorical vignettes left & right printed serials
Handsigned p Accountant & p Treasurer year printed as 185
1855 to 1858 **RARE**

Proof Black From 500 EF

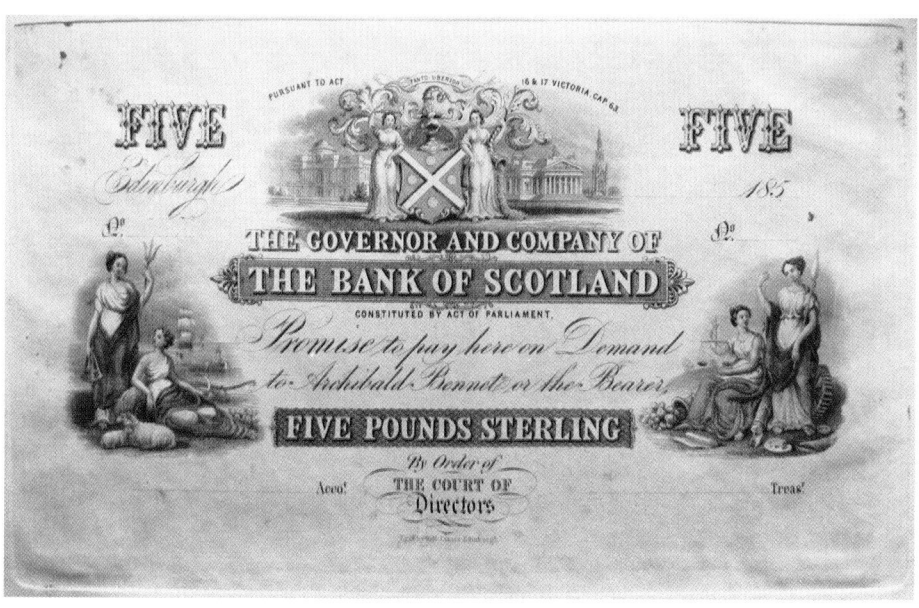

BA 71 Proof

Essay Black payable to James Simpson From 600 EF

FIRST PERKINS BACON ISSUE – 1827 *to* 1859

In early 1827 and thus about the same time as Lizars was commissioned to prepare new 1 Guinea and £5 notes on steel plate, the Bank also approached **Perkins & Heath** (later **Perkins & Bacon**) to prepare new notes for £1, £10, £20 and £100. The designs had many features in common and featured the Bank Arms top centre, an ornate panel to the left containing a vignette of Scotia, all within a machinework border. These notes were first issued in May 1827 and stayed in issue until 1860. Notes were made payable to George Sandy until 1854 then to Archibald Bennet. All issued notes continue to carry an impression of the Bank's seal. In 1849 the Bank switched their suppliers of watermarked paper for their higher value notes; Cowans of Penicuik were dropped in favour of Portals of Basingstoke. In 1856 W H Roberts of Laverock Bank, Edinburgh (who happened to be Perkins & Bacon's agent in Scotland), was commissioned to supply watermarked paper for the £1 notes.

A proof of the £1 note printed in blue ink was ordered from Perkins Bacon in 1856 following a spate of photographic forgeries. Three notes were delivered along with proofs in other colours (not seen) but it was decided not to put the blue version into circulation.

From 1827 the Bank's note registers are more or less complete so available details are set out in full. £1 notes started with plate letter F with 50,000 notes per plate letter and date. Letter J was not used.

BA 72a   £1   **Arms top centre flanked by ovals with ONE   Ornate panel left**
                     Pay George Sandy   Serials & dates by hand
                     Prefix letter engraved on plate
                     Imprint: **Perkins & Heath   Handsigned but no titles on plate**

Date	Prefix	Serial	Qty	
15 May 1827	F 1/1	- 100/500	50,000	
10 Dec 1827	G 1/1	- 100/500	50,000	
10 Nov 1829	H 1/1	- 100/500	50,000	
15 Dec 1830	I 1/1	- 100/500	50,000	**From 2000 F**
Proof undated plate F				**From 200 EF**

BA 72b   £1   **Similar to BA 72a**   *Imprint:* **Perkins & Bacon**

Date	Prefix	Serial	Qty	
25 May 1832	K 1/1	- 100/500	50,000	
15 May 1833	L 1/1	- 100/500	50,000	
2 Nov 1833	M 1/1	- 100/500	50,000	
9 Oct 1835	N 1/1	- 100/500	50,000	
6 Sep 1836	O 1/1	- 100/500	50,000	
2 Feb 1837	P 1/1	- 100/500	50,000	**From 2000 F**

BA 72c   £1   **Similar to BA 72a**   *Imprint:* **Perkins, Bacon & Petch**

Date	Prefix	Serial	Qty	
8 Jan 1838	Q 1/1	- 100/500	50,000	
4 Jun 1838	R 1/1	- 100/500	50,000	**From 2000 F**
Proof undated plate R				**From 200 EF**

BA 72d   £1   **Similar to BA 72a   Serials now printed**

Date	Prefix	Serial	Qty	
5 Apr 1839	S 1/1	- 100/500	50,000	
19 Aug 1839	T 1/1	- 100/500	50,000	
4 Dec 1840	U 1/1	- 100/500	50,000	
7 Jul 1842	V 1/1	- 100/500	50,000	
8 Mar 1844	W 1/1	- 100/500	50,000	
17 Jun 1845	X 1/1	- 100/500	50,000	
6 Nov 1845	Y 1/1	- 100/500	50,000	
16 Oct 1846	Z 1/1	- 100/500	50,000	

Fractional prefix

Date	Prefix	Serial	Qty	
4 Jan 1848	A/A 1/1	- 100/500	50,000	
27 Sep 1849	A/B 1/1	- 100/500	50,000	
23 Apr 1850	A/C 1/1	- 100/500	50,000	
19 Mar 1851	A/D 1/1	- 100/500	50,000	
20 Oct 1851	A/E 1/1	- 100/500	50,000	

Larger prefix letters

Date	Prefix	Serial	Qty	
3 Aug 1852	A/F 1/1	- 100/500	50,000	
8 Feb 1853	A/G 1/1	- 100/500	50,000	**From 2000 F**

BA 72d 1851

  Proof undated A/A A/E   **From 200 EF**

  Specimen undated T U A/C   **From 500 EF**

BA 72e   £1   Similar to BA 72a Payable to Archibald Bennet
       Imprint: **Perkins, Bacon and Co**
       Overprinted in Red:
       PURSUANT TO ACT 16 & 17 VICTORIA CAP. 63
       Prefixes are no longer engraved on the plate
       20 Apr 1854 A/H 1/1 - 100/500   50,000   **RARE**

BA 72f   £1   Similar to BA 72a Payable to Archibald Bennet
       PURSUANT TO ACT 16 & 17 VICTORIA CAP. 63 in upper border
       Signatory titles added p Accot & p Teller

6 Sep 1854	A/I 1/1	-	100/500	50,000
1 Mar 1855	A/K 1/1	-	100/500	50,000
21 Jun 1855	A/L 1/1	-	100/500	50,000
16 Oct 1855	A/M 1/1	-	100/500	50,000
22 Jan 1856	A/N 1/1	-	100/500	50,000
6 May 1856	A/O 1/1	-	100/500	50,000
12 Aug 1856	A/P 1/1	-	100/500	50,000
30 Apr 1857	A/Q 1/1	-	100/500	50,000
8 Oct 1857	A/R 1/1	-	100/500	50,000
16 Nov 1857	A/S 1/1	-	100/500	50,000
14 Dec 1857	A/T 1/1	-	100/500	50,000
4 May 1858	A/U 1/1	-	100/500	50,000
11 Nov 1858	A/V 1/1	-	100/500	50,000
8 Jun 1859	A/W 1/1	-	100/500	50,000
8 Jul 1859	A/X 1/1	-	100/500	50,000

                            From 1500 F

Proof undated Blue no prefix   From 500 EF

BA 72f Proof in blue

Specimen undated A/O 100/500 A/S 100/500   From 500 EF

BA 73a   £10   **Arms top centre flanked by ovals with TEN Ornate panel left**
Pay George Sandy Serials & date by hand
Prefix letter engraved on plate *Imprint:* **Perkins & Heath**
Handsigned but no titles on plate

10 Oct	1827	A	1/1	-	15/200	3,000
13 Oct	1829	A	16/1	-	25/200	2,000
1 Jun	1831	A	26/1	-	35/200	2,000
1 Nov	1833	A	36/1	-	50/200	3,000
23 Jul	1840	B	51/1	-	100/200	10,000
18 Sep	1850	C	101/1	-	120/200	4,000 RARE

Proof undated plate A   From 500 EF

A single issued £10 note has survived from the 1854 overprinted issue.

BA 73b £10 **Similar to BA 72a** *Imprint:* **Perkins & Heath**
printed serials **Overprinted in Red:**
PURSUANT TO ACT / 16 & 17 VICTORIA CAP. 63
Handsigned Acc^t & Treas^r **Titles engraved on plate**
18 Sep 1854   C 121/1   -   150/200   6,000   **RARE**

BA 73b 1854

BA 73c £10 **Similar to BA 72a Pay Archibald Bennet**
PURSUANT TO …. engraved on plate in upper border
6 Aug 1856   D 151/1   -   175/200   5,000

BA 74a £20 **Similar to BA 72a Pay George Sandy**
Imprint: **Perkins & Heath**
10 Apr 1828	A 1/1	-	5/200	1,000
1 Nov 1828	A 6/1	-	10/200	1,000
1 Oct 1829	A 11/1	-	15/200	1,000
1 Jul 1831	A 16/1	-	24/200	1,800
1 Nov 1833	A 25/1	-	25/200	200
22 Oct 1838	B 26/1	-	50/200	5,000
2 Nov 1843	B 51/1	-	75/200	5,000
4 Mar 1846	C 76/1	-	100/200	5,000
6 Apr 1853	D 101/1	-	105/200	1,000

Proof undated plate A   **From 500 EF**

BA 74b £20 Similar to BA 72a *Imprint:* **Perkins & Heath** printed serials
Overprinted in Red:
PURSUANT TO ACT 16 & 17 VICTORIA CAP. 63
Handsigned Acc^t & Treas^r **Titles engraved on plate**
26 Apr 1854   D 106/1   -   125/200   4,000

BA 74c £20 Similar to BA 72a **Pay Archibald Bennet**
PURSUANT TO ... engraved on plate in upper border
 4 Jun 1856   E 126/1   -   150/200   5,000
10 Nov 1858   F 151/1   -   160/200   2,000

Specimen undated F 160/200   **From 500 EF**

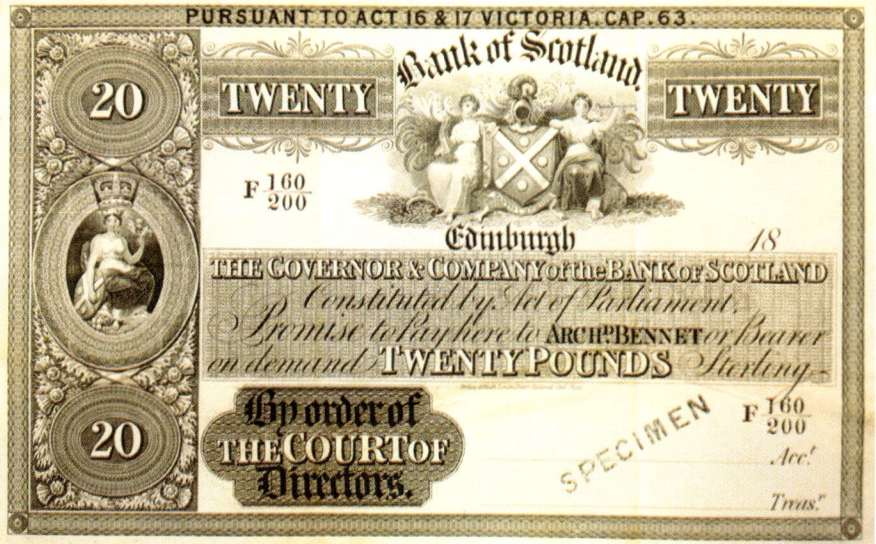

BA 74c Specimen

There were two designs of the £100 note, both prepared by **Perkins & Heath** around 1827-28. The adopted design is more similar in style to the £1 and £10 notes. There is little to choose aesthetically between the two designs and both featured the Bank Arms upper centre and a vignette of Caledonia to the left surmounted by a crown.

BA 75 £100 **Bank Arms upper centre ONE HUNDRED POUNDS curved above**
Vignette of Caledonia left Pay George Sandy
Imprint: **Perkins & Heath**

Proof/Essay Unadopted
From 600 EF

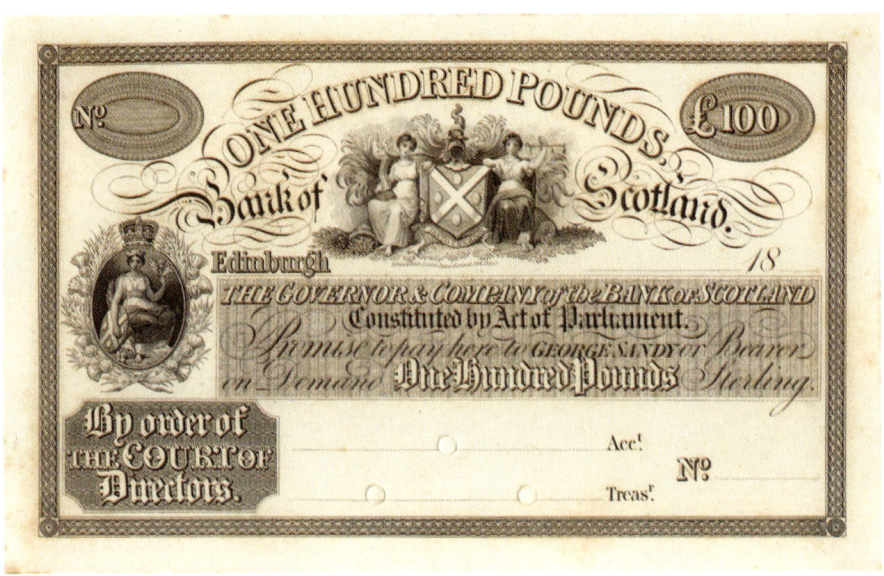

BA 75 Proof

BA 76a £100 Pay George Sandy Ornate vertical panel to left
Bank Arms below ONE HUNDRED POUNDS panel
Imprint: **Perkins & Heath**

10 Apr 1828	1/1	-	3/200	600
11 Nov 1829	4/1	-	5/200	400
2 Nov 1831	6/1	-	7/200	400
1 Nov 1833	8/1	-	10/200	600
5 Oct 1839	11/1	-	15/200	1,000
18 Nov 1845	16/1	-	20/200	1,000
28 Sep 1848	21/1	-	25/200	1,000
3 Dec 1852	26/1	-	29/200	800

Proof undated   From 600 EF

BA 76b £100 Similar to BA 76a *Imprint:* **Perkins & Heath** printed serials
Overprinted in Red:
PURSUANT TO ACT 16 & 17 VICTORIA CAP. 63
Handsigned Acc^t & Treas^r **Titles engraved on plate**

3 Oct 1854	30/1	-	30/200	200

BA 76c £100 Similar to BA 76a Pay Archibald Bennet
   PURSUANT TO …. engraved on plate in upper border
4 May 1855	31/1	- 35/200	1,000
4 Nov 1857	36/1	- 40/200	1,000
10 Aug 1858	41/1	- 45/200	1,000

   Specimen undated no prefix 43/200   **RARE**

BA 76c Specimen

BRADBURY & EVANS £100 ESSAYS – 1858 & 1880

By the mid-1850s the Bank was becoming increasingly concerned about forgeries using the new medium of photography and the minutes record a number of such forgeries of the £1 note in 1856. Reports on the problem were commissioned the same year from W H Lizars and George Wilson, Professor of Technology at Edinburgh University. The Bank also entered into detailed correspondence with Perkins Bacon & Co, the quality of whose notes they were clearly ambivalent about.

As a result the Bank decided to approach **Bradbury & Evans**, a London-based printing and engraving firm (and the predecessor of Bradbury Wilkinson & Co) to request the preparation of new notes using the best methods available to combat forgeries. The firm submitted artist's essays for each denomination but the Bank finally decided to order the engraving of just the £100 note, in February 1857. After some delay a number of proofs were despatched in April 1858. Some were printed in two colours, black and dark red, others were black only. All were printed using the intaglio method and carried the printers' imprint. On the choice of no more than two colours, Henry Bradbury wrote *'Then as few colours as possible should be used on account of the increased confusion to the public and expense and trouble in printing incurred.'*

Correspondence in the Bank's files indicates that the Bank was ready to order £5, £10 and £20 notes too, subject to agreement on price and terms. These terms were never agreed and discussions were ended in October 1858 when the Bank decided to resume negotiations with Perkins Bacon.

BA 77 **£100 Bank Arms top centre Black with Red panels Pay Bearer
Bank name in Roman capitals Ornate panel with Scotia to left**
Imprint: **Bradbury & Evans**

    Proof Black & Red
         Black Red 100 panel Pale Brown underlay
         Black   **From 300 EF**

BA 77 Proof with red panels

In 1880, according to Douglas, when the Bank embarked on a period of extensive research into methods of preventing forgery, it turned to the original Bradbury & Evans plate to have colour trials prepared using four different combinations of colour and overlay, all printed by lithography. Some changes to the earlier plate are evident but there is no record of who engraved the reworked plate. None of these experimental notes went into circulation of course and they do not carry the Bradbury & Evans imprint. No mention of these notes can be found in the Bank's records but the resulting essays are attractive and unusual for their time.

BA 78 **£100 Bank name in Gothic script Brown vertical panel left
No printers' imprint Pay Bearer**

    Colour Trial Large Red 100 underlay
                 Large Red £100 in script form
                 Large Olive-Green £100 in script form
                 Large Purple £100 in script form   **From 250 EF**

BA 78 Colour Trial in purple

SECOND PERKINS BACON ISSUE – 1860 *to* 1884

Pay Bearer

These designs are quite different from the earlier Perkins Bacon notes but are notable in that they see the introduction of a secondary coloured panel, the Bank's chosen method of deterring photographic forgeries. This followed a long examination of different anti-forgery methods in the late 1850s and the flirtation with Bradbury & Evans. The Bank commissioned Alexander Christie, Master of the Edinburgh School of Design to prepare the designs which were uniform across all five denominations. The value panel of the £100 note was however in green rather than red. The most striking change was to the vertical panel to the left which now included depictions of both sides of the Great Seal of Scotland as it appeared at the time the Bank was founded in 1695.

All notes are now payable to bearer and have printed prefix and serials. All notes carry the imprint of **Perkins, Bacon & Co London** on paper provided by Wyse & Co of Northampton. £1 notes were initially printed in 100 books of 500 notes for each prefix, but from prefix F this doubled to 200 books per prefix. All prefix letters are used. Proofs and specimens of all denominations have survived but the only issued notes of this series seen to date are £1 notes.

BA 79a	£1	Black Red ONE panel Handsigned p Acco^t & p Teller				
		Hand-written date				
		1 Mar 1860	A 1/1	-	100/500	50,000	
		4 Apr 1860	B 1/1	-	100/500	50,000	
		6 Jun 1860	C 1/1	-	100/500	50,000	
		23 Aug 1860	D 1/1	-	100/500	50,000	
		4 Sep 1860	E 1/1	-	100/500	50,000	**From 1500 F**
		Proof undated					**From 150 EF**

BA 79b £1 **Similar to BA 79a Handsigned** p Acco^t & p Teller printed date
   15 Oct 1860 F 1/1 - 200/500   100,000
                G 1/1 - 200/500   100,000
    5 Dec 1862 H 1/1 - 200/500   100,000
   14 Jul 1863 I 1/1 - 200/500   100,000
    5 Jan 1864 J 1/1 -   85/359   100,000   **From 1500 F**

The following **Proof** notes have been recorded:
15 Oct 1860   5 Dec 1862   14 Jul 1863   5 Jan 1864   **From 150 EF**

BA 79b Proof 1860 first printed date

A minor change in the designation of the signatories took place in 1864. The 'p' before Teller is dropped.

BA 79c £1 **Similar to BA 79a Handsigned** p Acco^t & Teller
    5 Jan 1864 J 104/160 - 200/500   included BA 79b
   30 Jun 1864 K 1/1 - 200/500   100,000
    2 Nov 1864 L 1/1 - 200/500   100,000
   10 May 1865 M 1/1 - 200/500   100,000
   22 Feb 1866 N 1/1 - 200/500   100,000
    8 Oct 1866 O 1/1 - 200/500   100,000
    6 Mar 1867 P 1/1 - 200/500   100,000
   22 Jul 1867 Q 1/1 - 200/500   100,000
    2 Jan 1868 R 1/1 - 200/500   100,000
    1 Aug 1868 S 1/1 - 200/500   100,000
   14 Dec 1868 T 1/1 - 200/500   100,000
    5 Apr 1869 U 1/1 - 200/500   100,000
   15 Sep 1869 V 1/1 - 200/500   100,000
    8 Aug 1872 W 1/1 - 200/500   100,000
   14 Nov 1872 X 1/1 - 200/500   100,000
    2 May 1873 Y 1/1 - 200/500   100,000   **From 1500 F**

Specimen 15 Sep 1869 no prefix/serials   **From 500 EF**

The following **Proof** notes have been recorded:
Undated	30 Jun 1864	2 Nov 1864	10 May 1865
22 Feb 1866	8 Oct 1866	6 Mar 1867	22 Jul 1867
2 Jan 1868	14 Dec 1868	5 Apr 1869	15 Sep 1869
8 Aug 1872	14 Nov 1872		

From 150 EF

In 1873 the Bank decided it was no longer necessary to emboss their seal on every £1 note issued.

BA 79d   £1   Similar to BA 79a **No embossed Bank Seal**
             3 Dec 1873   Z   1/1 - 200/500   100,000
             Fractional prefix
             2 Jan 1874 A/A 1/1 - 200/500   100,000
             12 Mar 1874 A/B 1/1 - 200/500   100,000
             16 Apr 1875 A/C 1/1 - 200/500   100,000
             8 Jul 1875 A/D 1/1 - 200/500   100,000
             30 Nov 1875 A/E 1/1 - 200/500   100,000   **From 1500 F**

BA 79d 1875

The following **Proof** notes have been recorded:
3 Dec 1873   2 Jan 1874   12 Mar 1874   8 Jul 1875   **From 150 EF**

In April 1876 it was decided to print the Accountant's signature on the £1 notes and have them hand signed only by, or on behalf of, the Teller. As part of the Bank's continuing experiments with coloured inks, an attractive colour trial of the £1 note was prepared in 1878 with the basic plate in blue and the value panel in red. The first printed signature was that of Edward Lothian but no issued notes with this signature have been seen (apart from a remnant in the Bank's mutilated notes register) and the only proofs are undated (but with pencil notations indicating they were prepared in May and June 1877 and 'awaiting a date').

BA 79e £1 **Similar to BA 79a Edward Lothian** printed signature Accountant
Handsigned Teller

4 Aug 1876	A/F 1/1	-	200/500	100,000
6 Dec 1876	A/G 1/1	-	200/500	100,000
19 Feb 1877	A/H 1/1	-	200/500	100,000
1 Jun 1877	A/I 1/1	-	200/500	100,000

RARE

Proof undated 19 Feb 1877 **From 250 EF**

BA 79e Proof Lothian signature

The earliest confirmed date of a note with the printed signature of Christopher Bell is 15th May 1878.

BA 79f   £1   **Similar to BA 79a Christopher Bell** printed signature Accountant
Handsigned Teller

Date	Serial		Range	Quantity	
15 May 1878	A/J 1/1	-	200/500	100,000	
30 Sep 1878	A/K 1/1	-	200/500	100,000	
17 Jan 1879	A/L 1/1	-	200/500	100,000	
9 Apr 1879	A/M 1/1	-	200/500	100,000	
7 Nov 1879	A/N 1/1	-	200/500	100,000	
5 Feb 1880	A/O 1/1	-	200/500	100,000	
23 Oct 1880	A/P 1/1	-	200/500	100,000	
10 Mar 1881	A/Q 1/1	-	200/500	100,000	
3 May 1881	A/R 1/1	-	200/500	100,000	
8 Dec 1881	A/S 1/1	-	200/500	100,000	
1 Jul 1882	A/T 1/1	-	200/500	100,000	
28 Sep 1882	A/U 1/1	-	200/500	100,000	
13 Nov 1882	A/V 1/1	-	200/500	100,000	
12 Apr 1883	A/W 1/1	-	200/500	100,000	
18 Aug 1883	A/X 1/1	-	200/500	100,000	
2 Oct 1883	A/Y 1/1	-	200/500	100,000	
14 Jan 1884	A/Z 1/1	-	200/500	100,000	
20 Jun 1884	B/A 1/1	-	200/500	100,000	
29 Jul 1884	B/B 1/1	-	200/500	100,000	
22 Sep 1884	B/C 1/1	-	200/500	100,000	**From 1250 F**

BA 79f 1879

Colour Trial Blue & Red 15 May 1878 **From 600 EF**

BA 79f Colour Trial in blue and red

Specimen 14 Jan 1884 no prefix/serials **From 500 EF**

The following **Proof** notes have been recorded:
Undated   15 May 1878   3 Apr 1879   7 Nov 1879
 5 Feb 1880   23 Oct 1880   10 Mar 1881   28 Sep 1882
13 Nov 1882   12 Apr 1883   18 Aug 1883   10 Sep 1883
 2 Oct 1883   14 Jan 1884   29 Jul 1884   22 Sep 1884   **From 150 EF**

Shortly after the first £5 notes were issued the Bank found that the 'FIVE' in the upper border was not sufficiently distinct and further printing from plate A was stopped and alterations made. Those issued were ordered to be called in and cancelled and new notes with prefixes B and C were issued in their place. No issued notes of £5 or higher are known to have survived.

BA 80a   £5   **Similar to BA 79a Black Red FIVE panel** Dated by hand
                   Handsigned Acco^t & Treas^r
                   1 Mar 1860 A 1/1 - 30/200   6,000

After 1870 £5 notes were no longer embossed with the Bank's Seal. The final ten books of prefix M (291 to 300) and all notes of prefix N (301 to 400) were not issued and burnt on 4th February 1886.

BA 80b   **£5**   **Similar to BA 79a** printed date

15 Oct 1860	B 101/1 -	200/200	20,000
	C 201/1 -	300/200	20,000
2 Apr 1863	D 301/1 -	400/200	20,000
3 Jan 1867	E 401/1 -	500/200	20,000
4 Aug 1868	F 501/1 -	600/200	20,000
4 Nov 1870	G 601/1 -	700/200	20,000
8 May 1872	H 701/1 -	800/200	20,000
12 Mar 1873	I 801/1 -	900/200	20,000
9 Sep 1874	J 901/1 -	1000/200	20,000
26 Feb 1880	K 1/1 -	100/200	20,000
17 Oct 1882	L 101/1 -	200/200	20,000
11 Apr 1883	M 201/1 -	300/200	20,000
5 Jul 1884	N 301/1 -	400/200	20,000

Specimen   3 Jan 1867   **From 600 EF**

BA 80b Specimen

The following **Proof** notes have been recorded:
Undated   15 Oct 1860   3 Jan 1867   4 Aug 1868
4 Nov 1870   8 May 1872   12 Mar 1873   11 Apr 1883   **From 200 EF**

As with other banks, issuance of £10 notes was very low and notes were often being issued long after the date on them. The last notes to be sealed were those dated 1867 implying that notes dated 1868 were not issued until after the Bank's decision to discontinue embossing a seal on their notes in 1873.

A famous and high quality forgery of the £10 note first came to light in October 1882. The forged notes appear to have emanated from France and a few of them were taken in by bookmakers at Musselburgh race course as well as elsewhere in Scotland. A total of 54 are recorded as having been submitted to the Bank for payment and after some debate the directors decided to honour only those uttered in Scotland, with the exception of ones taken in by '*betting men*'. One bookie did get his money back for having turned two others in. A few of these forgeries have come on to the market over the years, all prefix E dated 8th May 1872. The red 'TEN' panel has faded to yellow in most cases but they are instantly recognisable for having a notable error on them: the printers' imprint is spelt wrongly as 'PERKNIS BACON & CO LONDON'. As a result of the forgery the final print run of £10 notes with prefix F was destroyed unissued in December 1882.

BA 81a   £10   **Similar to BA 79a   Black   Red TEN panel**
              Handsigned Acco^t & Treas^r Dated by hand
              1 Mar 1860   A   1/1   -   50/200   10,000

BA 81b   £10   **Similar to BA 79a** printed date
              6 Nov 1863   B   51/1   -   100/200   10,000
              3 Jan 1867   C   101/1 -   150/200   10,000
              4 Aug 1868   D   151/1 -   200/200   10,000
              8 May 1872   E   201/1 -   250/200   10,000
              2 Oct 1874   F   251/1 -   300/200   10,000

              Specimen 2 Oct 1874   **From 750 EF**

BA 81b Specimen stamped CANCELLED

Forgery 8 May 1872 E   **From 500 F**

BA 81b Forgery

The following **Proof** notes have been recorded:
Undated   6 Nov 1863   3 Jan 1867   4 Aug 1868
8 May 1872 2 Oct 1874   **From 200 EF**

The last £20 notes to be sealed were those dated 1870. The final issues with prefix J and K were destroyed unissued in February 1886.

BA 82a	£20	Similar to BA 79a Black Red 20 panel			
		Handsigned Acco^t & Treas^r Dated by hand			
		1 Mar 1860 A 1/1 - 25/200			5,000
BA 82b	£20	Similar to BA 79a printed date			
		2 Nov 1860 A 26/1 - 50/200			5,000
		4 Dec 1862 B 51/1 - 75/200			5,000
		3 Jan 1867 C 76/1 - 100/200			5,000
		4 Aug 1868 D 101/1 - 125/200			5,000
		8 Nov 1870 E 126/1 - 150/200			5,000
		8 May 1872 F 151/1 - 175/200			5,000
		12 Mar 1873 G 176/1 - 200/200			5,000
		6 Oct 1874 H 201/1 - 225/200			5,000
		30 Sep 1882 I 226/1 - 250/200			5,000
		5 Apr 1883 J 251/1 - 275/200			5,000
		17 Jul 1884 K 276/1 - 300/200			5,000

Specimen 6 Oct 1874   **From 750 EF**

BA 82b Specimen stamped CANCELLED

The following **Proof** notes have been recorded:
Undated   4 Dec 1862   3 Jan 1867   4 Aug 1868
8 Nov 1870 8 May 1872   12 Mar 1873 6 Oct 1874
5 Apr 1883 17 Jul 1884   **From 200 EF**

The last £100 notes to be sealed were those dated July 1872.

BA 83a £100 Similar to BA 79a Black Green 100 panel
           Handsigned Acco^t & Treas^r Dated by hand
           1 Mar 1860   1/1   -   5/200   1,000

BA 83b £100 Similar to BA 79a printed date
           15 Oct 1860   6/1   -   10/200   1,000
            2 Nov 1860 11/1   -   15/200   1,000
           27 Feb 1861 16/1   -   20/200   1,000
           23 Apr 1861 21/1   -   25/200   1,000
            3 May 1864 26/1   -   30/200   1,000
            6 Jun 1865 31/1   -   35/200   1,000
            3 Jan 1867 36/1   -   40/200   1,000
            4 Aug 1868 41/1   -   45/200   1,000
            9 Nov 1870 46/1   -   50/200   1,000
            8 May 1872 51/1   -   55/200   1,000
            5 Jun 1872 56/1   -   60/200   1,000
           10 Jul 1872 61/1   -   65/200   1,000
           12 Mar 1873 66/1   -   70/200   1,000
            7 Apr 1874 71/1   -   75/200   1,000
            1 Sep 1874 76/1   -   80/200   1,000
           15 Jan 1879 81/1   -   85/200   1,000
           10 Feb 1879 86/1   -   90/200   1,000
            1 May 1883 91/1   -   95/200   1,000
           28 Oct 1884 96/1   - 100/200   1,000

Specimen 1 Sep 1874 **From 750 EF**

BA 83b Specimen stamped CANCELLED

The following **Proof** notes have been recorded:
Undated	23 Apr 1861	6 Jun 1865	3 Jan 1867
4 Aug 1868	9 Nov 1870	8 May 1872	5 Jun 1872
10 Jul 1872	12 Mar 1873	7 Apr 1874	1 Sep 1874
1 May 1883			

From 200 EF

FIRST WATERSTON ISSUE – 1885 *to* 1888

Celtic Pattern Watermark No medallion Royal Arms

As early as 1880 the Bank approached Alexander Crum Brown, Professor of Chemistry at Edinburgh University, to prepare a report (for which he was paid £500) on the best means of protecting banknotes from forgery, especially by photographic means. The forgeries of the £10 note in 1882 served only to add impetus to the Bank's concerns and Prof Crum Brown's researches into forgery-proof inks continued into 1883. The final results were adopted in October 1883: an entirely new series of notes with a unique combination of colours in shades of brown, yellow and blue-grey (technically using ultramarine, cadmium and vermilion pigments). Notes using Crum Brown's inks would remain in use for a remarkable 85 years from 1885 to 1969.

The notes were designed by William S Black, an Edinburgh artist and teacher. The design was common to all five denominations and featured the Bank's Arms upper centre in a panel with an ornate background, a vertical panel to the left with both sides of the Great Seal of Scotland as on the previous issue but now separated by the Royal Arms of Scotland. The central panel of the note containing the promissory text intentionally has no background ornamentation to enable the watermark to be clearly seen, on Crum Brown's recommendation.

A predominantly blue-grey essay by William Black can be found in the Bank's archives, similar to but with rather more elaborate flourishes than the final version.

The watermark itself, patented in 1885, is another departure from previous practice in that it consisted of a complex Celtic pattern designed specifically for the Bank. The paper supply contract was switched to Portals after a thorough review of alternatives. Security during the printing process was a key concern and the Bank consulted the Bank of England, whose banknote paper had long been supplied by Portals.

The notes were printed by **George Waterston & Sons**, an Edinburgh firm of stationers, from plates engraved by Mr F (Frederick?) Knights of London, about whom little is known. Once a set of master plates had been engraved they were despatched to Waterstons who made wax impressions from them and used these to make electrotypes from which the notes were printed. There was thus no need for the master plates to be re-engraved at any stage. Apart from being located in Edinburgh, thus reducing transport costs and risks, Waterstons were chosen as printers for two other reasons: they had worked closely with Crum Brown on his experiments with inks and they were able to give more convincing assurances about factory security - with notes no longer needing a physical signature to be complete and ready for issue, this aspect took on somewhat greater importance. Bank of England practice was carefully followed.

This was the first time a Scottish bank issued notes without a hand signature, the Bank again following Bank of England practice (and thus saving a small army of clerks from many tedious hours of note signing). £1 notes were printed on sheets of four notes, the higher denominations on sheets of two. The watermarks carried a four digit reference number, the first two digits indicating the month and the last two the year the paper was made. Very few issued notes of this series have survived. All those recorded are £1 notes but the records indicate that ninety-six £5 notes, nine £10 notes, eight £20 notes and two £100 notes are still outstanding.

William Black watercolour Essay

BA 84a   **£1**   **Brown/Yellow/Blue-Grey** uniface
John Forrest Stormonth Darling Secretary

1 Jan 1885	1/A 0001 - 10/A 10000	100,000	
20 Jan 1885	11/A 0001 - 20/A 10000	100,000	
2 Feb 1885	21/A 0001 - 23/A 10000	30,000	**From 1800 F**

BA 84a   1885   No patent number

When the watermark was patented it was decided to add the registration number to the notes below the border to the lower left of the note. On the £1 notes this probably took place at the start of prefix 24/A but this has not been absolutely confirmed. It appears to have been added to the higher value notes from the outset.

In November 1888 a serious and infamous forgery came to light. In the end a total of 56 forged notes appeared in circulation, the quality of which caused the Bank considerable concern. They were traced to 74 year-old John Hamilton Gray Mitchell, a retired artist and engraver who was finally arrested in July 1889. His steel plate engraving was of the highest quality and the notes themselves were flawed only in the poor quality of the paper. While the Bank had found the ideal combination of colours and inks to prevent photographic forgery it had not been able to stop forgery by more traditional methods. Mitchell pleaded guilty to passing six forged notes and was sentenced to seven years in jail, but served only one because of failing health. He died in 1892.

Of the 56 recorded forgeries, 34 are still held by the Bank and just three are believed to be in private hands, all with the date 9th March 1887 and prefix/serials 40/B 8813. Forgeries held by the Bank also include: 5th Sep 1885 90/A 2202, 18th Nov 1885 1/B 0552, 29th Jan 1887 22/B 3852 and 26th Feb 1887 35/B 1466. All these were used on genuine notes.

BA 84b	£1	Watermark registration number RD.NO 18970 lower left			
		2 Feb 1885	24/A 0001 -	30/A 10000	70,000
		19 Feb 1885	31/A 0001 -	40/A 10000	100,000
		3 Mar 1885	41/A 0001 -	50/A 10000	100,000
		16 Mar 1885	51/A 0001 -	60/A 10000	100,000
		4 Apr 1885	61/A 0001 -	70/A 10000	100,000
		22 Apr 1885	71/A 0001 -	80/A 10000	100,000
		5 Sep 1885	81/A 0001 -	90/A 10000	100,000
		7 Oct 1885	91/A 0001 -	100/A 10000	100,000
		18 Nov 1885	0/B 0001 -	9/B 10000	100,000
		31 Dec 1885	10/B 0001 -	19/B 10000	100,000
		29 Jan 1887	20/B 0001 -	29/B 10000	100,000
		26 Feb 1887	30/B 0001 -	39/B 10000	100,000
		9 Mar 1887	40/B 0001 -	49/B 10000	100,000
		24 Mar 1887	50/B 0001 -	59/B 10000	100,000
		13 Apr 1887	60/B 0001 -	69/B 10000	100,000
		14 May 1887	70/B 0001 -	79/B 10000	100,000
		23 May 1887	80/B 0001 -	89/B 10000	100,000
		10 Jun 1887	90/B 0001 -	99/B 10000	100,000
		6 Jul 1887	0/C 0001 -	9/C 10000	100,000
		27 Jul 1887	10/C 0001 -	19/C 10000	100,000
		8 Aug 1887	20/C 0001 -	29/C 10000	100,000
		17 Aug 1887	30/C 0001 -	39/C 10000	100,000
		15 May 1888	40/C 0001 -	49/C 10000	100,000
		30 May 1888	50/C 0001 -	59/C 10000	100,000
		12 Jun 1888	60/C 0001 -	69/C 10000	100,000
		25 Jun 1888	70/C 0001 -	79/C 10000	100,000
		11 Sep 1888	80/C 0001 -	89/C 10000	100,000
		28 Sep 1888	90/C 0001 -	99/C 10000	100,000	**From 1500 F**

Specimen 16 Mar 1885 & undated 00/A 0000 Brown/Yellow **From 800 EF**

Proof Uncut Sheet of four (with & without large punch holes) **From 4000 EF**

BA 84b Uncut sheet of four (not to same scale)

Forgery by Mitchell 9 Mar 1887 40/B 8813   **From 600 F**

BA 84b Mitchell forgery

BA 85   **£5**   **Brown/Yellow/Blue-Grey Black value panels** uniface
Watermark registration number RD.NO 18970 lower left
John Forrest Stormonth Darling Secretary

2 Jan 1885	1/A 0001	-	2/A 10000	20,000
6 Feb 1885	3/A 0001	-	4/A 10000	20,000
7 Mar 1885	5/A 0001	-	6/A 10000	20,000
9 Apr 1885	7/A 0001	-	8/A 10000	20,000
14 Sep 1885	9/A 0001	-	10/A 10000	20,000
13 Oct 1885	11/A 0001	-	12/A 10000	20,000
1 Jul 1887	13/A 0001	-	14/A 10000	20,000
16 Aug 1887	15/A 0001	-	16/A 10000	20,000
23 Jun 1888	17/A 0001	-	18/A 10000	20,000 **RARE**

Specimen undated   **From 2000 EF**

BA 85 Specimen undated

BA 86 £10 **Brown/Yellow/Blue-Grey Black value panels** uniface
Watermark registration number RD.NO 18970 lower left
John Forrest Stormonth Darling Secretary

3 Jan	1885	1/A 0001	- 10000	10,000	
5 Feb	1885	2/A 0001	- 10000	10,000	
12 Oct	1885	3/A 0001	- 10000	10,000	**RARE**

Specimen undated   **RARE**

BA 87 £20 **Brown/Yellow/Blue-Grey Red value panels** uniface
Watermark registration number RD.NO 18970 lower left
John Forrest Stormonth Darling Secretary

5 Jan	1885	1/A 0001	- 5000	5,000	
4 Feb	1885	2/A 0001	- 5000	5,000	
6 Mar	1885	3/A 0001	- 5000	5,000	
8 Apr	1885	4/A 0001	- 5000	5,000	
17 Sep	1885	5/A 0001	- 5000	5,000	
10 Oct	1885	6/A 0001	- 5000	5,000	
21 May	1888	7/A 0001	- 5000	5,000	
2 Jun	1888	8/A 0001	- 5000	5,000	**RARE**

Specimen undated   **RARE**

BA 88   **£100**   **Brown/Yellow/Blue-Grey   Red value panels** uniface
Watermark registration number RD.NO 18970 lower left
John Forrest Stormonth Darling Secretary

6 Jan 1885	1/A 0001	-	1000	1,000
3 Feb 1885	2/A 0001	-	1000	1,000
4 Mar 1885	3/A 0001	-	1000	1,000
7 Apr 1885	4/A 0001	-	1000	1,000
11 Sep 1885	5/A 0001	-	1000	1,000
15 Oct 1885	6/A 0001	-	1000	1,000
22 Nov 1886	7/A 0001	-	1000	1,000
30 Dec 1886	8/A 0001	-	1000	1,000
18 May 1887	9/A 0001	-	1000	1,000
20 Jun 1887	10/A 0001	-	1000	1,000
19 Jul 1887	1/B 0001	-	1000	1,000
5 Dec 1888	2/B 0001	-	1000	1,000
21 Dec 1888	3/B 0001	-	1000	1,000	**RARE**

Specimen *not seen but believed prepared*

SECOND WATERSTON ISSUE – 1889 *to* 1935

Medallion added Royal Arms

As a result of the Mitchell forgery the Bank decided to modify all five denominations of the notes. The panel containing the promissory text, originally with a white background to ensure the watermark was fully visible, was filled with a dense patterned underlay of engine turning, with a central medallion of the Bank's seal, predominantly in grey. These and other more minor changes were evidently successful as no further forgeries were recorded. A specimen of the modified £1 note was approved on 9th April 1889 and new notes of the other denominations followed. Despite all the work done on devising forgery-proof inks a number of variations in the yellow and brown shading have been observed throughout the period. None are significant enough to justify separate catalogue references and the variations appear to be at random. The colour ranges observed are from yellow-orange through to dark brown.

The watermark on all notes including undated specimens incorporates a four-number code. The last two digits of this indicate the year in which the paper was manufactured, a useful guide for dating the specimens.

An apparently unsolicited £1 note essay was submitted to the Bank by Bradbury Wilkinson & Co dated 27th November 1904. A black and white photograph is the only evidence of this essay and there is no mention of it in the Bank's records. While the style is very different from the issued note the overall design is not dissimilar.

Issued £1 notes prior to 1900 are scarce. This series is notable for the number of dates used. The frequency of date changes diminishes somewhat after the £1 note was reduced in size in 1929.

Bradbury Wilkinson photographic essay

BA 89a	**£1**	**Central medallion Royal Arms**						
		John Forrest Stormonth Darling Secretary					F	VF
		4 Jan 1889	0/D 0001	-	9/D 10000	100,000		
		31 Jan 1889	10/D 0001	-	19/D 10000	100,000		
		5 Feb 1889	20/D 0001	-	29/D 10000	100,000		
		28 Feb 1889	30/D 0001	-	39/D 10000	100,000		
		1 Mar 1889	40/D 0001	-	49/D 10000	100,000		
		27 Mar 1889	50/D 0001	-	59/D 10000	100,000		
		3 Aug 1889	60/D 0001	-	69/D 10000	100,000		
		21 Aug 1889	70/D 0001	-	79/D 10000	100,000		
		2 Oct 1889	80/D 0001	-	89/D 10000	100,000		
		19 Oct 1889	90/D 0001	-	99/D 10000	100,000		
		16 Nov 1889	0/E 0001	-	9/E 10000	100,000		
		22 Nov 1889	10/E 0001	-	19/E 10000	100,000		
		9 Dec 1889	20/E 0001	-	29/E 10000	100,000		
		20 Dec 1889	30/E 0001	-	39/E 10000	100,000		
		7 Jun 1890	40/E 0001	-	49/E 10000	100,000		
		24 Jun 1890	50/E 0001	-	59/E 10000	100,000		
		18 Jul 1890	60/E 0001	-	69/E 10000	100,000		
		29 Jul 1890	70/E 0001	-	79/E 10000	100,000		
		6 Sep 1890	80/E 0001	-	89/E 10000	100,000		
		30 Sep 1890	90/E 0001	-	99/E 10000	100,000		
		8 Oct 1890	0/F 0001	-	9/F 10000	100,000		
		23 Oct 1890	10/F 0001	-	19/F 10000	100,000		
		10 Nov 1890	20/F 0001	-	29/F 10000	100,000		
		21 Nov 1890	30/F 0001	-	39/F 10000	100,000		
		12 Dec 1890	40/F 0001	-	49/F 10000	100,000		
		26 Dec 1890	50/F 0001	-	59/F 10000	100,000		
		14 Jan 1891	60/F 0001	-	69/F 10000	100,000		
		11 Feb 1891	70/F 0001	-	79/F 10000	100,000	**1200**	**2000**

							F	VF
BA 89a	*Cont*							
	17 Mar 1891	80/F 0001	-	89/F 10000	100,000			
	25 Mar 1891	90/F 0001	-	99/F 10000	100,000			
	10 Apr 1891	0/G 0001	-	9/G 10000	100,000			
	28 Apr 1891	10/G 0001	-	19/G 10000	100,000			
	12 May 1891	20/G 0001	-	29/G 10000	100,000			
	29 May 1891	30/G 0001	-	39/G 10000	100,000			
	5 Jun 1891	40/G 0001	-	49/G 10000	100,000			
	22 Jun 1891	50/G 0001	-	59/G 10000	100,000			
	15 Jul 1892	60/G 0001	-	69/G 10000	100,000			
	26 Jul 1892	70/G 0001	-	79/G 10000	100,000			
	7 Jan 1893	80/G 0001	-	89/G 10000	100,000			
	10 Jan 1893	90/G 0001	-	99/G 10000	100,000			
	16 Jan 1893	0/H 0001	-	9/H 10000	100,000			
	24 Jan 1893	10/H 0001	-	19/H 10000	100,000			
	28 Jan 1893	20/H 0001	-	29/H 10000	100,000			
	1 Feb 1893	30/H 0001	-	39/H 10000	100,000			
	8 Feb 1893	40/H 0001	-	49/H 10000	100,000			
	13 Feb 1893	50/H 0001	-	59/H 10000	100,000			
	21 Feb 1893	60/H 0001	-	69/H 10000	100,000		1200	2000

BA 89a 1891

Specimen undated **From 800 EF**

BA 89b	£1	**Duncan McNeill** Secretary					F	VF
		15 Feb 1894	70/H 0001	-	79/H 10000	100,000		
		27 Feb 1894	80/H 0001	-	89/H 10000	100,000		
		2 Mar 1894	90/H 0001	-	99/H 10000	100,000		
		14 Mar 1894	0/I 0001	-	9/I 10000	100,000		
		30 Mar 1894	10/I 0001	-	19/I 10000	100,000		
		3 Apr 1894	20/I 0001	-	29/I 10000	100,000		
		19 Apr 1894	30/I 0001	-	39/I 10000	100,000		
		11 May 1894	40/I 0001	-	49/I 10000	100,000		
		22 Dec 1894	50/I 0001	-	59/I 10000	100,000		
		8 Mar 1895	60/I 0001	-	69/I 10000	100,000		
		15 Mar 1895	70/I 0001	-	79/I 10000	100,000		
		26 Mar 1895	80/I 0001	-	89/I 10000	100,000		
		6 Apr 1895	90/I 0001	-	99/I 10000	100,000		
		18 Apr 1895	0/J 0001	-	9/J 10000	100,000		
		4 May 1895	10/J 0001	-	19/J 10000	100,000		
		31 May 1895	20/J 0001	-	29/J 10000	100,000		
		3 Jun 1895	30/J 0001	-	39/J 10000	100,000		
		14 Jun 1895	40/J 0001	-	49/J 10000	100,000		
		10 Jul 1895	50/J 0001	-	59/J 10000	100,000		
		6 Aug 1895	60/J 0001	-	69/J 10000	100,000		
		3 Sep 1895	70/J 0001	-	79/J 10000	100,000		
		18 Sep 1895	80/J 0001	-	89/J 10000	100,000		
		4 Oct 1895	90/J 0001	-	99/J 10000	100,000		
		5 Nov 1895	0/K 0001	-	9/K 10000	100,000		
		27 Dec 1895	10/K 0001	-	19/K 10000	100,000		
		11 Jan 1896	20/K 0001	-	29/K 10000	100,000		
		24 Feb 1896	30/K 0001	-	39/K 10000	100,000		
		25 May 1896	40/K 0001	-	49/K 10000	100,000		
		27 May 1896	50/K 0001	-	59/K 10000	100,000		
		1 Jun 1896	60/K 0001	-	69/K 10000	100,000		
		4 Jun 1896	70/K 0001	-	79/K 10000	100,000		
		9 Jun 1896	80/K 0001	-	89/K 10000	100,000		
		17 Jun 1896	90/K 0001	-	99/K 10000	100,000		
		30 Jun 1896	0/L 0001	-	9/L 10000	100,000		
		3 Jul 1896	10/L 0001	-	19/L 10000	100,000		
		7 Jul 1896	20/L 0001	-	29/L 10000	100,000		
		16 Jul 1896	30/L 0001	-	39/L 10000	100,000		
		31 Jul 1896	40/L 0001	-	49/L 10000	100,000		
		5 Aug 1897	50/L 0001	-	59/L 10000	100,000		
		9 Aug 1897	60/L 0001	-	69/L 10000	100,000		
		12 Aug 1897	70/L 0001	-	79/L 10000	100,000		
		24 Aug 1897	80/L 0001	-	89/L 10000	100,000		
		31 Aug 1897	90/L 0001	-	99/L 10000	100,000		
		7 Sep 1897	0/M 0001	-	9/M 10000	100,000		
		15 Sep 1897	10/M 0001	-	19/M 10000	100,000		
		26 Oct 1897	20/M 0001	-	29/M 10000	100,000		
		13 Nov 1897	30/M 0001	-	39/M 10000	100,000		
		29 Dec 1897	40/M 0001	-	49/M 10000	100,000		
		6 Oct 1898	50/M 0001	-	59/M 10000	100,000		
		17 Oct 1898	60/M 0001	-	69/M 10000	100,000		
		25 Nov 1898	70/M 0001	-	79/M 10000	100,000		
		28 Nov 1898	80/M 0001	-	89/M 10000	100,000		
		1 Dec 1898	90/M 0001	-	99/M 10000	100,000	600	1200

						F	VF
BA 89b	Cont						
	2 Dec 1898	0/N 0001	-	9/N 10000	100,000		
	10 Dec 1898	10/N 0001	-	19/N 10000	100,000		
	14 Dec 1898	20/N 0001	-	29/N 10000	100,000	600	1200
	12 Jan 1900	30/N 0001	-	39/N 10000	100,000		
	17 Jan 1900	40/N 0001	-	49/N 10000	100,000		
	22 Feb 1900	50/N 0001	-	59/N 10000	100,000		
	10 Mar 1900	60/N 0001	-	69/N 10000	100,000		
	29 Mar 1900	70/N 0001	-	79/N 10000	100,000		
	5 Apr 1900	80/N 0001	-	89/N 10000	100,000		
	20 Apr 1900	90/N 0001	-	99/N 10000	100,000		
	8 May 1900	0/O 0001	-	9/O 10000	100,000		
	25 Jan 1901	10/O 0001	-	19/O 10000	100,000		
	11 Mar 1901	20/O 0001	-	29/O 10000	100,000		
	28 Mar 1901	30/O 0001	-	39/O 10000	100,000		
	1 Apr 1901	40/O 0001	-	49/O 10000	100,000		
	23 Apr 1901	50/O 0001	-	59/O 10000	100,000		
	3 May 1901	60/O 0001	-	69/O 10000	100,000		
	9 May 1901	70/O 0001	-	79/O 10000	100,000		
	16 May 1901	80/O 0001	-	89/O 10000	100,000		
	6 Jun 1901	90/O 0001	-	99/O 10000	100,000		
	21 Jun 1901	0/P 0001	-	9/P 10000	100,000		
	30 Jul 1901	10/P 0001	-	19/P 10000	100,000		
	19 Aug 1901	20/P 0001	-	29/P 10000	100,000		
	4 Sep 1901	30/P 0001	-	39/P 10000	100,000		
	18 Oct 1901	40/P 0001	-	49/P 10000	100,000		
	27 Nov 1901	50/P 0001	-	59/P 10000	100,000		
	15 Apr 1902	60/P 0001	-	69/P 10000	100,000		
	24 Apr 1902	70/P 0001	-	79/P 10000	100,000		
	7 May 1902	80/P 0001	-	89/P 10000	100,000		
	13 Jun 1902	90/P 0001	-	99/P 10000	100,000		
	26 Jun 1902	0/Q 0001	-	9/Q 10000	100,000		
	22 Jul 1902	10/Q 0001	-	19/Q 10000	100,000		
	6 Nov 1902	20/Q 0001	-	29/Q 10000	100,000		
	25 Feb 1903	30/Q 0001	-	39/Q 10000	100,000		
	21 Mar 1903	40/Q 0001	-	49/Q 10000	100,000		
	2 Apr 1903	50/Q 0001	-	59/Q 10000	100,000		
	11 Apr 1903	60/Q 0001	-	69/Q 10000	100,000		
	28 May 1903	70/Q 0001	-	79/Q 10000	100,000		
	19 Jun 1903	80/Q 0001	-	89/Q 10000	100,000		
	20 Jul 1903	90/Q 0001	-	99/Q 10000	100,000		
	7 Aug 1903	0/R 0001	-	9/R 10000	100,000		
	15 Aug 1903	10/R 0001	-	19/R 10000	100,000		
	12 Sep 1903	20/R 0001	-	29/R 10000	100,000		
	29 Sep 1903	30/R 0001	-	39/R 10000	100,000		
	9 Oct 1903	40/R 0001	-	49/R 10000	100,000		
	14 Nov 1903	50/R 0001	-	59/R 10000	100,000		
	23 Jan 1904	60/R 0001	-	69/R 10000	100,000		
	10 May 1904	70/R 0001	-	79/R 10000	100,000		
	27 Jun 1904	80/R 0001	-	89/R 10000	100,000		
	5 Jul 1904	90/R 0001	-	99/R 10000	100,000		
	28 Jul 1904	0/S 0001	-	9/S 10000	100,000		
	30 Aug 1904	10/S 0001	-	19/S 10000	100,000		
	23 Sep 1904	20/S 0001	-	29/S 10000	100,000	450	900

						F	VF
BA 89b	*Cont*						
	5 Oct 1904	30/S 0001	-	39/S 10000	100,000		
	11 Oct 1904	40/S 0001	-	49/S 10000	100,000		
	8 Nov 1904	50/S 0001	-	59/S 10000	100,000		
	15 Dec 1904	60/S 0001	-	69/S 10000	100,000		
	17 Jul 1905	70/S 0001	-	79/S 10000	100,000		
	24 Jul 1905	80/S 0001	-	89/S 10000	100,000		
	2 Nov 1905	90/S 0001	-	99/S 10000	100,000		
	16 Feb 1906	0/T 0001	-	9/T 10000	100,000		
	20 Mar 1906	10/T 0001	-	19/T 10000	100,000		
	22 Mar 1906	20/T 0001	-	29/T 10000	100,000		
	17 Apr 1906	30/T 0001	-	39/T 10000	100,000		
	26 Apr 1906	40/T 0001	-	49/T 10000	100,000		
	1 May 1906	50/T 0001	-	59/T 10000	100,000		
	10 Sep 1906	60/T 0001	-	69/T 10000	100,000		
	27 Sep 1906	70/T 0001	-	79/T 10000	100,000		
	20 Nov 1906	80/T 0001	-	89/T 10000	100,000		
	8 Dec 1906	90/T 0001	-	99/T 10000	100,000		
	11 Dec 1906	0/U 0001	-	9/U 10000	100,000		
	21 Jan 1907	10/U 0001	-	19/U 10000	100,000		
	12 Apr 1907	20/U 0001	-	29/U 10000	100,000		
	13 May 1907	30/U 0001	-	39/U 10000	100,000		
	22 May 1907	40/U 0001	-	49/U 10000	100,000		
	28 Jun 1907	50/U 0001	-	59/U 10000	100,000		
	13 Jul 1907	60/U 0001	-	69/U 10000	100,000		
	20 Sep 1907	70/U 0001	-	79/U 10000	100,000		
	9 Nov 1907	80/U 0001	-	89/U 10000	100,000		
	23 Nov 1907	90/U 0001	-	99/U 10000	100,000		
	18 Mar 1908	0/V 0001	-	9/V 10000	100,000		
	23 Mar 1908	10/V 0001	-	19/V 10000	100,000		
	25 Apr 1908	20/V 0001	-	29/V 10000	100,000		
	30 Apr 1908	30/V 0001	-	39/V 10000	100,000		
	2 Sep 1908	40/V 0001	-	49/V 10000	100,000		
	14 Sep 1908	50/V 0001	-	59/V 10000	100,000		
	13 Oct 1908	60/V 0001	-	69/V 10000	100,000		
	28 Oct 1908	70/V 0001	-	79/V 10000	100,000		
	3 Nov 1908	80/V 0001	-	89/V 10000	100,000		
	12 Nov 1908	90/V 0001	-	99/V 10000	100,000		
	4 Dec 1908	0/W 0001	-	9/W 10000	100,000		
	2 Jan 1909	10/W 0001	-	19/W 10000	100,000		
	8 Jan 1909	20/W 0001	-	29/W 10000	100,000		
	6 Feb 1909	30/W 0001	-	39/W 10000	100,000		
	10 Aug 1909	40/W 0001	-	49/W 10000	100,000		
	25 Aug 1909	50/W 0001	-	59/W 10000	100,000		
	9 Sep 1909	60/W 0001	-	69/W 10000	100,000		
	21 Oct 1909	70/W 0001	-	79/W 10000	100,000		
	19 Nov 1909	80/W 0001	-	89/W 10000	100,000		
	3 Dec 1909	90/W 0001	-	99/W 10000	100,000		
	28 Dec 1909	0/X 0001	-	9/X 10000	100,000		
	18 Jan 1910	10/X 0001	-	19/X 10000	100,000		
	26 Jan 1910	20/X 0001	-	29/X 10000	100,000		
	24 Oct 1910	30/X 0001	-	39/X 10000	100,000		
	1 Nov 1910	40/X 0001	-	49/X 10000	100,000		
	19 Dec 1910	50/X 0001	-	59/X 10000	100,000	**450**	**900**

BA 89b 1905

Trial undated (Trial watermark 1904)   From 500 EF

Specimen undated (prepared on 1892 & 1894 paper)   From 500 EF

BA 89c	£1	**Peter Macdonald** Secretary				F	VF
		3 Jan 1911	60/X 0001	-	69/X 10000	100,000	
		5 Jan 1911	70/X 0001	-	79/X 10000	100,000	
		27 Jan 1911	80/X 0001	-	89/X 10000	100,000	
		7 Feb 1911	90/X 0001	-	99/X 10000	100,000	
		14 Feb 1911	0/Y 0001	-	9/Y 10000	100,000	
		18 Feb 1911	10/Y 0001	-	19/Y 10000	100,000	
		20 Feb 1911	20/Y 0001	-	29/Y 10000	100,000	
		16 Aug 1911	30/Y 0001	-	39/Y 10000	100,000	
		13 Sep 1911	40/Y 0001	-	49/Y 10000	100,000	
		22 Sep 1911	50/Y 0001	-	59/Y 10000	100,000	
		12 Oct 1911	60/Y 0001	-	69/Y 10000	100,000	
		31 Oct 1911	70/Y 0001	-	79/Y 10000	100,000	
		15 Nov 1911	80/Y 0001	-	89/Y 10000	100,000	
		16 Dec 1911	90/Y 0001	-	99/Y 10000	100,000	
		23 Dec 1911	0/Z 0001	-	9/Z 10000	100,000	
		15 Jan 1912	10/Z 0001	-	19/Z 10000	100,000	
		9 Feb 1912	20/Z 0001	-	29/Z 10000	100,000	
		17 Feb 1912	30/Z 0001	-	39/Z 10000	100,000	
		25 Sep 1912	40/Z 0001	-	49/Z 10000	100,000	
		16 Oct 1912	50/Z 0001	-	59/Z 10000	100,000	
		22 Oct 1912	60/Z 0001	-	69/Z 10000	100,000	
		11 Nov 1912	70/Z 0001	-	79/Z 10000	100,000	
		7 Dec 1912	80/Z 0001	-	89/Z 10000	100,000	
		24 Dec 1912	90/Z 0001	-	99/Z 10000	100,000	400	750

					F	VF
BA 89c	*Cont*					
	Double Letter prefix					
	4 Jan 1913	0/AA 0001	-	9/AA 10000	100,000	
	8 Feb 1913	10/AA 0001	-	19/AA 10000	100,000	
	14 Mar 1913	20/AA 0001	-	29/AA 10000	100,000	
	10 Apr 1913	30/AA 0001	-	39/AA 10000	100,000	
	27 May 1913	40/AA 0001	-	49/AA 10000	100,000	
	5 Aug 1913	50/AA 0001	-	59/AA 10000	100,000	
	11 Sep 1913	60/AA 0001	-	69/AA 10000	100,000	
	6 Oct 1913	70/AA 0001	-	79/AA 10000	100,000	
	20 Nov 1913	80/AA 0001	-	89/AA 10000	100,000	
	2 Dec 1913	90/AA 0001	-	99/AA 10000	100,000	
	19 Jan 1914	0/AB 0001	-	9/AB 10000	100,000	
	28 Feb 1914	10/AB 0001	-	19/AB 10000	100,000	
	17 Mar 1914	20/AB 0001	-	29/AB 10000	100,000	
	14 Apr 1914	30/AB 0001	-	39/AB 10000	100,000	
	5 May 1914	40/AB 0001	-	49/AB 10000	100,000	**400**	**750**

BA 89c 1911

In 1914 the printers' imprint was modified on the £1 note, Waterston having adopted limited liability.

								F	VF
BA 89d	**£1**	**Peter Macdonald** Secretary		*Imprint:*	**G Waterston & Sons Ld.**				
		13 May 1914	50/AB 0001	-	59/AB 10000	100,000			
		1 Jun 1914	60/AB 0001	-	69/AB 10000	100,000			
		5 Jun 1914	70/AB 0001	-	79/AB 10000	100,000			
		10 Jun 1914	80/AB 0001	-	89/AB 10000	100,000			
		17 Jun 1914	90/AB 0001	-	99/AB 10000	100,000			
		2 Jul 1914	0/AC 0001	-	9/AC 10000	100,000			
		6 Jul 1914	10/AC 0001	-	19/AC 10000	100,000			
		7 Jul 1914	20/AC 0001	-	29/AC 10000	100,000			
		11 Jul 1914	30/AC 0001	-	39/AC 10000	100,000			
		15 Jul 1914	40/AC 0001	-	49/AC 10000	100,000			
		7 Aug 1914	50/AC 0001	-	59/AC 10000	100,000			
		18 Aug 1914	60/AC 0001	-	69/AC 10000	100,000			
		4 Sep 1914	70/AC 0001	-	79/AC 10000	100,000			
		9 Jan 1915	80/AC 0001	-	89/AC 10000	100,000			
		18 Jan 1915	90/AC 0001	-	99/AC 10000	100,000			
		1 Feb 1915	0/AD 0001	-	9/AD 10000	100,000			
		22 Mar 1915	10/AD 0001	-	19/AD 10000	100,000			
		1 Apr 1915	20/AD 0001	-	29/AD 10000	100,000			
		29 Apr 1915	30/AD 0001	-	39/AD 10000	100,000			
		19 May 1915	40/AD 0001	-	49/AD 10000	100,000			
		11 Jun 1915	50/AD 0001	-	59/AD 10000	100,000			
		3 Jul 1915	60/AD 0001	-	69/AD 10000	100,000			
		26 Aug 1915	70/AD 0001	-	79/AD 10000	100,000			
		31 Aug 1915	80/AD 0001	-	89/AD 10000	100,000			
		14 Sep 1915	90/AD 0001	-	99/AD 10000	100,000			
		13 Oct 1915	0/AE 0001	-	9/AE 10000	100,000			
		8 Nov 1915	10/AE 0001	-	19/AE 10000	100,000			
		24 Dec 1915	20/AE 0001	-	29/AE 10000	100,000			
		10 Jan 1916	30/AE 0001	-	39/AE 10000	100,000			
		15 Feb 1916	40/AE 0001	-	49/AE 10000	100,000			
		9 Mar 1916	50/AE 0001	-	59/AE 10000	100,000			
		24 Apr 1916	60/AE 0001	-	69/AE 10000	100,000			
		23 May 1916	70/AE 0001	-	79/AE 10000	100,000			
		3 Jun 1916	80/AE 0001	-	89/AE 10000	100,000			
		5 Jul 1916	90/AE 0001	-	99/AE 10000	100,000			
		26 Jul 1916	0/AF 0001	-	9/AF 10000	100,000			
		15 Aug 1916	10/AF 0001	-	19/AF 10000	100,000			
		19 Sep 1916	20/AF 0001	-	29/AF 10000	100,000			
		4 Oct 1916	30/AF 0001	-	39/AF 10000	100,000			
		23 Oct 1916	40/AF 0001	-	49/AF 10000	100,000			
		13 Nov 1916	50/AF 0001	-	59/AF 10000	100,000			
		1 Dec 1916	60/AF 0001	-	69/AF 10000	100,000			
		2 Jan 1917	70/AF 0001	-	79/AF 10000	100,000			
		3 Feb 1917	80/AF 0001	-	89/AF 10000	100,000			
		19 Mar 1917	90/AF 0001	-	99/AF 10000	100,000			
		20 Apr 1917	0/AG 0001	-	9/AG 10000	100,000			
		14 May 1917	10/AG 0001	-	19/AG 10000	100,000			
		26 May 1917	20/AG 0001	-	29/AG 10000	100,000			
		8 Jun 1917	30/AG 0001	-	39/AG 10000	100,000			
		25 Jun 1917	40/AG 0001	-	49/AG 10000	100,000			
		9 Jul 1917	50/AG 0001	-	59/AG 10000	100,000			**380**	**650**

BA 89d Cont   F   VF
23 Jul 1917 60/AG 0001 - 69/AG 10000 100,000
 9 Aug 1917 70/AG 0001 - 79/AG 10000 100,000
12 Sep 1917 80/AG 0001 - 89/AG 10000 100,000
 1 Oct 1917 90/AG 0001 - 99/AG 10000 100,000
16 Oct 1917   0/AH 0001 -   9/AH 10000 100,000
17 Nov 1917 10/AH 0001 - 19/AH 10000 100,000
 5 Dec 1917 20/AH 0001 - 29/AH 10000 100,000
17 Dec 1917 30/AH 0001 - 39/AH 10000 100,000
23 Jan 1918 40/AH 0001 - 49/AH 10000 100,000
16 Feb 1918 50/AH 0001 - 59/AH 10000 100,000
 5 Mar 1918 60/AH 0001 - 69/AH 10000 100,000
 8 Apr 1918 70/AH 0001 - 79/AH 10000 100,000
 1 May 1918 80/AH 0001 - 89/AH 10000 100,000
17 May 1918 90/AH 0001 - 99/AH 10000 100,000
 4 Jun 1918   0/AI 0001 -   9/AI 10000 100,000
22 Jun 1918 10/AI 0001 - 19/AI 10000 100,000
12 Jul 1918 20/AI 0001 - 29/AI 10000 100,000
27 Jul 1918 30/AI 0001 - 39/AI 10000 100,000
16 Aug 1918 40/AI 0001 - 49/AI 10000 100,000
 2 Sep 1918 50/AI 0001 - 59/AI 10000 100,000
25 Sep 1918 60/AI 0001 - 69/AI 10000 100,000
 9 Oct 1918 70/AI 0001 - 79/AI 10000 100,000
 7 Nov 1918 80/AI 0001 - 89/AI 10000 100,000
18 Nov 1918 90/AI 0001 - 99/AI 10000 100,000
11 Dec 1918   0/AJ 0001 -   9/AJ 10000 100,000
15 Jan 1919 10/AJ 0001 - 19/AJ 10000 100,000
20 Feb 1919 20/AJ 0001 - 29/AJ 10000 100,000
 3 Mar 1919 30/AJ 0001 - 39/AJ 10000 100,000
17 Apr 1919 40/AJ 0001 - 49/AJ 10000 100,000
28 Apr 1919 50/AJ 0001 - 59/AJ 10000 100,000
 8 May 1919 60/AJ 0001 - 69/AJ 10000 100,000
 6 Jun 1919 70/AJ 0001 - 79/AJ 10000 100,000
20 Jun 1919 80/AJ 0001 - 89/AJ 10000 100,000
16 Jul 1919 90/AJ 0001 - 99/AJ 10000 100,000
12 Aug 1919   0/AK 0001 -   9/AK 10000 100,000
 9 Sep 1919 10/AK 0001 - 19/AK 10000 100,000
 7 Oct 1919 20/AK 0001 - 29/AK 10000 100,000
22 Oct 1919 30/AK 0001 - 39/AK 10000 100,000
27 Nov 1919 40/AK 0001 - 49/AK 10000 100,000
 3 Dec 1919 50/AK 0001 - 59/AK 10000 100,000
10 Dec 1919 60/AK 0001 - 69/AK 10000 100,000
 8 Jan 1920 70/AK 0001 - 79/AK 10000 100,000
 4 Feb 1920 80/AK 0001 - 89/AK 10000 100,000
11 Mar 1920 90/AK 0001 - 99/AK 10000 100,000   380   650

BA 89c Detail of Waterston imprint

BA 89d Amended Waterston imprint

It can be confirmed that the Bank's final 'square' £1 note issue was dated 16th Nov 1927 with prefix/serials 9/AU 10000. This was also the last Scottish square of all to be issued, the Bank being the last one to reduce the size of its notes in conformity with the UK Treasury and Bank of England £1 notes.

BA 89e	**£1**	**Alexander Jolly Rose** Secretary						**F**	**VF**
		10 Sep 1920	0/AL 0001	-	9/AL 10000	100,000			
		21 Sep 1920	10/AL 0001	-	19/AL 10000	100,000			
		2 Oct 1920	20/AL 0001	-	29/AL 10000	100,000			
		19 Oct 1920	30/AL 0001	-	39/AL 10000	100,000			
		4 Nov 1920	40/AL 0001	-	49/AL 10000	100,000			
		24 Nov 1920	50/AL 0001	-	59/AL 10000	100,000			
		8 Dec 1920	60/AL 0001	-	69/AL 10000	100,000			
		22 Dec 1920	70/AL 0001	-	79/AL 10000	100,000			
		7 Jan 1921	80/AL 0001	-	89/AL 10000	100,000			
		25 Jan 1921	90/AL 0001	-	99/AL 10000	100,000			
		11 Feb 1921	0/AM 0001	-	9/AM 10000	100,000			
		18 Feb 1921	10/AM 0001	-	19/AM 10000	100,000			
		4 Aug 1921	20/AM 0001	-	29/AM 10000	100,000			
		23 Aug 1921	30/AM 0001	-	39/AM 10000	100,000			
		8 Sep 1921	40/AM 0001	-	49/AM 10000	100,000			
		20 Sep 1921	50/AM 0001	-	59/AM 10000	100,000			
		11 Oct 1921	60/AM 0001	-	69/AM 10000	100,000			
		27 Oct 1921	70/AM 0001	-	79/AM 10000	100,000			
		1 Nov 1921	80/AM 0001	-	89/AM 10000	100,000			
		14 Nov 1921	90/AM 0001	-	99/AM 10000	100,000			
		7 Dec 1921	0/AN 0001	-	9/AN 10000	100,000			
		19 Dec 1921	10/AN 0001	-	19/AN 10000	100,000			
		6 Jan 1922	20/AN 0001	-	29/AN 10000	100,000			
		19 Jul 1922	30/AN 0001	-	39/AN 10000	100,000			
		10 Aug 1922	40/AN 0001	-	49/AN 10000	100,000			
		24 Aug 1922	50/AN 0001	-	59/AN 10000	100,000			
		6 Sep 1922	60/AN 0001	-	69/AN 10000	100,000			
		27 Sep 1922	70/AN 0001	-	79/AN 10000	100,000			
		5 Oct 1922	80/AN 0001	-	89/AN 10000	100,000			
		31 Oct 1922	90/AN 0001	-	99/AN 10000	100,000			
		11 Nov 1922	0/AO 0001	-	9/AO 10000	100,000			
		23 Nov 1922	10/AO 0001	-	19/AO 10000	100,000			
		4 Dec 1922	20/AO 0001	-	29/AO 10000	100,000			
		18 Dec 1922	30/AO 0001	-	39/AO 10000	100,000			
		12 Jan 1923	40/AO 0001	-	49/AO 10000	100,000			
		6 Apr 1923	50/AO 0001	-	59/AO 10000	100,000			
		9 May 1923	60/AO 0001	-	69/AO 10000	100,000			
		28 May 1923	70/AO 0001	-	79/AO 10000	100,000			
		7 Jun 1923	80/AO 0001	-	89/AO 10000	100,000			
		14 Jun 1923	90/AO 0001	-	99/AO 10000	100,000			
		20 Jul 1923	1/AP 0001	-	9/AP 10000	100,000			
		28 Jul 1923	10/AP 0001	-	19/AP 10000	100,000			
		3 Aug 1923	20/AP 0001	-	29/AP 10000	100,000			
		21 Aug 1923	30/AP 0001	-	39/AP 10000	100,000			
		26 Oct 1923	40/AP 0001	-	49/AP 10000	100,000			
		29 Nov 1923	50/AP 0001	-	59/AP 10000	100,000			
		12 Dec 1923	60/AP 0001	-	69/AP 10000	100,000			
		2 Apr 1924	70/AP 0001	-	79/AP 10000	100,000			
		16 Apr 1924	80/AP 0001	-	89/AP 10000	100,000		**250**	**500**

						F	VF
BA 89e	Cont						
	15 May 1924	90/AP 0001	-	99/AP 10000	100,000		
	22 May 1924	0/AQ 0001	-	9/AQ 10000	100,000		
	9 Jun 1924	10/AQ 0001	-	19/AQ 10000	100,000		
	26 Jun 1924	20/AQ 0001	-	29/AQ 10000	100,000		
	4 Jul 1924	30/AQ 0001	-	39/AQ 10000	100,000		
	18 Jul 1924	40/AQ 0001	-	49/AQ 10000	100,000		
	14 Aug 1924	50/AQ 0001	-	59/AQ 10000	100,000		
	10 Nov 1924	60/AQ 0001	-	69/AQ 10000	100,000		
	23 Dec 1924	70/AQ 0001	-	79/AQ 10000	100,000		
	12 Mar 1925	80/AQ 0001	-	89/AQ 10000	100,000		
	4 Apr 1925	90/AQ 0001	-	99/AQ 10000	100,000		
	27 Apr 1925	0/AR 0001	-	9/AR 10000	100,000		
	7 May 1925	10/AR 0001	-	19/AR 10000	100,000		
	16 Jun 1925	20/AR 0001	-	29/AR 10000	100,000		
	24 Jul 1925	30/AR 0001	-	39/AR 10000	100,000		
	6 Aug 1925	40/AR 0001	-	49/AR 10000	100,000		
	16 Sep 1925	50/AR 0001	-	59/AR 10000	100,000		
	30 Oct 1925	60/AR 0001	-	69/AR 10000	100,000		
	25 Nov 1925	70/AR 0001	-	79/AR 10000	100,000		
	29 Dec 1925	80/AR 0001	-	89/AR 10000	100,000		
	11 Jan 1926	90/AR 0001	-	99/AR 10000	100,000		
	13 Feb 1926	0/AS 0001	-	9/AS 10000	100,000		
	8 Mar 1926	10/AS 0001	-	19/AS 10000	100,000		
	21 Apr 1926	20/AS 0001	-	29/AS 10000	100,000		
	4 May 1926	30/AS 0001	-	39/AS 10000	100,000		
	29 Jun 1926	40/AS 0001	-	49/AS 10000	100,000		
	1 Jul 1926	50/AS 0001	-	59/AS 10000	100,000		
	30 Aug 1926	60/AS 0001	-	69/AS 10000	100,000		
	13 Sep 1926	70/AS 0001	-	79/AS 10000	100,000		
	21 Oct 1926	80/AS 0001	-	89/AS 10000	100,000		
	13 Dec 1926	90/AS 0001	-	99/AS 10000	100,000		
	20 Jan 1927	0/AT 0001	-	9/AT 10000	100,000		
	14 Feb 1927	10/AT 0001	-	19/AT 10000	100,000		
	10 Mar 1927	20/AT 0001	-	29/AT 10000	100,000		
	19 Apr 1927	30/AT 0001	-	39/AT 10000	100,000		
	11 May 1927	40/AT 0001	-	49/AT 10000	100,000		
	2 Jun 1927	50/AT 0001	-	59/AT 10000	100,000		
	25 Jul 1927	60/AT 0001	-	69/AT 10000	100,000		
	2 Aug 1927	70/AT 0001	-	79/AT 10000	100,000		
	30 Sep 1927	80/AT 0001	-	89/AT 10000	100,000		
	10 Oct 1927	90/AT 0001	-	99/AT 10000	100,000		
	16 Nov 1927	0/AU 0001	-	9/AU 10000	100,000	**250**	**500**

Crum Brown inks - examples of colour variations

BA 89e Orange/Light Brown, Medallion Light Brown

BA 89e Dark Brown/Orange, Medallion Grey

Proof Uncut Sheet of four undated (with & without large punch holes)   **From 1500 EF**

The Bank's records indicate that 14 £5 notes with the Stormonth Darling signature remain unredeemed. Later records have not been maintained. Very few issued £5 notes dated prior to 1900 appear to have survived.

BA 90a   £5   **Central medallion Royal Arms Black value panels**
John Forrest Stormonth Darling Secretary

Date	From		To	Total		
24 May 1889	19/A 0001	-	20/A 10000	20,000		
25 Sep 1889	1/B 0001	-	2/B 10000	20,000		
3 Nov 1890	3/B 0001	-	4/B 10000	20,000		
4 Dec 1890	5/B 0001	-	6/B 10000	20,000		
8 Jan 1891	7/B 0001	-	8/B 10000	20,000		
12 Nov 1891	9/B 0001	-	10/B 10000	20,000		
28 Dec 1891	11/B 0001	-	12/B 10000	20,000		
18 Feb 1893	13/B 0001	-	14/B 10000	20,000		
20 Feb 1893	15/B 0001	-	16/B 10000	20,000		**RARE**

BA 90a 1889

BA 90b   £5   **Duncan McNeill** Secretary   F   VF

Date	From		To	Total	F	VF
5 May 1894	17/B 0001	-	18/B 10000	20,000		
10 Aug 1894	19/B 0001	-	20/B 10000	20,000		
22 Sep 1894	1/C 0001	-	2/C 10000	20,000		
31 Oct 1894	3/C 0001	-	4/C 10000	20,000		
7 Feb 1896	5/C 0001	-	6/C 10000	20,000		
21 Oct 1896	7/C 0001	-	8/C 10000	20,000		
28 Oct 1896	9/C 0001	-	10/C 10000	20,000		
15 Jan 1897	11/C 0001	-	12/C 10000	20,000		
26 Jan 1897	13/C 0001	-	14/C 10000	20,000		
12 Mar 1898	15/C 0001	-	16/C 10000	20,000		
14 Apr 1898	17/C 0001	-	18/C 10000	20,000		
2 Sep 1899	19/C 0001	-	20/C 10000	20,000	1400	-

BA 90b

						F	VF
	Cont						
	18 Jan 1901	1/D 0001	-	2/D 10000	20,000		
	5 Mar 1901	3/D 0001	-	4/D 10000	20,000		
	11 Jul 1901	5/D 0001	-	6/D 10000	20,000		
	24 Oct 1901	7/D 0001	-	8/D 10000	20,000		
	1 Nov 1902	9/D 0001	-	10/D 10000	20,000		
	19 Nov 1902	11/D 0001	-	12/D 10000	20,000		
	3 Dec 1903	13/D 0001	-	14/D 10000	20,000		
	16 Dec 1903	15/D 0001	-	16/D 10000	20,000		
	19 Dec 1904	17/D 0001	-	18/D 10000	20,000		
	14 Feb 1905	19/D 0001	-	20/D 10000	20,000		
	25 Aug 1905	1/E 0001	-	2/E 10000	20,000		
	9 Sep 1905	3/E 0001	-	4/E 10000	20,000		
	19 Mar 1906	5/E 0001	-	6/E 10000	20,000		
	21 Apr 1906	7/E 0001	-	8/E 10000	20,000		
	20 May 1907	9/E 0001	-	10/E 10000	20,000		
	29 Jun 1907	11/E 0001	-	12/E 10000	20,000		
	23 Jul 1907	13/E 0001	-	14/E 10000	20,000		
	4 Jan 1909	15/E 0001	-	16/E 10000	20,000		
	11 Jan 1909	17/E 0001	-	18/E 10000	20,000		
	9 Aug 1909	19/E 0001	-	20/E 10000	20,000		
	14 Jan 1910	1/F 0001	-	2/F 10000	20,000		
	6 Sep 1910	3/F 0001	-	4/F 10000	20,000	1200	1800

BA 90b 1901

Specimen undated (prepared on 1892 1894 1897 paper)   From 500 EF

								F	VF
BA 90c	£5	**Peter Macdonald** Secretary							
		15 Sep 1911	5/F 0001	-	6/F 10000	20,000			
		17 Oct 1911	7/F 0001	-	8/F 10000	20,000			
		18 Sep 1912	9/F 0001	-	10/F 10000	20,000			
		23 Oct 1912	11/F 0001	-	12/F 10000	20,000			
		27 Dec 1912	13/F 0001	-	14/F 10000	20,000			
		20 Sep 1913	15/F 0001	-	16/F 10000	20,000			
		18 Oct 1913	17/F 0001	-	10000	10,000		400	800

The printers' imprint was modified on the £5 note in 1913.

BA 90d	£5	**Peter Macdonald** Secretary *Imprint:* **G Waterston & Sons Ld**							
		18 Oct 1913	18/F 0001	-	10000	10,000			
		7 May 1914	19/F 0001	-	20/F 10000	20,000			
		22 Jun 1914	1/G 0001	-	2/G 10000	20,000			
		13 Jul 1914	3/G 0001	-	4/G 10000	20,000			
		18 Aug 1915	5/G 0001	-	6/G 10000	20,000			
		10 Dec 1915	7/G 0001	-	8/G 10000	20,000			
		25 Jan 1916	9/G 0001	-	10/G 10000	20,000			
		11 Feb 1916	11/G 0001	-	12/G 10000	20,000			
		4 Sep 1916	13/G 0001	-	14/G 10000	20,000			
		4 Oct 1916	15/G 0001	-	16/G 10000	20,000			
		2 Mar 1917	17/G 0001	-	18/G 10000	20,000			
		21 Nov 1917	19/G 0001	-	20/G 10000	20,000			
		21 Jan 1918	1/H 0001	-	2/H 10000	20,000			
		5 Apr 1918	3/H 0001	-	4/H 10000	20,000			
		7 Aug 1918	5/H 0001	-	6/H 10000	20,000			
		12 Sep 1918	7/H 0001	-	8/H 10000	20,000			
		23 Sep 1918	9/H 0001	-	10/H 10000	20,000			
		2 Oct 1918	11/H 0001	-	12/H 10000	20,000			
		12 Dec 1918	13/H 0001	-	14/H 10000	20,000			
		15 Mar 1919	15/H 0001	-	16/H 10000	20,000			
		2 Apr 1919	17/H 0001	-	18/H 10000	20,000			
		14 May 1919	19/H 0001	-	20/H 10000	20,000			
		3 Jun 1919	1/I 0001	-	2/I 10000	20,000		350	750

BA 90d 1914

BA 90e	**£5**	**Alexander Jolly Rose** Secretary				**F**	**VF**
		7 Oct 1920	3/I 0001	-	4/I 10000	20,000	
		8 Nov 1920	5/I 0001	-	6/I 10000	20,000	
		2 Dec 1920	7/I 0001	-	8/I 10000	20,000	
		14 Dec 1920	9/I 0001	-	10/I 10000	20,000	
		12 Jan 1921	11/I 0001	-	12/I 10000	20,000	
		6 Nov 1922	13/I 0001	-	14/I 10000	20,000	
		21 Dec 1922	15/I 0001	-	16/I 10000	20,000	
		9 Jan 1923	17/I 0001	-	18/I 10000	20,000	
		12 Apr 1923	19/I 0001	-	20/I 10000	20,000	
		16 Jun 1923	1/J 0001	-	2/J 10000	20,000	
		22 Aug 1923	3/J 0001	-	4/J 10000	20,000	
		25 Oct 1923	5/J 0001	-	6/J 10000	20,000	
		12 May 1924	7/J 0001	-	8/J 10000	20,000	
		14 Jun 1924	9/J 0001	-	10/J 10000	20,000	
		3 Sep 1924	11/J 0001	-	12/J 10000	20,000	
		20 Dec 1924	13/J 0001	-	14/J 10000	20,000	
		16 Jul 1925	15/J 0001	-	16/J 10000	20,000	
		27 Aug 1925	17/J 0001	-	18/J 10000	20,000	
		4 Nov 1925	19/J 0001	-	20/J 10000	20,000	
		8 Apr 1926	1/K 0001	-	2/K 10000	20,000	
		10 Jun 1926	3/K 0001	-	4/K 10000	20,000	
		1 Oct 1926	5/K 0001	-	6/K 10000	20,000	
		8 Mar 1927	7/K 0001	-	8/K 10000	20,000	
		11 May 1927	9/K 0001	-	10/K 10000	20,000	
		27 Jul 1928	11/K 0001	-	12/K 10000	20,000	
		1 Dec 1928	13/K 0001	-	14/K 10000	20,000	
		5 Jan 1929	15/K 0001	-	16/K 10000	20,000	**300**	**600**

BA 90e	Cont					F	VF
	2 Feb 1929	17/K 0001	-	18/K 10000	20,000		
	14 Aug 1929	19/K 0001	-	20/K 10000	20,000		
	30 Jun 1930	1/L 0001	-	2/L 10000	20,000		
	17 Sep 1930	3/L 0001	-	4/L 10000	20,000		
	22 Nov 1930	5/L 0001	-	6/L 10000	20,000		
	18 Dec 1930	7/L 0001	-	8/L 10000	20,000		
	19 May 1931	9/L 0001	-	10/L 10000	20,000		
	26 Jun 1931	11/L 0001	-	12/L 10000	20,000		
	28 Jul 1931	13/L 0001	-	14/L 10000	20,000	**300**	**600**

BA 90e 1926

In 1931 the Bank decided to replace the signature of the Secretary on their higher value notes with those of the Governor and Treasurer. This change was first applied to the £5 note in 1932.

BA 90f	£5	**Lord Elphinstone** Governor **George J Scott** Treasurer					
		7 Jan 1932	15/L 0001	-	16/L 10000	20,000	
		18 Apr 1932	17/L 0001	-	18/L 10000	20,000	
		11 Oct 1932	19/L 0001	-	20/L 10000	20,000	
		10 Feb 1933	1/M 0001	-	2/M 10000	20,000	
		25 Mar 1933	3/M 0001	-	4/M 10000	20,000	**400**	**750**

BA 90f 1932

The Bank's records indicate that 19 £10 notes with the Stormonth Darling signature remain unredeemed. Later records have not been maintained. No issued £10 notes dated prior to 1912 appear to have survived.

BA 91a	£10	**Central medallion Royal Arms Black value panels**					
		John Forrest Stormonth Darling Secretary					
		20 Aug 1889	4/A 0001	-	10000	10,000	
		15 Nov 1890	5/A 0001	-	10000	10,000	
		23 Dec 1890	6/A 0001	-	10000	10,000	**RARE**
BA 91b	£10	**Duncan McNeill** Secretary					
		16 Oct 1894	7/A 0001	-	10000	10,000	
		20 Oct 1896	8/A 0001	-	10000	10,000	
		19 May 1898	9/A 0001	-	10000	10,000	
		25 Jul 1901	10/A 0001	-	10000	10,000	
		17 Feb 1904	1/B 0001	-	10000	10,000	
		13 Sep 1905	2/B 0001	-	10000	10,000	
		27 Apr 1907	3/B 0001	-	10000	10,000	
		30 Sep 1909	4/B 0001	-	10000	10,000	**RARE**

Specimen undated (prepared on 1885 1892 1894 paper)   **From 500 EF**

BA 91b Specimen undated

BA 91c	£10	**Peter Macdonald** Secretary				
		20 Nov 1912	5/B 0001 - 10000	10,000		**RARE**

The printers' imprint was modified on the £10 note in 1914.

BA 91d	£10	**Peter Macdonald** Secretary	*Imprint:* **G Waterston & Sons Ld.**		**F**	**VF**
		24 Aug 1914	6/B 0001 - 10000	10,000		
		10 Sep 1917	7/B 0001 - 10000	10,000		
		5 Nov 1919	8/B 0001 - 10000	10,000	**1500**	-

BA 91d 1919

								F	VF
BA 91e	£10	**Alexander Jolly Rose** Secretary							
		15 Aug 1921	9/B 0001	-	10000		10,000		
		8 Aug 1924	10/B 0001	-	10000		10,000		
		9 Mar 1929	1/C 0001	-	10000		10,000	**1200**	-

BA 91e 1924

The Bank's records indicate that 21 £20 notes with the Stormonth Darling signature remain unredeemed. Later records have only partially been maintained. No issued £20 notes dated prior to 1910 are known to have survived.

BA 92a	£20	**Central medallion Royal Arms Red value panels**							
		John Forrest Stormonth Darling Secretary							
		9 Jul 1890	9/A 0001	-	5000		5,000		
		1 Aug 1890	10/A 0001	-	5000		5,000		
		11 Nov 1890	1/B 0001	-	5000		5,000		
		24 Dec 1890	2/B 0001	-	5000		5,000		
		7 Dec 1892	3/B 0001	-	5000		5,000		
		30 Jan 1893	4/B 0001	-	5000		5,000	**RARE**	
		Specimen undated						**RARE**	

BA 92b	**£20**	**Duncan McNeill** Secretary					
		26 May 1894	5/B 0001	-	5000	5,000	
		13 Aug 1894	6/B 0001	-	5000	5,000	
		19 Sep 1894	7/B 0001	-	5000	5,000	
		26 Aug 1895	8/B 0001	-	5000	5,000	
		1 Sep 1896	9/B 0001	-	5000	5,000	
		8 Sep 1896	10/B 0001	-	5000	5,000	
		13 Mar 1897	1/C 0001	-	5000	5,000	
		16 Apr 1898	2/C 0001	-	5000	5,000	
		29 Apr 1898	3/C 0001	-	5000	5,000	
		14 Jul 1899	4/C 0001	-	5000	5,000	
		9 Feb 1901	5/C 0001	-	5000	5,000	
		28 Aug 1901	6/C 0001	-	5000	5,000	
		22 Oct 1901	7/C 0001	-	5000	5,000	
		4 Jul 1902	8/C 0001	-	5000	5,000	
		13 Jan 1904	9/C 0001	-	5000	5,000	
		27 Jan 1904	10/C 0001	-	5000	5,000	
		23 Feb 1905	1/D 0001	-	5000	5,000	
		21 Sep 1905	2/D 0001	-	5000	5,000	
		2 May 1906	3/D 0001	-	5000	5,000	
		18 Jun 1907	4/D 0001	-	5000	5,000	
		30 Oct 1907	5/D 0001	-	5000	5,000	
		2 Nov 1910	6/D 0001	-	5000	5,000	**RARE**

Specimen undated (prepared on 1885 1892 1894 paper) From 500 EF

Records indicate that some 69 £20 notes with the Macdonald signature remain unredeemed.

							F	**VF**
BA 92c	**£20**	**Peter Macdonald** Secretary						
		26 Oct 1911	7/D 0001	-	5000	5,000		
		18 Nov 1911	8/D 0001	-	5000	5,000		
		15 Dec 1913	9/D 0001	-	5000	5,000	**1100**	-

BA 92c 1913

The printers' imprint was modified on the £20 note in 1914.

BA 92d	£20	**Peter Macdonald** Secretary		*Imprint:*	**G Waterston & Sons Ld**		**F**	**VF**
		25 Apr 1914	10/D 0001	-	5000	5,000		
		17 Jul 1915	1/E 0001	-	5000	5,000		
		6 Oct 1915	2/E 0001	-	5000	5,000		
		10 Jul 1917	3/E 0001	-	5000	5,000		
		19 Feb 1918	4/E 0001	-	5000	5,000		
		10 May 1918	5/E 0001	-	5000	5,000		
		3 Jul 1919	6/E 0001	-	5000	5,000		
		6 Aug 1919	7/E 0001	-	5000	5,000		
		8 Oct 1919	8/E 0001	-	2500	2,500	**1000**	-

BA 92d 1915

BA 92e	£20	**Alexander Jolly Rose** Secretary						
		11 Oct 1920	8/E 2501	-	5000	2,500		
		27 Nov 1920	9/E 0001	-	5000	5,000		
		29 Dec 1920	10/E 0001	-	5000	5,000		
		3 Nov 1922	1/F 0001	-	5000	5,000		
		22 Jan 1923	2/F 0001	-	5000	5,000		
		3 Apr 1924	3/F 0001	-	5000	5,000		
		24 Mar 1926	4/F 0001	-	5000	5,000		
		27 Jul 1926	5/F 0001	-	5000	5,000		
		2 Oct 1928	6/F 0001	-	5000	5,000		
		5 Nov 1928	7/F 0001	-	5000	5,000		
		30 May 1930	8/F 0001	-	5000	5,000		
		25 Sep 1930	9/F 0001	-	5000	5,000	**1000**	-

BA 92e 1926

In 1932 the signature of the Secretary on the £20 note was replaced with those of the Governor and Treasurer.

BA 92f   **£20**   **Lord Elphinstone** Governor   **George J Scott** Treasurer
           21 Jun 1932   10/F 0001   -   5000   5,000
           2 Dec 1932   1/G 0001   -   5000   5,000   **RARE**

The Bank's records indicate that just three £100 notes with the Stormonth Darling signature remain unredeemed. Later records have not been maintained. No issued £100 notes dated prior to 1935 are known to have survived.

BA 93a   **£100 Central medallion Royal Arms Red value panels**
          John Forrest Stormonth Darlin Secretary
               27 Aug 1889   4/B 0001   -   1000   1,000
               26 Sep 1889   5/B 0001   -   1000   1,000
               8 Jul 1890   6/B 0001   -   1000   1,000
               2 Aug 1890   7/B 0001   -   1000   1,000
               4 Nov 1890   8/B 0001   -   1000   1,000
               29 Nov 1890   9/B 0001   -   1000   1,000
               17 Dec 1890   10/B 0001   -   1000   1,000
               1 Oct 1891   1/C 0001   -   1000   1,000
               14 Oct 1891   2/C 0001   -   1000   1,000
               7 Nov 1891   3/C 0001   -   1000   1,000
               13 Dec 1892   4/C 0001   -   1000   1,000
               9 Jan 1893   5/C 0001   -   1000   1,000
               10 Feb 1893   6/C 0001   -   1000   1,000   **RARE**

BA 93b	**£100**	**Duncan McNeill** Secretary					
		12 Jul 1894	7/C 0001	-	1000	1,000	
		23 Aug 1894	8/C 0001	-	1000	1,000	
		24 Sep 1894	9/C 0001	-	1000	1,000	
		25 Oct 1894	10/C 0001	-	1000	1,000	
		2 Jul 1895	1/D 0001	-	1000	1,000	
		4 Aug 1896	2/D 0001	-	1000	1,000	
		11 Aug 1896	3/D 0001	-	1000	1,000	
		22 Aug 1896	4/D 0001	-	1000	1,000	
		31 Mar 1897	5/D 0001	-	1000	1,000	
		6 May 1897	6/D 0001	-	1000	1,000	
		17 May 1897	7/D 0001	-	1000	1,000	
		8 Jun 1898	8/D 0001	-	1000	1,000	
		15 Jun 1898	9/D 0001	-	1000	1,000	
		29 Aug 1899	10/D 0001	-	1000	1,000	
		16 Sep 1899	1/E 0001	-	1000	1,000	
		19 Jan 1901	2/E 0001	-	1000	1,000	
		3 Oct 1901	3/E 0001	-	1000	1,000	
		18 Dec 1901	4/E 0001	-	1000	1,000	
		14 Aug 1902	5/E 0001	-	1000	1,000	
		26 Nov 1902	6/E 0001	-	1000	1,000	
		22 Jan 1904	7/E 0001	-	1000	1,000	
		12 Feb 1904	8/E 0001	-	1000	1,000	
		29 Feb 1904	9/E 0001	-	1000	1,000	
		6 Dec 1904	10/E 0001	-	1000	1,000	
		17 Nov 1905	1/F 0001	-	1000	1,000	
		24 Nov 1905	2/F 0001	-	1000	1,000	
		11 Jun 1906	3/F 0001	-	1000	1,000	
		29 Oct 1907	4/F 0001	-	1000	1,000	
		30 Nov 1907	5/F 0001	-	1000	1,000	
		1 Feb 1909	6/F 0001	-	1000	1,000	
		8 Feb 1909	7/F 0001	-	1000	1,000	
		16 Nov 1909	8/F 0001	-	1000	1,000	
		8 Dec 1909	9/F 0001	-	1000	1,000	
		23 Nov 1910	10/F 0001	-	1000	1,000	
		9 Dec 1910	1/G 0001	-	1000	1,000	**RARE**

Specimen undated (prepared on 1885 1892 1894 paper)　　　　　**From 2000 EF**

BA 93b Specimen undated

BA 93c £100 **Peter Macdonald** Secretary
11 Dec 1911	2/G 0001	-	1000	1,000	
26 Dec 1911	3/G 0001	-	1000	1,000	
9 Oct 1912	4/G 0001	-	1000	1,000	
28 Nov 1912	5/G 0001	-	1000	1,000	
27 Sep 1913	6/G 0001	-	1000	1,000	
13 Nov 1913	7/G 0001	-	1000	1,000	**RARE**

The printers' imprint was modified on the £100 note in 1915.

BA 93d £100 **Peter Macdonald** Secretary *Imprint:* **G Waterston & Sons Ld**
7 Sep 1915	8/G 0001	-	1000	1,000	
19 Oct 1915	9/G 0001	-	1000	1,000	
9 Nov 1915	10/G 0001	-	1000	1,000	
17 Aug 1917	1/H 0001	-	1000	1,000	
1 Dec 1917	2/H 0001	-	1000	1,000	
11 Mar 1919	3/H 0001	-	1000	1,000	
17 Apr 1919	4/H 0001	-	1000	1,000	
7 Jul 1920	5/H 0001	-	1000	1,000	**RARE**

BA 93e   £100   **Alexander Jolly Rose** Secretary

	19 Aug 1920	6/H 0001	-	1000	1,000	
	5 Sep 1921	7/H 0001	-	1000	1,000	
	2 Dec 1922	8/H 0001	-	1000	1,000	
	16 Jan 1923	9/H 0001	-	1000	1,000	
	15 May 1923	10/H 0001	-	1000	1,000	
	24 Jul 1923	1/I 0001	-	1000	1,000	
	7 Oct 1925	2/I 0001	-	1000	1,000	
	4 Jan 1926	3/I 0001	-	1000	1,000	
	19 Apr 1927	4/I 0001	-	1000	1,000	
	16 Aug 1928	5/I 0001	-	1000	1,000	
	3 Sep 1928	6/I 0001	-	1000	1,000	
	18 Feb 1930	7/I 0001	-	1000	1,000	
	6 Jun 1930	8/I 0001	-	1000	1,000	**RARE**

In 1932 the signature of the Secretary on the £100 note was replaced with those of the Governor and Treasurer.

BA 93f   £100   **Lord Elphinstone** Governor   **George J Scott** Treasurer

	28 May 1932	9/I 0001	-	1000	1,000	
	8 Nov 1932	10/I 0001	-	1000	1,000	**RARE**

REDUCED SIZE £1 NOTES 1929 *to* 1933

In 1929 the Bank of Scotland was the last of the Scottish banks to reduce the size of its £1 note to Size B (exact dimensions varied from 151 to 155mm by 84 to 85mm) to conform to UK Treasury and Bank of England notes. The notes inevitably had to be redesigned but the essential features of the old 'square' notes were retained. The redesigns were prepared by Robert Burns, an Edinburgh artist and four new plates, each with eight impressions, were engraved by Thomas Macdonald & Son (Engravers) Ltd, of London. As before the notes were printed in Edinburgh by **George Waterston & Sons Ltd**, whose imprint is found on the notes in the lower right hand corner of the obverse. Paper continued to be supplied by Portals but the Celtic pattern watermark was modified and the patent registration number dropped.

For the first time the reverse of the note is also printed, with a depiction of the Bank's head office in Edinburgh and four '£1' symbols. The reverse is printed in grey-black. Also for the first time, the £1 note carries two printed signatures, those of the Governor and Treasurer.

BA 94	£1	Reduced size **Royal Arms Brown-Yellow** reverse grey-black			F	VF	EF
		Lord Elphinstone Governor **George J Scott** Treasurer					
		22 Jan 1929 A 0000001 - 1000000		1,000,000			
		28 Feb 1929 B 0000001 - 1000000		1,000,000			
		26 Sep 1929 C 0000001 - 1000000		1,000,000			
		14 Nov 1929 D 0000001 - 1000000		1,000,000			
		11 Mar 1930 E 0000001 - 1000000		1,000,000			
		19 Jun 1930 F 0000001 - 1000000		1,000,000			
		6 Aug 1931 G 0000001 - 1000000		1,000,000			
		15 Apr 1932 H 0000001 - 1000000		1,000,000			
		10 Oct 1932 I 0000001 - 1000000		1,000,000			
		17 Jul 1933 J 0000001 - 0900000		900,000	70	150	300
		Specimen 21 Jan 1929 A 0000000		25	From 250 UNC		
		Specimen 22 Jan 1929 A 0286147 <u>CANCELLED</u> twice in red punch holes			From 250 UNC		

BA 94a First prefix

BA 94 Reverse

THIRD WATERSTON ISSUE – 1935 *to* 1969

Bank Arms or Thistle Motif

In June 1934 the Lord Lyon, King of Arms, the supreme heraldic authority in Scotland, wrote to the Bank of Scotland objecting to the use of the Royal Arms on their notes (he similarly approached both the British Linen Bank and the National Bank of Scotland). Consequently all the notes had to be redesigned. Revised designs were approved in August 1934 and the printing of new notes authorised in January 1935. Colour variations from yellow-orange through to dark brown are noticeable throughout the series due to difficulties in maintaining quality control. Listing of all notes from 1935 onwards will be in order of denomination rather than split by signature pairs, better to illustrate the many changes as they took place.

On the £1 note the Royal Arms were replaced by a representation of the Bank's Arms. Other minor changes were made including a redesign of the central medallion and a frame added to the image of the Bank's head office on the reverse. Further size reductions to the £1 note took place during this series. In July 1934 the Bank received an offer from Waterlow & Sons to print their notes, but did not pursue it. There is no evidence that Waterlows submitted new note designs with their offer.

BA 95a	£1	Bank Arms Revised medallion Framed reverse			F	VF	EF
		Lord Elphinstone Governor					
		Alexander William Morton Beveridge Treasurer					
		15 Jan 1935 K 0000001 - 1000000		1,000,000			
		4 Feb 1935 L 0000001 - 1000000		1,000,000			
		18 May 1935 M 0000001 - 1000000		1,000,000			
		9 Dec 1935 N 0000001 - 1000000		1,000,000			
		30 Nov 1936 O 0000001 - 1000000		1,000,000			
		8 Mar 1937 P 0000001 - 1000000		1,000,000			
		15 Sep 1937 Q 0000001 - 1000000		1,000,000	25	70	170

BA 95a First prefix

BA 95 Framed reverse

Specimen undated no prefix/serials CANCELLED overprint **From 250 UNC**

							F	VF	EF
BA 95b	**£1**	**Lord Elphinstone** Governor							
		James Waddell Macfarlane Treasurer							
		5 Jan 1939	R 0000001	-	1000000	1,000,000			
		20 Apr 1939	S 0000001	-	1000000	1,000,000			
		12 Jun 1939	T 0000001	-	1000000	1,000,000			
		24 Aug 1939	U 0000001	-	1000000	1,000,000			
		15 Feb 1940	V 0000001	-	1000000	1,000,000			
		4 Jul 1940	W 0000001	-	1000000	1,000,000			
		1 Mar 1941	X 0000001	-	1000000	1,000,000			
		7 May 1941	Y 0000001	-	1000000	1,000,000	**20**	**60**	**140**

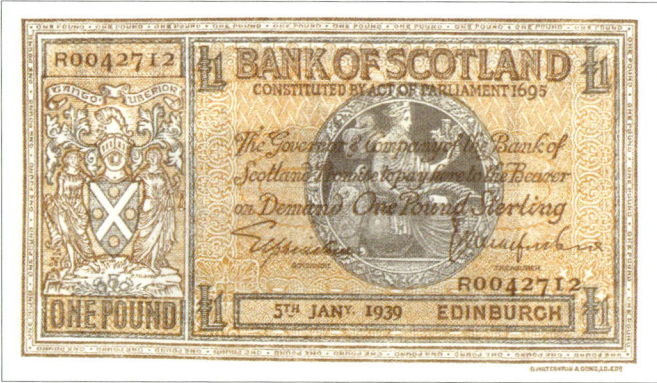

BA 95b First prefix

					F	VF	EF
BA 95c	£1	**Lord Elphinstone** Governor **John B Crawford** Treasurer					
		2 Jun 1942 Z 0000001 - 1000000		1,000,000	**20**	**60**	**130**

BA 95c

		Specimen undated no prefix/serials			30	**From 200 UNC**	
BA 95d	£1	**Bolder signature John B Crawford Six digit serials**					
		16 Oct 1943 AA 000001 - 1000000		1,000,000	**20**	**60**	**140**

BA 95d

In April 1943, ahead of the Bank's 250th anniversary in 1945, the Bank started to consider redesigning the £1 note. A committee was set up and several essays were presented by Waterstons involving a modified side panel and two redesigned reverses in different shades of grey. Proof reverses in several other colours have been seen.

Stanley Curister, Curator of the National Gallery, was consulted and expressed the view that none of these designs was suitable. He prepared several designs of his own but these were also rejected. His proposal for an entirely new reverse featuring the Bank's Arms against a lined background was however approved in May 1944 after several variants were submitted with four different reverse colours. The inks were adaptations of the Crum Brown originals by A B Fleming & Co Ltd, the long standing ink manufacturers for the Bank. Essays of both the Waterston and Curister designs have survived and are listed under BA 96 and BA 97.

Waterston Essay designs

BA 96 Tan reverse №2

BA 96 Blue reverse №6

BA 96a £1 **Side panel in revised colours**
Lord Elphinstone Governor **John B Crawford** Treasurer
Bank head office reverse dark olive-grey

Essay undated AA 962582   From 350 UNC

BA 96a/b/c Essay

BA 96b   £1   Similar to BA 96a reverse light olive-grey

                 Essay undated AA 962582   **From 350 UNC**

BA 96b Light olive-grey reverse

BA 96c   £1   Similar to BA 96a Side panel unchanged Blue medallion uniface

                 Essay undated no prefix/serials   **From 350 UNC**

BA 96d   £1   Similar to BA 96a Grey side panel & medallion uniface

                 Essay undated no prefix/serials   **From 350 UNC**

Curister Essay designs

BA 97a   £1   No side panel Grey medallion **Bank Arms** reverse dark grey **Lord Elphinstone** Governor **John B Crawford** Treasurer

                 Essay 1 Jan 1945 S 0247528   **From 250 UNC**

BA 97a/b/c/d

BA 97a Dark Grey reverse

BA 97b	**£1**	**Similar to BA 97a reverse green/grey**	
		Essay 1 Jan 1945 S 0247528	**From 250 UNC**
BA 97c	**£1**	**Similar to BA 97a reverse green**	
		Essay 1 Jan 1945 S 0247528	**From 250 UNC**
BA 97d	**£1**	**Similar to BA 97a reverse dark green**	
		Essay 1 Jan 1945 S 0247528	**From 250 UNC**

BA 97d Dark Green reverse

The adopted design was first issued in 1945. The side panel has been dropped and the whole obverse closely resembles the central area of the higher denomination notes containing the promissory text. The reverse features the Bank's Arms against a lined background.

BA 98a	£1	No side panel reverse dark brown				VF	EF	UNC
		Lord Elphinstone Governor **John B Crawford** Treasurer						
		4 Jan 1945	A 0000001	- 1000000	1,000,000			
		6 Feb 1945	B 0000001	- 0500000	500,000	50	120	250

BA 98a First prefix low serial

BA 98a Dark Brown reverse

It was quickly realised that the dark brown reverse was too heavy and obscured the watermark. A lighter yellow-ochre shade was adopted and introduced in late 1945.

BA 98b	£1	Yellow-Ochre reverse				VF	EF	UNC
		6 Feb 1945	B 0500001	- 1000000	500,000			
		4 Oct 1945	C 0000001	- 1000000	1,000,000			
		29 Nov 1945	D 0000001	- 1000000	1,000,000			
		11 Dec 1946	E 0000001	- 1000000	1,000,000			
		28 Jan 1947	F 0000001	- 1000000	1,000,000			
		9 Sep 1947	G 0000001	- 1000000	1,000,000			
		5 Jan 1948	H 0000001	- 1000000	1,000,000			
		10 Feb 1949	I 0000001	- 1000000	1,000,000			
		8 Mar 1949	J 0000001	- 1000000	1,000,000			
		16 Jan 1950	K 0000001	- 1000000	1,000,000			
		4 Dec 1950	L 0000001	- 1000000	1,000,000			
		5 Jan 1951	M0000001	- 1000000	1,000,000			
		12 Oct 1951	N 0000001	- 1000000	1,000,000			
		5 Nov 1951	O 0000001	- 1000000	1,000,000			
		17 Sep 1952	P 0000001	- 1000000	1,000,000			
		22 Oct 1952	Q 0000001	- 1000000	1,000,000			
		19 Nov 1952	R 0000001	- 0500000	500,000	**20**	**45**	**90**

BA 98b First Split Prefix

BA 98b Last Split Prefix

BA 98b Ochre reverse

Specimen undated no prefix/serials   25   **From 100 UNC**

BA 98c	**£1**	**Lord Elphinstone** Governor **William Watson** Treasurer				**VF**	**EF**	**UNC**
		4 Sep 1953	R 0500001	-	1000000	500,000		
		16 Oct 1953	S 0000001	-	1000000	1,000,000		
		9 Nov 1953	T 0000001	-	1000000	1,000,000	**25**	**50**	**110**

BA 98c First Split Prefix

In 1955 the Bank of Scotland absorbed the Union Bank of Scotland and it was felt desirable that some changes to the notes should be made to reflect this new combination. The decision to stay with Waterstons rather than move to Waterlows, who had been printing the Union Bank's notes, was made on cost grounds. It was also decided to source banknote paper locally and Cowans of Penicuik were selected after samples of their paper were tested. Remaining stocks of Portals paper were used up and notes of this issue used both paper types. Portals paper is slightly thinner than Cowans' but otherwise hard to distinguish. The small number of undated specimens printed on Union Bank watermarked paper may have been test printings using the different paper.

The only design change to the obverse was the adoption of a blue-grey medallion in place of the previous grey. A new reverse was designed with a circular vignette of the Union Bank's old ship motif set against an elaborate background of thistles.

BA 99a   **£1**   **Blue medallion Ship motif reverse**   VF   EF   UNC
Lord Elphinstone Governor   **William Watson** Treasurer

Date	Serial		Range	Quantity	VF	EF	UNC
1 Mar 1955	A 0000001	-	1000000	1,000,000			
2 Mar 1955	B 0000001	-	1000000	1,000,000			
3 Mar 1955	C 0000001	-	1000000	1,000,000			
4 Mar 1955	D 0000001	-	1000000	1,000,000	20	45	70

BA 99a First prefix

BA 99a Reverse

Specimen   1 Mar 1955 A 0000000   25   **From 180 UNC**
Union Bank watermark undated no prefix/serials 8   **From 200 UNC**

BA 99b   **£1**   **John Craig** Governor   **William Watson** Treasurer

Date	Serial		Range	Quantity	VF	EF	UNC
1 Sep 1955	E 0000001	-	1000000	1,000,000			
2 Sep 1955	F 0000001	-	1000000	1,000,000			
3 Sep 1955	G 0000001	-	1000000	1,000,000			
5 Sep 1955	H 0000001	-	1000000	1,000,000			
6 Sep 1955	I 0000001	-	1000000	1,000,000			
10 Sep 1956	J 0000001	-	1000000	1,000,000			
11 Sep 1956	K 0000001	-	1000000	1,000,000			
12 Sep 1956	L 0000001	-	1000000	1,000,000			
13 Sep 1956	M 0000001	-	1000000	1,000,000			
14 Sep 1956	N 0000001	-	1000000	1,000,000	15	40	60

BA 99b First prefix

Specimen undated no prefix/serials   30   **From 100 UNC**

						VF	**EF**	**UNC**
BA 99c	**£1**	**Lord Bilsland** Governor **William Watson** Treasurer						
		30 Aug 1957	O 0000001	-	1000000	1,000,000		
		1 Oct 1957	P 0000001	-	1000000	1,000,000		
		2 Oct 1957	Q 0000001	-	1000000	1,000,000		
		3 Oct 1957	R 0000001	-	1000000	1,000,000		
		4 Oct 1957	S 0000001	-	1000000	1,000,000		
		7 Oct 1957	T 0000001	-	1000000	1,000,000		
		22 Aug 1958	U 0000001	-	1000000	1,000,000		
		25 Aug 1958	V 0000001	-	1000000	1,000,000		
		26 Aug 1958	W 0000001	-	1000000	1,000,000		
		27 Aug 1958	X 0000001	-	1000000	1,000,000		
		28 Aug 1958	Y 0000001	-	1000000	1,000,000		
		29 Aug 1958	Z 0000001	-	1000000	1,000,000		
		Fractional prefix						
		1 Dec 1959	A/A 0000001	-	4500000	4,500,000		
		30 Nov 1960	B/A 0000001	-	4151500	4,148,000 *	**15**	**40**	**60**

BA 99c First prefix

BA 99c Last prefix

* Only 4,148,000 of these notes were actually issued. 5,000,000 were printed and highest serial number taken to cash was B/A 4151500.

Trial Modified border 30 Nov 1960 no prefix/serials			**From 170 UNC**
Specimen 29 Aug 1958 Z 0000000		5	
30 Nov 1960 B/A 0000000		n/k	**From 150 UNC**
undated no prefix/serials		30	**From 120 UNC**

In early 1959 the Bank first started to consider further reducing the size of its £1 notes. Some thought was given at this time to improving the designs and enhancing the security features which were still essentially Victorian in nature. Trials of new notes with different designs and in different colours can be found in the Bank's archives but none was considered acceptable. Reduced size notes adhering to the previous designs were first approved for issue in May 1961, the reduced size conforming to the smaller £1 notes first issued by the Bank of England in March 1960.

BA 100a	£1	Reduced size 152 x 71mm (Size C)				VF	EF	UNC
		Lord Bilsland Governor **William Watson** Treasurer						
		16 Nov 1961	A 0000001 - 1000000	1,000,000				
		17 Nov 1961	B 0000001 - 1000000	1,000,000				
		20 Nov 1961	C 0000001 - 1000000	1,000,000				
		21 Nov 1961	D 0000001 - 1000000	1,000,000				
		22 Nov 1961	E 0000001 - 1000000	1,000,000				
		23 Nov 1961	F 0000001 - 1000000	1,000,000				
		3 Dec 1962	G 0000001 - 1000000	1,000,000				
		4 Dec 1962	H 0000001 - 1000000	1,000,000				
		5 Dec 1962	I 0000001 - 1000000	1,000,000				
		6 Dec 1962	J 0000001 - 1000000	1,000,000				
		7 Dec 1962	K 0000001 - 1000000	1,000,000				
		10 Dec 1962	L 0000001 - 1000000	1,000,000				
		11 Dec 1962	M 0000001 - 1000000	1,000,000				
		12 Dec 1962	N 0000001 - 0790000	790,000		10	30	50

BA 100a First prefix

Trial Amended border 30 Nov 1960 B/A 0000000 **From 170 EF**

BA 100a Trial with amended border

Specimen 14 Sep 1961 30 Sep 1961 *both*
B/A 2357664 punch hole cancelled **From 130 UNC**
16 Nov 1961 A 0000000 30 **From 130 UNC**

During 1963 the first experiments took place with magnetic sorting codes to assist the daily note exchange to cope with the growing volumes of notes in circulation. Notes carrying experimental coding can be found overprinted SPECIMEN. They had probably been prepared for use by Crosfield Electronics Ltd who were developing sorting machines for the Scottish banks.

BA 100b £1 **Experimental Encoding within side margins of obverse**
Lord Bilsland Governor **William Watson** Treasurer

Trial undated stamped SPECIMEN 30 **From 300 UNC**

BA 100b Trial Experimental Encoding within side margins

New printing and numbering machines were introduced in August 1963 and the notes modified accordingly.

BA 100c £1 **Fractional Prefix Smaller serial numbers** VF EF UNC
Lord Bilsland Governor **William Watson** Treasurer

Date	Prefix	Range	Quantity	VF	EF	UNC
3 Feb 1964	A/A 0000001	- 1000000	1,000,000			
4 Feb 1964	A/B 0000001	- 1000000	1,000,000			
5 Feb 1964	A/C 0000001	- 1000000	1,000,000			
6 Feb 1964	A/D 0000001	- 1000000	1,000,000			
7 Feb 1964	A/E 0000001	- 1000000	1,000,000			
10 Feb 1964	A/F 0000001	- 1000000	1,000,000			
11 Feb 1964	A/G 0000001	- 1000000	1,000,000			
12 Feb 1964	A/H 0000001	- 1000000	1,000,000			
13 Feb 1964	A/I 0000001	- 1000000	1,000,000	10	25	50

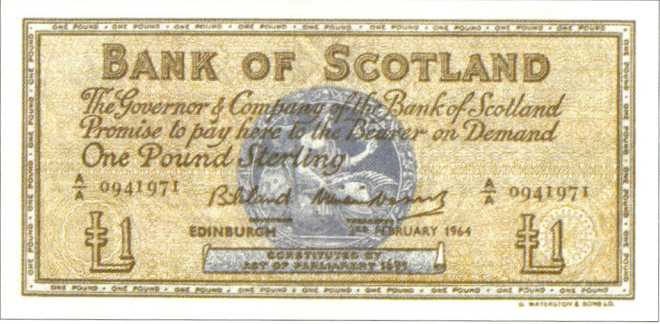

BA 100c First prefix

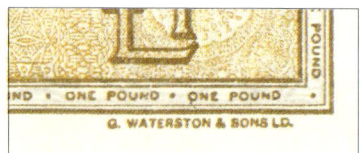   

Imprint with LD   Imprint with LTD

A minor amendment to the printers' imprint took place in 1965: 'LD' now reads 'LTD'.

BA 100d   **£1**   **Amended printers' imprint**   VF   EF   UNC

            4 May 1965   A/J 0000001   -   1000000   1,000,000
            5 May 1965   A/K 0000001   -   1000000   1,000,000
            6 May 1965   A/L 0000001   -   1000000   1,000,000
            7 May 1965   A/M 0000001   -   1000000   1,000,000
            10 May 1965 A/N 0000001   -   1000000   1,000,000
            11 May 1965 A/O 0000001   -   1000000   1,000,000   **10**   **25**   **50**

            Specimen undated A/M 0000000   7   **From 100 UNC**

In 1966 there was a further minor amendment to the layout of the note: 'EDINBURGH' and the date are now moved to the centre right of the note. Issue volumes are now rising and multiple prefixes are to be seen on each date. In 1967 Crosfield Electronics were finally able to offer a reliable electronic sorting machine and magnetic ink sorting codes appear on the notes from March 1967 onwards.

BA 100e   **£1**   **Revised layout EDINBURGH & date centre right**
            Lord Polwarth Governor
            James Letham Treasurer & General Manager
            1 Jun 1966 A/P 0000001   -   A/U 1000000   6,000,000   **10**   **25**   **50**

BA 100e First prefix

            Specimen 1 Jun 1966 A/P 0000000   25   **From 100 UNC**

BA 100f	£1	Magnetic Encoding on reverse				VF	EF	UNC
		3 Mar 1967 A/V 0000001 - A/Y 0834000			3,834,000	10	30	50

BA 100f/g Reverse with encoding

New paper with a thistle watermark was introduced in 1967, prepared for use in the new generation of notes the Bank was in the process of designing.

BA 100g	£1	Encoding on reverse Thistle watermark					VF	EF	UNC
		3 Mar 1967 A/Y 0834001 - B/C 0900000			4,066,000	*	10	25	50

* 900,000 notes printed with prefix B/C but only 866,000 taken to cash

On notes of £5 and above a thistle motif was chosen to replace the Royal Arms in the side panel. These 'horse blanket' notes were otherwise unchanged. The £5 was twice reduced in size during this series.

BA 101a	£5	Thistle motif Lord Elphinstone Governor uniface				F	VF	EF
		Alexander William Morton Beveridge Treasurer						
		17 Jan 1935	5/M 0001 -	6/M 10000	20,000			
		23 Jan 1935	7/M 0001 -	8/M 10000	20,000			
		9 Feb 1935	9/M 0001 -	10/M 10000	20,000			
		20 Mar 1935	11/M 0001 -	12/M 10000	20,000			
		16 Apr 1935	13/M 0001 -	14/M 10000	20,000			
		22 May 1935	15/M 0001 -	16/M 10000	20,000			
		15 Jun 1936	17/M 0001 -	18/M 10000	20,000			
		3 Jul 1936	19/M 0001 -	20/M 10000	20,000			
		29 Dec 1936	1/N 0001 -	2/N 10000	20,000			
		3 Aug 1937	3/N 0001 -	4/N 10000	20,000			
		13 Sep 1937	5/N 0001 -	6/N 10000	20,000			
		5 Oct 1937	7/N 0001 -	8/N 10000	20,000			
		19 Jan 1938	9/N 0001 -	10/N 10000	20,000			
		23 Feb 1938	11/N 0001 -	12/N 10000	20,000			
		17 Mar 1938	13/N 0001 -	14/N 10000	20,000	180	350	600

BA 101a 1938

Specimen undated stamped CANCELLED		20	**From 200 EF**

BA 101b	**£5**	**Lord Elphinstone** Governor **James Waddell Macfarlane** Treasurer					**F**	**VF**	**EF**
		24 Apr 1939	15/N 0001	-	16/N 10000	20,000			
		15 May 1939	17/N 0001	-	18/N 10000	20,000			
		8 Jun 1939	19/N 0001	-	20/N 10000	20,000			
		21 Jul 1939	1/O 0001	-	2/O 10000	20,000			
		24 Nov 1939	3/O 0001	-	4/O 10000	20,000			
		8 Dec 1939	5/O 0001	-	6/O 10000	20,000			
		22 Dec 1939	7/O 0001	-	8/O 10000	20,000			
		3 Jan 1940	9/O 0001	-	10/O 10000	20,000			
		29 Jan 1940	11/O 0001	-	12/O 10000	20,000			
		12 Feb 1940	13/O 0001	-	14/O 10000	20,000			
		4 Mar 1940	15/O 0001	-	16/O 10000	20,000			
		7 Jul 1941	17/O 0001	-	18/O 10000	20,000			
		12 Aug 1941	19/O 0001	-	20/O 10000	20,000			
		10 Sep 1941	1/P 0001	-	2/P 10000	20,000			
		16 Oct 1941	3/P 0001	-	4/P 10000	20,000	140	250	450

BA 101b 1940

A few issued £5 notes dated 1942 and 1944 have been seen with CANCELLED stamps. These may have been taken from circulation for use internally.

BA 101c	£5	**Lord Elphinstone** Governor		**John B Crawford** Treasurer	F	VF	EF
		5 Jun 1942	5/P 0001 -	6/P 10000	20,000		
		24 Jun 1942	7/P 0001 -	8/P 10000	20,000		
		10 Jul 1942	9/P 0001 -	10/P 10000	20,000		
		30 Jul 1942	11/P 0001 -	12/P 10000	20,000		
		6 Aug 1942	13/P 0001 -	14/P 10000	20,000		
		20 Aug 1942	15/P 0001 -	16/P 10000	20,000		
		11 Sep 1942	17/P 0001 -	18/P 10000	20,000		
		21 Sep 1942	19/P 0001 -	20/P 10000	20,000		
		6 Oct 1942	1/Q 0001 -	2/Q 10000	20,000		
		26 Oct 1942	3/Q 0001 -	4/Q 10000	20,000		
		10 Nov 1942	5/Q 0001 -	6/Q 10000	20,000		
		25 Nov 1942	7/Q 0001 -	8/Q 10000	20,000		
		6 Jan 1943	9/Q 0001 -	10/Q 10000	20,000		
		20 Jan 1943	11/Q 0001 -	12/Q 10000	20,000		
		8 Feb 1943	13/Q 0001 -	14/Q 10000	20,000		
		22 Feb 1943	15/Q 0001 -	16/Q 10000	20,000		
		10 Mar 1943	17/Q 0001 -	18/Q 10000	20,000		
		23 Mar 1943	19/Q 0001 -	20/Q 10000	20,000		
		7 Apr 1943	1/R 0001 -	2/R 10000	20,000		
		19 Apr 1943	3/R 0001 -	4/R 10000	20,000		
		4 May 1944	5/R 0001 -	6/R 10000	20,000		
		6 Jun 1944	7/R 0001 -	8/R 10000	20,000		
		12 Jul 1944	9/R 0001 -	10/R 10000	20,000		
		11 Aug 1944	11/R 0001 -	12/R 10000	20,000		
		26 Sep 1944	13/R 0001 -	14/R 10000	20,000	**140**	**250**	**450**

BA 101c 1942

Specimen undated   20   **From 200 EF**

In 1943 the Bank started to consider redesigning the £5 note. A committee was set up with a brief to examine ways of reducing the size of the £5 note and adding a printed reverse. Stanley Curister, Curator of the National Gallery, prepared designs for a printed reverse featuring the Bank's shield against a lined background which was approved in May 1944 after several variants were submitted experimenting with different coloured inks. The inks were produced by A B Fleming & Co Ltd, the long standing ink manufacturers for the Bank. A number of these essays have come on to the market, all in the reduced dimensions of 180 x 102mm.

Stanley Curister Essays

BA 102a   **£5**   **Reduced size Reverse Bank shield in dark brown**
                      Lord Elphinstone Governor   **John B Crawford** Treasurer

            Essay 4 May 1944 6/R 7135 Overprinted CANCELLED   **From 250 UNC**

BA 102a Essay 1944

BA 102b   **£5**   **Similar to BA 102a reverse dark grey**

       Essay 21 Jan 1945 8/Q 4233
           Overprinted CANCELLED or SPECIMEN   **From 250 UNC**

BA 102b Essay 1945

BA 102b Dark Grey reverse

BA 102c   £5   Similar to BA 102a reverse light grey-green

         Essay   21 Jan 1945 8/Q 4233
                Overprinted CANCELLED or SPECIMEN   **From 250 UNC**

BA 102d   £5   Similar to BA 102a reverse green

         Essay   21 Jan 1945 8/Q 4233
                Overprinted CANCELLED or SPECIMEN   **From 250 UNC**

BA 102d Green reverse

BA 102e   £5   Similar to BA 102a reverse olive-drab

         Essay   21 Jan 1945 8/Q 4233
                Overprinted CANCELLED or SPECIMEN   **From 250 UNC**

Paper Money of Scotland

The adopted designs were first issued in May 1945. The obverse retains all the features of the previous note while the printed reverse features the Bank's shield with floral flourishes against a lined background. Dimensions 180 x 102mm.

BA 103a	£5	**Brown value panels** dark brown reverse			**F**	**VF**	**EF**
		Lord Elphinstone Governor **John B Crawford** Treasurer					
		3 Jan 1945	1/A 0001 - 2/A 10000	20,000			
		15 Jan 1945	3/A 0001 - 4/A 10000	20,000			
		1 Feb 1945	5/A 0001 - 6/A 10000	20,000			
		16 Feb 1945	7/A 0001 - 8/A 10000	20,000			
		2 Mar 1945	9/A 0001 - 10/A 10000	20,000	**85**	**200**	**380**

BA 103a 1945 First date/prefix

BA 103a Dark Brown reverse

It was quickly realised that the dark brown reverse was too heavy and obscured the watermark. A lighter shade of yellow-ochre was adopted and introduced in late 1945.

							F	VF	EF
BA 103b	£5	**Brown value panels** yellow-ochre reverse							
		16 Mar 1945	11/A 0001	-	12/A 10000	20,000			
		3 Apr 1945	13/A 0001	-	14/A 10000	20,000			
		20 Apr 1945	15/A 0001	-	16/A 10000	20,000			
		3 May 1945	17/A 0001	-	18/A 10000	20,000			
		10 May 1945	19/A 0001	-	20/A 10000	20,000			
		4 Jun 1945	1/B 0001	-	2/B 10000	20,000			
		19 Jun 1945	3/B 0001	-	4/B 10000	20,000			
		4 Jul 1945	5/B 0001	-	6/B 10000	20,000			
		14 Jul 1945	7/B 0001	-	8/B 10000	20,000			
		1 Aug 1945	9/B 0001	-	10/B 10000	20,000			
		17 Aug 1945	11/B 0001	-	12/B 10000	20,000			
		1 Sep 1945	13/B 0001	-	14/B 10000	20,000			
		19 Sep 1945	15/B 0001	-	16/B 10000	20,000			
		10 Oct 1945	17/B 0001	-	18/B 10000	20,000			
		19 Oct 1945	19/B 0001	-	20/B 10000	20,000			
		2 Aug 1946	1/C 0001	-	2/C 10000	20,000			
		19 Aug 1946	3/C 0001	-	4/C 10000	20,000			
		5 Sep 1946	5/C 0001	-	6/C 10000	20,000			
		24 Sep 1946	7/C 0001	-	8/C 10000	20,000			
		8 Oct 1946	9/C 0001	-	10/C 10000	20,000			
		22 Oct 1946	11/C 0001	-	12/C 10000	20,000			
		5 Nov 1946	13/C 0001	-	14/C 10000	20,000			
		18 Nov 1946	15/C 0001	-	16/C 10000	20,000			
		6 Dec 1946	17/C 0001	-	18/C 10000	20,000			
		23 Dec 1946	19/C 0001	-	20/C 10000	20,000			
		9 Jun 1947	1/D 0001	-	2/D 10000	20,000			
		21 Jun 1947	3/D 0001	-	4/D 10000	20,000			
		2 Jul 1947	5/D 0001	-	6/D 10000	20,000			
		29 Jul 1947	7/D 0001	-	8/D 10000	20,000			
		5 Aug 1947	9/D 0001	-	10/D 10000	20,000			
		28 Aug 1947	11/D 0001	-	12/D 10000	20,000			
		8 Sep 1947	13/D 0001	-	14/D 10000	20,000			
		16 Sep 1947	15/D 0001	-	16/D 10000	20,000			
		9 Oct 1947	17/D 0001	-	18/D 10000	20,000			
		20 Oct 1947	19/D 0001	-	20/D 10000	20,000			
		7 Nov 1947	1/E 0001	-	2/E 10000	20,000			
		24 Nov 1947	3/E 0001	-	4/E 10000	20,000			
		5 Dec 1947	5/E 0001	-	6/E 10000	20,000			
		30 Dec 1947	7/E 0001	-	8/E 10000	20,000			
		10 Jan 1948	9/E 0001	-	10/E 10000	20,000	35	80	180

BA 103b Yellow-Ochre reverse

A further minor change took place in 1948 when the value panels were changed from brown to black.

BA 103c	£5	**Black value panels** yellow-ochre reverse				F	VF	EF
		16 Nov 1948	11/E 0001	-	12/E 10000	20,000		
		22 Dec 1948	13/E 0001	-	14/E 10000	20,000		
		12 Jan 1949	15/E 0001	-	16/E 10000	20,000		
		2 Feb 1949	17/E 0001	-	18/E 10000	20,000		
		4 Mar 1949	19/E 0001	-	20/E 10000	20,000		
		10 Mar 1949	1/F 0001	-	2/F 10000	20,000		
		2 Apr 1949	3/F 0001	-	4/F 10000	20,000		
		16 Apr 1949	5/F 0001	-	6/F 10000	20,000		
		12 May 1949	7/F 0001	-	8/F 10000	20,000		
		24 May 1949	9/F 0001	-	10/F 10000	20,000		
		10 Jun 1949	11/F 0001	-	12/F 10000	20,000		
		22 Jun 1949	13/F 0001	-	14/F 10000	20,000		
		6 Jul 1949	15/F 0001	-	16/F 10000	20,000		
		20 Jul 1949	17/F 0001	-	18/F 10000	20,000		
		24 Aug 1949	19/F 0001	-	20/F 10000	20,000		
		14 Sep 1949	1/G 0001	-	2/G 10000	20,000		
		17 Oct 1949	3/G 0001	-	4/G 10000	20,000		
		19 Nov 1949	5/G 0001	-	6/G 10000	20,000		
		1 Dec 1949	7/G 0001	-	8/G 10000	20,000		
		4 Jan 1950	9/G 0001	-	10/G 10000	20,000		
		6 Mar 1950	11/G 0001	-	12/G 10000	20,000		
		20 Mar 1950	13/G 0001	-	14/G 10000	20,000		
		4 Apr 1950	15/G 0001	-	16/G 10000	20,000		
		26 Apr 1950	17/G 0001	-	18/G 10000	20,000		
		5 May 1950	19/G 0001	-	20/G 10000	20,000		
		14 Jun 1950	1/H 0001	-	2/H 10000	20,000		
		18 Jul 1950	3/H 0001	-	4/H 10000	20,000	**30**	**70**	**145**

BA 103c | Cont | | | | F | VF | EF
10 Aug 1950	5/H 0001	-	6/H 10000	20,000			
6 Sep 1950	7/H 0001	-	8/H 10000	20,000			
16 Oct 1950	9/H 0001	-	10/H 10000	20,000			
3 Nov 1950	11/H 0001	-	12/H 10000	20,000			
17 Nov 1950	13/H 0001	-	14/H 10000	20,000			
8 Dec 1950	15/H 0001	-	16/H 10000	20,000			
19 Dec 1950	17/H 0001	-	18/H 10000	20,000			
18 Jan 1951	19/H 0001	-	20/H 10000	20,000			
7 Feb 1951	1/I 0001	-	2/I 10000	20,000			
22 Feb 1951	3/I 0001	-	4/I 10000	20,000			
8 Mar 1951	5/I 0001	-	6/I 10000	20,000			
22 Mar 1951	7/I 0001	-	8/I 10000	20,000			
9 Apr 1951	9/I 0001	-	10/I 10000	20,000			
18 Apr 1951	11/I 0001	-	12/I 10000	20,000			
1 May 1951	13/I 0001	-	14/I 10000	20,000			
11 May 1951	15/I 0001	-	16/I 10000	20,000			
7 Jun 1951	17/I 0001	-	18/I 10000	20,000			
27 Jun 1951	19/I 0001	-	20/I 10000	20,000			
3 Jul 1951	1/J 0001	-	2/J 10000	20,000			
13 Jul 1951	3/J 0001	-	4/J 10000	20,000			
11 Aug 1951	5/J 0001	-	6/J 10000	20,000			
27 Aug 1951	7/J 0001	-	8/J 10000	20,000			
12 Sep 1951	9/J 0001	-	10/J 10000	20,000			
25 Sep 1951	11/J 0001	-	12/J 10000	20,000			
2 Oct 1951	13/J 0001	-	14/J 10000	20,000			
26 Oct 1951	15/J 0001	-	16/J 10000	20,000			
12 Nov 1951	17/J 0001	-	18/J 10000	20,000			
28 Nov 1951	19/J 0001	-	20/J 10000	20,000			
3 Dec 1951	1/K 0001	-	2/K 10000	20,000			
14 Dec 1951	3/K 0001	-	4/K 10000	20,000			
27 Dec 1951	5/K 0001	-	6/K 10000	20,000			
11 Jan 1952	7/K 0001	-	8/K 10000	20,000			
25 Jan 1952	9/K 0001	-	10/K 10000	20,000			
6 Feb 1952	11/K 0001	-	12/K 10000	20,000			
25 Feb 1952	13/K 0001	-	14/K 10000	20,000			
7 Mar 1952	15/K 0001	-	16/K 10000	20,000			
24 Mar 1952	17/K 0001	-	18/K 10000	20,000			
8 Apr 1952	19/K 0001	-	20/K 10000	20,000			
23 Apr 1952	1/L 0001	-	2/L 10000	20,000			
7 May 1952	3/L 0001	-	4/L 10000	20,000			
27 May 1952	5/L 0001	-	6/L 10000	20,000			
12 Jun 1952	7/L 0001	-	8/L 10000	20,000			
30 Jun 1952	9/L 0001	-	10/L 10000	20,000			
17 Jul 1952	11/L 0001	-	12/L 10000	20,000			
24 Jul 1952	13/L 0001	-	14/L 10000	20,000			
8 Aug 1952	15/L 0001	-	16/L 10000	20,000			
22 Aug 1952	17/L 0001	-	18/L 10000	20,000			
10 Sep 1952	19/L 0001	-	20/L 10000	20,000			
26 Sep 1952	1/M 0001	-	2/M 10000	20,000			
14 Oct 1952	3/M 0001	-	4/M 10000	20,000			
31 Oct 1952	5/M 0001	-	6/M 10000	20,000			
6 Nov 1952	7/M 0001	-	8/M 10000	20,000			
21 Nov 1952	9/M 0001	-	10/M 10000	20,000	30	70	145

BA 103c 1949

BA 103d	£5	**Lord Elphinstone** Governor		**William Watson** Treasurer		F	VF	EF
		10 Dec 1952	11/M 0001	-	12/M 10000	20,000		
		8 Jan 1953	13/M 0001	-	14/M 10000	20,000		
		20 Jan 1953	15/M 0001	-	16/M 10000	20,000		
		10 Feb 1953	17/M 0001	-	18/M 10000	20,000		
		26 Feb 1953	19/M 0001	-	20/M 10000	20,000		
		5 Mar 1953	1/N 0001	-	2/N 10000	20,000		
		12 Mar 1953	3/N 0001	-	4/N 10000	20,000		
		10 Apr 1953	5/N 0001	-	6/N 10000	20,000		
		22 Apr 1953	7/N 0001	-	8/N 10000	20,000		
		6 May 1953	9/N 0001	-	10/N 10000	20,000		
		14 May 1953	11/N 0001	-	12/N 10000	20,000		
		1 Jun 1953	13/N 0001	-	14/N 10000	20,000		
		26 Jun 1953	15/N 0001	-	16/N 10000	20,000		
		7 Jul 1953	17/N 0001	-	18/N 10000	20,000		
		22 Jul 1953	19/N 0001	-	20/N 10000	20,000		
		13 Aug 1953	1/O 0001	-	2/O 10000	20,000		
		31 Aug 1953	3/O 0001	-	4/O 10000	20,000		
		2 Sep 1953	5/O 0001	-	6/O 10000	20,000		
		18 Sep 1953	7/O 0001	-	8/O 10000	20,000		
		1 Oct 1953	9/O 0001	-	10/O 10000	20,000		
		13 Oct 1953	11/O 0001	-	12/O 10000	20,000		
		2 Nov 1953	13/O 0001	-	14/O 10000	20,000		
		11 Nov 1953	15/O 0001	-	16/O 10000	20,000		
		2 Dec 1953	17/O 0001	-	18/O 10000	20,000		
		4 Dec 1953	19/O 0001	-	20/O 10000	20,000	30	70	145

BA 103d 1953

In 1955 the design was revised to reflect the absorption of the Union Bank of Scotland. Waterstons were retained as printers given the higher cost of the notes produced by Waterlows for the Union Bank. The first printings of the £5 note saw three changes: the medallion was amended to blue-grey, a light blue underlay was added to elements of the obverse and the watermark registration number was dropped. The reverse is unchanged.

BA 104a	**£5**	**Blue medallion** yellow-ochre reverse				**F**	**VF**	**EF**
		Lord Elphinstone Governor **William Watson** Treasurer						
		1 Mar 1955	1/A 0001	-	20/A 10000	200,000		
		2 Mar 1955	1/B 0001	-	20/B 10000	200,000		
		3 Mar 1955	1/C 0001	-	6/C 10000	60,000	35	80	160

BA 104a First Date

Proof Blue underlay in left panel 1 Mar 1955 0/A 00000			**From 250 UNC**
Specimen 1 Mar 1955 0/A 00000		30	**From 200 UNC**

As with the £1 note, the slightly thinner Portals paper was replaced with paper produced by Cowans of Penicuik, but not until the 6th April 1955 printing when the new Governor's signature was introduced.

BA 104b	£5	John Craig Governor William Watson Treasurer				F	VF	EF
		6 Apr 1955	7/C 0001 - 20/C 10000	140,000				
		7 Apr 1955	1/D 0001 - 20/D 10000	200,000				
		1 Sep 1955	1/E 0001 - 20/E 10000	200,000				
		2 Sep 1955	1/F 0001 - 20/F 10000	200,000				
		3 Sep 1955	1/G 0001 - 10/G 10000	100,000		35	80	160

BA 104b 1955

Specimen undated no prefix/serials SPECIMEN stamp   **From 150 UNC**

In August 1955 the Bank decided to have the reverse design amended to reflect the acquisition of the Union Bank. The new design featured two vignettes with circular frames, one with the Bank Arms and the second with the Union Bank's ship motif.

BA 105a	£5	John Craig Governor William Watson Treasurer						
		Ship & Arms reverse						
		9 Apr 1956	11/G 0001 - 20/G 10000	200,000				
		10 Apr 1956	1/H 0001 - 20/H 10000	200,000				
		11 Apr 1956	1/I 0001 - 20/I 10000	200,000				
		12 Apr 1956	1/J 0001 - 20/J 10000	200,000				
		13 Apr 1956	1/K 0001 - 20/K 10000	200,000				
		17 Apr 1956	1/L 0001 - 20/L 10000	200,000		35	70	150

BA 105a 1955

BA 105 Reverse

Specimen 9 Apr 1956 11/G 0000   30   **From 150 UNC**

BA 105b	£5	**Lord Bilsland** Governor		**William Watson** Treasurer		F	VF	EF
		1 May 1957	1/M 0001 -	20/M 10000	200,000			
		2 May 1957	1/N 0001 -	20/N 10000	200,000			
		3 May 1957	1/O 0001 -	20/O 10000	200,000			
		7 May 1957	1/P 0001 -	20/P 10000	200,000			
		8 May 1957	1/Q 0001 -	20/Q 10000	200,000			
		9 May 1957	1/R 0001 -	20/R 10000	200,000			
		10 Jun 1958	1/S 0001 -	20/S 10000	200,000			
		11 Jun 1958	1/T 0001 -	20/T 10000	200,000			
		12 Jun 1958	1/U 0001 -	20/U 10000	200,000			
		13 Jun 1958	1/V 0001 -	20/V 10000	200,000			
		16 Jun 1958	1/W 0001 -	20/W 10000	200,000			
		17 Jun 1958	1/X 0001 -	20/X 10000	200,000			
		29 Sep 1959	1/Y 0001 -	20/Y 10000	200,000			
		30 Sep 1959	1/Z 0001 -	20/Z 10000	200,000			
		Double Letter prefix						
		1 Oct 1959	1/AA 0001 -	20/AA 10000	200,000			
		2 Oct 1959	1/BA 0001 -	20/BA 10000	200,000			
		5 Oct 1959	1/CA 0001 -	20/CA 10000	200,000			
		6 Oct 1959	1/DA 0001 -	20/DA 10000	200,000			
		16 May 1960	1/EA 0001 -	20/EA 10000	200,000			
		17 May 1960	1/FA 0001 -	20/FA 10000	200,000			
		18 May 1960	1/GA 0001 -	20/GA 10000	200,000			
		19 May 1960	1/HA 0001 -	20/HA 10000	200,000			
		20 May 1960	1/IA 0001 -	20/IA 10000	200,000			
		23 May 1960	1/JA 0001 -	20/JA 10000	199,995			
		24 May 1960	1/KA 0001 -	20/KA 10000	200,000	15	35	75

BA 105b 1958

In 1960 five specimen notes dated 23rd May 1960 were prepared for use by the Bank's board, having been taken from the stock of notes ready for issue.

Specimen	23 May 1960	14/JA 4201 - 4205		5	**From 200 UNC**
	undated	no prefix/serials	SPECIMEN stamp		**From 150 UNC**

In 1961 the decision was taken to reduce the size of the £5 note to conform to the smaller Bank of England note. The design was unchanged including the hollow £5 denomination symbols.

BA 106a   **£5**   **Reduced size** 140 x 85mm   **Hollow £5 denomination symbols**   VF   EF   UNC
Lord Bilsland Governor   **William Watson** Treasurer

Date	From		To	Quantity	VF	EF	UNC
14 Sep 1961	1/A 0001	-	20/A 10000	200,000			
15 Sep 1961	1/B 0001	-	20/B 10000	200,000			
18 Sep 1961	1/C 0001	-	20/C 10000	200,000			
19 Sep 1961	1/D 0001	-	20/D 10000	200,000			
20 Sep 1961	1/E 0001	-	20/E 10000	200,000			
21 Sep 1961	1/F 0001	-	20/F 10000	200,000			
22 Sep 1961	1/G 0001	-	20/G 10000	200,000	**25**	**40**	**85**

BA 106a 1961

BA 106a-e Reverse

Specimen   14 Sep 1961 1/A 0000 20/KA 6597   40
                30 Sep 1961 20/WA 6597 20/WA 10000   **From 200 UNC**

BA 106a Specimen 30 Sep 1961

Solid £5 denomination symbols were introduced as a measure to improve differentiation from other denominations in the series.

BA 106b	£5	Solid £5 denomination symbols				VF	EF	UNC
		25 Sep 1961	1/H 0001	- 20/H 10000	200,000			
		7 Aug 1962	1/I 0001	- 20/I 10000	200,000			
		8 Aug 1962	1/J 0001	- 20/J 10000	200,000			
		9 Aug 1962	1/K 0001	- 20/K 10000	200,000			
		10 Aug 1962	1/L 0001	- 20/L 10000	200,000			
		13 Aug 1962	1/M 0001	- 20/M 10000	200,000			
		14 Aug 1962	1/N 0001	- 15/N 10000	150,000	**15**	**35**	**75**

BA 106b 1962

Specimen 25 Sep 1961 1/H 0000   40   **From 150 UNC**

Issued notes continued unchanged but a new prefix/serials system was introduced in 1963 due to ever rising issue volumes.

BA 106c	£5	Prefix / Six Digit Serials now run to 1 million				VF	EF	UNC
		7 Oct 1963 A 000001	-	1000000	1,000,000			
		8 Oct 1963 B 000001	-	1000000	1,000,000			
		11 Jan 1965 C 000001	-	1000000	1,000,000			
		12 Jan 1965 D 000001	-	600000	600,000	15	35	75

BA 106c First prefix 1963

BA 106d	£5	Lord Polwarth Governor William Watson Treasurer						
		7 Mar 1966 E 000001	-	1000000	1,000,000			
		8 Mar 1966 F 000001	-	600000	600,000	15	40	80

BA 106d 1966

					VF	EF	UNC
BA 106e	£5	**Lord Polwarth** Governor **James Letham** Treasurer & General Manager					
		1 Feb 1967 G 000001 - 1000000	1,000,000				
		2 Feb 1967 H 000001 - 600000	600,000		15	40	80

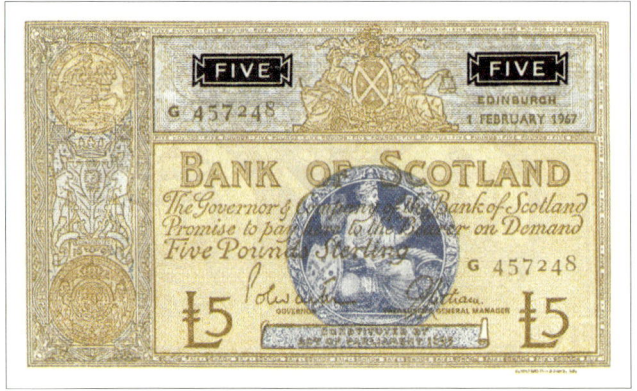

BA 106e First prefix 1967

Specimen 1 Feb 1967 G 000000   From 150 UNC

Magnetic sorting codes were added to the final issue of this £5 note.

					VF	EF	UNC
BA 106f	£5	**Magnetic Encoding on reverse Lord Polwarth** Governor **James Letham** Treasurer & General Manager					
		1 Nov 1967 I 000001 - 762000	762,000		15	55	100

BA 106f 1967

Blue Essays

Despite the introduction of solid £5 symbols it appears that the public continued to confuse £1 and £5 notes, so renewed experimentation with the colours of the £5 note was undertaken. In January 1963 it was agreed to prepare essays in blue, to reflect the chosen colour of Bank of England £5 notes. Notes in various shades of blue have been observed.

BA 107a £5 **Blue Deep Blue borders**

Essay 14 Aug 1962 10/N 1234 SPECIMEN stamp   From 300 UNC

BA 107a Essay Blue Deep Blue borders

BA 107b £5 **Pale Blue White borders**

Essay 14 Aug 1962 10/N 1234 SPECIMEN stamp   From 300 UNC

BA 107b Essay Pale Blue White borders

BA 107c   **£5**   **Blue White borders**

         Essay 14 Aug 1962 10/N 1234 SPECIMEN stamp   **From 300 UNC**

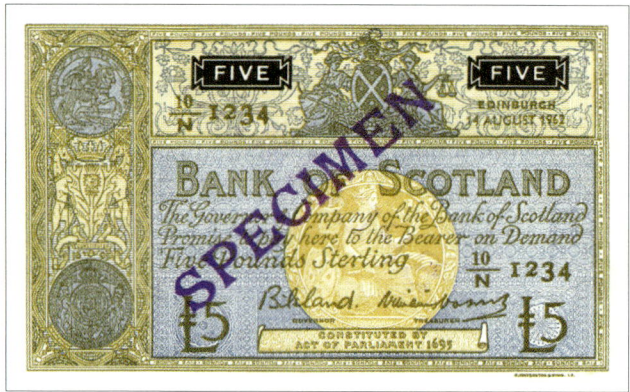

BA 107c Essay Blue White borders

There was only one minor change to the design of the £10 notes during this series, when the colour of the central medallion was changed to blue in 1963. Relatively few were issued due to the continuing unpopularity of this denomination.

						F	VF	EF
BA 108a	**£10**	**Thistle motif Lord Elphinstone** Governor uniface						
		Alexander William Morton Beveridge Treasurer						
		24 Jan 1935	2/C 0001	-	10000	10,000		
		28 Jun 1938	3/C 0001	-	10000	10,000	**300**	**650** **1200**

BA 108a 1938

BA 108b	£10	Lord Elphinstone Governor John B Crawford Treasurer				F	VF	EF
		16 Jul 1942	4/C 0001 - 10000		10,000			
		15 Oct 1942	5/C 0001 - 10000		10,000	**300**	**650**	**1200**

BA 108b First date

A small number of specimens with the October 1942 date were prepared for the board in 1962 when consideration was being given to preparing new designs.

Specimen 15 Oct 1942 5/C   5   **From 500 UNC**

Consideration of new designs in 1962 came to nothing but a short print run of 10,000 £10 notes was issued the following year. The notes now have machine-cut edges while the design was modified in two ways: the medallion was printed in blue-grey and the watermark registration number was dropped. The watermark indicates that the paper used for these notes dates from between 1939 and 1945.

BA 108c	£10	**Blue medallion Lord Bilsland** Governor **William Watson** Treasurer						
		26 Sep 1963	6/C 0001 - 5000		5,000			
		27 Sep 1963	7/C 0001 - 5000		5,000	**140**	**320**	**650**

BA 108c First date

Specimen undated no prefix/serials (on 1943 paper)   **From 350 UNC**

£20 notes were issued unchanged apart from the adoption of the thistle motif. There was only one minor change to the design of the £20 notes during this series, when the central medallion was changed to blue in 1955.

BA 109a	£20	**Thistle motif Lord Elphinstone** Governor uniface **Alexander William Morton Beveridge** Treasurer				F	VF	EF
		11 Jan 1935	2/G 0001	-	5000	5,000		
		16 Feb 1935	3/G 0001	-	5000	5,000		
		28 Mar 1936	4/G 0001	-	5000	5,000		
		5 Aug 1936	5/G 0001	-	5000	5,000		
		15 Apr 1938	6/G 0001	-	5000	5,000		
		22 Jul 1938	7/G 0001	-	5000	5,000	400	750	-

BA 109a First date 1935

BA 109b	**£20**	**Lord Elphinstone** Governor **James Waddell Macfarlane** Treasurer			**F**	**VF**	**EF**
		16 May 1939 8/G 0001 - 5000		5,000			
		12 Sep 1939 9/G 0001 - 5000		5,000	**450**	**850**	-

BA 109b Last date 1939

BA 109c	£20	Lord Elphinstone Governor			John B Crawford Treasurer		F	VF	EF
		5 Jun 1942	10/G 0001	-	5000	5,000			
		17 Aug 1942	1/H 0001	-	5000	5,000			
		12 Oct 1942	2/H 0001	-	5000	5,000			
		9 Nov 1942	3/H 0001	-	5000	5,000			
		4 Jan 1944	4/H 0001	-	5000	5,000			
		2 Feb 1944	5/H 0001	-	5000	5,000			
		16 Mar 1944	6/H 0001	-	5000	5,000			
		10 Apr 1944	7/H 0001	-	5000	5,000			
		9 May 1944	8/H 0001	-	5000	5,000			
		17 Nov 1947	9/H 0001	-	5000	5,000			
		4 Dec 1947	10/H 0001	-	5000	5,000			
		21 Jul 1949	1/I 0001	-	5000	5,000			
		9 Aug 1949	2/I 0001	-	5000	5,000			
		14 Sep 1949	3/I 0001	-	5000	5,000			
		19 Oct 1949	4/I 0001	-	5000	5,000			
		10 Nov 1949	5/I 0001	-	5000	5,000			
		16 Nov 1950	6/I 0001	-	5000	5,000			
		8 Dec 1950	7/I 0001	-	5000	5,000			
		26 Jan 1951	8/I 0001	-	5000	5,000			
		6 Feb 1951	9/I 0001	-	5000	5,000			
		2 Mar 1951	10/I 0001	-	5000	5,000			
		9 Apr 1952	1/J 0001	-	5000	5,000			
		8 May 1952	2/J 0001	-	5000	5,000			
		12 Jun 1952	3/J 0001	-	5000	5,000			
		8 Jul 1952	4/J 0001	-	5000	5,000			
		11 Aug 1952	5/J 0001	-	5000	5,000	**150**	**300**	**500**

BA 109c 1944

BA 109d	£20	**Lord Elphinstone** Governor **William Watson** Treasurer				F	VF	EF
		5 Dec 1952	6/J 0001	- 5000	5,000			
		8 Jan 1953	7/J 0001	- 5000	5,000			
		5 Feb 1953	8/J 0001	- 5000	5,000			
		18 Mar 1953	9/J 0001	- 5000	5,000			
		24 Apr 1953	10/J 0001	- 5000	5,000	**180**	**350**	**600**

BA 109d First date 1952

In 1955 the design was modified in two ways: the medallion was printed in blue-grey and the watermark registration number was dropped. Prefix letters started afresh from prefix A.

BA 109e	£20	**Blue medallion John Craig** Governor **William Watson** Treasurer				F	VF	EF
		6 Apr 1955	1/A 0001	- 5/A 5000	25,000			
		11 Jun 1956	6/A 0001	- 10/A 5000	25,000			
		12 Jun 1956	1/B 0001	- 5/B 5000	25,000	**60**	**120**	**240**

BA 109e First date/prefix

BA 109f **£20** **Lord Bilsland** Governor **William Watson** Treasurer   F   VF   EF

	21 Mar 1958	6/B 0001	-	10/B 5000	25,000		
	25 Mar 1958	1/C 0001	-	5/C 5000	25,000		
	26 Mar 1958	6/C 0001	-	10/C 5000	25,000		
	27 Mar 1958	1/D 0001	-	5/D 5000	25,000		
	12 Sep 1960	6/D 0001	-	10/D 5000	25,000		
	13 Sep 1960	1/E 0001	-	10/E 5000	50,000		
	14 Sep 1960	1/F 0001	-	5/F 5000	25,000	**50**	**110**	**220**

       Specimen 14 Sep 1960 3/F   20   **From 250 EF**

A change in the production process in 1963 resulted in the notes having guillotined edges on all four sides.

BA 109g **£20** **Guillotined Edges**

	1 Oct 1963	6/F 0001	-	10/F 5000	25,000		
	2 Oct 1963	1/G 0001	-	10/G 5000	50,000		
	3 Oct 1963	1/H 0001	-	4/H 5000	20,000	**50**	**110**	**220**

Bank of Scotland

BA 109g Guillotined edges 1963

In 1969, due to a shortage of supplies, the Bank felt it necessary to have another 25,000 notes printed. This emergency issue used the thistle watermarked paper prepared for the new £5 notes. The paper also contained a metal strip with 'B O S' in Morse code. The design was otherwise unchanged though the dimensions were very slightly smaller at 210 x 130mm.

				F	VF	EF
BA 109h	**£20**	**Lord Polwarth** Governor				
		James Letham Treasurer & General Manager				
		5 May 1969 5/H 0001 - 9/H 5000	25,000	60	180	380

BA 109h 1969

£100 notes were issued unchanged apart from the adoption of the thistle motif. There was only one minor change to the design of the £100 notes during this series, when the central medallion was changed to blue in 1956.

BA 110a £100 Thistle motif **Lord Elphinstone** Governor uniface
Alexander William Morton Beveridge Treasurer

8 Jan 1935	1/J 0001	-	1000	1,000
31 Jan 1935	2/J 0001	-	1000	1,000
23 Mar 1937	3/J 0001	-	1000	1,000
12 Aug 1937	4/J 0001	-	1000	1,000	**RARE**

BA 110b £100 **Lord Elphinstone** Governor
James Waddell Macfarlane Treasurer

2 Apr 1940	5/J 0001	-	1000	1,000
15 Jul 1940	6/J 0001	-	1000	1,000	**RARE**

BA 110c £100 **Lord Elphinstone** Governor **John B Crawford** Treasurer   F   VF   EF

10 Jun 1942	7/J 0001	-	1000	1,000			
15 Sep 1942	8/J 0001	-	1000	1,000			
10 Aug 1946	9/J 0001	-	1000	1,000			
4 Sep 1946	10/J 0001	-	1000	1,000			
16 Oct 1946	1/K 0001	-	1000	1,000			
12 Nov 1946	2/K 0001	-	1000	1,000			
4 Dec 1946	3/K 0001	-	1000	1,000			
4 Jul 1951	4/K 0001	-	1000	1,000			
15 Aug 1951	5/K 0001	-	1000	1,000			
18 Sep 1951	6/K 0001	-	1000	1,000			
4 Oct 1951	7/K 0001	-	1000	1,000			
15 Nov 1951	8/K 0001	-	1000	1,000			
14 Dec 1951	9/K 0001	-	1000	1,000	800	1600	-

BA 110c 1951

Specimen undated no prefix/serials   20   **From 750 EF**

In 1956 the design was modified in two ways: the medallion was printed in blue-grey and the watermark registration number was dropped.

BA 110d	£100	**Blue medallion John Craig** Governor **William Watson** Treasurer					F	VF	EF
		14 Sep 1956	10/K 0001	-	1000	1,000			
		17 Oct 1956	1/L 0001	-	1000	1,000			
		6 Nov 1956	2/L 0001	-	1000	1,000			
		3 Dec 1956	3/L 0001	-	1000	1,000	450	900	1750

BA 110d 1956

SCOTTISH UNC

A reminder to collectors that early Scottish 'Square' £1 notes and higher value 'Horse Blankets' will often be found with folds even if otherwise unused. The reason for this is the engrained habit of Scottish bank tellers of folding their notes at least once to fit them into their tills. Horse Blankets will often be found with two vertical folds, one third in on each side, while Squares will usually have a single vertical fold. As a result the top grade for a Scottish note is sometimes referred to as 'Scottish UNC', in reality this being between EF and AUNC depending on how heavy the folds are. Do not be put off buying this grade in the hope that a better one will come along as it is unlikely truly uncirculated notes exist.

The final print run of the £100 notes is remarkable for including large runs of consecutive dates. The Bank's records confirm that they were all taken to cash and issued. The records also suggest a further run starting with prefix 9/N was printed but destroyed unissued.

							F	VF	EF
BA 110e	**£100**	**Lord Bilsland** Governor		**William Watson** Treasurer					
		24 Mar 1959	4/L 0001	-	1000	1,000			
		25 Mar 1959	5/L 0001	-	1000	1,000			
		26 Mar 1959	6/L 0001	-	1000	1,000			
		27 Mar 1959	7/L 0001	-	1000	1,000			
		31 Mar 1959	8/L 0001	-	1000	1,000			
		1 Apr 1959	9/L 0001	-	1000	1,000			
		2 Apr 1959	10/L 0001	-	1000	1,000			
		3 Apr 1959	1/M 0001	-	1000	1,000			
		6 Apr 1959	2/M 0001	-	1000	1,000			
		7 Apr 1959	3/M 0001	-	1000	1,000			
		12 Nov 1962	4/M 0001	-	1000	1,000			
		13 Nov 1962	5/M 0001	-	1000	1,000			
		14 Nov 1962	6/M 0001	-	1000	1,000			
		15 Nov 1962	7/M 0001	-	1000	1,000			
		16 Nov 1962	8/M 0001	-	1000	1,000			
		19 Nov 1962	9/M 0001	-	1000	1,000			
		20 Nov 1962	10/M 0001	-	1000	1,000			
		21 Nov 1962	1/N 0001	-	1000	1,000			
		22 Nov 1962	2/N 0001	-	1000	1,000			
		23 Nov 1962	3/N 0001	-	1000	1,000			
		26 Nov 1962	4/N 0001	-	1000	1,000			
		27 Nov 1962	5/N 0001	-	1000	1,000			
		28 Nov 1962	6/N 0001	-	1000	1,000			
		29 Nov 1962	7/N 0001	-	1000	1,000			
		30 Nov 1962	8/N 0001	-	1000	1,000	400	800	1500

BA 110e 1962

Specimen 7 Apr 1959 3/M 0000   20   **From 1000 EF**

FINAL WATERSTON ISSUE – 1968 *to* 1969

'Modern' Multi-Coloured design

By the 1960s the William S Black designs of the 1880s had been in use, albeit with many modifications, for over 80 years and the threat of forgeries was becoming more of a problem. This was also a concern to the Bank of England so despite reassurances in 1966 from Waterstons and the plate engravers City Engraving Co. (Hull) Ltd the Bank decided it was time to prepare new designs. Waterstons had submitted a £1 essay as early as 1964 (denominated as 'One Royal Sterling') but new designs were not finally approved until June 1968. The new £1 notes were issued in late 1968 and the £5 notes in spring 1969. The plates were prepared in Holland by Joh. Enschede of Haarlem and printed by Waterstons in their Edinburgh factory. The printers' imprint was restricted to **WATERSTON** on the reverse of the notes.

The design featured the Bank's Arms within a geometric pattern and value panels upper right and lower left. Magnetic sorting marks, in the same pattern as the earlier issues, appear on the back. Paper with the thistle watermark continued to be supplied by Portals with a metallic strip reading 'B O S' in Morse code. This was the same paper and metallic strip used on the final issue of the £20 note. Essays of new £20 and £100 notes were also prepared in 1969 but not introduced as discussions for a merger with the British Linen Bank had by now started. Essays of all four denominations survive in the Bank's archives.

This series had a very short life because of the merger with the British Linen Bank. It was also the last series of banknotes printed by Waterston as the company felt unable to maintain the quality of printing with the huge increase in the quantity of notes required for the merged banks' new notes. Before Thomas De La Rue were appointed in their place they did manage to prepare essays of new £1 and £5 notes featuring the portrait of Sir Walter Scott which had been the distinguishing feature of the British Linen Bank's notes. These too are in the Bank's archives. All specimens with 000000 serials unless otherwise stated.

£100 Essay by Waterston 1969

£20 Essay by Waterston 1969

£20 Essay reverse showing workings

Waterston £1 Essay 1964

Waterston £1 Essay reverse

			VF	EF	UNC
BA 111a	£1	**Brown Blue centre Lord Polwarth** Governor **James Letham** Treasurer & General Manager **Small Date & EDINBURGH** 135 x 67mm reverse brown 17 Jul 1968 A/1 0000001 - A/6 1000000 6,000,000	8	22	60

BA 111a First prefix 1968

BA 111 Reverse

Specimen 17 Jul 1968 A/1   25   **From 200 UNC**

BA 111b	£1	Similar to BA 111a Large Date & EDINBURGH			VF	EF	UNC
		18 Aug 1969	A/7 0000001 - A/9 1000000	3,000,000			
			B/1 0000001 - B/4 0300000	3,300,000	8	22	60

BA 111b 1969

BA 112a	£5	Green Blue centre **Lord Polwarth** Governor					
		James Letham Treasurer & General Manager					
		Small Date & EDINBURGH 145 x 78mm reverse green					
		1 Nov 1968	A 0000001 - B 0600000	1,600,000	35	110	190

BA 112a 1968

BA 112 Reverse

Specimen 1 Nov 1968 A   25   **From 230 UNC**

					VF	EF	UNC
BA 112b	£5	Similar to BA 112a Large Date & EDINBURGH			35	110	190
		8 Dec 1969 C 0000001 - D 0640000 1,640,000					

BA 112b 1969

SIR WALTER SCOTT ISSUE – 1970 *to* 1994

Following the merger with the British Linen Bank it was felt important to design a new series of notes reflecting elements of both constituent banks' previous notes. After Waterstons had decided it no longer had the capability to handle the printing and security requirements of volume banknote production a new printing contract was awarded to the printers of the British Linen's notes, **Thomas De La Rue & Co Limited** (whose imprint does not appear on any notes of this issue). They were given five terms of reference when asked to design the new notes:

1. A portrait of Sir Walter Scott
2. A representation of the Bank's Arms
3. The Shield which forms part of these Arms
4. The Ship emblem of the Union Bank of Scotland
5. The figure of Pallas, the emblem of the British Linen Bank

The resulting designs have become modern classics of the Scottish series and are rightly very popular with collectors not only for the excellence of the designs but also for the number of varieties the series has thrown up. They were first issued on 5th November 1970 and are referred to by the Bank as 'Series D'. A number of stage proofs and essays have survived and occasionally appear on the market.

£1 notes were discontinued in 1988 and the £5, £10 and £20 notes were reduced in size between 1990 and 1992. 1,000,000 notes per prefix unless otherwise stated. Prefix letters I and O no longer used. The predominant colours of the £1, £5, £10 and £20 notes conformed to those adopted by the Bank of England.

Replacements, identified by De La Rue using a prefix combination including the letter Z, are first seen with this series and were produced for all denominations, except, it is believed, the £100 note. The Bank's records included details of most of the replacement serial ranges and these records are reproduced below. Some gaps in these ranges will be observed due to incomplete information. Firm sighting records have filled some gaps but the existence of notes with serials outside the ranges given is to be expected. Regular issue totals will include any replacements. All specimens with 000000 serials unless otherwise stated. A large number of specimens of this series have come on to the market since 2016.

							VF	EF	UNC
BA 113a	**£1**	**Green Encoded Lord Polwarth** Governor **Thomas W Walker** Treasurer & General Manager 135 x 67mm							
		10 Aug 1970	A/1	-	A/9				
			B/1	-	B/5	14,000,000			
		31 Aug 1971	B/6	-	B/20	15,000,000	5	18	40

BA 113a First prefix million serial

BA 113a/b/c/d/e Encoded reverse

Specimen 10 Aug 1970 A/1	100	**From 150 UNC**	
De La Rue Specimen 10 Aug 1970 A/1	n/k	**From 120 UNC**	

BA 113ar	**£1**	**Replacement**							
		10 Aug 1970	Z/1 0000001	-	0163000	163,000			
		31 Aug 1971	Z/1 0163001	-	0463000	300,000	35	65	120

BA 113ar Replacement

						VF	EF	UNC
BA 113b	£1	**Lord Clydesmuir** Governor **Thomas W Walker** Treasurer & General Manager						
		1 Nov 1972	C/1 - C/15		15,000,000			
		30 Aug 1973	C/16 - C/27		12,000,000	4	15	35

BA 113b First date/prefix

						VF	EF	UNC
BA 113br	£1	**Replacement**						
		1 Nov 1972	Z/1 0463001 - 0641000		178,000			
		30 Aug 1973	Z/1 0641001 - 0787000		146,000	30	65	120

						VF	EF	UNC
BA 113c	£1	**Lord Clydesmuir** Governor **Andrew M Russell** Treasurer & General Manager						
		28 Oct 1974	C/28 - C/39		12,000,000			
		26 Nov 1975	C/40 - C/54		15,000,000			
		8 Sep 1976	C/55 - C/69		15,000,000			
		25 Aug 1977	C/70 - C/85		16,000,000			
		3 Oct 1978	C/86 - C/99	D/1	15,000,000	3	10	20

BA 113c First date/prefix

Specimen 26 Nov 1975 C/40 25 Aug 1977 C/70
           3 Oct 1978 C/86   From 130 UNC

						VF	EF	UNC
BA 113cr	£1	**Replacement**						
		28 Oct 1974	Z/1 0787001 - Z/2 0027800		240,800			
		26 Nov 1975	Z/2 0027801 - 0142000		114,200			
		8 Sep 1976	Z/2 0142001 - 0501000		359,000			
		25 Aug 1977	Z/2 0501001 - 0680000		179,000			
		3 Oct 1978	Z/2 0680001 - 0780000		100,000	15	40	85

					VF	EF	UNC
BA 113d	£1	**Lord Clydesmuir** Governor **David Bruce Pattullo** Treasurer & General Manager					
		15 Oct 1979 D/2 - D/16		15,000,000			
		4 Nov 1980 D/17 - D/31		15,000,000	3	8	16

BA 113d Last date/prefix

Specimen 4 Nov 1980 D/17   From 120 UNC

BA 113dr	£1	**Replacement**					
		15 Oct 1979 Z/2 0781001 - 0940000		160,000			
		4 Nov 1980 Z/2 0941001 - Z/3 0091000		150,000	18	45	90

BA 113e	£1	**Sir Thomas Risk** Governor **David Bruce Pattullo** Treasurer & General Manager					
		30 Jul 1981 D/32 - D/42		11,000,000	3	8	15

BA 113e First prefix Error coat of arms green not black

BA 113e Last prefix

Specimen 30 Jul 1981 D/32   From 120 UNC

					VF	EF	UNC
BA 113er	£1	Replacement					
		30 Jul 1981 Z/3 0092001 - 0192000	100,000		**15**	**40**	**80**

BA 113f	£1	Similar to BA 113e No longer encoded					
		7 Oct 1983 D/43 - D/57	15,000,000				
		9 Nov 1984 D/58 - D/71	14,000,000				
		12 Dec 1985 D/72 - D/86	15,000,000				
		18 Nov 1986 D/87 - D/99					
		E/1 to 0650000	13,650,000		**3**	**6**	**12**

BA 113f Last Split Prefix

BA 113f/g Reverse No encoding

Specimen 7 Oct 1983 D/43 9 Nov 1984 D/58
18 Nov 1986 D/87   From 100 UNC

BA 113fr	£1	Replacement					
		7 Oct 1983 Z/3 0193001 - 0243000	50,000				
		9 Nov 1984 Z/3 0244001 - 0284000	40,000				
		12 Dec 1985 Z/3 0311408 - 0365000	n/k				
		18 Nov 1986 Z/3 0366001 - 0501000	135,000		**15**	**30**	**65**

					VF	EF	UNC
BA 113g	£1	**Sir Thomas Risk** Governor **Peter Burt** Treasurer & Chief General Manager 19 Aug 1988 E/1 0650001 - E/13 0650000 12,000,000			2	7	15

BA 113g First Split Prefix

Specimen   19 Aug 1988 E/1   From 100 UNC

					VF	EF	UNC
BA 113gr	£1	**Replacement** 19 Aug 1988 Z/3 0502001 - 0525000 * 50,000			20	50	100

BA 113gr Replacement final run

* highest number observed is Z/3 0524852

£5 notes were first issued in January 1971.

						VF	EF	UNC
BA 114a	£5	Blue Encoded **Lord Polwarth** Governor 146 x 78mm						
		Thomas W Walker Treasurer & General Manager						
		10 Aug 1970	A - E		5,000,000			
		2 Sep 1971	F - K		5,000,000	**15**	**70**	**140**

BA 114a First date/prefix

	Specimen 10 Aug 1970 A	100	**From 160 UNC**
	De La Rue Specimen 10 Aug 1970 A	n/k	**From 120 UNC**

BA 114ar	£5	Replacement						
		10 Aug 1970	ZA 000001	-	071023	180,000		
		2 Sep 1971	ZA 137638	-	180000	for both dates	**120**	**250**	-

BA 114ar Replacement

BA 114b	£5	Lord Clydesmuir Governor Thomas W Walker Treasurer & General Manager			VF	EF	UNC
		4 Dec 1972 L - Q		5,000,000			
		5 Sep 1973 R - X		7,000,000	15	60	130

De La Rue Specimen 5 Sep 1973 R From 140 UNC

BA 114b

BA 114br	£5	Replacement					
		4 Dec 1972 ZA 180001 - 321000	141,000				
		5 Sep 1973 ZA 339880 - 505000	n/k		100	220	-

BA 114c	£5	Lord Clydesmuir Governor Andrew M Russell Treasurer & General Manager					
		4 Nov 1974 Y - Z					
		Double Letter prefix					
		AA - AF	8,000,000				
		1 Dec 1975 AG - AP	8,000,000				
		21 Nov 1977 AQ - AU	5,000,000				
		19 Oct 1978 AV - BA	6,000,000		12	30	65

Specimen 1 Dec 1975 AG From 140 UNC

BA 114c Z last single letter prefix

BA 114cr	£5	Replacement					VF	EF	UNC
		4 Nov 1974	ZA 505001	-	678000	173,000			
		1 Dec 1975	ZA 678001	-	818000	140,000			
		21 Nov 1977	ZA 824001	-	920000	96,000			
		19 Oct 1978	ZA 920001	-	970000	50,000	55	110	220

BA 114cr Replacement

BA 114d	£5	**Lord Clydesmuir** Governor						
		David Bruce Pattullo Treasurer & General Manager						
		28 Sep 1979	BB	-	BJ	8,000,000			
		28 Nov 1980	BK	-	BS	8,000,000	12	30	65

Specimen 28 Nov 1980 BK   From 130 UNC

De La Rue Specimen 28 Nov 1980 BK   From 100 UNC

BA 114d

BA 114dr	£5	Replacement					VF	EF	UNC
		28 Sep 1979 ZA 971001	-	ZB 071000	100,000				
		28 Nov 1980 ZB 072001	-	167000	95,000		60	120	240

BA 114dr Replacement

BA 114e	£5	**Sir Thomas Risk** Governor							
		David Bruce Pattullo Treasurer & General Manager							
		27 Jul 1981 BT	-	CC	10,000,000				
		25 Jun 1982 CD	-	CK	7,000,000		10	30	55

Specimen 27 Jul 1981 BT 25 Jun 1982 CD   From 130 UNC

BA 114e First date/prefix

BA 114er	£5	Replacement							
		27 Jul 1981 ZB 168001	-	270000	102,000				
		25 Jun 1982 ZB 271001	-	341000	70,000		40	100	200

BA 114f	£5	No longer encoded							
		13 Oct 1983 CL	-	CR	6,000,000				
		12 Sep 1984 CS	-	DB	10,000,000				
		3 Dec 1985 DC	-	DL	9,000,000				
		15 Jan 1987 DM	-	DT	7,000,000				
		29 Feb 1988 DU	-	DZ	6,000,000		10	25	45

BA 114f Last high serial

BA 114f Reverse No encoding

Specimen 13 Oct 1983 CL 12 Sep 1984 CS
 3 Dec 1985 DC 29 Feb 1988 DU   From 120 UNC

						VF	**EF**	**UNC**
BA 114fr	**£5**	Replacement						
		13 Oct 1983	ZB 344186	-	398510	n/k		
		12 Sep 1984	ZB 428704	-	464276	n/k		
		3 Dec 1985	ZB 469001	-	519000	50,000		
		15 Jan 1987	ZB 520001	-	555000	35,000		
		29 Feb 1988	ZB 556001	-	616000	60,000	20	40	80

BA 114fr Replacement

In 1990 the £5 note was reduced in size and 'STERLING' was added under the central denomination wording.

					VF	EF	UNC
BA 115a	£5	**Reduced size** 135 x 70mm **Sir Thomas Risk** Governor **Peter Burt** Treasurer & Chief General Manager					
		20 Jun 1990 EA - EJ		9,000,000	8	25	40
		Specimen 20 Jun 1990 EA			From 120 UNC		

BA 115a First prefix

BA 115ar	£5	**Replacement**					
		20 Jun 1990 ZB 617001 - 638000		21,000	35	70	150

BA 115ar Replacement

BA 115b	£5	**David Bruce Pattullo** Governor **Peter Burt** Treasurer & Chief General Manager					
		6 Nov 1991 EK - EQ		6,000,000			
		18 Jan 1993 ER - EW		6,000,000			
		7 Jan 1994 EX - FB		5,000,000	7	15	35

BA 115b First date/prefix low serial

BA 115b Last date, final prefix high serial

    Specimen 6 Nov 1991 EK 18 Jan 1993 ER 7 Jan 1994 EX   **From 120 UNC**

							VF	EF	UNC
BA 115br	**£5**	**Replacement**							
		6 Nov 1991	ZB 639001	-	659000	20,000			
		18 Jan 1993	ZB 660001	-	680000	20,000			
		7 Jan 1994	ZB 698673			n/k	30	60	120

£10 notes were not introduced until 1974, three years later than the £1 note.

							VF	EF	UNC
BA 116a	**£10**	**Brown Lord Clydesmuir** Governor 150 x 85mm							
		Andrew M Russell Treasurer & General Manager							
		1 May 1974	A			1,000,000			
		3 Jul 1975	B	-	E	4,000,000			
		12 Jan 1977	F	-	G	2,000,000			
		2 Dec 1977	H	-	J	2,000,000			
		29 Sep 1978	K	-	L	2,000,000	45	110	250

    Specimen 1 May 1974 A 12 Jan 1977 F
                2 Dec 1977 H 29 Sep 1978 K   **From 130 UNC**

BA 116a First date/prefix

BA 116 Reverse

BA 116ar	£10	Replacement					VF	EF	UNC
		1 May 1974	ZB 000001	-	025000	25,000			
		3 Jul 1975	ZB 025001	-	085000	60,000			
		12 Jan 1977	ZB 085001	-	105000	20,000			
		2 Dec 1977	ZB 105001	-	125000	20,000			
		29 Sep 1978	ZB 125001	-	145000	20,000	**150**	**300**	-

BA 116ar Replacement

						VF	EF	UNC
BA 116b	£10	Lord Clydesmuir Governor						
		David Bruce Pattullo Treasurer & General Manager						
		10 Oct 1979	M	- N	2,000,000			
		5 Feb 1981	P	- W	8,000,000	40	100	220
		Specimen 10 Oct 1979 M 5 Feb 1981 P					From 120	UNC

BA 116b First date/prefix low serial

BA 116br	£10	**Replacement**						
		10 Oct 1979	ZB 146001	-	160000	14,000		
		5 Feb 1981	ZB 161001	-	241000	80,000	150	300	-

BA 116c	£10	Sir Thomas Risk Governor						
		David Bruce Pattullo Treasurer & General Manager						
		22 Jul 1981	X	-	Z			
		Double Letter prefix						
			AA			4,000,000		
		16 Jun 1982	AB	-	AH	7,000,000		
		14 Oct 1983	AJ	-	AR	8,000,000		
		17 Sep 1984	AS	-	BB 500000	9,500,000		
		8 Jan 1986	BB 500001	-	BK 500000	8,000,000		
		20 Oct 1986	BK 500001	-	BZ 500000	14,000,000		
		6 Aug 1987	BZ 500001	-	CX 600000	22,100,000	20	35	75
		Specimen 22 Jul 1981 X 16 Jun 1982 AB 14 Oct 1983 AJ						
		17 Sep 1984 AS 8 Jan 1986 BB 20 Oct 1986 BK						
		6 Aug 1987 BZ					From 120 UNC	

BA 116c Specimen

							VF	EF	UNC
BA 116cr	**£10**	**Replacement**							
		22 Jul 1981	ZB 242001	-	282000	40,000			
		16 Jun 1982	ZB 283001	-	355000	72,000			
		14 Oct 1983	ZB 368045	-	385519	n/k			
		17 Sep 1984	ZB 489638	-	501706	n/k			
		8 Jan 1986	ZB 503001	-	531000	28,000			
		20 Oct 1986	ZB 532001	-	564000	32,000			
		6 Aug 1987	ZB 565001	-	645000	80,000	35	70	140

BA 116cr Replacement

							VF	EF	UNC
BA 116d	**£10**	**Sir Thomas Risk** Governor							
		Peter Burt Treasurer & Chief General Manager							
		1 Sep 1989	CX 600001	-	DT	20,400,000			
		31 Oct 1990	DU	-	EP	20,000,000	15	30	70

BA 116d Last date final prefix high serial

Specimen 1 Sep 1989 CX 31 Oct 1990 DU   From 120 UNC

							VF	EF	UNC
BA 116dr	**£10**	Replacement							
		1 Sep 1989	ZB 646001	-	692000	46,000			
		31 Oct 1990	ZB 693001	-	717000	24,000	**35**	**60**	**120**

In 1992 the £10 note was reduced in size and 'STERLING' was added under the central denomination wording.

BA 117	**£10**	**Reduced size** 142 x 75mm							
		David Bruce Pattullo Governor							
		Peter Burt Treasurer & Chief General Manager							
		7 May 1992	EQ	-	FP	24,000,000			
		9 Mar 1993	FQ	-	GE	15,000,000			
		13 Apr 1994	GF	-	GG	2,000,000	**15**	**35**	**70**

Specimen 7 May 1992 EQ 9 Mar 1993 FQ 13 Apr 1994 GF   From 100 UNC

BA 117 First date/prefix low serial

						VF	EF	UNC
BA 117r	£10	Replacement						
		7 May 1992	ZB 718001	-	768000	50,000		
		9 Mar 1993	ZB 769001	-	790000	21,000	**35**	**60**	**120**
		13 Apr 1994	ZB *none traced to date*					

BA 117r Replacement

£20 notes were first issued in March 1971.

BA 118a	£20	**Purple Lord Polwarth** Governor 160 x 90mm						
		Thomas W Walker Treasurer & General Manager						
		1 Oct 1970	A 000001	-	275000	275,000	**90**	**240**	**450**

BA 118a 1970

BA 118 Reverse

Specimen 1 Oct 1970 A			From 200 UNC
De La Rue Specimen 1 Oct 1970 A			From 150 UNC

BA 118b	**£20**	**Lord Clydesmuir Governor**			VF	EF	UNC
		Thomas W Walker Treasurer & General Manager					
		3 Jan 1973 A 275001 - 450000		175,000	**90**	**250**	**450**

BA 118b 1973

BA 118c	**£20**	**Lord Clydesmuir** Governor					
		Andrew M Russell Treasurer & General Manager					
		8 Nov 1974 A 450001 - 650000		200,000			
		14 Jan 1977 A 650001 - 900000		250,000	**80**	**170**	**320**

BA 118c 1977

BA 118d	£20	**Lord Clydesmuir** Governor			VF	EF	UNC
		David Bruce Pattullo Treasurer & General Manager					
		16 Jul 1979 A 900001 - B 400000		500,000			
		2 Feb 1981 B 400001 - 750000		350,000	50	110	220
		Specimen 16 Jul 1979 A 2 Feb 1981 B			From 180 UNC		

BA 118d 1981

BA 118e	£20	**Sir Thomas Risk** Governor					
		David Bruce Pattullo Treasurer & General Manager					
		4 Aug 1981 B 750001 - C 300000		550,000			
		9 Jun 1982 C 300001 - 800000		500,000			
		EDINBURGH & Date move to centre left					
		30 Sep 1983 C 800001 - D 400000		600,000			
		11 Oct 1984 D 400001 - E 150000		750,000			
		5 Nov 1985 E 150001 - F 650000		1,500,000			
		6 Jan 1987 F 650001 - H 150000		1,500,000			
		15 Dec 1987 H 150001 - K 150000		2,000,000	35	85	170

BA 118e Last Split Prefix

Specimen 4 Aug 1981 B 9 Jun 1982 C 30 Sep 1983 C
11 Oct 1984 D 5 Nov 1985 E 6 Jan 1987 F
15 Dec 1987 H   **From 160 UNC**

De La Rue Specimen 4 Aug 1981 B   **From 120 UNC**

In 1991 the £20 note was reduced in size and 'STERLING' was added under the central denomination wording. The first £20 note replacements were recorded in 1991. All prefix Z notes will be replacements and are not part of the regular issue.

BA 119	£20	Reduced size 150 x 80mm				VF	EF	UNC
		David Bruce Pattullo Governor						
		Peter Burt Treasurer & Chief General Manager						
		1 Jul 1991	K 150001	-	U 150000	9,000,000		
		3 Feb 1992	U 150001	-	Y			
		Double Letter prefix						
			AA	-	AG 150000	11,000,000		
		12 Jan 1993	AG 150001	-	AU 150000	12,000,000	35	70	130

Specimen 1 Jul 1991 K 3 Feb 1992 U 12 Jan 1993 AG   **From 150 UNC**

BA 119 First Split Prefix

BA 119 Last Split Prefix

BA 119r	£20	Replacement				VF	EF	UNC
		1 Jul 1991	Z 000001	-	011000	11,000		
		3 Feb 1992	Z 012001	-	030000	18,000		
		12 Jan 1993	Z 031001	-	049000	18,000	**150**	**350**	**650**

BA 119r Replacement 1992

£100 notes were first issued in late 1971. No replacements are known to have been issued.

BA 120a	£100	Red Lord Polwarth Governor 160 x 90mm Thomas W Walker Treasurer & General Manager 6 Dec 1971 A 000001 - 020000	20,000	**VF** **320**	**EF** **600**	**UNC** **1300**

BA 120a 1971

BA 120 Reverse

Specimen 6 Dec 1971 A	100	**From 280 UNC**
De La Rue Specimen 6 Dec 1971 A		**From 220 UNC**

BA 120b	£100	Lord Clydesmuir Governor Thomas W Walker Treasurer & General Manager 6 Sep 1973 A 020001 - 045000	25,000	**280**	**600**	**1150**

Specimen 6 Sep 1973 A		**From 260 UNC**

				VF	EF	UNC
BA 120c	**£100**	**Lord Clydesmuir** Governor **Andrew M Russell** Treasurer & General Manager				
		11 Oct 1978 A 045001 - 070000	25,000	**250**	**500**	**1200**
		Specimen 11 Oct 1978 A		From 250 UNC		

BA 120c 1978

				VF	EF	UNC
BA 120d	**£100**	**Lord Clydesmuir** Governor **David Bruce Pattullo** Treasurer & General Manager				
		26 Jan 1981 A 070001 - 095000	25,000	**220**	**460**	**1000**
		Specimen 26 Jan 1981 A		From 250 UNC		

BA 120d 1981

					VF	EF	UNC
BA 120e	**£100**	**Sir Thomas Risk** Governor **David Bruce Pattullo** Treasurer & General Manager					
		10 Jun 1982 A 095001 - 125000		30,000			
		15 Oct 1984 A 125001 - 155000		30,000			
		18 Dec 1985 A 155001 - 190000		35,000			
		26 Nov 1986 A 190001 - 225000		35,000	220	420	850

Specimen 10 Jun 1982 A 15 Oct 1984 A 26 Nov 1986 A   From 250 UNC

BA 120e 1985

					VF	EF	UNC
BA 120f	**£100**	**Sir Thomas Risk** Governor **Peter Burt** Treasurer & Chief General Manager					
		14 Feb 1990 A 225001 - 260000		35,000	210	380	750

Specimen 14 Feb 1990 A   From 250 UNC

BA 120f 1990

In 1992 'STERLING' was added under the central denomination wording. Dimensions unchanged.

						VF	EF	UNC
BA 121	£100	STERLING added **David Bruce Pattullo** Governor						
		Peter Burt Treasurer & Chief General Manager						
		22 Jan 1992	A 260001 - 300000		40,000			
		2 Dec 1992	A 300001 - 350000		50,000			
		9 Feb 1994	A 350001 - 390000 *		40,000	180	320	650

Specimen 22 Jan 1992 A   2 Dec 1992 A   9 Feb 1994 A   From 250 UNC

BA 121 Last date high serial

* Notes up to A 387500 were taken to cash and put into circulation, but possibly 100 of the final print run of notes up to A 390000 were issued direct to collectors, some as part of sets with matching final serials.

TERCENTENARY ISSUE – 1995 *to* 2006

The Bank celebrated its 300th anniversary in 1995 and commissioned a new series of notes in recognition of this significant milestone. The designs were the product of a design committee and are felt by many to be among the least impressive of modern Scottish notes. They were engraved by **Thomas De La Rue & Co Limited** whose imprint as before does not appear on any issued notes of this series.

A new portrait of Sir Walter Scott now appears on the left of each obverse with the former portrait now relegated to the watermark. A small panel lower centre contains the words '*300 years of Service to the Community 1695-1995*'. Each denomination continues to use the predominant colours of the previous series with green chosen for the newly re-introduced £50 note (the first of this denomination for over 200 years).

Common features of the reverse include a small vignette of the Bank's head office on the Mound, in Edinburgh, and the symbols of the three constituent banks to the right: Pallas for the British Linen Bank, the Bank's own stylised logo and the Union Bank's ship vignette. The principal feature of each denomination is a different scene from the many Scottish industries and activities supported by the Bank:

£5	Oil & Energy
£10	Distilling & Brewing
£20	Education & Research (featuring the chemical scientist Janet Mullen)
£50	Arts & Culture
£100	Leisure & Tourism

A number of enhanced security features are deployed including a metal security thread which repeats 'BOS' and the denomination. There are two bar codes printed on the front of each denomination horizontally and vertically using fluorescent ink to act as both security and to aid high speed note sorting. A 'see through' feature in exact register is seen in the form of a thistle image upper right on the obverse and upper left on the reverse. Each denomination carries a distinct symbol in the lower left corner to aid the visually impaired.

The £5 note was first issued on 4th January 1995 followed by the £10 on 20th February, the £20 and £50 on 2nd May and finally the £100 on the Tercentenary date itself, 17th July 1995. Bruce Pattullo was knighted in 1995 and his title is now stated in the listings.

Prefix letters I and O are not used. Replacements have been recorded on all denominations but only partial information has been found on replacement serial ranges after 1995 so gaps have been filled by firm sightings as reported by collectors. All specimens with 000000 serials unless otherwise stated.

A few De La Rue essays have come on to the market including a superb £100 featuring the former British Linen Bank head office on the reverse.

BA 122a	£5	**Blue Sir Bruce Pattullo** Governor 135 x 70mm		VF	EF	UNC
		Peter Burt Treasurer & Chief General Manager				
		4 Jan 1995 AA - AM	12,000,000	10	25	50

BA 122a First prefix

BA 122 Reverse

Specimen 4 Jan 1995 AA   **From 100 UNC**

					VF	EF	UNC
BA 122ar	£5	Replacement					
		4 Jan 1995 ZZ 000001 - 020000		20,000	25	60	120

BA 122ar Replacement

BA 122b	£5	**Sir Bruce Pattullo** Governor					
		Gavin Masterton Treasurer & Chief General Manager					
		13 Sep 1996 AN - AZ		12,000,000	10	15	30

BA 122b First prefix low serial

BA 122br	£5	Replacement					
		13 Sep 1996 ZZ 021001 - 041000		20,000	25	60	120

BA 122c	£5	**Sir Alistair M A Grant** Governor					
		Gavin Masterton Treasurer & Chief General Manager					
		5 Aug 1998 BA - BR		16,000,000	10	15	30
		De La Rue Specimen 5 Aug 1998 BA			From 70 UNC		

BA 122c First prefix low serial

BA 122cr **£5** **Replacement**   **VF** **EF** **UNC**
              5 Aug 1998 ZZ 042001 - 077000   35,000   **25**   **60**   **120**

BA 122cr Replacement

BA 122d **£5** **Sir Peter Burt** Governor
              George Mitchell Treasurer & Managing Director
              25 Jun 2002 BS - CB   10,000,000   **8**   **15**   **25**

BA 122d First prefix low serial

						VF	EF	UNC
BA 122dr	**£5**	Replacement						
		25 Jun 2002 ZZ 085602 - 090983			n/k	25	60	120

						VF	EF	UNC
BA 122e	**£5**	**Dennis Stevenson** Governor **Colin Matthew** Treasurer						
		1 Jan 2006 CC - CH 600000			5,600,000	8	10	22
		Specimen 1 Jan 2006 CC					From 90	UNC

BA 122e Last prefix penultimate serial

						VF	EF	UNC
BA 122er	**£5**	Replacement						
		1 Jan 2006 ZZ 103903 - 105508			n/k	15	35	80

						VF	EF	UNC
BA 123a	**£10**	Brown **Sir Bruce Pattullo** Governor 142 x 75mm						
		Peter Burt Treasurer & Chief General Manager						
		1 Feb 1995 AA - BM			36,000,000	15	30	60
		Specimen 1 Feb 1995 AA					From 120	UNC

BA 123a First prefix

BA 123 Reverse

BA 123ar £10 **Replacement**   **VF EF UNC**
1 Feb 1995 ZZ 000001 - 035000   35,000   **25 65 130**

BA 123ar Replacement

BA 123b £10 **Sir Bruce Pattullo** Governor
Gavin Masterton Treasurer & Chief General Manager
5 Aug 1997 BN - CF   18,000,000   **13 20 40**

BA 123b First prefix low serial

Specimen 5 Aug 1997 CE   **From 100 UNC**

					VF	EF	UNC
BA 123br	**£10**	**Replacement** 5 Aug 1997 ZZ 036001 - 071000		35,000	**25**	**65**	**130**

BA 123c	**£10**	**Sir Alistair M A Grant** Governor **Gavin Masterton** Treasurer & Chief General Manager 18 Aug 1998 CG - DT		36,000,000	**13**	**20**	**40**
		Specimen 18 Aug 1998 CG				**From 100 UNC**	

BA 123c First prefix 100 serial

BA 123cr	**£10**	**Replacement** 18 Aug 1998 ZZ 072001 - 097000		25,000	**25**	**65**	**130**

BA 123d	**£10**	**John C Shaw** Governor **George C Mitchell** Treasurer & Managing Director 18 Jun 2001 DU - EU		25,000,000	**13**	**20**	**35**
		Specimen 18 Jun 2001 DU				**From 100 UNC**	

BA 123d First prefix

							VF	EF	UNC
BA 123dr	**£10**	**Replacement**							
		18 Jun 2001 ZZ 098001	-	114926		n/k	25	65	130

BA 123e **£10** **George C Mitchell** Governor
  26 Nov 2003 EV - FB   7,000,000
  24 Sep 2004 FC - FM   10,000,000   **13 20 40**

  Specimen 26 Nov 2003 EV   **From 100 UNC**

BA 123e First prefix

BA 123er **£10** **Replacement**
  26 Nov 2003 ZZ 116863 - 116915   n/k
  24 Sep 2004 ZZ 120042 - 143685   n/k   **25 65 130**

BA 123er Replacement

BA 123f **£10** **Dennis Stevenson** Governor **Colin Matthew** Treasurer
  1 Jan 2006 FN - FX   10,000,000   **13 20 40**

  Specimen 1 Jan 2006 FN   **From 100 UNC**

BA 123f Last prefix penultimate serial (solid)

					VF	EF	UNC
BA 123fr	**£10**	**Replacement**					
		1 Jan 2006 ZZ 145831 - 147909		n/k	25	65	130

BA 124a **£20** **Purple Sir Bruce Pattullo** Governor 150 x 80mm
Peter Burt Treasurer & Chief General Manager

		1 May 1995 AA - AY	23,000,000	25	40	70

Specimen 1 May 1995 AA   From 110 UNC

BA 124a First prefix

BA 124 Reverse

Bank of Scotland

						VF	EF	UNC
BA 124ar	£20	Replacement						
		1 May 1995 ZZ 000001	-	037000	37,000	60	120	200

BA 124b £20 **Sir Bruce Pattullo** Governor
Gavin Masterton Treasurer & Chief Gen Manager

					VF	EF	UNC
25 Oct 1996	AZ	-	BL 900000	11,900,000			
1 Apr 1998	BL 900001	-	CE 550000	17,650,000	25	40	70

Specimen 25 Oct 1996 AZ 1 Apr 1998 BL   From 110 UNC

BA 124b First prefix low serial

BA 124b Final Split Prefix highest serial

BA 124br £20 Replacement

					VF	EF	UNC
25 Oct 1996	ZZ 038001	-	058000	20,000			
1 Apr 1998	ZZ 059001	-	089000	30,000	60	120	200

BA 124c £20 **Sir Alistair M A Grant** Governor
Gavin Masterton Treasurer & Managing Director

				VF	EF	UNC
22 Mar 1999 CE 550001	-	DL	30,450,000	25	35	50

BA 124c   First Split Prefix low serial

Specimen 22 Mar 1999 CE   From 110 UNC

						VF	EF	UNC
BA 124cr	£20	Replacement						
		22 Mar 1999 ZZ 090001 - 107931			n/k	45	90	180
BA 124d	£20	**John C Shaw** Governor						
		George C Mitchell Treasurer & Managing Director						
		18 Jun 2001 DM - DW 900000		9,900,000		23	30	50

BA 124d First prefix low serial

						VF	EF	UNC
BA 124dr	£20	Replacement						
		18 Jun 2001 ZZ 111015 - 130689			n/k	45	90	180

BA 124dr Replacement

The Bank's museum, the Museum on the Mound, had a block of 50,000 £20 notes specially printed for display purposes to illustrate the physical scale of £1,000,000 of notes. They were all dated 26th November 2003, carried the prefix YY and were stamped CANCELLED.

BA 124e	£20	George C Mitchell Governor				VF	EF	UNC
		26 Nov 2003 DW 900001	-	EG 550000	9,650,000			
		24 Sep 2004 EG 550001	-	FN	30,450,000	22	30	50
		Specimen 24 Sep 2004 EG					From 110	UNC

BA 124e First Split Prefix low serial

BA 124e Last prefix penultimate serial (solid)

Prefix YY bundles in Museum on the Mound

BA 124er	£20	Replacement			VF	EF	UNC
		26 Nov 2003 ZZ 132534	-	140280	n/k		
		24 Sep 2004 ZZ 142679	-	170913	n/k	35	70	140

BA 124er Replacement

					VF	EF	UNC
BA 125a	£50	Green Sir Bruce Pattullo Governor 155 x 85mm Peter Burt Treasurer & Chief General Manager					
		1 May 1995 AA 000001 - 800000		800,000	60	120	230
		Specimen 1 May 1995 AA				From 160 UNC	

BA 125a First prefix

BA 125 Reverse

BA 125ar	£50	Replacement			
		1 May 1995 ZZ 000108		n/k	**RARE**

					VF	EF	UNC
BA 125b	**£50**	**Sir Alistair M A Grant** Governor **Gavin Masterton** Treasurer & Managing Director 15 Apr 1999 AA 800001 - AB 400000 600,000			60	100	180

BA 125b First Split Prefix low serial

BA 125br	**£50**	**Replacement** 15 Apr 1999 *none traced to date*		

					VF	EF	UNC
BA 125c	**£50**	**George C Mitchell** Governor 29 Jan 2003 AB 400001 - 1000000 600,000 24 Sep 2004 AC 000001 - 500000 500,000			-	70	140

BA 125c 2004 Last prefix low serial

BA 125cr	**£50**	**Replacement** 29 Jan 2003 ZZ 005120 24 Sep 2004 *none traced to date*	n/k	**From 300 VF**

							VF	EF	UNC
BA 125d	**£50**	**Dennis Stevenson** Governor **Colin Matthew** Treasurer							
		1 Jan 2006 AC 500001	-	AD 100000	600,000		-	70	140
		Specimen 1 Jan 2006 AC						From 160	UNC
BA 125dr	**£50**	**Replacement**							
		1 Jan 2006 ZZ 010005	-	010253		n/k	200	400	-

BA 125dr Replacement

BA 126 Essay of reverse

BA 126a	£100	Red Sir Bruce Pattullo Governor 163 x 90mm		VF	EF	UNC
		Peter Burt Treasurer & Chief General Manager				
		17 Jul 1995 AA 000001 - 250000	250,000	150	300	500
		Specimen 17 Jul 1995 AA			From 180 UNC	

BA 126a First Prefix

BA 126 Reverse

BA 126ar	£100	Replacement				
		17 Jul 1995 ZZ 000001 - 001220	1,220			RARE

BA 126b	£100	Sir Bruce Pattullo Governor				
		Gavin Masterton Treasurer & Chief General Manager				
		18 Aug 1997 AA 250001 - 550000	300,000	140	260	450
		Specimen 18 Aug 1997 AA			From 160 UNC	

BA 126b First Split Prefix low serial

						VF	EF	UNC
BA 126br	**£100**	Replacement						
		18 Aug 1997 ZZ 002001 - 002167			n/k	**150**	**230**	**480**

BA 126c	**£100**	**Sir Alistair M A Grant** Governor						
		Gavin Masterton Treasurer & Managing Director						
		19 May 1999 AA 550001 - 850000			300,000	**130**	**170**	**320**

BA 126c First Split Prefix

BA 126cr	**£100**	Replacement			
		19 May 1999 ZZ 004168		n/k	**From 350 EF**

BA 126d	**£100**	**George C Mitchell** Governor					
		26 Nov 2003 AA 850001 - AB 150000	300,000				
		24 Sep 2004 AB 150001 - 400000	250,000	**130**	**170**	**320**	

BA 126d First Split Prefix

BA 126dr **£100** **Replacement**
26 Nov 2003 *none traced to date*
24 Sep 2004 *none traced to date*

BA 126e **£100** **Dennis Stevenson** Governor **Colin Matthew** Treasurer **VF** **EF** **UNC**
1 Jan 2006 AB 400001 - 720000 320,000 **120** **150** **250**

Specimen 1 Jan 2006 AB **From 180 UNC**

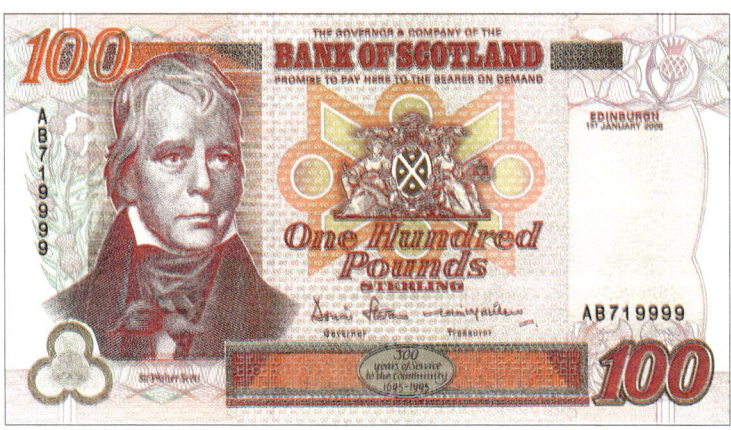

BA 126e Last prefix penultimate serial

BA 126er **£100** **Replacement**
1 Jan 2006 ZZ 010115 - 010210 n/k **From 300 VF**

BRIDGES ISSUE – 2007 *to* date

Issuer: Bank of Scotland plc

In 2006 the Bank decided to replace its Tercentenary notes, prompted by an internal reorganisation which transferred the note issue licence to a new corporate entity, Bank of Scotland plc. This arose from the 2001 merger of the Bank of Scotland with the former Halifax Building Society (founded 1853) which had been floated on the Stock Exchange in 1997. The new group was known as HBOS and the resulting headlong expansion brought about the group's collapse in the 2008 credit crunch. The group is now part of Lloyds Banking Group plc, technically registered as a Scottish bank though with its head office in London. The change of issuing entity broke the direct link with the bank created in 1695.

As before, the notes were printed and engraved by **Thomas De La Rue & Co Limited** (no imprint on the notes). The principal designer of the new series was Stuart Rost whose work on the £50 note won the International Bank Note Society's Banknote of the Year award for 2007. The latest security features were incorporated into the note designs including an iridescent band, a hologram and a security thread which, on the £20, £50 and £100 notes, changes colour when tilted. For the first time the plates were digitally engraved, rather than by the human hand.

To emphasise the continuity despite the change in legal issuer, the Bank refers to this issue as their 47th. The obverse of the new design continues to feature Sir Walter Scott, his portrait now based on the famous painting of him from 1822 by Sir Henry Raeburn, while each reverse focuses on a famous Scottish bridge:

£5	Brig o' Doon, Alloway, Ayrshire, made famous by Robert Burns
£10	Glenfinnan Viaduct, on the West Highland Line, featured in the Harry Potter films
£20	Forth Bridge, between North and South Queensferry
£50	Falkirk Wheel, the world's only rotating boat lift built to restore the canal link between Glasgow and Edinburgh
£100	Kessock Bridge, spanning the Moray and Beauly Firths near Inverness

Prefix letters I and O are not used. All details of replacements are from firm sightings as reported by collectors. Full serial number ranges are not known. The Museum on the Mound had another block of 50,000 £20 notes specially printed for display purposes to illustrate the physical scale of £1,000,000 of notes. They were all dated 17th September 2007, carried the prefix YY and were stamped CANCELLED. They sit in the Museum alongside the earlier set of specially printed £20 notes. All specimens with 000000 serials unless otherwise stated.

Stage proofs have surfaced from the De La Rue archives. Specimens without the usual 'SPECIMEN' stamp come from sheets of uncut notes sold by the Bank in a charity auction.

					EF	UNC
BA 127a	**£5**	**Blue** 135 x 70mm				
		Dennis Stevenson Governor **Colin Matthew** Treasurer				
		17 Sep 2007 AA - AP		14,000,000	8	16
		Proof 17 Sep 2007 AA 123456			From 160 UNC	
		Specimen 17 Sep 2007 AA			From 80 UNC	

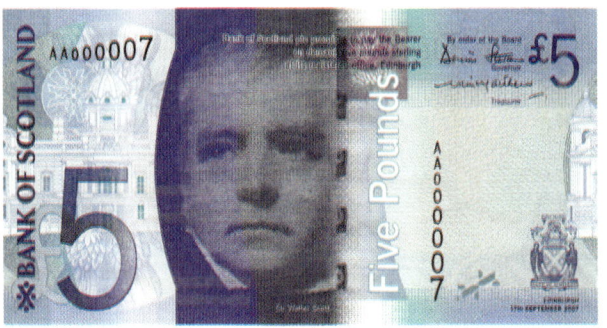

BA 127a First prefix 7 serial

BA 127 Reverse

BA 127ar	**£5**	**Replacement**				
		17 Sep 2007 ZZ 000001 - 014007			40	80

BA 127ar Replacement

				EF	UNC
BA 127b	£5	**Eric Daniels** Governor **Archie Kane** Treasurer 19 Jan 2009 AQ - AZ	10,000,000	8	15
BA 127br	£5	**Replacement** 19 Jan 2009 ZZ 021353 - 021881		40	80
BA 127c	£5	**Antonio Horta-Osorio** Governor **Philip Grant** Treasurer 1 Aug 2011 BA - BE	5,000,000	8	15

BA 127c 2011

BA 127cr	£5	**Replacement** 1 Aug 2011 ZZ 041984 - 047535		40	80
BA 128a	£10	**Brown** 142 x 75mm **Dennis Stevenson** Governor **Colin Matthew** Treasurer 17 Sep 2007 AA - BM	36,000,000	15	25
		Specimen 17 Sep 2007 AA		From 100	UNC

BA 128a First prefix 7 serial

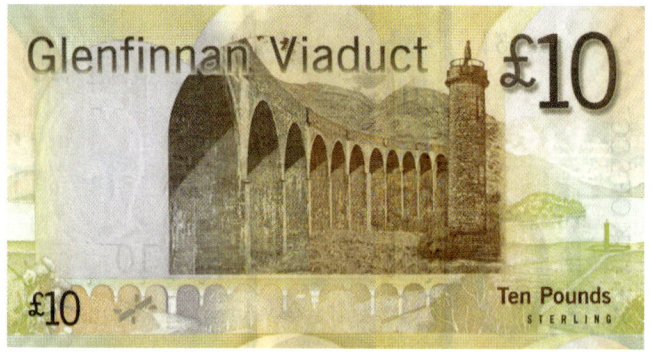

BA 128 Reverse

						EF	UNC
BA 128ar	£10	**Replacement** 17 Sep 2007 ZZ 000001 - 019543				**35**	**75**

BA 128ar Replacement

BA 128b	£10	**Eric Daniels** Governor **Archie Kane** Treasurer 19 Jan 2009 BN - DD			40,000,000	**15**	**20**
BA 128br	£10	**Replacement** 19 Jan 2009 ZZ 050451 - 125165				**35**	**75**
BA 129a	£20	**Purple** 150 x 80mm **Dennis Stevenson** Governor **Colin Matthew** Treasurer 17 Sep 2007 AA - BW			45,000,000	**25**	**45**
		Specimen 17 Sep 2007 AA				**From 100 UNC**	

BA 129a First prefix 7 serial

BA 129 Reverse

Prefix YY display in Museum on the Mound

					EF	UNC
BA 129ar	£20	**Replacement** 17 Sep 2007 ZZ 000001 - 061245 overlap with BA 129br			40	80

BA 129ar Replacement

					EF	UNC
BA 129b	£20	**Eric Daniels** Governor **Archie Kane** Treasurer 19 Jan 2009 BX - DT *continuing*		21,000,000	25	40
BA 129br	£20	**Replacement** 19 Jan 2009 ZZ 056716 - 069537 overlap with BA 129ar			40	80
BA 130a	£50	**Green** 155 x 85mm **Dennis Stevenson** Governor **Colin Matthew** Treasurer 17 Sep 2007 AA - AB 700000		1,700,000	90	160
		Specimen 17 Sep 2007 AA			From 120 UNC	

BA 130a First prefix 7 serial

BA 130a Reverse

| BA 130ar | £50 | Replacement 17 Sep 2007 ZZ 000001 - 007373 | | **EF** 80 | **UNC** 160 |

BA 130ar Replacement

| BA 130b | £50 | **Eric Daniels** Governor **Archie Kane** Treasurer 19 Jan 2009 AB 700001 - 900000 | 200,000 | 80 | 160 |

| BA 130br | £50 | Replacement 19 Jan 2009 ZZ 010908 - 012057 | | 100 | 180 |

| BA 130c | £50 | **Antonio Horta-Osorio** Governor **Philip Grant** Treasurer 1 Aug 2011 AB 900001 - AC 1000000   1,100,000 29 Mar 2016 AD 000001 -   700000   700,000 | | 65 | 100 |

Specimen 1 Aug 2011 AC   From 140 UNC

BA 130cr   **£50**   **Replacement**   **EF**   **UNC**
                        1 Aug 2011   ZZ 015681   -   020780   **80**   **160**
                        29 Mar 2016   *none traced to date*

BA 130cr   Replacement

BA 131a   **£100**   **Red**   163 x 90mm
                     Dennis Stevenson Governor   **Colin Matthew** Treasurer
                     17 Sep 2007   AA 000001   -   900000   900,000   **130**   **250**

                     Proof   17 Sep 2007 AA 123456   **From 200 UNC**

                     Specimen   17 Sep 2007 AA   **From 160 UNC**

                     De La Rue Specimen   17 Sep 2007 AA   **From 130 UNC**

BA 131a   First prefix 7 serial

BA 131 Reverse

					EF	UNC
BA 131ar	**£100**	**Replacement**				
		17 Sep 2007 ZZ 000001	-	004347	**150**	**300**

BA 131ar Replacement

BA 131b	**£100**	**Eric Daniels** Governor **Archie Kane** Treasurer					
		19 Jan 2009 AA 900001	-	1000000	100,000	**120**	**250**
BA 131br	**£100**	**Replacement**					
		19 Jan 2009 ZZ 005603	-	007183		**130**	**250**
BA 131c	**£100**	**Antonio Horta-Osorio** Governor **Philip Grant** Treasurer					
		1 Aug 2011 AB 000001	-	250000	250,000		
		19 Aug 2014 AB 250001	-	750000	500,000	**120**	**220**
BA 131cr	**£100**	**Replacement**					
		1 Aug 2011 ZZ 007199	-	007857		**130**	**250**
		19 Aug 2014 *none traced to date*					

POLYMER ISSUE

Reduced Size

On 1st June 2015 the Bank announced that it was going to follow the Bank of England and the Clydesdale in issuing reduced size polymer £5 and £10 notes, commencing with the £5 note. The notes were to be printed by **De La Rue** using their Safeguard® polymer material. At the same time they announced that a limited edition of fifty notes featuring Pudsey the Bear would be printed and auctioned off for the charity BBC Children in Need. As a special feature ten of these notes would come with the purchaser's right to have their own choice of prefix/serials added. Most were sold in auctions in December 2015 and October 2016 and the total raised for charity exceeded £80,000. One of the personalised notes sold for £15,500 (+ 20% buyers premium), to date a record price for any Scottish banknote. The image on the reverse of the note of Pudsey holding the Saltire aloft was designed by Kayla Robson, then aged twelve. The obverse continues to feature Sir Walter Scott.

The first regular issue of £5 notes took place on 4th October 2016 with low and special serials again being sold for charity. The Number One note, AA 000001, sold for £12,500 + buyers premium. The reverse design reverts to the image of Brig o' Doon.

Polymer £10 notes were first issued on 10th October 2017 accompanied by a charity auction of notes with low and special numbers. The design was similar to the preceding paper £10 note but as with the £5 note the Bank's iconic former head office on The Mound in Edinburgh featured more prominently on the front. Glenfinnan Viaduct is again the main feature on the reverse of the £10 note but now depicts a steam train crossing it. An uncut sheet of 45 specimen £10 notes (no overprint) was also auctioned. Prefix letters I and O not used.

BA 132   **£5**   **Blue Pudsey the Bear Commemorative** 125 x 65mm
Antonio Horta-Osorio Governor **Philip Grant** Treasurer
17 Jul 2015 PUDSEY 01 - 40   10 with personalised serials   **RARE**

BA 132 Pudsey Commemorative 1 serial

BA 132 Reverse

BA 133a	**£5**	**Blue** 125 x 65mm				**EF**	**UNC**
		Antonio Horta-Osorio Governor **Philip Grant** Treasurer					
		25 Mar 2016 AA - AJ 900000			8,900,000	7	12
		continuing					

BA 133a First prefix 000001 serial

BA 133 Reverse

A few £5 and £10 pre-production test notes prefix XX, dated 19th May 2015 and 1st June 2016 respectively, were prepared for internal use. Blocks of these notes were issued to note handling companies and should have been returned, but one or two have entered into circulation. The £5 note varies from the issued notes in that the 'Spark' metallic ink orientation of the '5' on the lower right of the obverse differs (left-right) from the issued note (up-down).

Prefix XX £5 pre-production test note

BA 133ar	**£5**	**Replacement**			
		25 Mar 2016 ZZ 000807 - 098249		15	35

BA 133ar Replacement

BA 134a   £10   **Brown** 132 x 69mm   EF   UNC
              Antonio Horta-Osorio Governor **Philip Grant** Treasurer
              1 Jun 2016   AA   -   BC   27,000,000   12   15
                           continuing

BA 134a First prefix serial 000001

BA 134 Reverse

BA 134ar £10 **Replacement**
              1 Jun 2016 ZZ 005658   -   176898   15   35

BA 134ar Replacement

In November 2017 the Bank produced a limited edition set of 38 polymer £10 notes for sale in a charity auction for Mental Health UK. The notes, their prefixes (LMS: London, Midland & Scotland Railway; BR: British Rail) and their serial numbers have a railway theme reflecting the reverse design of a Stanier 'Black 5' locomotive pulling a train over the Glenfinnan Viaduct. The name of a West Highland Line station was added to the reverse of each prefix LMS note in the style of an old station sign (known as a 'Totem'). The notes were otherwise unchanged from the regular issues. Two were sold with the purchaser's right to have their own choice of prefix/serials added.

BA 134b £10   **Railway themed charity issue Special prefixes**
              1 Jun 2016   BR   LMS   18 per prefix   From 300 UNC

British Linen Bank

British Linen Company 1746 *to* 1904
British Linen Bank 1905 *to* 1970

The British Linen Bank began life as the British Linen Company and was incorporated by Royal Charter on 5th July 1746, as the crest on most of its notes in the 19th and 20th centuries proudly proclaimed. It was set up in the aftermath of the Jacobite Rebellion (hence, it is suggested, the name 'British' rather than 'Scottish' or even 'North British') to acquire the business of the Edinburgh Linen Co-Partnery which had been founded in 1722.

A key figure involved in establishing the Company was its first Governor, Archibald Campbell, the 3rd Duke of Argyll and the 1st Earl of Ilay. He is perhaps better known as the first Governor of the Royal Bank of Scotland, no doubt due to his featuring on all of that bank's notes from 1987 to date. Other key figures included the Deputy Governor Andrew Fletcher, later Lord Milton, who was influential in London circles, and founding directors Patrick Crawford, William Beckford, later twice Lord Mayor of London, John Coutts, founder of the predecessor firm to Forbes, Hunter & Co and the Edinburgh merchants Thomas Allan and Alexander Sharp. Other important proprietors (i.e. shareholders) included William Maule, 1st Earl Panmure and George Middleton, a partner of Coutts & Co in London. Ebernezer McCulloch and William Tod were jointly appointed the first Managers.

The Company set nominal capital at £100,000 though the amount initially subscribed was much lower. Nominal capital did not need increasing until 1806 when it was doubled. From the outset it was agreed *'that a seal be made for the Company in the figure of Pallas'*, this emblem subsequently appearing on many of the Company's notes. As the name implies the Company was not a bank at all in the beginning, it was a trader and manufacturer of linen. In 1763 the Company formally decided to give these activities up and concentrate solely on banking, thus making it the third oldest of the Chartered Banks in Scotland. It was formally acknowledged as a bank by its two main competitors, the Royal Bank of Scotland and the Bank of Scotland in 1765 and 1771 respectively.

The bank set up a wide network of agencies across Scotland, one of the first institutions to do so. Many of these later became branches and the Company even ventured south of the border to Berwick-on-Tweed and Wooler in Northumberland. During the earlier part of the 19th century it began to call itself the British Linen Company Bank but while this designation appeared on its cheques and other instruments, it appeared on its notes only as a watermark. A single acquisition was made, that of the Paisley Banking Company in 1836. Authorised Circulation under the 1845 Act was £438,024, the highest of all the Scottish banks.

The logical name change to British Linen Bank finally took place on 11th June 1906. The bank lost its independence in 1919 to Barclays Bank when the wave of banking amalgamations across the United Kingdom was at its peak, but maintained its autonomy and separate identity until 1970. In that year Barclays sold its stake to the Bank of Scotland. The legal use of the name was also acquired and in 1977 it resumed business as the merchant banking arm of the Bank of Scotland. It continued as such until September 1999 when it was bought out by its management and re-launched as British Linen Advisers. This firm finally closed its doors in 2008.

The Company's earliest notes are extremely rare and were issued while it was still principally engaged in linen manufacture and trading, so the promissory clause added the words '*value received in goods*' to the usual promise to pay the bearer on demand. They were very simple designs and inevitably forgeries appeared. The Pallas vignette is first seen in 1754 and was later accompanied by the Latin word '*Ditat*', meaning '*She Enriches*'. In 1822 new and elaborate steel-engraved designs by **Perkins Fairman & Heath** (later **Perkins Bacon**) were first issued. These classic designs remained in use right through to 1970 with remarkably little variation. The first **Perkins** notes were printed solely in black but blue ink was later introduced with the bank's initials across the centre in red, as a better protection against forgery. The essential features of the Perkins design were continued after the firm lost the printing contract to **Waterlow & Sons** in 1904, although the plates were re-engraved to a noticeably higher standard. All notes were impressed with the Company's seal prior to 1878 and were fully handsigned until 1885 when a printed signature first appeared on the £1 notes.

In 1935 all the notes were modified when the Royal Arms in use for over 100 years were replaced with arms specially created for the bank, on the insistence of the Lord Lyon King of Arms, a court official with wide heraldic powers in Scotland. In 1961 **Thomas De La Rue & Co Ltd** took over Waterlow & Sons. The old designs were retained but the final issues featured a portrait of Sir Walter Scott, perhaps the bank's most famous customer, whose tracts written in 1825 under the pseudonym of Malachi Malagrowther helped save the Scottish £1 note from oblivion.

FIRST ISSUE – 1747

Hand-written notes

The Company first decided to issue promissory notes in 1747 to facilitate its trading activities. Notes for £5, £10 and £20 were prepared by hand using a promissory text set out in the minutes of the Court of Directors. They were made payable to a specific person or to bearer on demand. A £100 note was also prepared bearing interest at a rate decreed not to exceed 4% p.a., payable up to three months from date of issue. These early notes were all hand written and none appear to have survived.

BL 1	£5	Hand-written
BL 2	£10	Hand-written
BL 3	£20	Hand-written
BL 4	£100	Hand-written Interest clause

SECOND ISSUE – 1750 *to* 1751

Printed notes payable on demand 'value received in goods'

After attempting to obtain a legal opinion to confirm the Directors' wish to add the words '*value received in goods*' to the promissory text, the Company went ahead anyway in June 1750 and decided to have plates prepared for the issue of 10 Shillings, 20 Shillings (i.e. £1 Sterling) and £5 notes. A total of 2,063 10s notes, 1,010 £1 notes and 200 £5 notes were issued, the 10s bound into books of 400 notes, the £1 into books of 250 and the £5 into a single book of 200. By November there had been reports that the paper used was too thick causing the notes to wear out too quickly in circulation. A new printing of 4,000 10s notes and 400 £1 notes followed and the earlier ones were withdrawn and destroyed. Further printings followed in 1751, now using watermarked paper, and a very small printing of £10 notes was undertaken (but none were issued in the end and they were probably destroyed in 1770). The Company appointed John Stewart as its first Cashier in April 1751. It is not recorded who engraved the plates or which paper mill provided the paper. It is not believed any of these notes have survived. The numbering system conforms to the Scottish practice of book number over sequential number. Notes were dated and numbered by hand.

BL 5	10s	**Black**	uniface
BL 6	£1	**Black**	uniface
BL 7	£5	**Black**	uniface
BL 8	£10	**Black**	uniface

THIRD ISSUE – 1751 *to* 1762

Pallas vignette

In October 1751 new 10s, £1 and £5 notes were issued with the Pallas vignette on them. Pallas was well chosen - she is the Greek Goddess of Weaving as well as Wisdom - and appears seated on a bale of flax, a weaver's shuttle in one hand and linen yarn in the other. In some vignettes she sits next to a bleaching field with a ship on the horizon. The promissory text was unchanged and continued to have the additional words '*value received in goods*'. A revised watermark was also adopted. The first reference to the paper mill used to produce the paper for the notes came in 1754 when an order for new notes was placed with the Springfield Paper Mill near Lasswade. The first mention of an engraver is in 1758 when a Mr Cooper asked to take the £1 plates home for him to work on them. The request was denied. In August 1759 a new paper supplier was engaged, the price of paper from Redhall Paper Mills being 1s 8d per 100 sheets compared to the 2s 6d charged by the Springfield mill. An initial order of 43,000 sheets for 10s, £1 and £5 notes indicates how issue volumes were rising but the mill put its prices up to 2s per 100 sheets four months later.

The earliest recorded surviving note of the British Linen Company is a £1 note with the handwritten date 6th September 1754, though probably not issued until some years later (the minutes record that a final issue of notes with this date was agreed in May 1770). It is illustrated in Malcolm's history and Graham but its present whereabouts are unknown. '*Linen*' is spelt '*Linnen*' but it is not known if this occurred on all these early notes.

By 1762 total note issuance had reached:

10s	38,400 notes	128	books of 300 notes each
£1	33,600 notes	112	books of 300 notes each
£5	4,750 notes	19	books of 250 notes each
£10	250 notes	1	book of 250 notes

BL 9   10s   Black Pallas vignette Dated by hand uniface

BL 10   £1   Black Pallas vignette Dated by hand uniface
                     6 Sep 1754   **RARE**

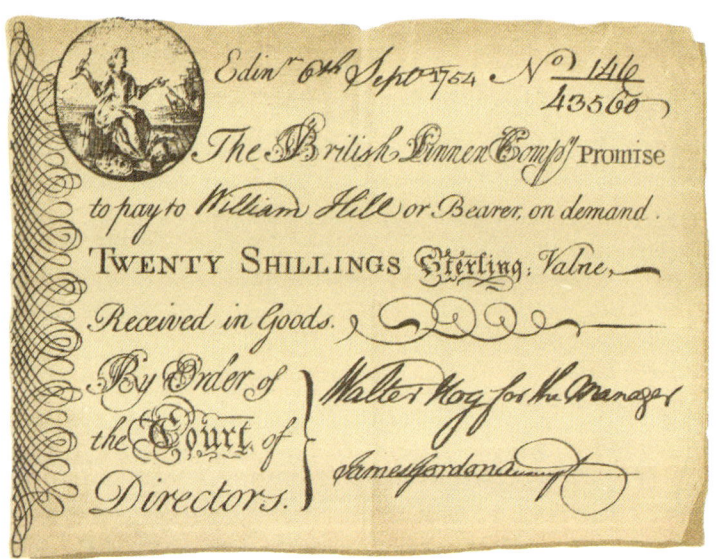

BL 10 Illustrated in Malcolm (whereabouts unknown)

BL 11   £5   Black Pallas vignette Dated by hand uniface
                     6 Sep 1754

FOURTH ISSUE – 1762 to 1765

Option Clause

In June 1762 the British Linen Company felt compelled to follow suit when they realised that not only the two 'Chartered' banks (i.e. the Bank of Scotland and the Royal Bank) but also most private bank note issuers had adopted the notorious Option Clause, whereby notes were payable either on demand or at the issuer's option six months after presentation (plus interest). The Company was at a clear disadvantage and quickly commissioned **Andrew Bell**, an established Edinburgh engraver who also engraved notes for the Royal Bank, to prepare new 10s, £1 and £5 notes with the option clause. By 1764 note total note circulation was capped at £80,000. The issue of 10s notes was discontinued in April 1765 following a change in the law. No issued option notes are known to have survived.

Option clause note issuance:

	10s	18,600 notes	62 books of 300 notes each
	£1	63,900 notes	213 books of 300 notes each
	£5	6,850 notes	13 books of 250 & 12 books of 300 notes each

BL 12	10s	**Pallas vignette** **Option clause** printed date uniface 1 Jun 1763	
		Proof	**RARE**

BL 13	£1	**Pallas vignette** **Option clause** printed date uniface 5 Jul 1762 1 Jun 1763	
		Proof undated	**RARE**

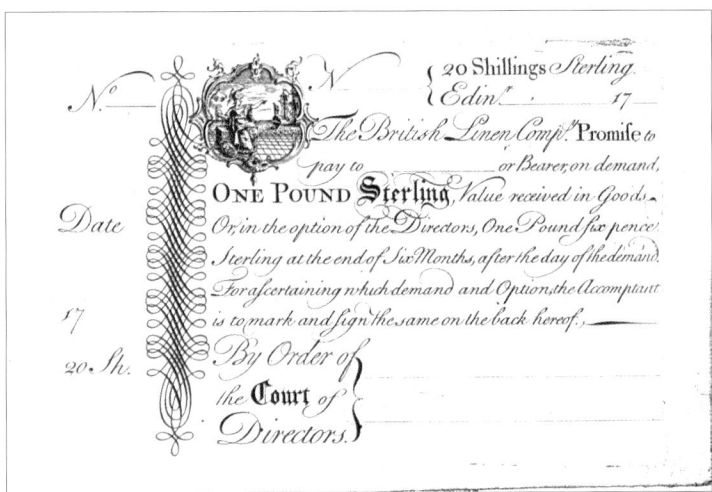

BL 13 Proof Option clause note

BL 14	£5	**Pallas vignette** **Option clause** printed date uniface 1 Jun 1763

FIFTH ISSUE – 1765 *to* 1815

Demand Notes Pallas vignette with panel of thistles

After the option clause was prohibited new notes payable to the bearer on demand were clearly required. The £1 note from the pre-option clause issue was re-used initially, with another 7,200 being printed. New notes, now without the words '*value received in goods*' were however quickly ordered, starting a long lasting series during which several new denominations were added. The words '*value received*' remained on some notes but gradually disappeared. The transition from linen manufacture and trading to pure banking was decided on in 1763 and took place gradually in the years thereafter. Better relationships with the major banks were established, these earlier having often refused to accept the Company's notes, while the Company's note issue continued to grow.

By 1796 the average total notes in issuance had reached £218,886 with these notes being in circulation for an average of forty-five days. An inventory of outstanding notes dated prior to August 1781 was carried out in 1803 and found that these totalled £2,112 12s 3d, this odd sum reflecting the fact that on some mutilated notes only a fraction of the face value was paid out. Some of this total was eventually written off (to profit) on the assumption the notes had been lost or destroyed.

For the first time a 1 Guinea note was issued, appearing in 1768. From 1773 plate letters were introduced on 1 Guinea notes, starting with plate B. From 1770 onwards there appear to have been frequent changes of paper suppliers, more than one of which may have been supplying paper at the same time: Polton Paper Mill in 1770, London-based Herbert & Durnford in 1774, John Balfour & Co, Edinburgh in 1777, London-based Wright, Gill & Co in 1780 and Charles Cowan of Penicuik in 1783. For a trial period in 1772 notes distributed to the Company's agents were marked in red ink to ascertain how long they stayed in circulation and hence their profitability.

Stamp duty was payable on new notes of over 1 Guinea from 1st August 1783 and a dry (i.e. embossed) stamp applied to each note. Notes with earlier dates but not issued until after that date also had to be stamped (e.g. £5 notes dated 1st August 1780). £1 notes had to be stamped from July 1799. From December 1804 a further change in the Stamp Act restricted the validity of a note to three years from the date of issue, resulting in all notes being dated by hand thereafter. There is only one recorded exception to this, the £2 note with the printed date 11th October 1808.

In 1774 a forgery of £1 notes led to those dated 6th September 1770 being withdrawn and the design amended. Forgeries were a constant problem, especially of £1 and 1 Guinea notes. The minutes record in full an advertisement inserted in January 1774 in the Edinburgh Courant, Mercury & Advertiser newspapers:

'*The British Linen Company give notice that a forgery has appeared of their £1 notes dated 6th Sept 1770. The forged notes are done on common paper, the figure of the woman & ship are ill executed and appears faint and the Strokes of the letters in the Copperplate print are less full or broad than in the real ones. The Waving Watermark round the edges of the real notes is imperfectly imitated by draughts with an instrument, which are so deep in the forged notes that have already appeared as to cut the paper in some places quite through. The words of the Watermark in the Real notes are 'BRITISH', 'LINEN' vertical, L under the H, 'COMPANY' upside-down, C adjacent to N, forming three sides of a square. And these can be easily distinguished from the forged notes by holding them to the light when the word LINEN which runs across the note appears distinctly. The Seal is also attempted to be imitated but very imperfectly. If any person can give information so as the Forger or issuer of these notes may be traced he shall be amply rewarded and his name concealed if desired. And any person or persons who shall apprehend the forger so as he may be brought to Justice shall upon his conviction be paid £100 stg by the said Linen Company.*'

The Bank Suspension period was imposed on 1st March 1797 as a result of the Napoleonic Wars, prohibiting banks from paying out in gold or silver. Legislation was passed permitting the issuance of notes for sums under £1. As a result the Company joined several other Scottish banks in issuing 5s notes for a few years until 1801. Their issuing instructions were recorded as follows:

'These Notes are not to be issued for any other purpose than that of giving Change to the holder of the British Linen Company Notes, they are not to be given to any person in exchange for other Bank Notes nor are they to be given to any Public Company or Banking Society without value being paid for them in Specie.'

In 1765 Andrew Bell was appointed to engrave the £1 and 1 Guinea notes but none carry his imprint. Other engravers used included Edwin Butterworth, Mr Farmer and Mr Ellis (further details unknown) while James Kirkwood was contracted to engrave a new plate for the £5 note in 1783. Several new denominations were added during this long and complex series, including £10 and £20 notes in 1783 and a £50 note in 1789, all engraved by James Kirkwood. A £100 note was also added in 1789. Very few £50 and £100 notes were issued. 1798 sees the first mention of 2 Guineas note and in 1808 a £2 note was issued for the first and only time. The first recorded engraver's imprint on any notes is that of John Beugo on the 1 Guinea note of 1799.

All the notes in this series feature the Pallas vignette in an ornate frame with some anti-forgery ornamentation in the form of a single panel of thistles. A number of detail changes took place, the principal one being the introduction of a simplified circular vignette of Pallas to replace the earlier more ornate frame and image. The new version was gradually standardised across all denominations. All notes are uniface and have an impression of the Company's seal. Issued notes will have a 'BLC' or 'BRITISH LINEN CO' watermark.

Notes are listed in order of denomination rather than the order in which the different values first appeared.

BL 15　　**5s**　　**Pay David Sime Pallas vignette** in ornate frame
　　　　　　　　　Scrollwork across top   127 x 90mm
　　　　　　　　　31 Mar 1797 printed date　　　　　　　　　　　　　　**From 1000 F**

　　　　　　　　　Unissued　　　　　　　　　　　　　　　　　　　　**From 800 VF**

BL 15 1797

BL 16	**5s**	Pay David Sime *Printer:* **J Beugo** **Circular Pallas vignette** **Panel of thistles** across top 1 Jan 1800 printed date	**From 1000 F**

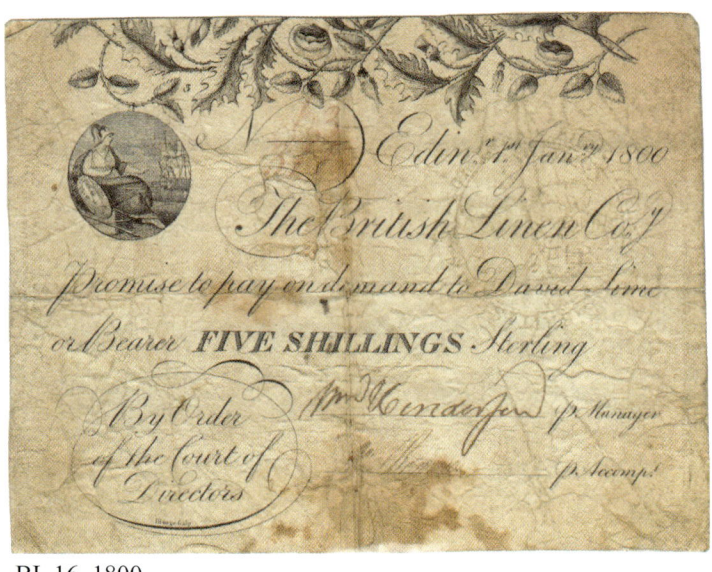

BL 16 1800

BL 17a	**£1**	Twenty Shillings **Panel of thistles** across top **Scrollwork** panel left 1 Aug 1765 printed date	**RARE**
BL 17b	**£1**	Similar to BL 17a **Pay James Rowe** 6 Sep 1770 printed date	**RARE**
BL 18	**£1**	**Circular Pallas vignette** **Panel of thistles** across top 13 May 1774 & 2 Aug 1781 printed dates	**RARE**
BL 19a	**£1**	Pay David Sime Engraved by J Beugo Twenty Shillings in Gothic **Circular Pallas vignette** **Panel of thistles** on left 2 Dec 1799 printed date	**RARE**
BL 19b	**£1**	**Similar** to BL 19a **Pay David Sime** 1805 to 1811 Dated by hand	**RARE**
BL 19c	**£1**	Similar to BL 19a **Pay William Fleming** 1811 Dated by hand	**RARE**
		Forgery 1811	**From 200 F**

BL 20a   1gn   **Pallas vignette** upper centre   **One Guinea** upper right
                       Panel of thistles across top
                       5 Apr 1768   printed date   No plate letter   **RARE**

BL 20a   1768   (heavily trimmed)

BL 20b   1gn   Similar to BL 20a   Pay James Rowe   Minor design changes
                       6 Sep 1770   printed date   plate E   **RARE**

BL 20b   1770

BL 20c	**1gn**	**Similar to BL 20a Pay William Fleming**		
		1 May 1778 printed date	plate K	**RARE**
		Pull (2006) plate K		**From 25 UNC**

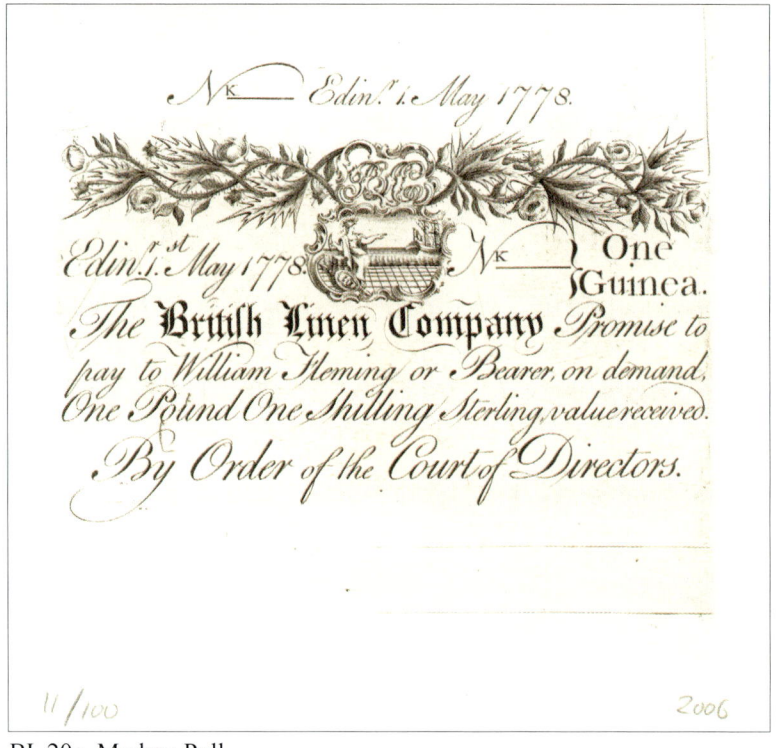

BL 20c Modern Pull

BL 20d	**1gn**	**BLCo monogram Circular Pallas vignette** upper centre	
		Panel of thistles across top with **BLCo monogram**	
		1 Aug 1783 printed date	**RARE**

In 1799 the 1 Guinea note was reworked and the revised design carries the printer's imprint for the first time. The watermark 'BLC' is to be found on the lower right of the note.

BL 21a　　1gn　　**One Guinea in Gothic** *Imprint:* **J Beugo**
　　　　　　　　　Circular Pallas vignette upper left **Panel of thistles** across top
　　　　　　　　　Payee & serials in red
　　　　　　　　　　2 Dec 1799 printed date　　　　　　plate D　　　　　　　　**From 2000 F**

BL 21a 1799

BL 21b　　1gn　　**Similar to BL 21a Pay William Rennie**
　　　　　　　　　Dated by hand　　　　　　　　　　　　　　　　　　　　　　　**From 2000 F**

BL 21c　　1gn　　**Similar to BL 21a Pay William Fleming**
　　　　　　　　　Amended panel of thistles with 1808 in oval
　　　　　　　　　　1808 printed date Oct 180 (completed by hand)　　plate D F　　**From 2000 F**

　　　　　　　　　Specimen plate F　　　　　　　　　　　　　　　　　　　　**From 600 EF**

BL 21d　　1gn　　**Similar to BL 21a Pay William Fleming**
　　　　　　　　　Larger panel of thistles with small oval **BLCo monogram**
　　　　　　　　　　1815 Dated by hand　　　　　　　　　　　　　　　　　　　**From 2000 F**

　　　　　　　　　Forgery 1815 to 1819　　　　　　　　　　　　　　　　　　**From 200 F**

BL 21d Forgery 1815

BL 22	£2	Pay George Mill Value received *Imprint:* J Beugo		
		Circular Pallas vignette Panel of thistles on left		
		11 Oct 1808 printed date	plate A	**RARE**
		Pull undated (2006)	No plate letter	**From 25 UNC**

BL 22 1808

BL 23 2gn **Pay William Fleming TWO GUINEAS** in capitals
Circular Pallas vignette Panel of thistles on left
1811 Dated by hand   **RARE**

BL 24 £5 **Pay James Rowe Panel of thistles** on left
3 Sep 1766 printed date
6 Sep 1770 printed date   **RARE**

In December 1802 the minutes refer to a forged £5 note discovered in London. John Mackay and John Pyper were '*suspected of having uttered the forged note ... and had been traced and found they had taken passage on board a vessel from London to Dundee*'. While the two were apprehended, James Webster, a cabin boy on the ship, reported that he had found a bundle in the bed that Mackay had slept in. Of these twelve notes (all with the printed date 1st August 1780) six were signed and six unsigned. The strong presumption is that the signatures had been forged, not the notes themselves, most of which appear to be impressed with genuine seals and revenue stamps. Several have come on to the market over the years, all annotated with a declaration on the reverse dated 17th December 1802. They carry the watermark 'BRITISH LINEN Co'

BL 25a £5 **Circular Pallas vignette Panel of thistles** on left
Payee inserted by hand
1 Aug 1780 printed date   plate B
1 Aug 1783 printed date   **From 1500 F**

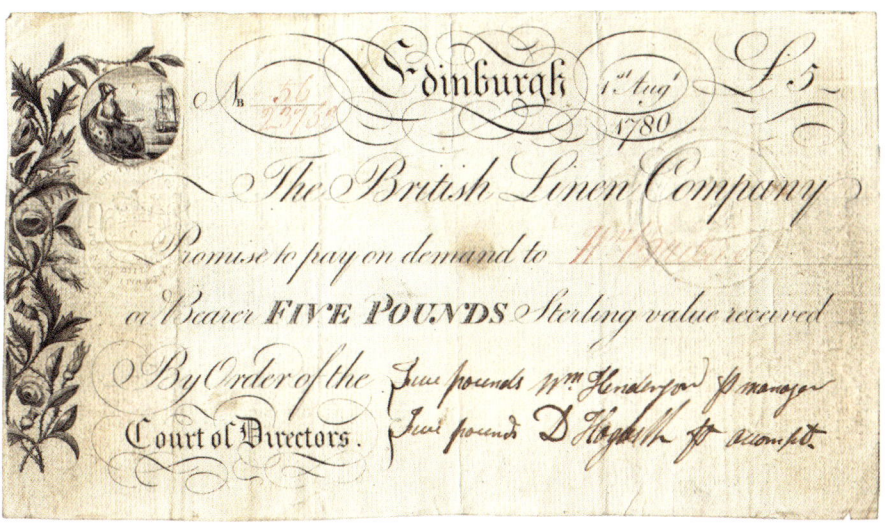

BL 25a 1780

BL 25b £5 **Similar to BL 25a** *Printer:* **J Beugo**
1806 year printed as 180   plate A   **From 1500 F**

BL 25b 1806

BL 26 £10 **1 Aug 1783** printed date
No issued notes recorded, design unconfirmed

BL 27 £20 **1 Aug 1783** printed date
No issued notes recorded, design unconfirmed

BL 28 £50 **1 Sep 1789** printed date
No issued notes recorded, design unconfirmed

BL 29 £100 **1 Sep 1789** printed date
No issued notes recorded, design unconfirmed

BL 30 **£100** **Circular Pallas vignette Panel of thistles** on left
Dated by hand

Specimen undated (1810) **RARE**

BL 30 £100 Specimen for Stamp Office 1810

SIXTH ISSUE – 1819 *to* 1824

Vignette of two females with lion and unicorn

This short lived design has been confirmed only on the £1 and 1 Guinea denominations though it is possible others were prepared. These are the last notes to be engraved on copper plate and most carry the imprints of **Forrester** as designer and **John Beugo** as engraver. The design is dominated by a central vignette of two females with lion and unicorn and a reworked panel of thistles to the left. The 1821 £5, £20 and £100 notes referred to by Douglas are believed to be notes of the previous issue. This was the last time Beugo engraved notes for the Company and in December 1823 he was given a 'present' of £20. He died in 1842.

A £1 essay has survived displaying elements of this design. It may have been engraved on steel plate and although there is no imprint it could possibly have been prepared by **Perkins & Heath**.

BL 31 **£1** **Pay David Dow**
Vignette flanked by Twenty & Shillings in gothic script
1821 Dated & numbered by hand **RARE**

Essay **From 350 EF**

Forgery 1820 to 1824 plate F **From 250 F**

BL 32	1gn	**Pay David Dow Vignette** with **ONE GUINEA** above in capitals	
		1821 Dated & numbered by hand plate A	**RARE**
		Proof *Printer:* **Forrester & Suffield**	From 350 EF
		Forgery 1819 to 1821	From 250 F
		Pull no plate letter (2007)	From 25 UNC

BL 32 Forgery 1819

FIRST PERKINS BACON ISSUE – 1822 *to* 1860

Royal Arms Steel plate engraving by Perkins & Heath

This issue marks the start of the **Perkins & Heath** (later **Perkins Bacon & Petch**) designs, the first to be prepared on hardened steel plates. The basics of the designs lasted right through to 1970 despite two changes of printer, size reductions and new colours. The initial designs were uniface and in black only. They featured the Royal Arms top centre flanked by value panels, with an ornate panel down the left hand side incorporating a small vignette of Britannia with shield and lion.

An inventory of notes issued prior to 1850 and still outstanding was drawn up in July 1881:

Five Shillings	1797 & 1800	£1,041 13s 9d
Ten Shillings		£401 10s
One Pound	1 Nov 1849 & before	£12,230 7s 8d
One Guinea	1 Nov 1838 & before	£2,480 2s
Two Pounds	11 Oct 1808 & before	£256
Two Guineas	2 Dec 1811	£68 5s
Five Pounds	1 Jul 1848 & before	£2,125
Ten Pounds	1 Jul 1848 & before	£435
Twenty Pounds	1 Jul 1848 & before	£500
Fifty Pounds	17 Sep 1789	£50
Total		**£19,587 18s 5d**

The Company then '*Ordered that a sum of £18,032 18s 5d be written to the debit of said Note Accounts and a like sum carried to the credit of the Current year's Profit and Loss Account leaving a sum of £2,368 10s 6d at the credit of the Note Accounts above mentioned.*'

Notes of the 1822 series were payable to bearer or a named official and carried two hand-written signatures. Prefix and serials were initially applied by hand but were later printed. All notes of this issue are dated by hand. Of the named officials Alexander Blair was Joint Manager until July 1832 when he left to join the Bank of Scotland; James Wilson was appointed Accountant in 1836, later became Cashier and retired in 1852 after 53 years with the Company; and William Spence was promoted to Secretary in 1859 and retired in 1871.

The 1 Guinea note was in issue only for a few years and survivors are rare. Total circulation continued to rise and averaged £458,886 by 1836, slightly higher than the Authorised Circulation under the 1845 Act. Proof notes from the extensive Perkins Bacon archive have enabled us to follow the development of this and subsequent issues. The printers' imprint progresses from **Perkins & Heath** (1822-1829), to **Perkins & Bacon** (1829-1834), to **Perkins Bacon & Petch** (1834-1852) and to **Perkins Bacon & Co** (after 1852). Dates of changes to the imprints will vary and not all imprints have been recorded on every denomination. A number of poor forgeries of the £1 note have been seen.

BL 33a	£1	**Pay Alex^r Blair** *Printer:* **Perkins & Heath** 1826 to 1829 Dated & numbered by hand	**RARE**
		Proof undated	**From 250 EF**
		Forgeries 1826 to 1829	**From 100 F**
BL 33b	£1	**Pay James Wilson** *Printer:* **Perkins Bacon & Petch** 1842 Dated & numbered by hand	**RARE**
		Proof undated	**From 250 EF**

BL 33b Proof payable to James Wilson

BL 33c   £1   **Pay William Spence Handsigned** Manager & Accountant
Printer: **Perkins Bacon & Co**
Printed prefix/serials on background panels
9 Sep 1853 A 78/296 Dated by hand   **From 2500 F**

Proof undated   **From 250 EF**

BL 33c 1853

BL 34   1gn   **Pay Alexander Blair** (not abbreviated) *Printer:* **Perkins & Heath**
1822 Dated & numbered by hand   **RARE**

Proof undated   **From 300 EF**

BL 34 1822

BL 35a	**£5**	**Pay Alex^r Blair** *Printer:* **Perkins & Heath** Dated & numbered by hand		
		Proof undated		From 300 EF

BL 35b	**£5**	**Pay William Spence** *Printer:* **Perkins, Bacon & Co**		
		Proof undated		From 300 EF

BL 36a	**£10**	**Pay Alex^r Blair** *Printer:* **Perkins & Heath** Dated & numbered by hand		
		Proof undated		From 300 EF

BL 36b	**£10**	**Pay William Spence** *Printer:* **Perkins, Bacon & Co**		
		Proof undated		From 300 EF

BL 37a	**£20**	**Pay Alex^r Blair** *Printer:* **Perkins & Heath** Dated & numbered by hand		
		Proof undated		From 300 EF

BL 37a Proof payable to Alex^r Blair

BL 37b	**£20**	**Pay William Spence** *Printer:* **Perkins, Bacon & Co**	
		Proof undated	From 300 EF

BL 38	**£100**	**Pay Alex^r Blair** *Printer:* **Perkins & Heath** Dated & numbered by hand	
		Proof undated	From 300 EF

SECOND PERKINS BACON ISSUE – 1860 *to* 1871

Blue with Red 'B. L. C^o' panel Notes payable to William Spence or bearer

The designs are essentially unchanged but the basic plate is now printed in blue with a red panel with 'B.L.Co.' overlaid across the centre of the notes. A curiosity of the £1 and £100 notes is the addition of two small florettes (called 'buttons' in Company correspondence) either side of the Royal Arms, starting in 1865 on the £1 and 1866 on the £100. No reason has yet been established for their appearance. From about 1865 small plate numbers can be observed on most notes in the upper left hand corner just outside the border. A defect in the blue ink led to a change of paper in 1862. The paper supplier throughout this period was I H Saunders & Co Ltd, London.

All notes have printed prefix and serials while printed dates were first introduced during this issue. All notes continue to be signed by hand p Manager and p Accountant. At some point prior to 1870 (and possibly earlier as the use of the word 'Bank' started to appear on Company documents as early as 1828) the watermark was amended to 'BRITISH LINEN COMPANY BANK'. Printers' imprint is **Perkins Bacon & Co.**

BL 39a	**£1**	**Pay William Spence** **No florettes** Dated by hand	
		Proof undated Black	From 200 EF

BL 39b	**£1**	**Pay William Spence** **No florettes** printed date 1 Aug 1863 H 4/69	From 2000 F
		The following **Proof** notes have been recorded: Black or Blue, no red panel Undated 4 Jun 1860 1 Nov 1860 1861 (year only printed) 6 Apr 1861 1 Mar 1863 1 Feb 1864 4 Oct 1864 2 Jan 1865 1 Apr 1865 2 Aug 1865	From 200 EF

BL 39b No florettes

BL 39c   £1   **Pay William Spence Two Florettes** printed date
              4 Feb 1870   U 111/400   **From 2000 F**

The following **Proof** notes have been recorded: Black or Blue, no red panel
1 Jan 1866   2 Apr 1867   3 Feb 1868   4 Mar 1869
4 Feb 1870   6 Mar 1871   **From 200 EF**

BL 39c Two florettes

BL 40 £5 **Pay William Spence**

The following **Proof** notes have been recorded: Black or Blue, no red panel
Undated   7 Jun 1864   2 Jan 1865   1 Jul 1865
3 Feb 1868   1 Jan 1869   1 Mar 1870   3 Aug 1871   **From 200 EF**

Specimen 3 Aug 1871   **From 500 VF**

BL 40 Specimen pen cancelled

BL 41 £10 **Pay William Spence**

The following **Proof** notes have been recorded: in Black
Undated   7 Oct 1861   1 Feb 1867   1 May 1869
6 May 1870   1 Nov 1871   **From 200 EF**

Specimen 1 Nov 1871   **From 500 VF**

BL 42 £20 **Pay William Spence**

The following **Proof** notes have been recorded: in Black
Undated   3 Jan 1865   1 Jan 1867   2 Mar 1868
1 Apr 1869   4 May 1870   3 Aug 1871   **From 200 EF**

BL 43a £100 Pay William Spence No florettes

> The following **Proof** notes have been recorded: in Black
> Undated   1 Jul 1862   1 Jan 1863   1 Jun 1863
> 3 Dec 1863   1 Nov 1864   1 Feb 1865   **From 200 EF**

BL 43b £100 Pay William Spence Two Florettes

> The following **Proof** notes have been recorded: in Black
> 2 Oct 1865   18 Dec 1865   1 Jun 1868   1 Apr 1869
> 3 May 1870   3 Aug 1871   **From 200 EF**

BL 43b Proof Two florettes

THIRD PERKINS BACON ISSUE – 1871 to 1904

Blue with Red 'B. L. Cº' panel   Notes payable to bearer

In December 1871 the board agreed that notes should no longer be made payable to a named official or bearer but to the bearer only, a decision possibly prompted by the retirement of William Spence. The small florettes on the £1 note were discontinued about 1883 but they continued on the £100 note throughout this issue (and indeed until 1933). Further problems with the blue ink became evident, with the blue turning almost black on some notes. Improved quality ink was introduced in 1875. From 1878 the use of the Company's seal was discontinued.

From 1886 one of the two signatures was printed on the £1 notes, a decision occasioned by the continuing rise in issue volumes. Prior to this, notes carried two hand-written signatures for the Manager and Accountant. The watermark on all denominations remained 'BRITISH LINEN COMPANY BANK' but on the £1 note had been amended to an ornate 'B L Cº / ONE POUND' by 1889.

The full note registers are available from 1872 but earlier ones have not been located and may have been destroyed. Each prefix of the £1 notes comprised 150 books of 1,000 notes each. Prefix letter J not used. Printers' imprint is **Perkins Bacon & Co** until some time after May 1887 when the firm took on limited liability and became **Perkins Bacon & Co Ltd**. Some early notes will have initial zeroes on the sequential numbers (e.g. W 1/001 rather than W 1/1) but the initial zeroes were later dropped.

BL 44a	**£1**	**Handsigned**	Manager & Accot.	**Two florettes**				
		2 Feb 1872	W	1/1	–	150/1000	150,000	
		2 Nov 1872	X	1/1	–	150/1000	150,000	
		4 Jul 1873	Y	1/1	–	150/1000	150,000	
		1 Jun 1874	Z	1/1	–	150/1000	150,000	
		1 May 1875	A	1/1	–	150/1000	150,000	
		2 Mar 1876	B	1/1	–	150/1000	150,000	
		1 Nov 1876	C	1/1	–	150/1000	150,000	
		3 May 1877	D	1/1	–	150/1000	150,000	
		5 Nov 1877	E	1/1	–	150/1000	150,000	
		2 Nov 1878	F	1/1	–	150/1000	150,000	
		2 Jan 1879	G	1/1	–	150/1000	150,000	
		1 Aug 1879	H	1/1	–	150/1000	150,000	
		2 Jul 1880	I	1/1	–	150/1000	150,000	
		2 Feb 1881	K	1/1	–	150/1000	150,000	
		3 Oct 1881	L	1/1	–	150/1000	150,000	
		1 Apr 1882	M	1/1	–	150/1000	150,000	
		1 Jan 1883	N	1/1	–	150/1000	150,000	**From 1500 F**

The following **Proof** notes have been recorded: Black or Blue, no red panel
Undated   2 Feb 1872   2 Nov 1872   4 Jul 1873
1 Jun 1874   1 May 1875   2 Mar 1876   1 Nov 1876
2 Nov 1878   1 Aug 1879   2 Feb 1881   **From 200 EF**

BL 44a Two florettes

BL 44b	£1	**Handsigned**	Manager & Acco!	**No florettes**			
		2 May 1883	O	1/1	-	150/1000	150,000
		1 Dec 1883	P	1/1	-	150/1000	150,000
		15 Apr 1884	Q	1/1	-	150/1000	150,000
		8 Nov 1884	R	1/1	-	150/1000	150,000
		16 May 1885	S	1/1	-	150/1000	150,000
		17 Oct 1885	T	1/1	-	150/1000	150,000

From 1500 F

The following **Proof** notes have been recorded: Black or Blue, no red panel
15 Apr 1884   17 Oct 1885

From 200 EF

BL 44b No florettes

BL 44c	£1	**John S K Maclean** Printed signature p Manager
		Handsigned p Acco!

24 May 1886   U   1/1   -   150/1000   150,000   **RARE**

The following **Proof** note has been recorded: Black, no red panel
24 May 1886   **From 250 EF**

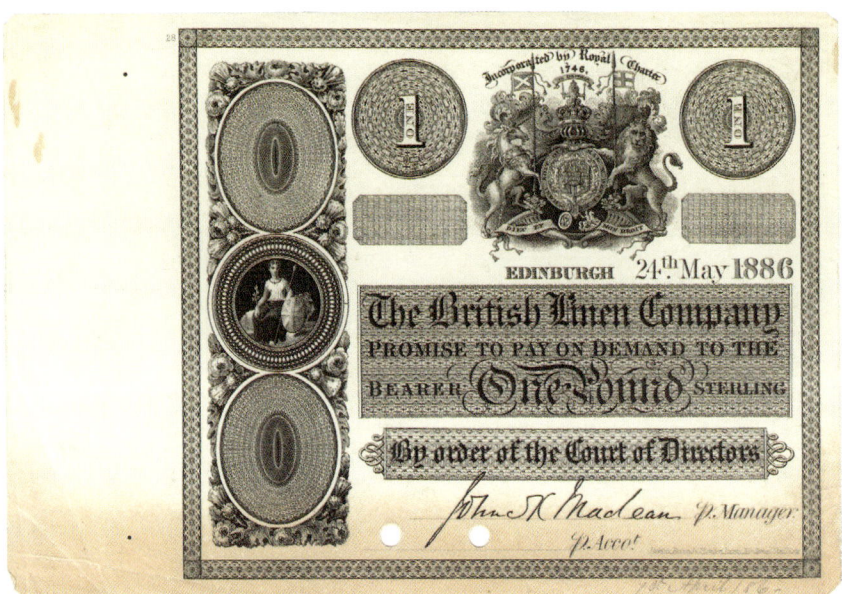

BL 44c Proof Maclean signature

BL 44d	£1	**P Martine** Printed signature p Manager **Handsigned** p Acco!
		Printer: **Perkins Bacon & Co**

25 Jan 1887   V   1/1   -   150/1000   150,000
 7 Apr 1887   W   1/1   -   150/1000   150,000
10 Feb 1888   X   1/1   -   150/1000   150,000   **From 1000 F**

The following **Proof** notes have been recorded: Black or Blue, no red panel
25 Jan 1887   7 Apr 1887   **From 150 EF**

BL 44e	£1	**P Martine** Printed signature p Manager **Handsigned** p Acco!
		Printer: **Perkins Bacon & Co Ld**

12 Sep 1888   Y   1/1   -   150/1000   150,000
14 Mar 1889   Z   1/1   -   150/1000   150,000
12 Oct 1889   A   1/1   -   150/1000   150,000
20 Dec 1889   B   1/1   -   150/1000   150,000
30 Jun 1890   C   1/1   -   150/1000   150,000
22 Jul 1890   D   1/1   -   150/1000   150,000
10 Sep 1891   E   1/1   -   150/1000   150,000
10 Mar 1892   F   1/1   -   150/1000   150,000
20 Jul 1892   G   1/1   -   150/1000   150,000
24 Jan 1893   H   1/1   -   150/1000   150,000

BL 44e *Cont*

Date	Letter			Range	Count	
17 Aug 1893	I	1/1	-	150/1000	150,000	
22 Feb 1894	K	1/1	-	150/1000	150,000	
23 May 1894	L	1/1	-	150/1000	150,000	
22 Nov 1894	M	1/1	-	150/1000	150,000	
22 Apr 1895	N	1/1	-	150/1000	150,000	
24 Jan 1896	O	1/1	-	150/1000	150,000	
24 Mar 1896	P	1/1	-	150/1000	150,000	
22 Oct 1896	Q	1/1	-	150/1000	150,000	
18 Dec 1896	R	1/1	-	150/1000	150,000	
26 Feb 1897	S	1/1	-	150/1000	150,000	
30 Nov 1897	T	1/1	-	150/1000	150,000	
18 Jun 1898	U	1/1	-	150/1000	150,000	
26 Aug 1898	V	1/1	-	150/1000	150,000	
22 Sep 1898	W	1/1	-	150/1000	150,000	
28 Mar 1899	X	1/1	-	150/1000	150,000	
23 Aug 1899	Y	1/1	-	150/1000	150,000	
25 Oct 1899	Z	1/1	-	150/1000	150,000	**From 1000 F**

The following **Proof** notes have been recorded: Black or Blue, no red panel

12 Sep 1888   14 Mar 1889   12 Oct 1889   20 Dec 1889
30 Jun 1890   22 Jul 1890   10 Sep 1891   10 Mar 1892
24 Jan 1893   22 Feb 1894   22 Nov 1894   24 Jan 1896
24 Mar 1896   26 Feb 1897   18 Jun 1898   22 Sep 1898
23 Aug 1899   25 Oct 1899   **From 150 EF**

BL 44e Martine signature

BL 44f	£1	C Hogg Printed signature p Manager **Handsigned** p Acco!					
		23 Jan 1900	A	1/1	- 150/1000	150,000	
		10 Apr 1900	B	1/1	- 150/1000	150,000	
		15 Sep 1900	C	1/1	- 150/1000	150,000	
		12 Nov 1900	D	1/1	- 150/1000	150,000	
		1 Feb 1901	E	1/1	- 150/1000	150,000	
		15 May 1901	F	1/1	- 150/1000	150,000	
		1 Oct 1901	G	1/1	- 150/1000	150,000	
		9 Dec 1901	H	1/1	- 150/1000	150,000	
		4 Mar 1902	I	1/1	- 150/1000	150,000	
		15 Jul 1902	K	1/1	- 150/1000	150,000	
		9 Aug 1902	L	1/1	- 150/1000	150,000	
		2 Jan 1903	M	1/1	- 150/1000	150,000	
		3 Jun 1903	N	1/1	- 150/1000	150,000	
		1 Dec 1903	O	1/1	- 150/1000	150,000	
		6 Apr 1904	P	1/1	- 150/1000	150,000	**From 850 F**

The following **Proof** notes have been recorded: Black or Blue, no red panel
23 Jan 1900   12 Nov 1900   1 Feb 1901   15 May 1901
9 Dec 1901   4 Mar 1902   15 Jul 1902   2 Jan 1903
1 Dec 1903   **From 150 EF**

Specimen   1 Feb 1901 E 140/327 & E 141/235   **From 600 EF**

BL 44f Hogg signature

Issued notes with the printed signature of F Gordon Brown are very scarce with only two recorded. Specimens and proofs are however regularly seen.

BL 44g	£1	F Gordon Brown Printed signature p Manager **Handsigned** p Acco!					
		31 May 1904	Q	1/1	- 150/1000	150,000	**From 2000 F**

The following **Proof** note has been recorded: in Blue
31 May 1904 Q   **From 250 EF**

Specimen   31 May 1904 no prefix/serials & Q 40/396   **From 350 EF**

BL 44g F Gordon Brown signature

The £5 issues comprise 20 books of 500 notes each per prefix. Possibly as few as three issued notes have survived.

BL 45a   **£5**   **Handsigned** Manager & Acco!
                            Printer: **Perkins Bacon & Co**

2 Nov 1872	K 1/1	-	20/500	10,000
2 Apr 1874	L 1/1	-	20/500	10,000
1 Feb 1876	M 1/1	-	20/500	10,000
1 Feb 1877	N 1/1	-	20/500	10,000
4 Jun 1878	O 1/1	-	20/500	10,000
5 Nov 1878	P 1/1	-	20/500	10,000
4 Jul 1879	Q 1/1	-	20/500	10,000
2 Aug 1880	R 1/1	-	20/500	10,000
7 Oct 1881	S 1/1	-	20/500	10,000
1 Sep 1882	T 1/1	-	20/500	10,000
2 Apr 1883	U 1/1	-	20/500	10,000
6 Mar 1884	V 1/1	-	20/500	10,000
8 Nov 1884	W 1/1	-	20/500	10,000
15 Sep 1885	X 1/1	-	20/500	10,000
15 Feb 1886	Y 1/1	-	20/500	10,000
26 Oct 1886	Z 1/1	-	20/500	10,000
4 May 1887	A/2 1/1	-	20/500	10,000 **RARE**

The following **Proof** notes have been recorded: Black or Blue, no red panel
2 Nov 1872   2 Apr 1874   **From 200 EF**

BL 45b	£5	**Handsigned** p Manager & p Acco!					
		Printer: **Perkins Bacon & Co Ld**					
		10 Jan 1889	B/2	1/1	-	20/500	10,000
		14 Mar 1890	C/2	1/1	-	20/500	10,000
		10 Oct 1890	D/2	1/1	-	20/500	10,000
		22 Aug 1891	E/2	1/1	-	20/500	10,000
		20 Jun 1892	F/2	1/1	-	20/500	10,000
		23 Feb 1894	G/2	1/1	-	20/500	10,000
		27 Dec 1894	H/2	1/1	-	20/500	10,000
		18 Jan 1896	I/2	1/1	-	20/500	10,000
		20 Apr 1897	K/2	1/1	-	20/500	10,000
		28 Mar 1898	L/2	1/1	-	20/500	10,000
		16 Feb 1899	M/2	1/1	-	20/500	10,000
		22 May 1899	N/2	1/1	-	20/500	10,000
		29 Sep 1899	O/2	1/1	-	20/500	10,000
		15 Mar 1900	P/2	1/1	-	20/500	10,000
		4 Apr 1901	Q/2	1/1	-	20/500	10,000
		14 Oct 1901	R/2	1/1	-	20/500	10,000
		28 Feb 1902	S/2	1/1	-	20/500	10,000
		30 Jan 1903	T/2	1/1	-	20/500	10,000
		24 Jul 1903	U/2	1/1	-	20/500	10,000
		15 Aug 1904	V/2	1/1	-	20/500	10,000	**From 2000 F**

The following **Proof** note has been recorded: Black or Blue, no red panel
18 Jan 1896   **From 200 EF**

Specimen 14 Oct 1901 no prefix & R/2   **From 500 EF**

BL 45b 1903

The £10 plates were not modified when Perkins Bacon took on limited liability. 10 books of 500 notes each. Only one issued £10 note is known to have survived, dated 25th October 1898 P 7/175.

BL 46a	**£10**	**Handsigned** Manager & Acco!					
		Printer: **Perkins Bacon & Co**					
		1 Mar 1877	G 1/1	-	10/500	5,000	
		5 Nov 1878	H 1/1	-	10/500	5,000	
		4 Jul 1879	I 1/1	-	10/500	5,000	
		2 Apr 1883	K 1/1	-	10/500	5,000	
		15 Oct 1885	L 1/1	-	10/500	5,000	
		14 Sep 1886	M 1/1	-	10/500	5,000	**RARE**
BL 46b	**£10**	**Similar to BL46a Handsigned** p Manager & p Acco!					
		10 Jun 1890	N 1/1	-	10/500	5,000	
		17 Aug 1894	O 1/1	-	10/500	5,000	
		25 Oct 1898	P 1/1	-	10/500	5,000	
		2 Sep 1901	Q 1/1	-	10/500	5,000	**RARE**

The following **Proof** notes have been recorded: Black or Blue, no red panel
Undated   10 Jun 1890   17 Aug 1894   25 Oct 1898
2 Sep 1901   **From 200 EF**

Specimen 2 Sep 1901 no prefix & Q   **From 500 EF**

BL 46b 1898

Each prefix of the £20 note comprised five books of 500 notes each. Only two issued £20 notes are known to have survived, T/2 4/157 and T/2 5/137, both dated 14th July 1903.

BL 47a   £20   **Handsigned** Manager & Acco!
   Printer: **Perkins Bacon & Co**
1 Nov 1872	L 1/1	-	5/500	2,500
2 Apr 1875	M 1/1	-	5/500	2,500
3 Jan 1876	N 1/1	-	5/500	2,500
date unrecorded	O 1/1	-	5/500	2,500
date unrecorded	P 1/1	-	5/500	2,500
5 Nov 1878	Q 1/1	-	5/500	2,500
4 Jul 1879	R 1/1	-	5/500	2,500
1 Oct 1880	S 1/1	-	5/500	2,500
9 May 1881	T 1/1	-	5/500	2,500
1 Sep 1882	U 1/1	-	5/500	2,500
2 Apr 1883	V 1/1	-	5/500	2,500
9 Jun 1884	W 1/1	-	5/500	2,500
1 Jan 1885	X 1/1	-	5/500	2,500
15 Oct 1885	Y 1/1	-	5/500	2,500
16 Mar 1886	Z 1/1	-	5/500	2,500
6 Sep 1886	A/2 1/1	-	5/500	2,500
8 Jul 1887	B/2 1/1	-	5/500	2,500 **RARE**

The following **Proof** notes have been recorded: Black or Blue, no red panel
1 Nov 1872   2 Apr 1875   3 Jan 1876   8 Jul 1887

Specimen 1 Nov 1872 L   **From 1000 EF**

BL 47b   £20   **Handsigned** p Manager & p Acco!
   Printer: **Perkins Bacon & Co Ld**
12 Aug 1889	C/2 1/1	-	5/500	2,500
14 Oct 1890	D/2 1/1	-	5/500	2,500
10 Sep 1891	E/2 1/1	-	5/500	2,500
20 Nov 1892	F/2 1/1	-	5/500	2,500
24 Nov 1893	G/2 1/1	-	5/500	2,500
22 Feb 1895	H/2 1/1	-	5/500	2,500
15 Jan 1896	I/2 1/1	-	5/500	2,500
30 Jun 1897	K/2 1/1	-	5/500	2,500
23 Aug 1898	L/2 1/1	-	5/500	2,500
28 Feb 1899	M/2 1/1	-	5/500	2,500
29 Sep 1899	N/2 1/1	-	5/500	2,500
1 Oct 1900	O/2 1/1	-	5/500	2,500
16 Apr 1901	P/2 1/1	-	5/500	2,500
31 Aug 1901	Q/2 1/1	-	5/500	2,500
6 Mar 1902	R/2 1/1	-	5/500	2,500
1 May 1903	S/2 1/1	-	5/500	2,500
14 Jul 1903	T/2 1/1	-	5/500	2,500
1 Nov 1904	U/2 1/1	-	5/500	2,500 **RARE**

The following **Proof** notes have been recorded: Black or Blue, no red panel
12 Aug 1889   22 Feb 1895   14 Oct 1890   15 Jan 1896
28 Feb 1899   **From 200 EF**

Specimen undated 31 Aug 1901 no prefix & Q/2   **From 600 EF**

BL 47b 1903

The £100 plates were also modified when Perkins Bacon took on limited liability. One book of 500 notes each per prefix. No issued £100 notes are known to have survived.

BL 48a   **£100** **Handsigned** Manager & Accountant Titles not printed
              Printer: **Perkins Bacon & Co**

	date unrecorded	G	1/1	-	1/500	500
	date unrecorded	H	1/1	-	1/500	500
	7 May 1879	I	1/1	-	1/500	500
	date unrecorded	K	1/1	-	1/500	500
	1 Apr 1882	L	1/1	-	1/500	500
	date unrecorded	M	1/1	-	1/500	500
	date unrecorded	N	1/1	-	1/500	500
	date unrecorded	O	1/1	-	1/500	500
	date unrecorded	P	1/1	-	1/500	500
	date unrecorded	Q	1/1	-	1/500	500
	date unrecorded	R	1/1	-	1/500	500
	1 Nov 1884	S	1/1	-	1/500	500
	date unrecorded	T	1/1	-	1/500	500
	1 Apr 1886	U	1/1	-	1/500	500
	16 Aug 1886	V	1/1	-	1/500	500
	15 Dec 1886	W	1/1	-	1/500	500
	12 Jun 1888	X	1/1	-	1/500	500
	15 May 1889	Y	1/1	-	1/500	500	**RARE**

          Specimen undated no prefix   From 700 EF

BL 48a Specimen

BL 48b   £100   **Handsigned** Manager & Accountant Titles not printed
Printer: **Perkins Bacon & Co Ld**

Date	Prefix	Range	Qty
15 Oct 1889	Z 1/1	- 1/500	500
12 Jun 1890	A/2 1/1	- 1/500	500
10 Sep 1890	B/2 1/1	- 1/500	500
20 Jul 1891	C/2 1/1	- 1/500	500
17 Aug 1892	D/2 1/1	- 1/500	500
20 Jan 1893	E/2 1/1	- 1/500	500
22 Dec 1893	F/2 1/1	- 1/500	500
22 May 1894	G/2 1/1	- 1/500	500
16 Oct 1894	H/2 1/1	- 1/500	500
22 Feb 1896	I/2 1/1	- 1/500	500
23 Mar 1896	K/2 1/1	- 1/500	500
28 Apr 1897	L/2 1/1	- 1/500	500
24 Nov 1898	M/2 1/1	- 1/500	500
28 Jul 1899	N/2 1/1	- 1/500	500
23 Aug 1899	O/2 1/1	- 1/500	500
20 Mar 1900	P/2 1/1	- 1/500	500
1 Sep 1900	Q/2 1/1	- 1/500	500
1 Apr 1901	R/2 1/1	- 1/500	500
1 Oct 1901	S/2 1/1	- 1/500	500
5 May 1902	T/2 1/1	- 1/500	500
1 Nov 1902	U/2 1/1	- 1/500	500
8 Jan 1903	V/2 1/1	- 1/500	500
6 Jul 1903	W/2 1/1	- 1/500	500
31 Aug 1904	X/2 1/1	- 1/500	500 **RARE**

The following **Proof** notes have been recorded: Blue, no red panel
1 Mar 1872   5 Jun 1872   1 Jul 1874   3 May 1875   **From 250 EF**

Specimen undated no prefix & S/2 1 Oct 1901 S/2   **From 700 EF**

FIRST WATERLOW ISSUE – 1905 *to* 1907

Heading: British Linen Company

The decision to change printers was made in September 1904 and came about as a result of a dispute between directors of Perkins Bacon & Co Ltd. Receivers had been appointed and the Company understandably became concerned that its supply of notes might be interrupted. Other printers were approached including Bradbury Wilkinson who prepared a superb essay dated 9th August 1904. This retained elements of the Perkins design and could be described as artistically superior to Waterlow's efforts. Sadly only a black and white photograph of it has survived. **Waterlow & Sons Limited**, however, agreed to rework the existing designs '*without materially altering the general appearance and characteristics of the old notes*' and won the contract on this basis. The new note order was placed in January 1905 and the first notes were issued in April the same year. Within a few months it became evident there were faults with the notes and Waterlow had to move quickly to correct them under threat of losing their new contract. The exact nature of the faults is not clear from the minutes.

The engraving and print quality of the new notes were clearly a considerable improvement on the Perkins notes, about which Waterlow had been very critical. The watermark on the new £1 notes reads 'B L Cº / ONE POUND' but cannot be confirmed on higher denominations. A small number of unissued but numbered £1 notes appear to have been taken aside for use as specimens (though not marked as such) and were punch hole cancelled. The usual Waterlow positional plate letters can be found in the lower left hand corner of the notes. This short lived issue has thrown up some real rarities to challenge collectors. Some records of notes outstanding have survived for this issue: 28 £5 notes, 20 £10 notes, a mere three £20 notes and just five £100 notes. There are only two recorded survivors of issued £1 notes.

Bradbury Wilkinson photographic essay

BL 49   **£1**   **F Gordon Brown** Printed signature p Manager
             Handsigned p Acco!
             28 Feb 1905   R 1/1   -   500/1000   500,000
             30 Mar 1906   S 1/1   -   417/750   416,750   **From 2000 F**

             Specimen 28 Feb 1905 R 222/159 & 327/147 *to* 327/190   **From 300 EF**

BL 49 Specimen

BL 50	**£5**	**Handsigned** p Manager & p Acco!				
		8 Mar 1905	W/2 1/1 - 20/500	10,000		
		1 Jun 1905	X/2 1/1 - 20/500	10,000		
		14 Apr 1906	Y/2 1/1 - 20/500	10,000	**From 2000 F**	
		Specimen 8 Mar 1905 W/2			**From 500 EF**	

BL 50 Specimen

BL 51	**£10**	**Handsigned** p Manager & p Acco!			
		15 Apr 1905 R 1/1 - 10/500	5,000	**From 2500 F**	
		Specimen 15 Apr 1905		**From 600 EF**	

BL 51 1905

BL 52	£20	**Handsigned** p Manager p Acco!			
		7 Jun 1905	V/2 1/1 - 5/500	2,500	
		20 Feb 1906	W/2 1/1 - 5/500	2,500	**From 2500 F**
		Specimen 7 Jun 1905			**From 750 EF**

BL 52 1905

BL 53	**£100**	**Handsigned**	Manager & Accountant		Titles not printed			
		14 Feb 1905	Y/2	1/1	-	1/500	500	
		18 Mar 1905	Z/2	1/1	-	1/500	500	
		3 Aug 1905	A/3	1/1	-	2/500	1,000	
		30 Sep 1905	B/3	1/1	-	2/500	1,000	
		5 Oct 1905	C/3	1/1	-	2/500	1,000	
		23 Nov 1905	D/3	1/1	-	2/500	1,000	
		2 Jan 1906	E/3	1/1	-	2/500	1,000	**From 3000 F**
	Specimen	30 Sep 1905 B/3						**From 850 EF**

BL 53 1905

SECOND WATERLOW ISSUE - 1907 *to* 1914

Heading: British Linen Bank

The British Linen Company finally changed its name to the British Linen Bank in 1906. New notes were prepared by **Waterlow & Sons Limited** including an amended 'B L B' watermark. Some paper with the old watermark 'B L Co' was left over from the previous printing of the £1 note and this was used up. On the higher denominations the only watermark observed reads 'BRITISH LINEN / BANK' but earlier paper may also have been used on some printings. Prefix J not used. Positional plate letters as before. Again, we have some records of notes outstanding: well over a hundred £5 notes, but just 45 £10 notes, 46 £20 notes and a mere four £100 notes. Survivors of the higher denominations in collectors' hands will be far fewer.

BL 54a   £1   **F Gordon Brown** Printed signature p Manager
                 Handsigned p Acco!
                 15 Jan 1907   T   1/1   -   500/1000   500,000   **RARE**

                 Specimen 15 Jan 1907 T   **From 450 EF**

BL 54b   £1   **Andrew Young** Printed signature p Manager   F   VF
                 Handsigned p Acco!
                 26 Dec 1907   U   1/1   -   500/1000   500,000   **750 1250**

BL 54b 1907

BL 54c	£1	**Alexander S Aikman** Printed signature p Manager **Handsigned** p Acco!			**F**	**VF**
		2 Nov 1908 V 1/1 - 500/1000	500,000		**600**	**1200**
		Specimen 2 Nov 1908 15 Jul 1910			**From 1000 EF**	

BL 54c 1908

BL 54d	£1	**Edwin G Galletly** Printed signature p Manager **Handsigned** p Acco!				
		15 Jul 1910 W 1/1 - 500/1000	500,000			
		11 Aug 1911 X 1/1 - 500/1000	500,000		**350**	**850**

BL 54d 1911

BL 54e	£1	Edwin G Galletly Printed signature p General Manager Handsigned p Acco!					F	VF	EF
		29 Oct 1912	Y 1/1	-	500/1000	500,000			
		17 Sep 1913	Z 1/1	-	350/1000	350,000	350	850	1500

BL 54e 1913

												F	VF
BL 55a	£5	**Handsigned**	p Manager & p Acco!										
		4 Feb 1907	Z/2	1/1	-	20/500			10,000				
		3 Sep 1907	A/3	1/1	-	20/500			10,000				
		2 Jan 1908	B/3	1/1	-	20/500			10,000				
		15 May 1909	C/3	1/1	-	20/500			10,000				
		15 Nov 1909	D/3	1/1	-	20/500			10,000				
		3 Jan 1910	E/3	1/1	-	20/500			10,000				
		6 Jul 1910	F/3	1/1	-	20/500			10,000				
		1 Aug 1911	G/3	1/1	-	20/500			10,000				
		4 Dec 1911	H/3	1/1	-	20/500			10,000			**650**	**1250**
		Specimen 3 Sep 1907 15 May 1909										**From 750 EF**	

BL 55a 1911

BL 55b	£5	**Handsigned**	p General Manager & p Acco!						
		31 Oct 1912	I/3	1/1	-	20/500	10,000		
		15 Apr 1914	K/3	1/1	-	20/500	10,000	**650**	**1250**

BL 56	£10	**Handsigned** p Manager & p Acco^t			
		30 Jan 1907 S/1 1/1 - 10/500		5,000	**From 2000 F**
		Specimen 30 Jan 1907			**From 750 EF**

BL 56 1907

BL 57a	**£20**	**Handsigned** p Manager & p Acco!				
		2 Jan 1907	X/2 1/1	-	5/500	2,500
		7 Sep 1907	Y/2 1/1	-	5/500	2,500
		18 Apr 1908	Z/2 1/1	-	5/500	2,500
		5 Dec 1910	A/3 1/1	-	5/500	2,500
		31 Mar 1911	B/3 1/1	-	5/500	2,500
		20 Oct 1912	C/3 1/1	-	5/500	2,500	**From 2000 F**
		Specimen 2 Jan 1907					**From 750 EF**

BL 57a 1912

BL 57b	**£20**	**Handsigned** p General Manager & p Acco!				
		18 Nov 1912	D/3 1/1	-	5/500	2,500	**From 2000 F**

BL 58	**£100**	**Handsigned** Manager & Accountant Titles not printed				
		11 Feb 1907	F/3 1/1	-	2/500	1,000
		2 Apr 1908	G/3 1/1	-	2/500	1,000
		15 May 1912	H/3 1/1	-	2/500	1,000	**From 3000 F**
		Specimen 11 Feb 1907					**From 850 EF**

THIRD WATERLOW ISSUE – 1914 *to* 1934

Blue with Red sunburst underlay Royal Arms

In 1913 Waterlow recommended that additional protection against forgery be introduced. They suggested that an '*anti-photographic ground tint*' in the form of a red sunburst underlay be added to the obverse while a printed reverse should also be adopted. The bank accepted their recommendations and proofs were prepared. The reverse design of Pallas was based on a sketch by the artist Morris Meredith Williams. Watermarked paper was no longer felt necessary and was discontinued. The cost of the new plates was £213 for the £1 plate and £196 for each of the higher values. Printing costs rose sharply from £3 14s 6d per 1,000 notes for the £1 notes in 1914 to £8 6s 6d in 1920, though they had fallen back to £4 15s 0d by 1924. The higher value printing costs rose from £6 18s 0d to £14 18s 6d per 1,000 notes and back to £12 5s 0d over the same period. No prefix J except one £5 note issue (see BL 60). Positional plate letters as before.

BL 59a	£1	**Edwin G Galletly** Printed signature p General Manager				F	VF	EF
		Handsigned p Acco!						
		23 Sep 1914	A 1/1 - 500/1000	500,000			
		10 May 1915	B 1/1 - 500/1000	500,000			
		9 Feb 1916	C 1/1 - 500/1000	500,000			
		3 Aug 1916	D 1/1 - 500/1000	500,000			
		18 Jul 1917	E 1/1 - 500/1000	500,000			
		5 Apr 1918	F 1/1 - 500/1000	500,000			
		5 Nov 1918	G 1/1 - 500/1000	500,000	250	450	900
		Waterlow Colour Trial Brown, Green underprint undated				From 500 EF		
		Specimen undated				From 550 EF		

BL 59a 1915

BL 59 £1 Reverse

BL 59b	£1	Calvert John Grant Printed signature p General Manager Handsigned p Acco!				F	VF	EF
		19 Aug 1919	H 1/1 -	500/1000	500,000			
		7 Jan 1921	I 1/1 -	1000/1000	1,000,000			
		19 Mar 1923	K 1/1 -	1000/1000	1,000,000			
		31 Jul 1924	L 1/1 -	500/1000	500,000	200	400	750
		Specimen undated					From 550 EF	

BL 59b 1921

BL 59c	£1	**John Waugh** Printed signature p General Manager				F	VF	EF
		Handsigned p Acco!						
		15 Oct 1925	M 1/1 - 250/1000		250,000	**250**	**500**	**800**

BL 59c 1925

The long series of £5 notes contains one anomaly in that prefix J was used for the July 1929 printing. This appears to have been an error by Waterlow who should have used prefix I to conform to standard British Linen practice. This is the only recorded use of prefix J on a British Linen note.

BL 60	£5	**Handsigned** p General Manager & p Acco!					
		8 Jan 1915	L/3 1/1	-	20/500	10,000	
		13 Sep 1915	M/3 1/1	-	20/500	10,000	
		1 Feb 1916	N/3 1/1	-	20/500	10,000	
		15 Aug 1916	O/3 1/1	-	20/500	10,000	
		4 Apr 1917	P/3 1/1	-	20/500	10,000	
		20 Dec 1917	Q/3 1/1	-	20/500	10,000	
		3 Jan 1918	R/3 1/1	-	20/500	10,000	
		13 Mar 1918	S/3 1/1	-	20/500	10,000	
		4 Jun 1918	T/3 1/1	-	20/500	10,000	
		6 Sep 1918	U/3 1/1	-	20/500	10,000	
		30 Jan 1919	V/3 1/1	-	20/500	10,000	
		4 Mar 1919	W/3 1/1	-	20/500	10,000	
		30 Apr 1919	X/3 1/1	-	20/500	10,000	
		13 Jun 1919	Y/3 1/1	-	20/500	10,000	
		18 Jul 1919	Z/3 1/1	-	20/500	10,000	
		12 Sep 1919	A/4 1/1	-	20/500	10,000	
		15 Oct 1919	B/4 1/1	-	20/500	10,000	
		19 Nov 1919	C/4 1/1	-	20/500	10,000	**300 650 1200**

							F	VF	EF
BL 60	£5	*Cont*							
		16 Jan 1920	D/4 1/1	-	20/500	10,000			
		21 Feb 1920	E/4 1/1	-	20/500	10,000			
		18 Mar 1920	F/4 1/1	-	20/500	10,000			
		29 Apr 1920	G/4 1/1	-	20/500	10,000			
		22 Jun 1920	H/4 1/1	-	20/500	10,000			
		14 Sep 1920	I/4 1/1	-	20/500	10,000			
		7 Jan 1921	K/4 1/1	-	20/500	10,000			
		24 Feb 1921	L/4 1/1	-	20/500	10,000			
		21 Sep 1921	M/4 1/1	-	20/500	10,000			
		7 Nov 1921	N/4 1/1	-	20/500	10,000			
		17 Oct 1922	O/4 1/1	-	20/500	10,000			
		5 Dec 1922	P/4 1/1	-	20/500	10,000			
		31 Oct 1923	Q/4 1/1	-	20/500	10,000			
		26 Nov 1923	R/4 1/1	-	20/500	10,000			
		17 Jun 1924	S/4 1/1	-	20/500	10,000			
		10 Jul 1924	T/4 1/1	-	20/500	10,000			
		13 Feb 1925	U/4 1/1	-	20/500	10,000			
		18 Mar 1925	V/4 1/1	-	20/500	10,000			
		1 Dec 1925	W/4 1/1	-	20/500	10,000			
		16 Jan 1926	X/4 1/1	-	20/500	10,000			
		12 Oct 1926	Y/4 1/1	-	20/500	10,000			
		10 Jan 1927	Z/4 1/1	-	20/500	10,000			
		11 Feb 1927	A/5 1/1	-	20/500	10,000			
		12 Mar 1927	B/5 1/1	-	20/500	10,000			
		13 Apr 1927	C/5 1/1	-	20/500	10,000			
		14 May 1927	D/5 1/1	-	20/500	10,000			
		4 Mar 1929	E/5 1/1	-	20/500	10,000			
		4 Apr 1929	F/5 1/1	-	20/500	10,000			
		9 May 1929	G/5 1/1	-	20/500	10,000			
		6 Jun 1929	H/5 1/1	-	20/500	10,000			
		9 Jul 1929	J/5 1/1	-	20/500	10,000			
		8 Aug 1929	K/5 1/1	-	20/500	10,000			
		10 Jan 1931	L/5 1/1	-	20/500	10,000			
		11 Mar 1931	M/5 1/1	-	20/500	10,000			
		14 Apr 1931	N/5 1/1	-	20/500	10,000			
		15 May 1931	O/5 1/1	-	20/500	10,000			
		16 Jun 1931	P/5 1/1	-	20/500	10,000			
		17 Jul 1931	Q/5 1/1	-	20/500	10,000			
		15 Mar 1933	R/5 1/1	-	20/500	10,000			
		17 Apr 1933	S/5 1/1	-	20/500	10,000			
		18 May 1933	T/5 1/1	-	20/500	10,000			
		20 Jun 1933	U/5 1/1	-	20/500	10,000			
		27 Jul 1933	V/5 1/1	-	20/500	10,000			
		3 Aug 1933	W/5 1/1	-	20/500	10,000	300	650	1200

Waterlow Colour Trial Brown Green underprint undated
Dark Brown Pale Red underprint
undated & 16 Jan 1926   From 700 EF

BL 60 1924

BL 60 £5 Reverse

The £10 note issue was discontinued in 1920, further evidence of the lack of demand for this denomination. A number of notes of the final printing in the range V/1 6/212 to V/1 6/326 (and possibly more) have survived in uncirculated condition although fully signed and taken to cash. From this range 25 notes were stamped SPECIMEN and punch hole cancelled.

BL 61	£10	**Handsigned** p General Manager & p Acco!				F	VF	EF
		15 Feb 1916	T/1 1/1	-	10/500	5,000		
		9 Feb 1920	U/1 1/1	-	10/500	5,000		
		15 Mar 1920	V/1 1/1	-	10/500	4,975	**900 1600 2800**	
		Specimen 15 Mar 1920				25	**From 1500 EF**	

BL 61 1920

BL 61 £10 Reverse

BL 62	**£20**	**Handsigned**	p General Manager & p Acco!				
		3 May 1916	E/3	1/1	- 5/500	2,500	
		30 Jan 1918	F/3	1/1	- 5/500	2,500	
		27 Feb 1918	G/3	1/1	- 5/500	2,500	
		26 Jul 1918	H/3	1/1	- 5/500	2,500	
		12 Aug 1918	I/3	1/1	- 5/500	2,500	
		5 May 1919	K/3	1/1	- 5/500	2,500	
		19 Sep 1919	L/3	1/1	- 5/500	2,500	
		7 Apr 1920	M/3	1/1	- 5/500	2,500	
		5 May 1920	N/3	1/1	- 5/500	2,500	
		15 Jan 1924	O/3	1/1	- 5/500	2,500	
		15 Mar 1924	P/3	1/1	- 5/500	2,500	
		8 Feb 1929	Q/3	1/1	- 5/500	2,500	
		6 Apr 1929	R/3	1/1	- 5/500	2,500	**From 750 F**
		9 Mar 1931	S/3	1/1	- 5/500	2,500	
		5 May 1931	T/3	1/1	- 5/500	2,500	
		24 Nov 1931	U/3	1/1	- 5/500	2,500	
		15 Dec 1931	V/3	1/1	- 5/500	2,500	
		31 Jul 1933	W/3	1/1	- 5/500	2,500	
		4 Sep 1933	X/3	1/1	- 5/500	2,500	**From 500 F**

BL 63	**£100**	**Handsigned**	p General Manager & p Acco! **Plain paper**				
		7 Jan 1916	I/3	1/1	- 2/500	1,000	
		12 Dec 1916	K/3	1/1	- 2/500	1,000	
		15 Jan 1918	L/3	1/1	- 2/500	1,000	
		1 Mar 1918	M/3	1/1	- 2/500	1,000	**From 2500 F**
		28 Jul 1933	N/3	1/1	- 2/500	1,000	**From 1200 F**

BL 63 1916

In 1925 the British Linen Bank decided to follow other Scottish banks in reducing the size of their £1 note to size B, 151-155mm by 84-85mm, to conform to the standard size of UK Treasury notes issued after 1917. The £1 note now carries a single printed signature of the Cashier. The plates initially consisted of 16 notes per sheet but this was increased to 20 per sheet with the 30th November 1931 printing. Positional plate letters as before.

BL 64	£1	John Waugh Printed signature Cashier						F	VF	EF
		Reduced size								
		1 May 1926	N	000001	-	1000000	1,000,000	50	120	250
		1 Mar 1927	O	000001	-	1000000	1,000,000			
		31 Oct 1928	P	000001	-	1000000	1,000,000			
		2 Dec 1929	Q	000001	-	1000000	1,000,000			
		2 Mar 1931	R	000001	-	250000	250,000			
		5 May 1931	S	000001	-	250000	250,000			
		8 Jun 1931	T	000001	-	250000	250,000			
		6 Jul 1931	U	000001	-	250000	250,000			
		30 Nov 1931	V	000001	-	250000	250,000			
		8 Dec 1931	W	000001	-	250000	250,000			
		5 Jan 1932	X	000001	-	250000	250,000			
		8 Feb 1932	Y	000001	-	250000	250,000			
		26 Jan 1933	Z	000001	-	250000	250,000			
		3 Apr 1933	A	000001	-	250000	250,000			
		12 Jun 1933	B	000001	-	250000	250,000			
		10 Aug 1933	C	000001	-	250000	250,000			
		1 Feb 1934	D	000001	-	250000	250,000			
		10 Apr 1934	E	000001	-	250000	250,000			
		4 Jun 1934	F	000001	-	250000	250,000			
		2 Aug 1934	G	000001	-	250000	250,000	30	60	150
		Specimen 1 May 1926 N no serials					25	**From 200 EF**		

BL 64 N First prefix

FOURTH WATERLOW ISSUE – 1934 *to* 1960

Bank Arms

Following an objection by the Lord Lyon King of Arms to the continued use (since 1822) of the Royal Arms on the notes, Waterlows were asked to prepare new notes with the British Linen Bank's newly designed Coat of Arms, but leaving the rest of the notes unchanged. In 1937 as an additional security device the paper on all the notes was changed from plain to 'granite' paper, containing red and blue silk fibres. In 1945 the decision was taken that all notes should bear only a single signature, that of the General Manager. The opportunity was taken in 1935 finally to remove the two florettes, now described in the bank's records as *'white line stars'*, from the £100 note. Positional code letters as before. No prefix J.

An interesting essay £1 note was submitted by Thomas De La Rue in 1937 featuring a vignette of the Scott Monument on Princes Street, Edinburgh. This attractive design was not adopted but the note was on display for a time in the Bank of Scotland's museum and is now held in their archives.

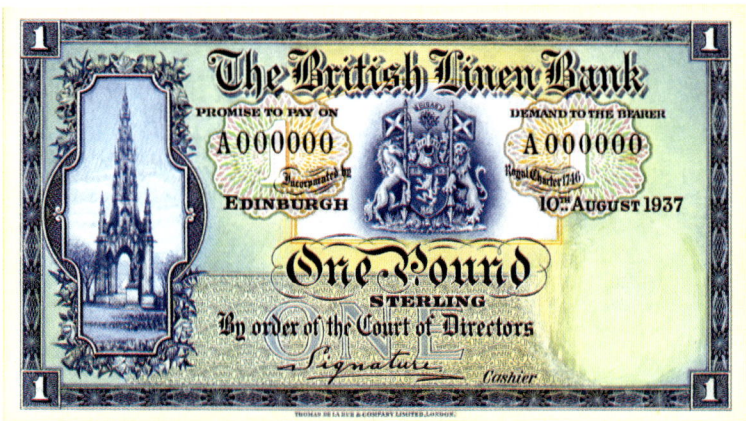

Thomas De La Rue 1937 Essay (enlarged)

BL 65a O prefix serial 8

BL 65a	£1	John Waugh Printed signature Cashier **Plain paper**					F	VF	EF
		18 Jan 1935	H	000001	-	250000	250,000		
		20 Feb 1935	I	000001	-	250000	250,000		
		15 Mar 1935	K	000001	-	250000	250,000		
		22 Apr 1935	L	000001	-	250000	250,000		
		5 Sep 1935	M	000001	-	250000	250,000		
		30 Oct 1935	N	000001	-	250000	250,000		
		28 Nov 1935	O	000001	-	250000	250,000		
		5 Dec 1935	P	000001	-	250000	250,000		
		9 Feb 1937	Q	000001	-	250000	250,000		
		26 Apr 1937	R	000001	-	250000	250,000	30	55	110

BL 65a H First

BL 65a R Last

Granite paper was introduced in 1937 starting with prefix S. A fractional prefix was introduced with the March 1940 printing.

BL 65b £1 **John Waugh** Printed signature Cashier **Granite paper**   F   VF   EF

Single prefix letter

Date	Prefix	Serial Range	Quantity
2 Jul 1937	S	000001 - 250000	250,000
10 Aug 1937	T	000001 - 250000	250,000
20 Sep 1937	U	000001 - 250000	250,000
4 Oct 1937	V	000001 - 250000	250,000
10 Aug 1938	W	000001 - 250000	250,000
15 Sep 1938	X	000001 - 250000	250,000
12 Oct 1938	Y	000001 - 250000	250,000
8 Nov 1938	Z	000001 - 250000	250,000
12 Jun 1939	A	000001 - 250000	250,000
2 Aug 1939	B	000001 - 250000	250,000
3 Oct 1939	C	000001 - 250000	250,000
13 Nov 1939	D	000001 - 250000	250,000

Fractional prefix

Date	Prefix	Serial Range	Quantity
7 Mar 1940	E/1	000001 - 250000	250,000
16 May 1940	F/1	000001 - 250000	250,000
18 Jul 1940	G/1	000001 - 250000	250,000
3 Oct 1940	H/1	000001 - 250000	250,000
20 May 1941	I/1	000001 - 250000	250,000
23 Jun 1941	K/1	000001 - 250000	250,000
25 Jul 1941	L/1	000001 - 250000	250,000
27 Aug 1941	M/1	000001 - 250000	250,000
3 Sep 1942	N/1	000001 - 250000	250,000
7 Oct 1942	O/1	000001 - 250000	250,000
9 Nov 1942	P/1	000001 - 250000	250,000
1 Dec 1942	Q/1	000001 - 250000	250,000
3 Jan 1944	R/1	000001 - 250000	250,000
4 Feb 1944	S/1	000001 - 250000	250,000
6 Mar 1944	T/1	000001 - 250000	250,000
8 Apr 1944	U/1	000001 - 250000	250,000	20 45 90

Proof Blue/Red 6 Mar 1944 & 8 Apr 1944 no prefix/serials   **From 150 EF**

BL 65b Single prefix letter

BL 65b Fractional prefix, final date

In 1950 the first seven digit serial numbers are seen, the so-called 'overs'. This came about as a result of a desire to reduce spoilage - Waterlow stated that they allowed for 15% spoilage but this could be reduced by printing 1,000,000 notes for each date and prefix, as had been done with the initial B size £1 printings up to 1929. Good notes rescued from spoiled but uncut sheets were then numbered and issued.

BL 65c £1 **George Mackenzie** Printed signature General Manager **VF EF UNC**

4 Jan 1946	V/1	000001	-	250000	250,000		
5 Feb 1946	W/1	000001	-	250000	250,000		
8 Mar 1946	X/1	000001	-	250000	250,000		
9 Apr 1946	Y/1	000001	-	250000	250,000		
3 Feb 1947	Z/1	000001	-	250000	250,000		
4 Mar 1947	A/2	000001	-	250000	250,000		
6 May 1947	B/2	000001	-	250000	250,000		
7 Jul 1947	C/2	000001	-	250000	250,000		
14 Aug 1947	D/2	000001	-	250000	250,000		
16 Sep 1947	E/2	000001	-	250000	250,000		
17 Oct 1947	F/2	000001	-	250000	250,000		
18 Nov 1947	G/2	000001	-	250000	250,000		
10 Jun 1948	H/2	000001	-	250000	250,000		
14 Sep 1948	I/2	000001	-	250000	250,000		
15 Dec 1948	K/2	000001	-	250000	250,000		
20 Jan 1949	L/2	000001	-	250000	250,000		
15 Jul 1949	M/2	000001	-	250000	250,000		
16 Aug 1949	N/2	000001	-	250000	250,000		
17 Sep 1949	O/2	000001	-	250000	250,000		
18 Oct 1949	P/2	000001	-	250000	250,000		
17 Apr 1950	Q/2	000001	-	1000000	1,000,000		
	Q/2	1000001	-	1020000	20,000 Overs		
5 Aug 1950	R/2	000001	-	1000000	1,000,000	20 45 90	
	R/2	1000001	-	1020000	20,000 Overs		

Overs   35 60 135

Specimen 5 Feb 1946 W/1 040211   From 120 UNC

BL 65c V/1 First date/prefix

BL 65c R/2 Last

BL 65d £1 **Andrew Philip Anderson** Printed signature General Manager VF EF UNC

Date	Prefix	Range		Quantity	
4 Jun 1951	S/2	000001	-	1000000	1,000,000
	S/2	1000001	-	1008000	8,000 Overs
12 Feb 1952	T/2	000001	-	1000000	1,000,000
	T/2	1000001	-	1012000	12,000 Overs
4 Nov 1952	U/2	000001	-	1000000	1,000,000
	U/2	1000001	-	1012000	12,000 Overs
21 Oct 1953	V/2	000001	-	1000000	1,000,000
	V/2	1000001	-	1008000	8,000 Overs
16 Feb 1954	W/2	000001	-	1000000	1,000,000
12 Jan 1955	X/2	000001	-	1200000	1,200,000 *
	X/2	1200001	-	1215000	15,000 Overs
9 Aug 1955	Y/2	000001	-	800000	800,000
28 Dec 1955	Z/2	000001	-	1000000	1,000,000
	A/3	000001	-	1000000	1,000,000
	A/3	1000001	-	1003000	3,000 Overs
4 Jun 1956	B/3	000001	-	1000000	1,000,000
	C/3	000001	-	1000000	1,000,000
5 Apr 1957	D/3	000001	-	1000000	1,000,000
	E/3	000001	-	1000000	1,000,000
	E/3	1000001	-	1010000	10,000 Overs
10 Dec 1957	F/3	000001	-	1000000	1,000,000
	G/3	000001	-	1000000	1,000,000
	G/3	1000001	-	1010000	10,000 Overs
28 Aug 1958	H/3	000001	-	1000000	1,000,000
	I/3	000001	-	1000000	1,000,000
	I/3	1000001	-	1010000	10,000 Overs
12 May 1959	K/3	000001	-	1000000	1,000,000
	L/3	000001	-	1000000	1,000,000	20 45 90
	L/3	1000001	-	1010000	10,000 Overs
Overs					25 55 120

* The original print run of prefix X/2 was for 1,200,000 notes, an accidental excess of 200,000 notes which was adjusted for in the Y/2 print run. Technically these are not 'overs'.

BL 65d S/2 First

BL 65d L/3 Last

BL 65d E/3 Over

A few specimens of the final Waterlow printing were taken from notes ready for issue.

						VF	EF	UNC
BL 65e	**£1**	**Andrew Philip Anderson** Printed signature General Manager						
		Sans serif prefix/serials N°. omitted						
		15 Apr 1960	M/3 000001 - 1000000	1,000,000				
			N/3 000001 - 1000000	1,000,000				
			O/3 000001 - 1000000	999,975				
			P/3 000001 - 1000000	1,000,000		20	45	90
			P/3 1000001 - 1200000	200,000 Overs				
		Overs				25	50	100
		Specimen 15 Apr 1960 O/3 000000 & 389561-565			25	From 100 EF		

BL 65e Over

BL 64 & 65 £1 Reverse

Size of ths £5 note remained unchanged at 210 x 120mm.

BL 66a	£5	**Adam Dempster** Printed signature General Manager					F	VF	EF
		Handsigned p Acco! **Plain paper**							
		16 Sep 1935	X/5	1/1	-	20/500	10,000		
		12 Nov 1935	Y/5	1/1	-	20/500	10,000		
		3 Dec 1935	Z/5	1/1	-	20/500	10,000		
		20 Dec 1935	A/6	1/1	-	20/500	10,000		
		3 Jan 1936	B/6	1/1	-	20/500	10,000		
		6 Feb 1936	C/6	1/1	-	20/500	10,000	180	350	-

Specimen No hand signature Punch hole cancelled
20 Dec 1935 A/6 20/500   3 Jan 1936 B/6 20/500   **From 300 EF**

BL 66a 1935

BL 66b	£5	**Adam Dempster** Printed signature General Manager					F	VF	EF
		Handsigned p Acco! **Granite paper**							
		6 Jul 1938	D/6	1/1	-	20/500	10,000		
		10 Aug 1938	E/6	1/1	-	20/500	10,000		
		14 Sep 1938	F/6	1/1	-	20/500	10,000		
		12 Oct 1938	G/6	1/1	-	20/500	10,000		
		15 Nov 1938	H/6	1/1	-	20/500	10,000		
		14 Dec 1938	I/6	1/1	-	20/500	10,000		
		8 Jun 1940	K/6	1/1	-	20/500	10,000		
		10 Jul 1940	L/6	1/1	-	20/500	10,000		
		6 Aug 1940	M/6	1/1	-	20/500	10,000		
		16 Sep 1940	N/6	1/1	-	20/500	10,000		
		12 Nov 1940	O/6	1/1	-	20/500	10,000		
		30 Dec 1940	P/6	1/1	-	20/500	10,000	150	250	450

BL 66b 1940

BL 66c   **£5**   **George Mackenzie** Printed signature General Manager   F   VF   EF
Handsigned p Acco!

Date	Serial				
16 Jun 1941	Q/6	1/1	-	20/500	10,000
17 Jul 1941	R/6	1/1	-	20/500	10,000
19 Aug 1941	S/6	1/1	-	20/500	10,000
3 Sep 1941	T/6	1/1	-	20/500	10,000
4 Oct 1941	U/6	1/1	-	20/500	10,000
5 Nov 1941	V/6	1/1	-	20/500	10,000
14 Jul 1942	W/6	1/1	-	20/500	10,000
20 Aug 1942	X/6	1/1	-	20/500	10,000
30 Sep 1942	Y/6	1/1	-	20/500	10,000
4 Nov 1942	Z/6	1/1	-	20/500	10,000
10 Dec 1942	A/7	1/1	-	20/500	10,000
12 Jan 1943	B/7	1/1	-	20/500	10,000	**150 250 450**

BL 66c 1942

BL 66d	£5	George Mackenzie General Manager					F	VF	EF
		John Waugh Printed signature Accountant and Cashier							
		11 Feb 1943	C/7	1/1	-	40/500	20,000		
		13 Mar 1943	D/7	1/1	-	40/500	20,000		
		16 Apr 1943	E/7	1/1	-	40/500	20,000		
		17 May 1943	F/7	1/1	-	40/500	20,000		
		18 Jun 1943	G/7	1/1	-	40/500	20,000		
		19 Jul 1943	H/7	1/1	-	40/500	20,000		
		21 Aug 1943	I/7	1/1	-	40/500	20,000		
		22 Sep 1943	K/7	1/1	-	40/500	20,000		
		23 Oct 1943	L/7	1/1	-	40/500	20,000		
		24 Nov 1943	M/7	1/1	-	40/500	20,000		
		27 Dec 1943	N/7	1/1	-	40/500	500 *		
		28 Jan 1944	O/7	1/1	-	40/500	20,000	150	250	450

* Notes N/7 11/1 to 11/500 were stolen from the printers. As a result the bank decided that the rest of the N/7 print run, a total of 19,500 notes (39 books of 500 notes each) should be destroyed unissued. This was done in July 1945. It seems none of the stolen notes entered circulation but they may have survived as they have not been redeemed.

BL 66d 1943

In 1944 the £5 was reduced in size to 180 x 102mm, size X. The value panels either side of the bank's arms were redesigned with the FIVE now in white on a blue background and the panels for the prefix/serials were removed. There were other minor modifications to the design.

BL 67a £5 **George Mackenzie** General Manager F VF EF
John Waugh Printed signature Accountant and Cashier
Reduced size

Date	Prefix			Numbers	Quantity	F	VF	EF
29 May 1944	P/7	1/1	-	40/500	20,000			
30 Jun 1944	Q/7	1/1	-	40/500	20,000			
31 Jul 1944	R/7	1/1	-	40/500	20,000			
1 Sep 1944	S/7	1/1	-	40/500	20,000			
2 Oct 1944	T/7	1/1	-	40/500	20,000			
3 Nov 1944	U/7	1/1	-	40/500	20,000	180	350	550

Specimen 31 Jul 1944 R/7 39/1 n/a From 200 EF

BL 67a Last

BL 67b £5 **George Mackenzie** Printed signature General Manager
No Before prefix Fractional book/sequential numbers

Date	Prefix			Numbers	Quantity	F	VF	EF
10 Sep 1946	V/7	1/1	-	40/500	20,000			
11 Oct 1946	W/7	1/1	-	40/500	20,000			
13 Nov 1946	X/7	1/1	-	40/500	20,000			
16 Dec 1946	Y/7	1/1	-	40/500	20,000			
15 Jan 1947	Z/7	1/1	-	40/500	20,000			
15 Feb 1947	A/8	1/1	-	40/500	20,000			
11 Aug 1947	B/8	1/1	-	40/500	20,000			
11 Sep 1947	C/8	1/1	-	40/500	20,000			
15 Oct 1947	D/8	1/1	-	40/500	20,000			
11 Nov 1947	E/8	1/1	-	40/500	20,000			
12 Dec 1947	F/8	1/1	-	40/500	20,000			
14 Jan 1948	G/8	1/1	-	40/500	20,000			
10 Feb 1948	H/8	1/1	-	40/500	20,000			
10 Mar 1948	I/8	1/1	-	40/500	20,000	90	180	300

								F	VF	EF
BL 67b	£5	Cont								
		6 Apr 1949	K/8	1/1	-	40/500	20,000			
		16 May 1948	L/8	1/1	-	40/500	20,000			
		4 Jun 1949	M/8	1/1	-	40/500	20,000			
		11 Jul 1949	N/8	1/1	-	40/500	20,000			
		10 Aug 1949	O/8	1/1	-	40/500	20,000			
		2 Sep 1949	P/8	1/1	-	40/500	20,000			
		1 Oct 1949	Q/8	1/1	-	40/500	20,000			
		2 Nov 1949	R/8	1/1	-	40/500	20,000			
		10 Jan 1950	S/8	1/1	-	40/500	20,000			
		20 Feb 1950	T/8	1/1	-	40/500	20,000			
		20 Mar 1950	U/8	1/1	-	40/500	20,000			
		20 Apr 1950	V/8	1/1	-	40/500	20,000			
		10 May 1950	W/8	1/1	-	40/500	20,000			
		10 Jun 1950	X/8	1/1	-	40/500	20,000			
		10 Jul 1950	Y/8	1/1	-	40/500	20,000			
		2 Aug 1950	Z/8	1/1	-	40/500	20,000	90	180	300

BL 67c	£5	**Andrew Philip Anderson** Printed signature General Manager								
		No Before prefix Fractional book/sequential numbers								
		5 Dec 1950	A/9	1/1	-	40/500	20,000			
		3 Jan 1951	B/9	1/1	-	40/500	20,000			
		6 Feb 1951	C/9	1/1	-	40/500	20,000	100	200	350

BL 67c Last

BL 67d	**£5**	**Andrew Philip Anderson** Printed signature General Manager					F	VF	EF
		In-line sans serif book/sequential numbers							
		Initial zeroes added No omitted							
		7 Mar 1951	D/9	01/001	-	40/500	20,000		
		11 Apr 1951	E/9	01/001	-	40/500	20,000		
		8 May 1951	F/9	01/001	-	40/500	20,000		
		18 Jun 1951	G/9	01/001	-	40/500	20,000		
		4 Jul 1951	H/9	01/001	-	40/500	20,000		
		22 Aug 1951	I/9	01/001	-	40/500	20,000		
		20 Sep 1951	K/9	01/001	-	40/500	20,000		
		22 Oct 1951	L/9	01/001	-	40/500	20,000		
		23 Nov 1951	M/9	01/001	-	40/500	20,000		
		27 Dec 1951	N/9	01/001	-	40/500	20,000		
		21 Jan 1952	O/9	01/001	-	40/500	20,000		
		25 Feb 1952	P/9	01/001	-	40/500	20,000		
		12 Mar 1952	Q/9	01/001	-	40/500	20,000		
		24 Apr 1952	R/9	01/001	-	40/500	20,000		
		22 May 1952	S/9	01/001	-	40/500	20,000		
		6 Jun 1952	T/9	01/001	-	40/500	20,000		
		23 Jul 1952	U/9	01/001	-	40/500	20,000		
		27 Oct 1952	V/9	01/001	-	40/500	20,000		
		26 Nov 1952	W/9	01/001	-	40/500	20,000		
		3 Dec 1952	X/9	01/001	-	40/500	20,000		
		7 Jan 1953	Y/9	01/001	-	40/500	20,000		
		4 Feb 1953	Z/9	01/001	-	40/500	20,000		
		3 Mar 1953	A/10	01/001	-	40/500	20,000		
		2 Apr 1953	B/10	01/001	-	40/500	20,000		
		7 May 1953	C/10	01/001	-	40/500	20,000		
		2 Jun 1953	D/10	01/001	-	40/500	20,000		
		7 Jul 1953	E/10	01/001	-	40/500	20,000		
		5 Aug 1953	F/10	01/001	-	40/500	20,000		
		7 Sep 1953	G/10	01/001	-	40/500	20,000		
		7 Oct 1953	H/10	01/001	-	40/500	20,000		
		4 Nov 1953	I/10	01/001	-	40/500	20,000		
		7 Dec 1953	K/10	01/001	-	40/500	20,000		
		26 Jan 1954	L/10	01/001	-	40/500	20,000		
		12 Feb 1954	M/10	01/001	-	40/500	20,000		
		25 Mar 1954	N/10	01/001	-	40/500	20,000		
		7 Apr 1954	O/10	01/001	-	40/500	20,000		
		14 May 1954	P/10	01/001	-	40/500	20,000		
		22 Jun 1954	Q/10	01/001	-	40/500	20,000		
		15 Jul 1954	R/10	01/001	-	40/500	20,000		
		17 Aug 1954	S/10	01/001	-	40/500	20,000		
		15 Sep 1954	T/10	01/001	-	40/500	20,000		
		19 Oct 1954	U/10	01/001	-	40/500	20,000		
		16 Nov 1954	V/10	01/001	-	40/500	20,000		
		21 Dec 1954	W/10	01/001	-	40/500	20,000		
		19 Jan 1955	X/10	01/001	-	40/500	20,000		
		17 Feb 1955	Y/10	01/001	-	40/500	20,000		
		16 Mar 1955	Z/10	01/001	-	40/500	20,000	**30**	**60**	**120**

BL 67d D/9 First

BL 67e	£5	**Andrew Philip Anderson** Printed signature General Manager **Sequential serial numbers** Book numbers discontinued				VF	EF	UNC
		15 Apr 1955	A/11 000001	- 100000	100,000			
		12 May 1955	B/11 000001	- 100000	100,000			
		8 Jun 1955	C/11 000001	- 100000	100,000			
		6 Jul 1955	D/11 000001	- 100000	100,000			
		4 May 1956	E/11 000001	- 100000	100,000			
		6 Jun 1956	F/11 000001	- 100000	100,000			
		9 Jul 1956	G/11 000001	- 100000	100,000			
		10 Aug 1956	H/11 000001	- 100000	100,000			
		10 Apr 1957	I/11 000001	- 100000	100,000			
		15 May 1957	K/11 000001	- 100000	100,000			
		5 Jun 1957	L/11 000001	- 100000	100,000			
		3 Jul 1957	M/11 000001	- 100000	100,000			
		30 Sep 1957	N/11 000001	- 100000	100,000			
		18 Oct 1957	O/11 000001	- 100000	100,000			
		20 Nov 1957	P/11 000001	- 100000	100,000			
		9 Dec 1957	Q/11 000001	- 100000	100,000			
		7 Jan 1959	R/11 000001	- 100000	100,000			
		11 Feb 1959	S/11 000001	- 100000	100,000			
		18 Mar 1959	T/11 000001	- 100000	100,000			
		8 Apr 1959	U/11 000001	- 100000	100,000			
		2 May 1959	V/11 000001	- 200000	200,000			
		3 Jun 1959	W/11 000001	- 200000	200,000			
		2 Jul 1959	X/11 000001	- 200000	199,975			
		4 Aug 1959	Y/11 000001	- 200000	200,000	30	60	120
		Specimen 2 Jul 1959 X/11 000000 & 055001			25	From 140 EF		

BL 67e A/11 First

BL 67e Y/11 Last

£20 specimen notes of this issue are in some cases fully numbered notes ready for issue and taken aside to be overprinted 'SPECIMEN' with the signatures cancelled with punch holes. It has not been possible to identify the exact serial ranges used in this way but those which have been observed are recorded below. Size of the £20 note remained unchanged at 210 x 120mm.

BL 68a	£20	**Adam Dempster** Printed signature General Manager		**F**	**VF**
		Handsigned p Acco! **Plain paper**			
		6 Aug 1935 Y/3 1/1 - 5/500	2,500		
		3 Oct 1935 Z/3 1/1 - 5/500	2,500	**350**	**650**
		Specimen 6 Aug 1935 Y/3 5/500 Punch hole cancelled		**From 300 EF**	

BL 68a Y/3 First

BL 68 Reverse

BL 68b	£20	**Adam Dempster** Printed signature General Manager				F	VF	EF
		Handsigned p Acco! **Granite paper**						
		31 Jul 1939	A/4 1/1	-	5/500	2,500		
		24 Aug 1939	B/4 1/1	-	5/500	2,500		
		29 Jun 1940	C/4 1/1	-	5/500	2,500		
		2 Aug 1940	D/4 1/1	-	5/500	2,500	200	400	-

BL 68b D/4 Last

BL 68c	£20	**George Mackenzie** Printed signature General Manager						
		Handsigned p Acco!						
		25 May 1942	E/4 1/1	-	10/500	5,000		
		2 Jul 1942	F/4 1/1	-	10/500	5,000		
		10 Mar 1943	G/4 1/1	-	10/500	5,000		
		7 Apr 1943	H/4 1/1	-	10/500	5,000		
		23 Jan 1945	I/4 1/1	-	10/500	5,000		
		24 Feb 1945	K/4 1/1	-	10/500	5,000	150	300	500

Specimen 23 Jan 1945 I/4 10/301 Punch hole cancelled   From 300 EF

BL 68c 1942

BL 68d	£20	George Mackenzie Printed signature General Manager			F	VF	EF
		Panels for prefix/serials					
		2 Sep 1946	L/4 1/1 - 10/500	5,000			
		4 Oct 1946	M/4 1/1 - 10/500	5,000			
		4 Nov 1946	N/4 1/1 - 10/500	5,000			
		25 Jun 1949	O/4 1/1 - 10/500	5,000			
		18 Jul 1949	P/4 1/1 - 10/500	5,000			
		4 Aug 1949	Q/4 1/1 - 10/500	5,000	100	200	450

BL 68d 1949 Last

BL 68e	£20	Andrew Philip Anderson Printed signature General Manager				F	VF	EF
		Serials in line Initial zeroes added Nº omitted						
		No prefix/serial panels						
		12 May 1952	R/4 01/001	- 10/500	5,000			
		16 Jun 1952	S/4 01/001	- 10/500	5,000			
		15 Jul 1952	T/4 01/001	- 10/500	5,000			
		30 Dec 1952	U/4 01/001	- 10/500	5,000			
		20 Jan 1953	V/4 01/001	- 10/500	5,000			
		10 Feb 1953	W/4 01/001	- 10/500	5,000			
		18 May 1954	X/4 01/001	- 10/500	5,000			
		8 Jun 1954	Y/4 01/001	- 10/500	5,000			
		6 Jul 1954	Z/4 01/001	- 10/500	5,000			
		7 Oct 1955	A/5 01/001	- 20/500	10,000			
		9 Nov 1955	B/5 01/001	- 20/500	10,000			
		7 Dec 1955	C/5 01/001	- 20/500	10,000			
		17 Oct 1957	D/5 01/001	- 20/500	10,000			
		15 Nov 1957	E/5 01/001	- 20/500	9,975			
		11 Dec 1957	F/5 01/001	- 20/500	10,000	80	180	430
		Specimen	15 Nov 1957 E/5 00/000		25			
			15 Nov 1957 E/5 17/476 to 17/485		25		From 200 EF	

BL 68e R/4 First Serials in line Initial zeroes added

The amended £100 note issued in 1935 finally had the 'florettes' removed. As with the £20 notes some £100 specimen notes have been fully numbered notes ready for issue and taken aside to be overprinted 'SPECIMEN' and the signatures cancelled with punch holes. It has not been possible to identify the exact serial ranges used in this way but those which have been observed are recorded below. Size of the £100 note remained unchanged at 210 x 120mm.

BL 69a £100 **Adam Dempster** Printed signature General Manager
              Handsigned p Acco! **Plain paper**
              24 Jun 1935   O/3 1/1 - 2/500   1,000   **From 1500 F**

              Proof undated No printed signature Title p General Manager   **From 1000 EF**

              Specimen 24 Jun 1935 O/3 2/500 Punch hole cancelled   **From 1000 EF**

BL 69b £100 **George Mackenzie** Printed signature General Manager   **F   VF   EF**
              Handsigned p Acco! **Granite paper**
              Panels for prefix/serials
              4 Feb 1942   P/3 1/1 - 2/500   1,000
              3 Mar 1943   Q/3 1/1 - 2/500   1,000   **800 1500 3000**

              Specimen 4 Feb 1942 P/3 2/86 Punch hole cancelled   **From 1000 EF**

BL 69b 1943

BL 69c £100 **Andrew Philip Anderson** Printed signature General Manager
              No & Fractional book/sequential numbers
              No prefix/serial panels
              5 Apr 1951   R/3 1/1 - 2/500   1,000   **700 1400 2500**

              Specimen 5 Apr 1951 R/3 1/201 Punch hole cancelled   **From 1000 EF**

BL 69c 1951

BL 69d	£100	**Andrew Philip Anderson** Printed signature General Manager				F	VF	EF
		Serials in line Initial zero added N⁰ omitted						
	5 Aug 1954	S/3 01/001	-	02/500	975			
	27 Nov 1957	T/3 01/001	-	02/500	1,000	500	950	2000
	Specimen	5 Aug 1954 S/3 00/000			25			
		5 Aug 1954 S/3 02/106 *to* 02/114			25		From 500 EF	

BL 69d Serials in line Initial zeroes added

FIRST THOMAS DE LA RUE ISSUE – 1961 *to* 1967

Unchanged designs Size reductions

After **Thomas De La Rue & Co Limited** took over the security printing business of Waterlow & Sons Ltd in January 1961 the note issues were initially continued unchanged apart from the new imprint. Size reductions to the £1 followed very quickly and the £5 issue was reduced in size from the outset. Around 1962 the bank started experimenting with electronic sorting codes, working with Crosfield Electronics who had developed the CMC7 encoding system of small parallel lines, and De La Rue who were responsible for the magnetic ink essential to make the technology work. It took until late 1967 for the electronic sorting of notes to go live after a long series of technical setbacks.

An experimental £1 'Test Note' note dated 31st March 1962 has survived in reasonable numbers. The coding symbols on it were outside the left and right hand margins on the reverse of the note and were not those finally adopted; these comprised seven horizontal lines printed twice in mirror format in the body of the reverse designs of the £1 and £5 notes, in the format 2-3-2 on the £1 note and 4-2-1 on the £5 note. All specimens have 000000 serials unless otherwise stated.

BL 70	£1	**Andrew Philip Anderson** General Manager				VF	EF	UNC
		B size 151 x 84mm						
		30 Sep 1961	Q/3 000001 - 1000000	1,000,000				
			R/3 000001 - 1000000	1,000,000				
			S/3 000001 - 1000000	1,000,000				
			T/3 000001 - 1000000	1,000,000		15	40	80
		Specimen 30 Sep 1961 Q/3			100		From 120 UNC	
		De La Rue Specimen 30 Sep 1961 Q/3					From 110 UNC	

BL 70 Q/3 First

BL 70 £1 Reverse

BL 71a	£1	**Andrew Philip Anderson** General Manager				**VF**	**EF**	**UNC**
		Reduced size C 151 x 71mm						
		31 Mar 1962	U/3 000001 - 1000000	1,000,000				
			V/3 000001 - 1000000	1,000,000				
			W/3 000001 - 1000000	1,000,000				
			X/3 000001 - 1000000	1,000,000				
			Y/3 000001 - 1000000	1,000,000		**10**	**30**	**60**

BL 71a Y/3 Last

BL 71a Reduced size reverse

Specimen 31 Mar 1962 U/3	100		**From 120 UNC**
De La Rue Specimen 31 Mar 1962 U/3			**From 100 UNC**
Test Note 31 Mar 1962 **Encoded** no prefix/serials			**From 200 UNC**

BL 71a Test Note

BL 71a Test Note reverse Encoded

Technically, the final run of £1 notes dated 13th June 1967 with prefix P/4, are all error notes! The bank had expected these to be delivered with the backs encoded but De La Rue omitted to add the coding.

BL 71b	**£1**	**Thomas W Walker** General Manager					**VF**	**EF**	**UNC**
		1 Jul 1963	Z/3 000001	-	1000000	1,000,000			
			A/4 000001	-	1000000	1,000,000			
			B/4 000001	-	1000000	1,000,000			
			C/4 000001	-	1000000	1,000,000			
			D/4 000001	-	1000000	1,000,000			
		4 May 1964	E/4 000001	-	1000000	1,000,000			
			F/4 000001	-	1000000	1,000,000			
			G/4 000001	-	1000000	1,000,000			
			H/4 000001	-	1000000	1,000,000			
			I/4 000001	-	1000000	1,000,000			
		25 Jan 1966	K/4 000001	-	1000000	1,000,000			
			L/4 000001	-	1000000	1,000,000			
			M/4 000001	-	1000000	1,000,000			
			N/4 000001	-	1000000	1,000,000			
			O/4 000001	-	1000000	1,000,000			
		13 Jun 1967	P/4 000001	-	1000000	1,000,000	10	30	60

		Specimen 1 Jul 1963 Z/3 13 Jun 1967 P/4			100 (each)		**From 100 UNC**
		De La Rue Specimen 1 Jul 1963 Z/3 4 May 1964 E/4 25 Jan 1966 K/4 13 Jun 1967 P/4					**From 80 UNC**

BL 71b P/4 Last

BL 71c	**£1**	**Thomas W Walker** General Manager **Encoded** **Modified design reverse**						**VF EF UNC**
		13 Jun 1967	Q/4 000001	-	1000000	1,000,000		
			R/4 000001	-	1000000	1,000,000		
			S/4 000001	-	1000000	1,000,000		
			T/4 000001	-	1000000	1,000,000		10 35 70
		Specimen 13 Jun 1967 no prefix/serials				100		**From 100 UNC**
		De La Rue Specimen 13 Jun 1967 S/4						**From 80 UNC**

BL 71c T/4 Last

BL 71c Modified design reverse Encoded

The first De La Rue £5 note was smaller than its Waterlows predecessor but not all the notes of this short interim issue were released as work had already started on the new Sir Walter Scott design.

BL 72	£5	**Andrew Philip Anderson** General Manager			VF	EF	UNC
		Reduced size 160 x 90mm					
		2 Jan 1961 Z/11 000001 - 250000	250,000				
		3 Feb 1961 A/12 000001 - 250000	250,000		50	180	360
		4 Mar 1961 B/12 000001 - 250000	250,000 *				
		5 Apr 1961 C/12 000001 - 380000	380,000 *				

* Printed but not issued

      Specimen 2 Jan 1961 Z/11   100   **From 120 UNC**

      De La Rue Specimen 2 Jan 1961 Z/11   **From 100 UNC**

BL 72 Z/11 First

BL 72 A/12 Last confirmed issued

The £20 note was unchanged apart from the revised printers' imprint.

						VF	EF	UNC
BL 73	**£20**	**Andrew Philip Anderson** General Manager						
		14 Feb 1962	G/5 01/001 - 20/500		10,000			
		5 Mar 1962	H/5 01/001 - 20/500		10,000			
		4 Apr 1962	I/5 01/001 - 20/500		10,000	130	350	-
		Specimen 14 Feb 1962 G/5 00/000			100		From 300 UNC	
		De La Rue Specimen 14 Feb 1962 G/5 00/000					From 200 UNC	

BL 73 1962

SCOTTISH UNC

A reminder to collectors that early Scottish 'Square' £1 notes and higher value 'Horse Blankets' will often be found with folds even if otherwise unused. The reason for this is the engrained habit of Scottish bank tellers of folding their notes at least once to fit them into their tills. Horse Blankets will often be found with two vertical folds, one third in on each side, while Squares will usually have a single vertical fold. As a result the top grade for a Scottish note is sometimes referred to as 'Scottish UNC', in reality this being between EF and AUNC depending on how heavy the folds are. Do not be put off buying this grade in the hope that a better one will come along as it is unlikely truly uncirculated notes exist.

The £100 note was also unchanged apart from the revised printers' imprint. A long run of £100 notes in 'Scottish UNC' with the final date 1st June 1962 has been coming on to the market in recent years. Notes in the range V/3 02/143 to 02/190 have been observed to date (early November 2017). Previously, issued notes of this type had been rare and there was doubt as to how many had been issued.

BL 74	**£100**	**Andrew Philip Anderson** General Manager					**VF**	**EF**
		9 May 1962	U/3 01/001	-	02/500	1,000		
		1 Jun 1962	V/3 01/001	-	02/500	1,000	**650**	**1500**
		Specimen 9 May 1962 U/3 00/000				100	**From 300 UNC**	
		De La Rue Specimen 9 May 1962 U/3 00/000					**From 200 UNC**	

BL 74 V/3 Last 1962

SECOND THOMAS DE LA RUE ISSUE – 1962 *to* 1970

Sir Walter Scott portrait

The British Linen Bank made the inspired and ground-breaking decision to feature the portrait of Sir Walter Scott on its final note issues prior to being acquired by the Bank of Scotland. Essays of £1 and £5 notes with the Scott portrait have emerged from the De La Rue archives, dated 31st December 1961 and 30th September 1961 respectively. Both carry the printed signature of A P Anderson. The very first issued £1 note U/4 000001 and one of the first £5 notes D/12 100000 were donated by the bank to Mrs Patricia Maxwell-Scott and are now on display at Scott's former home in Abbotsford. Discussions had started with De La Rue in January 1969 to produce a new reduced size £20 note with the Scott portrait but these did not proceed due to the imminent merger with the Bank of Scotland.

There was only one variety of the £1 note, now further reduced in size to size D, but the £5 notes were further reduced from size X in 1968. The last issues look as if they are printed on plain rather than granite paper but the coloured fibres are now in invisible fluorescent form. A metallic security strip was introduced in 1962 on the £5 notes with the £1 notes following suit in 1968.

The final £1 notes were taken into cash on 8th December 1970 and were thus the very last notes the bank issued and the only ones dated 1970. All specimens have 000000 serials unless otherwise stated.

De La Rue Essay 1961 (enlarged)

BL 75 £1 **Thomas W Walker** General Manager **Encoded**   VF   EF   UNC
Metallic Strip 134 x 67mm

					VF	EF	UNC
29 Feb 1968	U/4 000001	-	1000000	1,000,000			
	V/4 000001	-	1000000	1,000,000			
	W/4 000001	-	1000000	1,000,000			
	X/4 000001	-	1000000	1,000,000			
	Y/4 000001	-	1000000	1,000,000			
5 Nov 1969	Z/4 000001	-	1000000	1,000,000			
	A/5 000001	-	1000000	1,000,000			
	B/5 000001	-	1000000	1,000,000			
	C/5 000001	-	1000000	1,000,000	10	30	60
20 Jul 1970	D/5 000001	-	1000000	1,000,000	10	35	70

Specimen 29 Feb 1968 U/4   100   **From 100 UNC**

De La Rue Specimen 29 Feb 1968 U/4
                 5 Nov 1969 Z/4   20 Jul 1970 D/5   **From 80 UNC**

BL 75 D/5 Last 1970

BL 75 Reverse Encoded

British Linen Bank

BL 76a   £5   **Andrew Philip Anderson** General Manager   VF   EF   UNC
Metallic Strip 140 x 85mm

21 Sep 1962	D/12 000001	-	1000000	1,000,000
20 Oct 1962	E/12 000001	-	1000000	1,000,000
19 Nov 1962	F/12 000001	-	1000000	1,000,000

                                                                         15   45   90

Specimen 21 Sep 1962 D/12   100   **From 120 UNC**

De La Rue Specimen 21 Sep 1962 D/12   **From 100 UNC**

BL 76a

BL 76a Reverse

BL 76b   £5   **Thomas W Walker** General Manager **Metallic strip**

16 Jun 1964	G/12 000001	-	1000000	1,000,000
17 Jul 1964	H/12 000001	-	100000	100,000
	H/12 200001	-	1000000	800,000
18 Aug 1964	I/12 000001	-	1000000	1,000,000

                                                                         15   45   90

De La Rue Specimen 16 Jun 1964 G/12   **From 100 UNC**

A portion of the H/12 printing was prepared with electronic sorting codes added. This had been done on an experimental basis but as the coding was in the finally adopted format the notes were issued, although not until late 1967.

BL 76c	**£5**	**Thomas W Walker** General Manager **Encoded**			**VF**	**EF**	**UNC**
		17 Jul 1964 H/12 100001 - 200000		100,000	**100**	**180**	**300**

BL 76c 1964

BL 76c Reverse Encoded

The final printing of the £5 note saw a further size reduction. 1,000,000 notes of this issue dated 24th May 1968 with prefix M/12 were printed but not delivered and were later destroyed.

BL 77	£5	**Thomas W Walker** General Manager **Encoded** **Metallic Strip** 145 x 78mm					VF	EF	UNC
		22 Mar 1968	K/12 000001	-	1000000	1,000,000			
		23 Apr 1968	L/12 000001	-	1000000	1,000,000	20	55	120
		24 May 1968	M/12 000001	-	1000000	1,000,000 ∗			

∗ Printed but not issued

        Specimen 22 Mar 1968 K/12   100   **From 120 UNC**

        De La Rue Specimen 22 Mar 1968 K/12   **From 100 UNC**

BL 77 L/12 Last issued prefix

BL 77 Reverse Encoded

Caledonian Bank

Caledonian Banking Company 1836 *to* 1882
Caledonian Bank Limited 1882 *to* 1906

The Caledonian Banking Company was established as a joint stock company in Inverness in 1838 with a nominal capital of £125,000, of which only one quarter was initially paid up. In the early years of its development the bank opened a number of branches mostly in the Inverness area though it did eventually venture further afield. Its expansion eastwards, however, caused friction with and was probably halted by the Aberdeen-based North of Scotland Bank, which saw the Caledonian as encroaching on its patch.

The bank thus kept to its Highlands heartlands and remained the only bank ever to be based in Inverness. Its directors, shareholders and employees were overwhelmingly from the Highlands themselves. With pre-railway communications slow and difficult the Highland community of the time was close-knit and self-reliant, both a strength and a weakness for the bank. The bank traded successfully until 1878 when it was hit by the City of Glasgow Bank debacle. It held £400 of the City of Glasgow's stock as security for a loan. There was rumour and panic, forcing the Caledonian to close its doors on 5th December 1878. The Bank of Scotland agreed to provide assistance and this, along with the news that their City of Glasgow Bank liability stood at only £11,000, enabled the Caledonian to reopen its doors for business eight months later in August 1879.

The damage had been done, however, and the bank did not subsequently prosper. By the turn of the century its decline had become increasingly evident. A few major bad debts did not help and by 1907 the bank's reserves were down to £195,000, its net profits barely over £12,000 and it had clearly become too small and weak to survive alone. The Caledonian Bank directors approached the Bank of Scotland in 1906 to propose an amalgamation which the shareholders duly agreed to at a special meeting in July 1907. At the time of its absorption the bank had a total of thirty four branches making it the smallest of the ten note-issuing banks operating in Scotland at the turn of the century. Today, the most tangible evidence of its history is its former head office on the High Street in Inverness, a beautiful example of Victorian classical architecture built in 1847 to the design of Mackenzie and Matthews. It was for many years the main Inverness branch of the Bank of Scotland but is now a glorified pub.

There were only two basic banknote designs, one for the £1 note and another for the higher denominations. Almost uniquely for Scottish notes, all the notes carry a Gaelic motto (spelt slightly differently on some notes), 'Tir nam Beann, nan Gleann, s'nan Gaisgeach' which translates as 'Land of the Mountains, the Glens and the Heroes'. The Authorised Circulation under the 1845 Bankers Act was £53,434.

FIRST ISSUE – 1839 *to* 1862

W H Lizars Designs

The original designs were prepared by **W H Lizars** and count amongst the most delightful of all Scottish notes, especially the higher values. The vignette of Inverness on the £1 note was engraved from a drawing by William Banks, who was Lizars's works manager before starting out on his own as an engraver, printer and lithographer. An identical vignette of Inverness attributed to Banks appears in The Scottish Tourist, a guide book of Scotland published by Lizars in the 1840s. There are two other vignettes, symbolic depictions of Hunting and Agriculture. These also appear on the higher denomination notes which feature a central vignette of Inverness Castle with a sweeping panorama of the town (a city since 2000) and the mountains. A number of early essays by Lizars have survived, showing how the final designs evolved.

The note registers of the bank have survived more or less intact in the archives of the Lloyds Banking Group in Edinburgh and available details are listed. All notes have printed prefix and serials. All notes handsigned by the Accountant and Manager unless otherwise stated.

The £1 notes were printed in books of 500, the first batch numbered fom A 1/1 to A 152/500 (76,000 notes) and the second B 1/1 to B 100/500 (50,000 notes). The dates of issue are recorded as ranging from 8th February 1839 to 1st May 1857. These may not necessarily have been the dates actually on the notes.

CA 1a	£1	Black	**Dated by hand**	uniface	Congreve		
			16 Apr 1839	plate A	50/292		
			1 Jun 1839	plate A	52/236		
			10 Jul 1839	plate A	69/223 – 70/411		**From 3000 F**
		Proof	undated	plate A B B/A (plate letter B left & A right)			**From 350 EF**

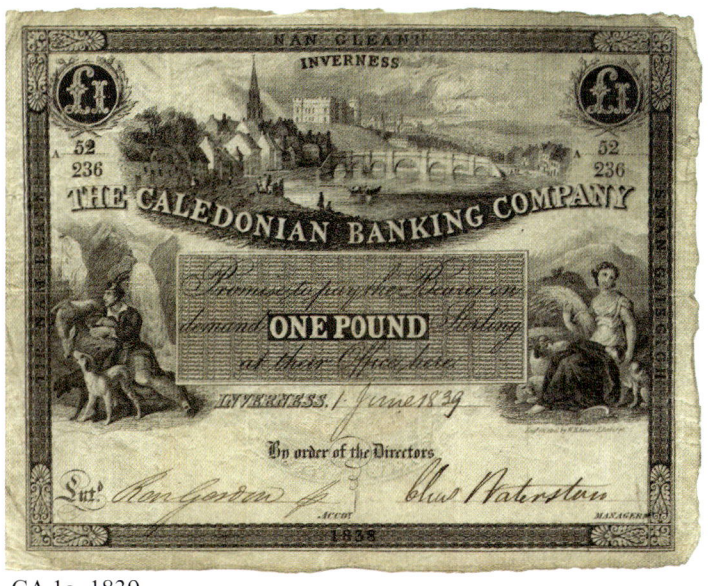

CA 1a 1839

Prior to 1859 a blue reverse was added to the £1 note by Lizars. The design comprised the arms of Inverness surrounded by, in clockwise order from the one o'clock position, those of Dingwall, Nairn, Forres, Cromarty, Dornoch and Elgin, all towns where the bank had opened branches. Issued notes ran from C 1/1 to C 70/500 (35,000 notes).

CA 1b £1 **Black** blue reverse

Proof blue reverse **From 250 EF**

CA 1b Reverse in blue

£5 notes were issued from 8th February 1839 to 1st June 1840 and numbered A 1/1 to A 29/250 in books of 250 (7,250 notes).

CA 2a £5 **Black Dated by hand** uniface Congreve

Proof undated plate A **From 500 EF**

The blue reverse was added to plate B in 1859. Notes were issued from 1st October 1859 to 1st July 1872 and were numbered B 1/1 to B 50/200 in books of 200 (10,000 notes). Two varieties known.

CA 2b £5 **Black Dated by hand** blue reverse
1 Oct 1859   plate B   2/63
1 Nov 1865   plate B   27/130 - 50/76 **From 2500 F**

CA 2c £5 **Black Ornate Red initials C B Co over central panel
Dated by hand** blue reverse
1 Oct 1859   plate B   18/19 - 21/172 **From 2500 F**

£10 notes were issued from 25th February 1839 to 23rd May 1892 and numbered A 1/1 to A 16/250 in books of 250 (4,000 notes). Remarkably, only one issued note has survived. Although printed by Lizars it was not issued until 1892, so limited was the demand for this denomination. As the bank had adopted limited liability and changed its name long before 1892, the note was overprinted accordingly.

CA 3	£10	Black Dated by hand uniface	
		23 May 1892 plate A 15/194	RARE
		Proof undated plate A	From 500 EF

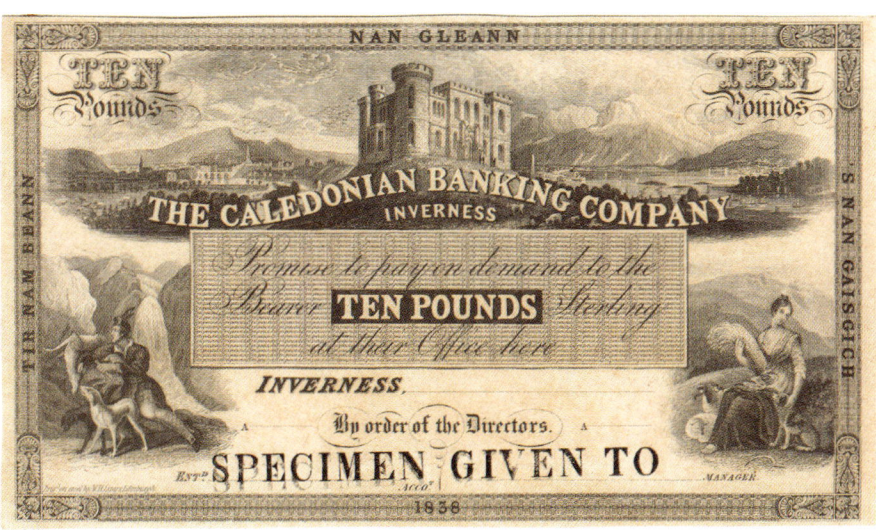

CA 3 £10 Proof

£20 notes were issued from 25th February 1839 to 1st November 1888 and were numbered A 1/1 to A 22/250 in books of 250 (5,500 notes). At some point these notes may have had a change of printers' imprint but no issued notes have survived to ascertain where the change came.

CA 4	£20	**Black Dated by hand** uniface	
		No issued notes recorded	
		Proof undated plate A	**From 600 EF**

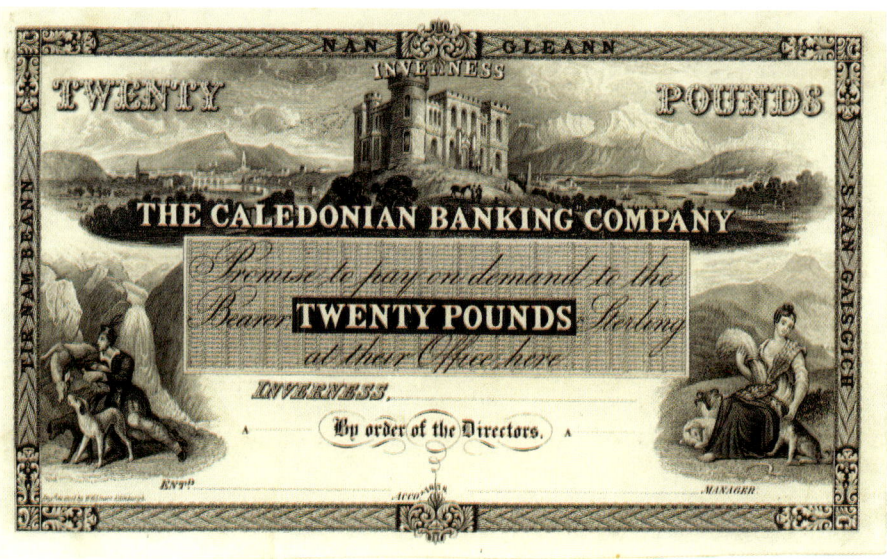

CA 4 £20 Proof

£100 notes were issued from 9th December 1857 to 1st May 1874 and numbered A 1/1 to A 5/1 in books of 100 (401 notes). A change of printers' imprint may also have occurred but no issued notes have survived to confirm this.

CA 5	£100	**Black Dated by hand** uniface	
		No issued notes recorded	
		Proof undated plate A	**From 750 EF**

SECOND ISSUE – 1862 *to* 1891

Printer: **W & A K Johnston**

The Lizars plates were taken over by **W & A K Johnston** when they acquired Lizars's business after his death in 1859. Initially the only change they made to the obverse was to the printers' imprint.

The £1 note was however re-engraved with a revised vignette of Inverness featuring the new suspension bridge opened in 1855. A red central panel was added to the obverse and the blue reverse was dropped from the £1 note. The text 'Incorporated by Act of Parliament' was added inside the upper border. An anomaly seen on one note dated 15th May 1876 shows the engraved plate letters G to the left and F to the right. Notes signed p. Acct and p Manager. Note issue totals shown where known.

CA 6	£1	Black Suspension bridge vignette printed date uniface Central panel with Red text				
		1 Jan 1863	D 1/1	- 100/500	50,000	
		1 Nov 1865	E 1/1	- 100/500	50,000	
		1 Jul 1872	F 1/1	- 100/500	50,000	
		15 May 1876	G 1/1	- 100/500	50,000	
			H 1/1	- 100/500	50,000	
			I 1/1	- 92/500	46,000	**From 2000 F**

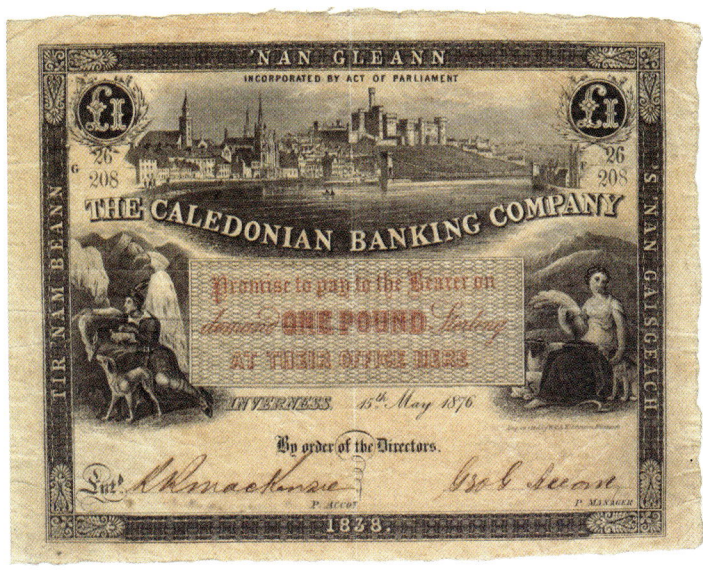

CA 6   1876

Proof 1 Jan 1863 plate D no red panel   **From 400 EF**

Specimen 1 Jan 1863 plate D   **From 600 EF**

CA 7a	**£5**	**Black Dated by hand** blue reverse
		No issued notes recorded may not have been issued

The £5 note was further modified in 1872 and the blue reverse discontinued on the issued note.

CA 7b	**£5**	**Black Red central panel with outline FIVE** printed date uniface		
		1 Jul 1872 C 1/1 - 45/200	9,000	**From 2000 F**
		Proof with and without outline Red FIVE plate C		**From 500 EF**
		Proof Blue reverse plate C *Printer:* **W H Lizars**		**From 600 EF**

W & A K Johnston prepared £10, £20 and £100 notes but it is not known if any were issued with their imprint.

CA 8	**£10**	**Black Dated by hand** blue reverse
		Proof uniface plate A — **From 600 EF**
		Proof Blue reverse plate A *Printer:* **W H Lizars** — **From 750 EF**

CA 9	**£20**	**Black Dated by hand** blue reverse
		Proof uniface plate A — **From 600 EF**
		Proof Blue reverse plate A *Printer:* **W H Lizars** — **From 750 EF**

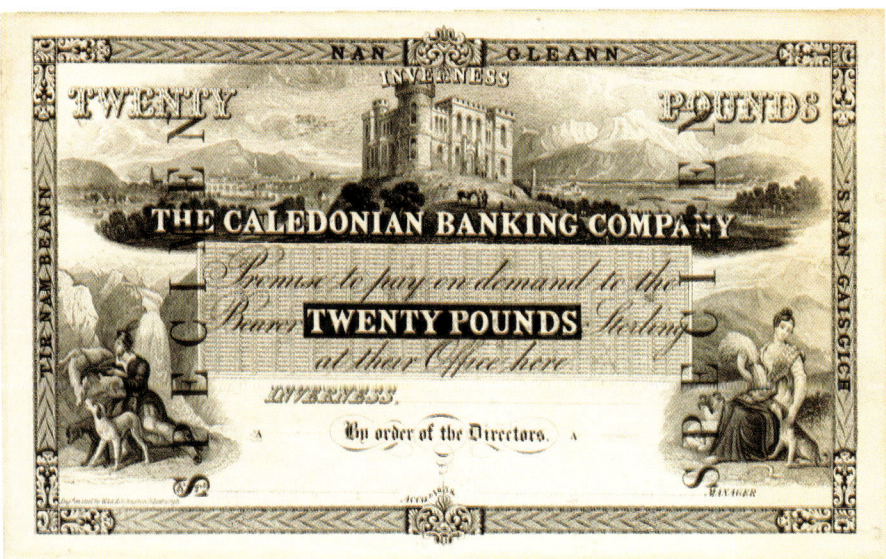

CA 9 £20 Proof

CA 10   **£100** **Black** **Dated by hand** blue reverse

        Proof uniface plate A   **From 700 EF**
        Proof Blue reverse plate A *Printer:* **W H Lizars**   **From 850 EF**

CA 10 £100 Proof

PROVISIONAL ISSUE – 1882

Second Issue Overprinted: 𝔗𝔥𝔢 ℭ𝔞𝔩𝔢𝔡𝔬𝔫𝔦𝔞𝔫 𝔅𝔞𝔫𝔨𝔦𝔫𝔤 ℭ𝔬𝔶., 𝔏𝔦𝔪𝔦𝔱𝔢𝔡.

The Caledonian Bank adopted limited liability in 1882. Consequently a vertical or diagonal overprint in Gothic script in either black or blue was applied to all notes outstanding at that time. The overprint simply stated the bank's revised name 'The Caledonian Banking Coy., Limited.' and has been observed on £1 and £5 notes as well as on the one surviving £10 note.

Enlargement of overprint

CA 11   £1   Overprint on: CA 6   From 1500 F

CA 11 Overprint on CA6 £1 1876

CA 12a   £5   Overprint on: CA 2b & CA 2c   From 2000 F

CA 12b   £5   Overprint on: CA 7b   From 2000 F

CA 12b Overprint on CA7b £5 1872, ink cancelled

CA 13   £10   Overprint on: CA 3   RARE

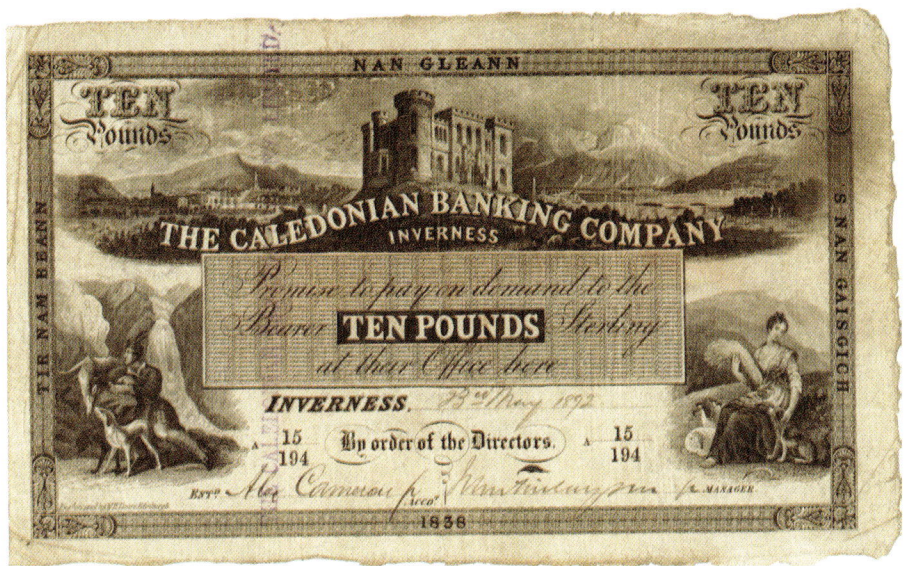

CA 13 Overprint on CA 3 1892

THIRD ISSUE – 1891 *to* 1906

Printer: **George Waterston & Sons Orange Overlay**

In 1891 the bank turned to **George Waterston & Sons of Edinburgh** who made minor changes to the original designs, introduced new colours and added a lithographic orange and yellow overlay. This series remained in issue until 1906 with only one minor change to the bank title in 1904 when the initial 'THE' was dropped. The value panels on the £10, £20 and £100 notes were printed in blue. All notes now carry the wording 'Incorporated under the Companies Acts 1862 to 1880'. The notes continued to circulate long after the Caledonian had been absorbed by the Bank of Scotland. £1 notes are signed p Acct and p Manager. An unsolicited essay was prepared by Bradbury Wilkinson in 1904 using the same view of Inverness as the Waterston note but with an additional vignette of an unidentified Highland gentleman. A reverse featuring a view of the River Ness from the castle was also prepared. Sadly only black and white photographs of the note have survived.

The vignette of Inverness on the £1 note initially remained unchanged and continued to feature the suspension bridge. No issued notes of this type have been seen, though proofs (possibly later pulls) survive.

CA 14   **£1**   **Black & Orange Suspension bridge vignette** printed date uniface
No issued notes recorded

15 May 1891	I 93/1 - 100/500		40,000
	J 1/1 - 32/500		16,000

Proof 15 May 1891 I   **From 700 EF**
Proof Uncut sheet of four 15 May 1891 I   **From 4800 EF**

CA 14 £1 Proof 1891

Proof uncut sheet of four 1891 (not to same scale)

The vignette of Inverness was modified in 1893 when the earlier view of the stone bridge was re-introduced.

CA 15a **£1** **Black & Orange Stone bridge vignette** printed date uniface

16 Jan 1893	J 33/1	- 100/500	34,000	
15 Jan 1895	K 1/1	- 100/500	50,000	
	L 1/1	- 100/500	50,000	
3 Jan 1898	M 1/1	- 100/500	50,000	
2 Jul 1900	N 1/1	- 100/500	50,000	**From 1500 F**

CA 15a 1900

Specimen 16 Jan 1893 J **From 1000 EF**

The bulk of the final print run, from P 5/1 to P 100/500 was destroyed unissued in December 1907.

CA 15b	£1	Black & Orange	Shortened bank title	uniface		
		4 Jan 1904	O	1/1 - 100/500	50,000	
		2 Jan 1906	P	1/1 - 4/500	2,000	**From 1500 F**

CA 15b 1906

Pull Black & Orange undated limited issue by HBOS 2007

**UNC
30**

Photographic Essay c.1904

A few issued £5 notes can be found in the Lloyds archive.

CA 16a	£5	**Black & Orange** Dated by hand uniface		
		16 Jan 1893 D 1/1 - 10/200	2,000	
		18 Jun 1894 D 11/1 - 20/200	2,000	
		1 Jan 1896 D 21/1 - 44/200	4,800	**RARE**
		Specimen undated A		**From 1500 EF**

CA 16b	£5	**Black & Orange** printed date uniface		
		11 Nov 1897 D 45/1 - 50/200	1,200	
		E 1/1 - 15/200	3,000	
		2 Jul 1900 E 16/1 - 35/200	4,000	**RARE**

CA 16b 1897

The final print run of the £5 note carries the shorter title, but the notes themselves, while apparently issued, have not been seen.

CA 16c	£5	**Black & Orange Shortened bank title** printed date uniface	
		4 Jan 1904 E 36/1 - 50/200	3,000
		F 1/1 - 15/200	3,000
		2 Jan 1906 F 16/1 - 22/200	1,400
		Specimen 2 Jan 1906 F 50/50 Lloyds archive	

No issued £10 notes have been seen though a small number of specimens exist.

CA 17a	£10	Black & Orange Blue value panels			
		3 Jan 1898 A 17/1 - 18/200	400		
		2 Jan 1900 A 19/1 - 21/200	600		**RARE**
		Specimen undated A & A 22/101 Lloyds archive			From 2000 EF

CA 17a Specimen A prefix

A single specimen has survived of the £10 note with the shortened title. It is un-numbered but hand annotations on the reverse suggest that 1,000 notes in the range A 31/1 to A 35/200 were prepared and sent to the bank on 2nd August 1904. There is no evidence any of these notes were issued.

CA 17b   **£10**   **Black & Orange   Blue value panels   Shortened bank title**
No issued notes recorded

         Specimen   4 Jan 1904 A   **From 2000 EF**

CA 17b Specimen shortened title

£20 notes were issued from 16th January 1893 to 20th April 1903 and were numbered A 33/1 to A 45/200 in books of 200 (2,600 notes). None has survived.

CA 18a £20 **Black & Orange Blue value panels** Dated by hand uniface
No issued notes recorded

CA 18b £20 **Black & Orange Blue value panels Shortened bank title**
No issued notes recorded

Specimen undated plate B Lloyds archive

£100 notes were issued from 16th January 1893 to 3rd January 1898 and were numbered A 11/1 to A 12/100 in books of 100 (200 notes). None has survived.

CA 19a £100 **Black & Orange Blue value panels**
No issued notes recorded

A final issue was dated 1 October 1904, numbered A 13/1 to A 13/100 (100 notes).

CA 19b £100 **Black & Orange Blue value panels Shortened bank title**
No issued notes recorded

Specimen undated A Lloyds archive

CA 19b Specimen

Union Bank of Scotland

Union Bank of Scotland 1843 *to* 1880
Union Bank of Scotland Limited 1882 *to* 1954

The Union Bank of Scotland grew out of the Glasgow Union Banking Company, a bank founded in 1830 to provide a counterweight to the dominance of the Edinburgh-based 'Chartered' or public banks which the increasing industrial power of Glasgow – and municipal pride – demanded be challenged. The Glasgow Union had already absorbed three other banks before the decision was taken to reconstitute and re-launch the bank in May 1843. The name change was motivated by the desire of the bank to project its stronger position across the banking map of Scotland as it had gained a solid reputation for reliability and conservatism. The new bank opened its doors for buisness on 1st July 1843.

Unusually, the new bank had two head offices from the outset. To the original one in Glasgow was added a second in Edinburgh, all the directors of which were former partners of Sir William Forbes, James Hunter & Co, the leading private bank of the time which had merged with the Glasgow Union in April 1838. There were now a total of twelve directors, six in Glasgow and six in Edinburgh, although administrative control remained in Glasgow. Paid-up capital was increased from £350,000 to £500,000 in April, and again to £1,000,000 in November. There were now several hundred shareholders and the formation document, signed by every single one of them, was nearly fifteen metres long.

Two further amalgamations took place just after the Union Bank had been established in 1843: Hunters & Co of Ayr was absorbed in August and the Glasgow & Ship Bank in December. This bank had itself been created by an amalgamation, of the venerable Ship Bank and the Glasgow Bank Company of Dennistoun & Co. In 1849 the Banking Company in Aberdeen was also absorbed. This bank had suffered substantial losses as a result of which its nominal capital of £300,000 had reduced to a mere £7,049 5s 1d. The name of the Aberdeen bank did not disappear until 1854 but its absorption did give the Union Bank entry into the regional market of northeast Scotland. The final acquisition took place in 1857 when the Perth Banking Company was taken over. This was the Union Bank's last acquisition and resulted in the bank having both the highest Authorised Circulation in Scotland (£454,346) and the highest number of branches (ninety seven) at that time. The branch network now extended throughout Scotland.

In November 1862 the bank was incorporated under the Companies Act of that year. Its further progress was much slower and it lost its early dynamism to gradually slip down the rankings until by the time of its acquisition by the Bank of Scotland in 1955 it was only the sixth largest of the seven remaining Scottish banks.

The early note issues of the Union Bank are as complex as its early history. The first notes were designed in 1843 by **W H Lizars**. These notes were originally thought to have been prepared for issue only in Edinburgh until proofs prepared for issue in Glasgow also came to light. The Glasgow Committee's minutes, on re-examination, confirmed most if not all denominations of the Lizars designs were issued payable in both cities. A single issued Glasgow note, a £1 note from 1845, has been recorded.

From 1846 new designs were prepared by **Perkins Bacon & Petch** and it can be confirmed that these were made payable only in Glasgow. The two series of notes were issued in parallel until 1863 though the Lizars Glasgow issue was probably discontinued when the Perkins notes were first issued in 1846. The designs of the two series are quite different and it remains a unique circumstance in Scottish banking history that a single bank had concurrent note issues payable in different offices.

It must have made procedures at the regular note exchanges with other banks somewhat problematic, not to mention the preparation of the periodic note issue returns to the Stamp Office. In fact there were further complexities: Forbes Hunter continued to issue its own notes until October 1845 and these too had to be separately exchanged with the other banks. The Union Bank's Edinburgh balance sheet in June 1846 showed Forbes Hunter notes amounting to £183,820 still in issue as well as £194,000 of Union Bank notes. Moreover the Banking Company in Aberdeen's final note issue from 1849 to 1854 took place after that bank had been absorbed by the Union Bank and carries both banks' names.

According to the Edinburgh Committee minute books of the Union Bank, W H Lizars presented specimens of the £1 note design on 25th May 1843. These were approved and passed to the Glasgow Committee for their approval. Two years later the minutes of the Glasgow Committee record that on 13th August 1845 a request was received from Perkins Bacon & Co to design a new 20 Shillings note. Sketches were approved on 19th November and the finished proofs on 25th March 1846. The new notes were payable in Glasgow and were authorised for issue on 29th April 1846.

There is no clear reason why separate issues payable in different cities were prepared. There is no evidence of any disagreement between the two Committees on this matter so perhaps it was just down to a desire to preserve some degree of independence from each other.

The separate issues were replaced in 1863 by a new issue payable at both the bank's head offices in 'Glasgow or Edinburgh'. The Union was the only Scottish bank to make its notes payable in more than one location and continued this practice until its final issues in 1954. The new notes quickly replaced the earlier issues which were withdrawn and as a result are very rare in issued form. The 1863 issue was prepared by **Perkins Bacon & Co** who retained the contract until 1904 when a dispute between the partners prompted the bank to switch the contract to **Waterlow & Sons**. Waterlows remained the bank's engravers and printers until the merger with the Bank of Scotland.

All note issue details have been extracted from the Union Bank's minute books. Some of the earlier records are however not precise enough to be applied to specific dates or even denominations so we have given authorisation dates for the issue if the date on the note is not otherwise recorded. The numbering of all notes conforms to the established Scottish fractional system of book number over sequential number, except where stated.

Dimensions of notes conform to the Scottish standard Size A 'square' for the £1 (~ 155 x 125mm) and Size W 'horse blanket' for the higher denominations (~ 210 x 125mm). The £1 note was reduced to Size B in 1924 (~ 150 x 85mm) while size reductions of the higher values took place in 1950.

FIRST LIZARS ISSUE – 1843

Four bank names in borders Separate Edinburgh and Glasgow Issues

Common features of this magnificent series are vignettes of two equestrian statues, Charles II in Parliament Square, Edinburgh, and William of Orange in the Trongate, Glasgow.

The four banks are:

- **Sir William Forbes, J Hunter & Co** (top border of Edinburgh issue & bottom border of Glasgow issue)
- **Paisley Union Bank Co** (right border)
- **Glasgow Union Banking Company** (bottom of the Edinburgh issue and top of the Glasgow issue)
- **Glasgow Thistle Bank Co** (left border)

The £1 note features two female figures lower left and right, representing the Arts (left) and Commerce and Industry (right). The vignettes are transposed on the Glasgow issues. All notes are handsigned and carry the imprint **Drawn and Engraved by W H Lizars, Edinburgh**. Issued £1 notes are printed on watermarked paper. No issued notes of any higher denomination have survived.

A few issued £1 notes have a black stamped letter **L** on the front. This may have been a control mark applied for internal purposes. The small red stamps seen applied either side of the ONE on some notes may also have been control marks. It is possible both were applied to check how the notes were in practice circulating. The **L** has not, for example, been seen on the Perkins Bacon Glasgow issues. These symbols do not appear to have had the same function as the star applied to Glasgow notes of the Perkins issue from 1854 to indicate the absence of a revenue stamp on the reverse. The **L** has been seen on both stamped and unstamped Lizars notes. A number of notes of the 1st Issue had to be withdrawn and replaced due to the inferior quality of the paper.

EDINBURGH ISSUE

UB 1   £1   **Payable in Edinburgh Handsigned** Accountant & Cashier
              printed serials   year printed as 184 Congreve
                 1 Jul 1843   21/81   20,000   **RARE**

UB 1 Black stamped letter L

Proof undated   From 500 EF

On the £5 note the female vignettes represent Justice (left) and Industry/Commerce (right).

UB 2	**£5**	**Payable in Edinburgh Handsigned** Accountant & Cashier year printed as 184	
		Proof undated	**From 600 EF**

The £10 note is similar but the central vignette is of an allegorical male and two females with the two equestrian statues moved to the lower left and right.

UB 3	**£10**	**Payable in Edinburgh Handsigned** Accountant & Cashier year printed as 184	
		Proof undated	**From 600 EF**

On the £20 note the equestrian statues are facing forward and located upper centre, either side of a plinth inscribed with a 20 and the shields of Edinburgh and Glasgow.

UB 4	**£20**	**Payable in Edinburgh Handsigned** Accountant & Cashier year printed as 184	
		Proof year printed as 184	**From 600 EF**

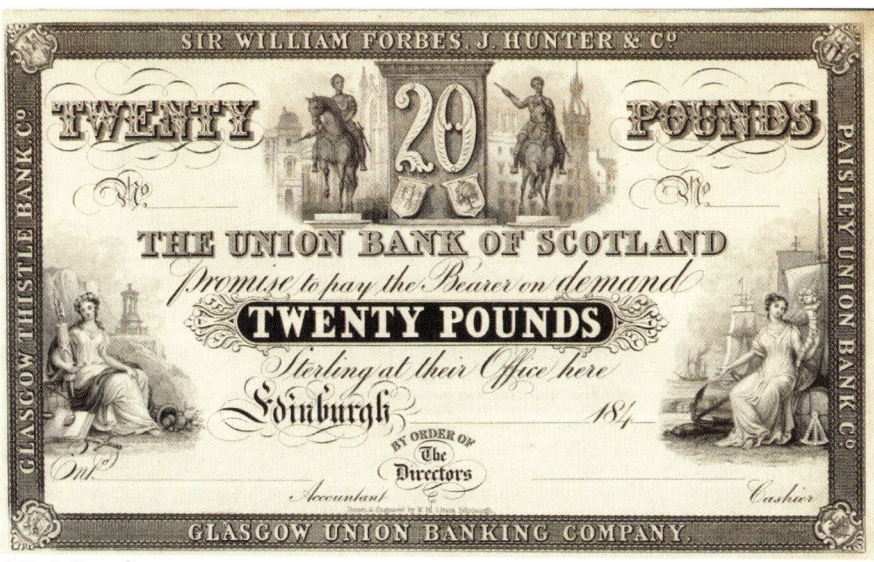

UB 4 Proof

The £100 note has a central vignette of Queen Victoria with large 100 panels either side. A proof with the 100 panels missing has also been recorded.

UB 5	**£100**	**Payable in Edinburgh Handsigned** Accountant & Cashier year printed as 184	
		Proof undated	**From 700 EF**

GLASGOW ISSUE

UB 6   £1   **Payable in Glasgow**   Bank names & vignettes transposed

                       Proof   year printed as 184   **From 1000 EF**

UB 6   Proof   marked SPECIMEN

UB 7   £5   **Payable in Glasgow**   Bank names & vignettes transposed
                       Confirmed issued   Not seen

UB 8   £10   **Payable in Glasgow**   Bank names & vignettes transposed
                       Confirmed issued   Not seen

UB 9   £20   **Payable in Glasgow**   Bank names & vignettes transposed
                       Confirmed issued   Not seen

UB 10	£100	**Payable in Glasgow** Bank names & vignettes transposed		
		Proof year printed as 184		**RARE**

UB 10 Proof

SECOND LIZARS ISSUE – 1844 *to* 1860

Six bank names in borders Separate Edinburgh and Glasgow Issues

Design as before but with two additional banks in borders: Hunters & Comp^y Ayr (left) and Glasgow & Ship Bank (right). Printed Congreve revenue stamp on reverse of issued £1 notes. No issued notes of any higher denomination have survived. It is believed that the Glasgow issues were discontinued when the Perkins Bacon notes were introduced in 1846. Issue records are incomplete and in some cases only the totals authorised (auth) are recorded. n/a = not available n/k = not known

EDINBURGH ISSUE – 1844 *to* 1860

UB 11	£1	**Payable in Edinburgh** Congreve		
		Handsigned Acco^t & Cashier		
		2 Jan 1844		14,000
		Oct - Nov 1844 (auth)		30,000
		Apr - Dec 1845 (auth)		100,000
		5 Oct 1846	24/226	30,000
		1848 (auth)		15,000	**From 2500 F**

UB 11 Punch cancelled Stamped L top left

Proof undated   From 500 EF

UB 12	£5	Payable in Edinburgh Handsigned Accountant & Cashier	
		Year printed as 184	
		2 Jan 1844	8,000
		1845 (auth)	7,994
		1860 (auth)	3,000

Proof year printed as 184   From 600 EF

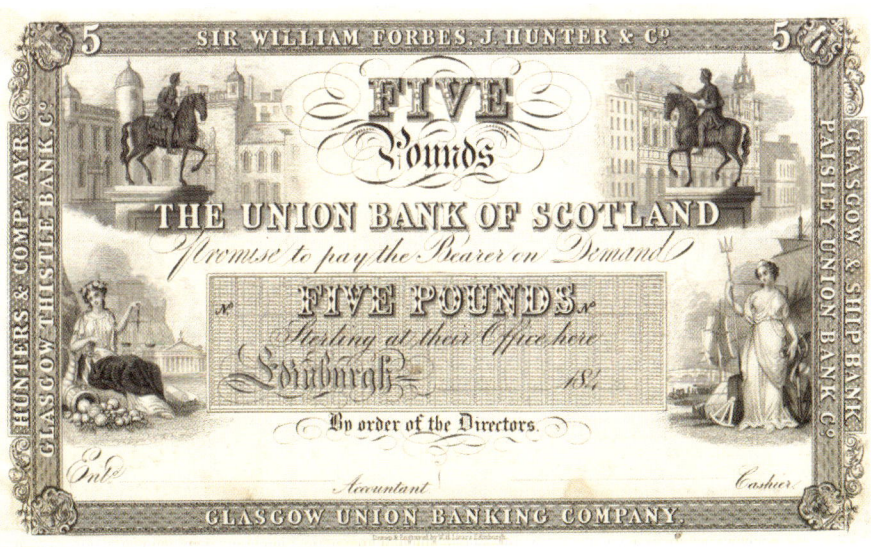

UB 12 Proof

UB 13   £10   **Payable in Edinburgh   Handsigned** Acco! & Cashier
                         Year printed as 184
                            2 Jan 1844   2,000

                      Proof   year printed as 184   **From 600 EF**

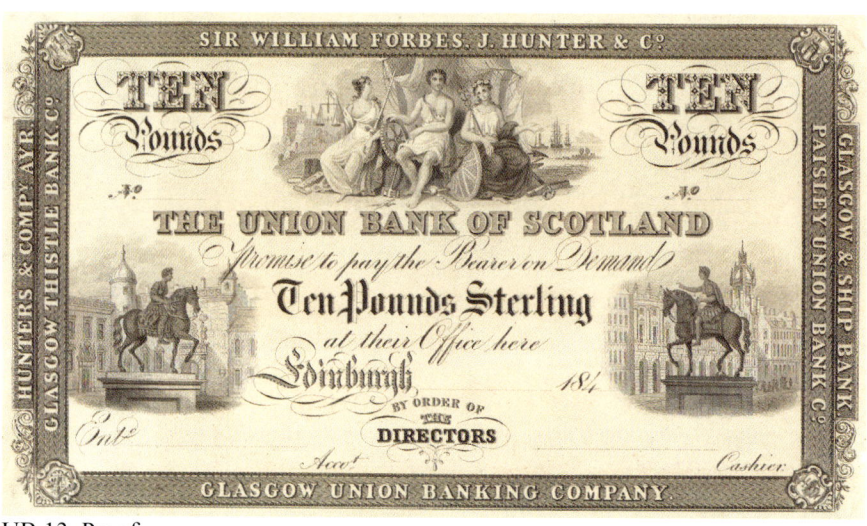

UB 13   Proof

UB 14   £20   **Payable in Edinburgh   Handsigned** Accountant & Cashier
                         Year printed as 184
                            2 Jan 1844   1,000
                                 1846 (auth)   2,600

                      Proof   year printed as 184   **From 600 EF**

UB 15   £100   **Payable in Edinburgh   Handsigned** Accountant & Manager
                         Year printed as 184
                            2 Jan 1844   500
                                1846 (auth)   500

                      Proof   year printed as 184   **From 700 EF**

UB 15 Proof

GLASGOW ISSUE 1844 *to* 1846

The Glasgow Committee minutes confirm that 20,000 £1 notes were issued in Glasgow running from book 249 to book 288, all dated 1st May 1845. Each book contained 500 notes.

UB 16	£1	**Payable in Glasgow** Bank names and vignettes transposed **Serials hand-written** year of date printed as 184 Congreve		
		1 May 1845 277/157	20,000	**From 3000 F**

UB 16 1845

UB 17	£5	**Payable in Glasgow** Bank names & vignettes transposed *Confirmed issued Not seen*
UB 18	£10	**Payable in Glasgow** Bank names & vignettes transposed *Confirmed issued Not seen*
UB 19	£20	**Payable in Glasgow** Bank names & vignettes transposed

UB 19   £20   Proof year printed as 184   **RARE**

UB 19 Proof

UB 20   £100   **Payable in Glasgow** Bank names & vignettes transposed
Confirmed issued Not seen

THIRD LIZARS ISSUE – 1850 *to* 1857

Seven bank names in borders Payable in Edinburgh

Only the £1 note is known to have been further modified by adding a seventh bank, the Banking Co. in Aberdeen, below the lower border. Only the 18 of the date is printed while the printers' imprint is amended to **W H Lizars, Edinburgh** and is moved inside the lower border. On 8th January 1850 the Minutes record a report that '*there was a probability of getting rid of the Government coloured stamp on £5 and £1 notes, and having a dry stamp imposed instead*'. However, a surviving issued note dated 4 June 1850 has neither Congreve nor embossed stamp on it and is clearly uniface. A few notes dated 1854 and 1856 have been recorded with two small red control marks upper centre. The significance of these is unclear.

UB 21	£1	Payable in Edinburgh Handsigned Acco! & Cashier

Dated by hand printed serials uniface

4 Jun 1850	41/230			n/k
1 May 1854	42/157	-	72/57	30,000
1 Mar 1856	37/82			10,000

From 2500 F

UB 21 1850 Stamped L top left

UB 21 Red control marks

Proof undated (stamped SPECIMEN) **From 500 EF**

FOURTH LIZARS ISSUE – 1858 *to* 1859

PERTH BANKING CO *replaces* **GLASGOW THISTLE BANK** in left border
Additional Text: **PURSUANT TO ACT OF PARLIAMENT Blue reverse**

A change in the law permitted banks to incorporate with limited liability but banks were required to reaffirm their unlimited liability for the note issue. This caused the Union Bank to add **PURSUANT TO ACT OF PARLIAMENT** inside the upper border. It is possible that this text was added to the plate before it was further amended to include the Perth Banking Co. If so then a further variety may exist. Imprint of **W H Lizars, Edinburgh**.

A blue reverse is now added, featuring an equestrian statue of William of Orange surrounded by an ornate thistle design with the Lizars imprint below. A proof in blue of the reverse design can be found in the British Museum.

UB 22	£1	**Payable in Edinburgh** blue reverse		
		Handsigned Accountant & Cashier **Dated by hand**		
		1 May 1858 88/23	n/k	**From 2500 F**
		Proof undated uniface		**From 600 EF**

UB 22 Proof reverse in the British Museum

W & A K JOHNSTON ISSUE – 1860 *to* 1861

Printer: **W & A K Johnston Payable in Edinburgh Blue reverse**

The Lizars design remains unchanged but following his death in 1859 and the taking over of his business by W & A K Johnston, the printers' imprint was amended to **Engraved on Steel by / W & A K Johnston, Edinburgh**. This appears below the lower border. The imprint on the blue reverse was also amended.

UB 23a	£1	Handsigned	Acco! & Cashier year printed as 18		
		1 May1860	14/155	12,000	**From 2500 F**

UB 23a 1860

UB 23b	£1	Handsigned	Acco! & Cashier **Date printed in full**		
		1 Jan 1861	82/152 - 198/49	n/k	**From 2500 F**

UB 23b

UB 24   £5   **Handsigned** Accountant & Manager
No 7ᵗʰ bank added below border

Colour Trials undated part coloured uniface:
Key text in Light Red
Value & bank title in Deep Red central panel Light Blue
Value & bank title in Blue
Value & central panel in Blue   **From 800 EF**

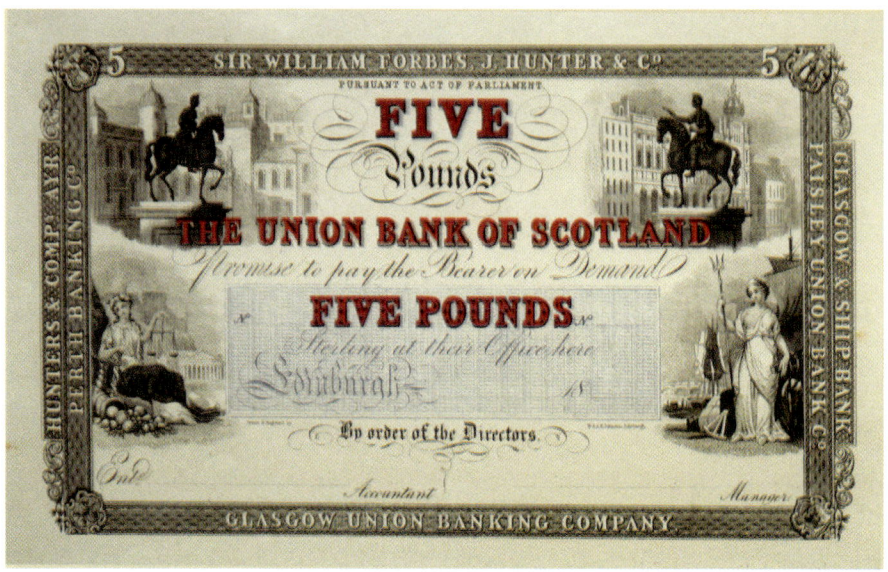

UB 24 Colour Trial value & bank title in deep red central panel light blue

Proof undated uniface   **From 600 EF**

No other denominations known with the Johnston imprint, the blue reverse or with the date printed in full.

FIRST PERKINS BACON & PETCH ISSUE – 1846 *to* 1854

Six banks in oval frames forming left hand border Uniface

On 25th March 1846 the bank's Glasgow Committee approved proofs of new designs submitted by **Perkins, Bacon & Petch**. The new notes were payable in Glasgow and were authorised for issue on 29th April 1846. They shared a common design featuring the names of the six constituent banks as at 1843 in oval frames down the left hand side of the note: Glasgow Union Banking Co, Sir W Forbes J Hunter & Co, Glasgow Thistle Banking Co, Paisley Union Bank Co, Hunters & Comp^y Ayr, and Glasgow & Ship Bank Co. There are three vignettes: the statue of William of Orange in Glasgow's Trongate upper centre, along with female figures representing Scotland and Ireland (lower left, with shield with thistle emblem, plus harp) and Britannia (lower right, with Royal Navy ensign and lion).

Unlike the Lizars issues, the bank names were not amended or added to during the life of this series and the words **PURSUANT TO ACT OF PARLIAMENT** were not added at any stage. All notes have the printers' imprint **Perkins, Bacon & Petch, London, Patent Hardened Steel Plate**.

Issued £1 notes have hand-written in-line serials, a stylistic departure from the standard Scottish fractional system. No issued notes of higher denominations have survived to confirm if they were similarly numbered.

UB 25a £1 **Handsigned** Acco! & Cashier Congreve
Year printed as 184
1 Apr 1846		40,000
2 Nov 1846	94.329	20,000
1846 (auth)		10,000
1 Apr 1847		21,850
1847 (auth)		20,000
1848 (auth)		19,895
1 Nov 1848		20,000
1849 (auth)		60,000

From 2500 F

Proof undated   **From 300 EF**

UB 25b £1 **Handsigned** Acco! & Cashier Congreve
Year printed as 18
1850 (auth)	40,000
1 Nov 1850	40,000
1851 (auth)	40,000
1 Nov 1852	20,000
2 May 1853	20,000

RARE

Proof undated   **From 300 EF**

£5 notes were first issued in 1848. Those authorised for issue in 1855 may have had a star added by hand.

UB 26	£5	**Handsigned** Acco! & Cashier year printed as 18	
		1850 to 1851 (auth)	13,000
		1855 (auth)	2,000

Proof year printed as 18   **From 500 EF**

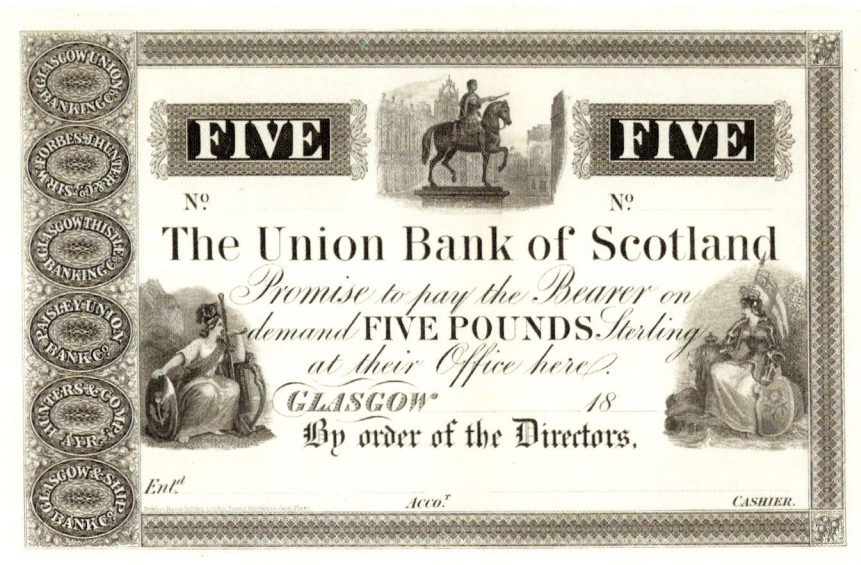

UB 26 Proof

£10 notes were first issued in 1848.

UB 27	£10	**Handsigned** p Acco! & p Cashier year printed as 18	
		1850 (auth)	1,000

Proof undated uniface   **From 500 EF**

Specimen year printed as 18 on watermarked bank paper   **From 750 EF**

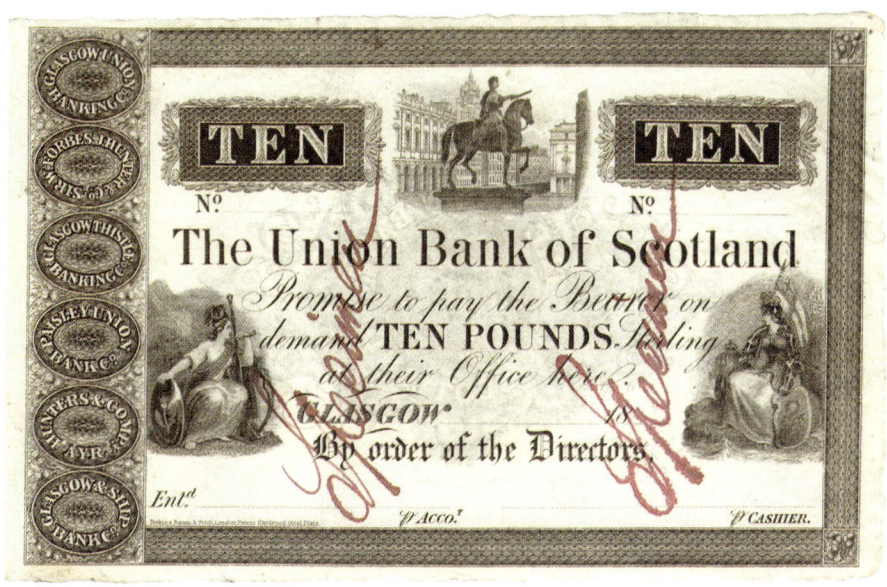

UB 27 Specimen hand-written

£20 notes were first issued in 1848. Those authorised for issue in 1855 may have had a star added by hand.

UB 28	£20	**Handsigned** Acco! & Cashier year printed as 18	
		1850 (auth)	3,000
		1855 (auth)	1,200
		Proof year printed as 18 uniface	**From 500 EF**

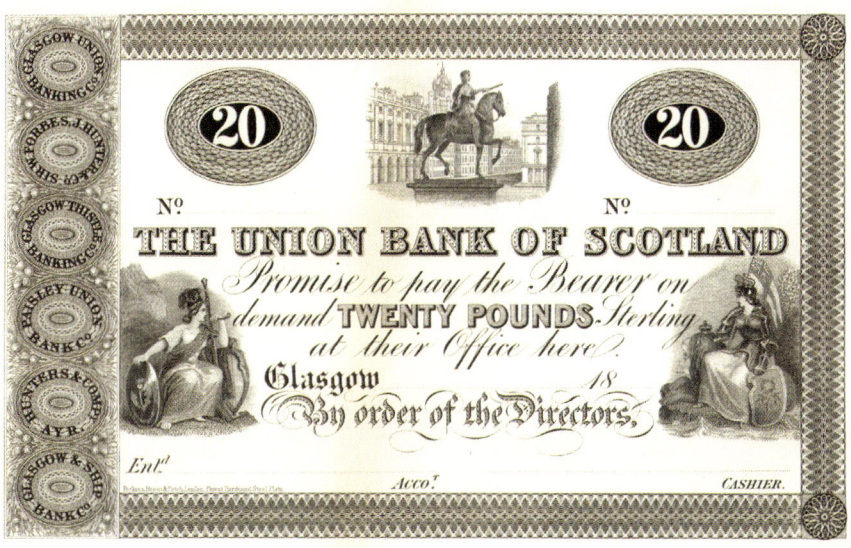

UB 28 Proof

£100 notes were first issued in 1848. Those authorised for issue in 1854 may have had a star added by hand. No £100 notes of this type have have yet to be seen to confirm other details.

UB 29	£100	Handsigned Acco! & Cashier	
		1850 to 1851 (auth)	2,300
		2 May 1853	500
		1 Apr 1854	500

SECOND PERKINS BACON & PETCH ISSUE – 1854 *to* 1862

Star added to plate Printed reverse

The reason the star was added to the Perkins Bacon notes payable in Glasgow is explained in a letter to branches from the Glasgow Head Office dated 1st April 1854, asking for it to be *'impressed upon the left hand corner of all the Unstamped notes… in consequence of this Bank's having arranged to avail itself of the privilege granted to all Scotch Banks, by a recent Act of Parliament, of paying a fixed rate of Composition in lieu of the Stamp Duty payable on their Notes.'* The need to identify these notes was to assist in completing correct weekly returns to Edinburgh. The letter does not refer specifically to either the Glasgow or Edinburgh issues but there is no indication that these stars were ever applied to Edinburgh notes.

The first £1 notes of this issue had the star added by hand ahead of the plates being modified. The only £1 note seen modified in this way is uniface, unlike all later notes which carry the printed reverse common to this issue. It is possible that the higher denominations of the First Perkins Bacon Issue were also issued with the hand stamped star but it has only been confirmed on the £1 note. Two trial £1 notes with an additional colour value panel exist in the Bank of Scotland's archive.

During this issue, the signatories were amended to **p** Accountant and **p** Cashier. All notes have the printers' imprint **Perkins, Bacon & Petch, London, Patent Hardened Steel Plate**. The printed reverse is in black with the bank name in a circular design and abbreviated printers' imprint **Perkins Bacon & Co London**. A forgery of £1 notes of this issue was reported in the Glasgow Committee minutes of 23rd July 1856.

Total notes issued from 1st April 1854 to 1st August 1862 recorded as follows:

£1	1,040,000
£5	74,000
£10	7,000
£20	19,050
£100	5,000

UB 30 **£1** **INTERIM ISSUE: Hand stamped star**
Handsigned Acco! & Cashier **Dated by hand**
Hand-written In-line serials uniface
   1 Apr 1854   57.421   20,000   **RARE**

UB 30 Hand stamped star

UB 31 to 35 Reverse

UB 31a	£1	**Printed star Printed reverse**

Handsigned Acco! & Cashier **Dated by hand**
Hand-written In-line serials

1855 (auth)		40,000	
1 Nov 1855		10,000	
1 Oct 1856		20,000	
1 Oct 1857	559.465	n/k	**From 2500 F**

UB 31a

Proof undated uniface   **From 300 EF**

Colour Trial undated central ONE panel in Blue or Red uniface

UB 31a Colour Trial with blue panel

UB 31b	£1	**Handsigned** p Acco! & p Cashier		
		1 Jun 1859 183 977	n/k	
		1 Nov 1860 437 793	n/k	**From 2500 F**
		Proof undated uniface		**From 300 EF**

Printed serial numbers in the traditional style of book number over sequential number appear to have been introduced in January 1861 according to surviving Perkins Bacon ledgers. The earliest printed serial number is 517/001 but it is not clear if this note had a printed date or not. The Perkins records are incomplete, hence gaps in the serial number sequences.

UB 31c	£1	**Handsigned** p Acco! & p Cashier printed date		
		Fractional serials printed		
		2 Aug 1861 747/501 - 795/1000	n/k	
		1 Feb 1862 849/501 - 940/1000	n/k	
		1 Aug 1862 1041/501 - 1080/1000	n/k	**From 2500 F**

UB 31c 1862

The following **Proof** notes have been recorded:
Undated   2 Aug 1861   1 Feb 1862   1 Aug 1862   **From 300 EF**

UB 32	**£5**	**Handsigned** p Acco! & p Cashier		
		Proof undated		From 500 EF
		Specimen on bank paper		From 750 EF

UB 32 Specimen hand-written

UB 33	**£10**	**Handsigned** p Acco! & p Cashier		
		Proof undated no star on plate		From 500 EF
		Specimen on watermarked bank paper		From 750 EF

UB 34	**£20**	**Handsigned** p Acco! & p Cashier	
		1855 (auth)	1,200
		1856 to 1858 (auth)	17,850

UB 35	**£100**	**Handsigned** p Acco! & p Cashier		
		Proof undated		From 600 EF
		Specimen on bank paper		From 950 EF

UB 35 Specimen hand-written

FIRST GENERAL ISSUE – 1863 *to* 1866

Heading in Gothic Script: Incorporated by Act of Parliament

In November 1862 The Union Bank of Scotland was incorporated under the Companies Act of that year and on 30th March 1863 new note designs were authorised to replace the still separate Edinburgh and Glasgow issues. The new notes were payable, uniquely in Scottish banking history, in Glasgow or Edinburgh. They prominently displayed the words *Incorporated by Act of Parliament*. The new note designs were much simpler, with no borders and no reference to the old constituent banks. The principal design feature is the Coat of Arms adopted by the bank featuring a shield halved between the arms of Glasgow and Edinburgh supported by allegorical females representing Commerce and Justice. This sits between oval value panels with machinework patterns which vary with the denominations. Colour was introduced for the first time, the basic plate being in blue overlaid by a green value panel on the issued £1 note.

All notes now have printed dates. As with the earlier notes, no issued notes of £5 or above have survived. Printers' imprint is now **Perkins Bacon & Co London**. The numerous Perkins proofs (and in some cases part proofs of just the upper half of the note) have come from the extensive Perkins Bacon archive. Most proofs are printed in black but some are in the blue of the issued notes.

A notorious forgery of the £1 note by a Glasgow photographer, John Henry Greatrex, took place in 1866 and led to the early replacement of this note series. Photography was used to create the image and the forgeries then printed by lithography. Greatrex and his accomplices, the brothers Thomas and Sewell Grimshaw, were caught after suspicions were raised in Dalkeith when the Grimshaws tried to pass forged notes in local shops. Greatrex absconded to New York but was caught and brought back to Scotland for his trial. He was imprisoned for twenty years. The bank burnt 1,325 forged notes after the trial and thus very few of his forgeries have survived. All are dated 1st November 1865.

Total notes issued from 1st May 1863 to November 1866 recorded as follows:

£1	737,000
£5	30,000
£10	5,000
£20	10,000
£100	n/k

UB 36   £1   **Blue Green ONE Handsigned** p Acco! & p Cashier
Printed serials uniface
1 May 1863   plate A
2 Feb 1864   plate A   130/155 A
2 Nov 1864   plate A   262/887 A   -   280/508
2 Jan 1865   plate A   396/95 A   -   439/370
1 Nov 1865   plate A
15 May 1866   plate A   **From 1500 F**

UB 36   1864

Forgery (by Greatrex) 1 Nov 1865   **From 800 F**

The following **Proof** notes have been recorded: all plate A
Undated   1 May 1863   2 Nov 1863   2 Feb 1864
2 May 1864   1 Aug 1864   2 Nov 1864   2 Jan 1865
1 Nov 1865   15 May 1866   **From 200 EF**

Specimen 2 Nov 1864 plate A   **From 750 EF**

UB 36 Forgery by Greatrex

UB 37	**£5**	**Handsigned** p Acco! & p Cashier	
		The following **Proof** notes have been recorded: 1 May 1863 2 Nov 1866	**From 250 EF**
UB 38	**£10**	**Similar to UB 37**	
		The following **Proof** note has been recorded: 1 May 1863	**From 250 EF**
UB 39	**£20**	**Similar to UB 37**	
		The following **Proof** notes have been recorded: 1 May 1863 2 Nov 1865	**From 250 EF**
UB 40	**£100**	**Similar to UB 37**	
		The following **Proof** notes have been recorded: 1 May 1863 11 Nov 1864 1 Nov 1865 2 Nov 1866	**From 350 EF**

SECOND GENERAL ISSUE – 1867 *to* 1880

Framed Designs Black plate Green value panels

This series was introduced as a result of the Greatrex forgeries. The new notes still have the Coat of Arms as the principal design feature, with the same value panels either side, except for the £1 note where these have been modified. The two equestrian statues are restored and appear on the lower left and right. In addition the whole design is now framed within machinework borders. The words **INCORPORATED BY ACT OF PARLIAMENT** are in smaller capitals curved over the central vignette. The basic plate is printed in black on all notes, with green central value panels on issued notes and specimens. Printers' imprint is in capitals: **PERKINS, BACON & CO LONDON**. Perkins' plate numbers probably first appeared on this issue and are to be found at the top left hand corner of the note just outside the border. Watermarked paper.

Total notes issued from 2nd April 1867 to 4th October 1878 recorded as follows:

£1	plate A B C	1,000,000 *each*
	plate D	250,000
£5	plate A	200,000
	plate B	10,000
£10	plate A	33,000
£20	plate A	51,600
£100	plate A (1867)	n/a
£100	plate A (1872)	17,500

UB 41 1870

UB 41	£1	Black Green ONE uniface

Handsigned p Cashier & p Acco!
Small plate letter
  2 Apr 1867 plate A
  2 Apr 1870 plate A   802/380 A
Larger plate letter
  3 Apr 1871 plate B   126/981 B
  1 Oct 1872 plate B   626/689 B - 671/597
  1 May 1873 plate B   749/196 B
  1 Aug 1874 plate C   205/228 C
  3 Jan 1876 plate C   458/094 C - 630/191
  1 Jul 1878 plate D   221/291 D

From 1300 F

UB 41 1878 large plate letter D

Forgery plate C 1 Aug 1874 3 Jan 1876   **From 150 F**

Essay 1 Aug 1879 Vignette of three females plate D
    Amended value panels   **From 300 EF**

The following **Proof** notes have been recorded: no green ONE
Plate A
Undated   2 Apr 1867   11 Nov 1867   1 May 1868
2 Nov 1868   1 Nov 1869   2 Apr 1870   1 Nov 1870
Plate B
Undated   3 Apr 1871   1 Nov 1871   1 Oct 1872
1 May 1873
Plate C
1 Aug 1874   3 Jan 1876   1 Sep 1877
Plate D
1 Jul 1878   **From 200 EF**

Specimen Green ONE 2 Apr 1867 plate A
                             3 Apr 1871 plate B   **From 600 EF**

UB 42	**£5**	**Black Green FIVE Handsigned** p Cashier & p Acco!

The following **Proof** notes have been recorded: no green FIVE
Plate A
2 Apr 1867   1 May 1868   2 Nov 1868   1 Nov 1869
2 Apr 1870   3 Apr 1871   2 Apr 1872   2 Sep 1873
2 Apr 1875   1 May 1877
Plate B
4 Oct 1878   **From 250 EF**

Specimen 2 Apr 1867 1 May 1877 Green FIVE plate A   **From 650 EF**

UB 42 Specimen

UB 43 **£10** Black Green TEN Handsigned p Cashier & p Acco!

The following **Proof** notes have been recorded: all plate A no green TEN
2 Apr 1867   1 Nov 1869   1 Oct 1870   11 Nov 1871
1 Oct 1873   2 May 1876   1 Oct 1878   **From 250 EF**

Specimen 2 May 1876 Green TEN plate A   **From 650 EF**

UB 43 Specimen

UB 44   **£20**   Black Green TWENTY **Handsigned** p Cashier & p Acco!

The following **Proof** notes have been recorded: all plate A no green TWENTY
2 Apr 1867	2 Nov 1868	1 May 1869	2 Apr 1870
1 Nov 1873	2 Apr 1875	1 May 1877	1 May 1869

From 250 EF

Specimen Green TWENTY plate A
2 Apr 1867   1 May 1869   2 Apr 1870   1 May 1877   **From 650 EF**

UB 44 Specimen £20

UB 45   **£100** Black Green £100 **Handsigned** Cashier & Acco!

The following **Proof** notes have been recorded: all plate A no green £100
2 Apr 1867   1 May 1869   2 Apr 1870   2 Oct 1871   **From 300 EF**

Specimen 2 Apr 1867 1 May 1869 Green £100 plate A   **From 1000 EF**

UB 45 Specimen £100

The £100 note was extensively redesigned in 1872 with the bank's name now much bolder and curved over the vignette of the bank's arms. The coloured value panel is now in red.

UB 46   **£100   Black   Red £100   Handsigned** Cashier & Acco!

        The following **Proof** notes have been recorded: all plate A no red £100
        1 Mar 1872   11 Nov 1873   1 May 1875   1 Aug 1877
        7 Oct 1878   **From 300 EF**

        Specimen 1 Aug 1877 Red £100 plate A   **From 1000 EF**

UB 46 Specimen £100

Early in 1880 the designs of all denominations were amended, the principal change being to the value panels either side of the bank arms. The basic plate is now printed in blue and the coloured value panel overlay is dark red. All notes are believed to be uniface. No issued notes of this series are known to have survived though proofs exist and the bank's records confirm the following notes were issued:

£1	650,000
£5	32,000
£10	7,000
£20	9,000
£100	1,000

UB 47   £1   Amended value panels Dark Red ONE

        Proof 2 Jan 1880 plate A
                undated plate A   **From 200 EF**

UB 48   £5   Amended value panels Dark Red FIVE

        Proof 2 Jan 1880 plate A
                undated plate A   **From 250 EF**

UB 48 Proof signature removed

UB 49   £10   Amended value panels Dark Red TEN

        Proof 2 Jan 1880 plate A   **From 250 EF**

UB 50	£20	Amended value panels Dark Red TWENTY	
		Proof 2 Jan 1880 plate A	From 250 EF
UB 51	£100	Value panels as UB 46	
		Proof 2 Jan 1880 plate A	From 300 EF

THIRD GENERAL ISSUE – 1882 *to* 1903

Heading: UNION BANK OF SCOTLAND, LIMITED

In 1882 the bank registered under the Companies Act of 1879 to take limited liability. The bank's name was amended accordingly and new notes prepared. The blue plate and dark red value panel combination of the 1880 series was retained. A blue reverse is introduced displaying the bank's name within a circular machinework design. Printers' imprint unchanged: **PERKINS, BACON & CO LONDON** though this was amended after the printers also adopted limited liability in May 1887. All notes hand signed p Cashier and p Accountant except for the £100 note where the officials signed in person. All notes are printed on watermarked paper. The prefix/suffix letters are engraved on the plate with the serial numbers applied separately in red. A printed signature first appears on the final £1 notes of 1903 to 1904.

A small florette has been added on these notes in the top left hand corner just inside the border, for reasons yet to be determined. It is possible the florettes were applied to identify the notes as having been issued by the bank under its new name, with Limited added to the title, but even this is not clear as it appears some notes with the first date were prepared without the florette.

Dates and issue numbers are taken from the bank's note registers. Apart from a few issued £5 notes only £1 notes are known to have survived. The many Perkins proofs are mainly in black only.

UB 52 to 56 Reverse

UB 52a	£1	**Blue Dark Red ONE Florette hand stamped** blue reverse

Printer: **Perkins, Bacon & Co London**
Small Roman prefix Serials in red

15 Apr 1882   A   1/001   -   650/1000   650,000   **From 1200 F**
                                                 shared with UB 52b

UB 52a Florette hand stamped

Florette enlarged

UB 52b	£1	**Blue Dark Red ONE Florette added to plate** blue reverse

Printer: **Perkins, Bacon & Co London**
Roman prefix/suffix
Small prefix Serials in red   shared with UB 52a
15 Apr 1882   A   1/001   -   650/1000   650,000
 2 Jun 1884   A 651/001   -   1000/1000   350,000
Larger suffix
 4 Nov 1885   1/001 B   -   450/1000   450,000
16 May 1887   451/001 B   -   950/1000   500,000   **From 1000 F**

UB 52b Small Roman prefix

The following **Proof** notes have been recorded:
Undated   15 Apr 1882   2 Jun 1884   4 Nov 1885
16 May 1887   **From 200 EF**

UB 52c   £1   *Printer:* **Perkins, Bacon & Co Ld London**
                Roman suffix Serials in red
                  1 Apr 1889   951/001 B   -   1000/1000   50,000
                  6 Jul 1889   1/001 C   -   600/1000   600,000
                  2 Apr 1891   601/001 C   -   1000/1000   400,000
                Imprint on reverse: **Perkins, Bacon & Co Ld London**
                 19 Jul 1892   1/001 D   -   325/1000   325,000
                 20 Jul 1893   326/001 D   -   574/1000   249,000
                  7 Jul 1894   1/001 E   -   400/1000   400,000
                 15 Jul 1895   401/001 E   -   600/1000   200,000
                  2 Apr 1896   601/001 E   -   1000/1000   400,000
                Gothic suffix
                  5 Mar 1897   1/001 𝔉   -   350/1000   350,000
                 18 Feb 1898   351/001 𝔉   -   750/1000   400,000
                 31 Jan 1899   751/001 𝔉   -   1000/1000   250,000
                 28 Feb 1899   1/001 𝔊   -   450/1000   450,000
                 24 Oct 1900   451/001 𝔊   -   1000/1000   550,000
                Roman suffix
                 13 Sep 1901   1/001 H   -   300/1000   300,000
                 29 Aug 1902   301/001 H   -   550/1000   250,000   **From 750 F**

                The following **Proof** notes have been recorded: all with suffix
                Undated   1 Apr 1889   6 Jul 1889   2 Apr 1891
                19 Jul 1892   20 Jul 1893   7 Jul 1894   15 Jul 1895
                 2 Apr 1896   5 Mar 1897   18 Feb 1898   31 Jan 1899
                28 Feb 1899   24 Oct 1900   13 Sep 1901   29 Aug 1902   **From 200 EF**

UB 52c Roman suffix

Specimen 20 Jul 1893 suffix D   25   **From 250 EF**

UB 52d	£1	**J R Wood** Printed signature Acco.! **Handsigned** p Cashier				
		Serials in Red				
		10 Mar 1903	551/001 H	-	1000/1000	450,000
		Bolder suffix				
		3 May 1904	1/001 I	-	400/1000	400,000	**From 1000 F**

UB 52d Bolder suffix Printed signature of Accountant

The following **Proof** notes have been recorded:
10 Mar 1903   3 May 1904   3 May 1905 suffix I   **From 200 EF**

Specimen 10 Mar 1903 suffix H   25   **From 250 EF**

UB 53a	£5	**Blue Dark Red FIVE** blue reverse					
		Printer: **Perkins, Bacon & Co London**					
		Serials in Red					
		15 Apr 1882	A 1/001	-	230/200	46,000	
		2 Sep 1884	A 231/001	-	330/200	20,000	
		4 Nov 1885	A 331/001	-	430/200	20,000	
		16 May 1887	A 431/001	-	620/200	38,000	
		1 Apr 1889	A 621/001	-	750/200	26,000	
		2 Apr 1891	A 751/001	-	900/200	30,000	
		3 Apr 1893	A 901/001	-	1000/200	20,000	**RARE**

The following **Proof** notes have been recorded: all with A prefix
Undated   15 Apr 1882   2 Sep 1884   4 Nov 1885
16 May 1887   1 Apr 1889   2 Apr 1891   3 Apr 1893   **From 250 EF**

Specimen 4 Nov 1885   n/k
              3 Apr 1893   25   **From 300 EF**

UB 53b	£5	*Printer:* **Perkins, Bacon & Co Ld London**					
		10 Jul 1894	B 1/001	-	130/200	26,000	
		2 Apr 1896	B 131/001	-	300/200	34,000	
		2 Mar 1898	B 301/001	-	520/200	44,000	
		27 Jan 1900	B 521/001	-	720/200	40,000	
		29 Aug 1902	B 721/001	-	1000/200	56,000	**From 2000 F**

UB 53b 1898

The following **Proof** notes have been recorded: all with B prefix
10 Jul 1894   2 Apr 1896   2 Mar 1898   27 Jan 1900   **From 250 EF**

UB 54a	£10	**Blue Dark Red TEN** blue reverse					
		Printer: **Perkins, Bacon & Co London**					
		15 Apr 1882	A 1/001	-	15/200	3,000	
		15 Sep 1887	A 16/001	-	25/200	2,000	
		1 Feb 1890	A 26/001	-	35/200	2,000	
		2 Apr 1891	A 36/001	-	55/200	4,000	
		3 Apr 1893	A 56/001	-	60/200	1,000	**RARE**

The following **Proof** notes have been recorded:
15 Apr 1882   15 Sep 1887   1 Feb 1890   2 Apr 1891
3 Apr 1893   **From 250 EF**

Specimen 3 Apr 1893   25   **From 300 EF**

UB 54a Specimen 1893

UB 54b	£10	*Printer:* **Perkins, Bacon & Co Ld London**					
		10 Jul 1894	A 61/001	-	70/200	2,000	
		15 Jul 1895	A 71/001	-	100/200	6,000	
		4 Aug 1899	A 101/001	-	130/200	6,000	
		18 Mar 1904	A 131/001	-	135/200	1,000	**RARE**

The following **Proof** notes have been recorded:
10 Jul 1894   15 Jul 1895   4 Aug 1899   10 Mar 1904   **From 250 EF**

UB 55a	£20	Blue Dark Red TWENTY blue reverse				
		Printer: **Perkins, Bacon & Co London**				
		15 Apr 1882	A 1/001 - 40/200	8,000		
		2 Sep 1884	A 41/001 - 60/200	4,000		
		4 Nov 1885	A 61/001 - 80/200	4,000		
		16 May 1887	A 81/001 - 118/200	7,600		
		1 Apr 1889	A 119/001 - 148/200	6,000		
		2 Apr 1891	A 149/001 - 195/200	9,400	**RARE**	

The following **Proof** notes have been recorded:
15 Apr 1882 no florette   2 Sep 1884   4 Nov 1885
16 May 1887   1 Apr 1889   2 Apr 1891   **From 250 EF**

Specimen 2 Apr 1891   25   **From 350 EF**

UB 55a Specimen 1891

UB 55b	£20	*Printer:* **Perkins, Bacon & Co Ld London**				
		2 Apr 1895	A 196/001 - 230/200	7,000		
		20 Jul 1897	A 231/001 - 250/200	4,000		
		3 Aug 1898	B 1/001 - 35/200	7,000		
		29 Aug 1902	B 36/001 - 85/200	10,000	**RARE**	

The following **Proof** notes have been recorded:
2 Apr 1895   20 Jul 1897   3 Aug 1898   29 Aug 1902   **From 250 EF**

UB 56a	£100	**Blue Dark Red £100** blue reverse					
		Printer: **Perkins, Bacon & Co London**					
		15 Apr 1882	A 1/001	-	10/100	1,000	
		2 Sep 1884	A 11/001	-	20/100	1,000	
		4 Mar 1886	A 21/001	-	55/100	3,500	
		1 May 1888	A 56/001	-	75/100	2,000	
		2 Apr 1891	A 76/001	-	100/100	2,500	**RARE**

The following **Proof** notes have been recorded:
15 Apr 1882   2 Sep 1884   4 Mar 1886   1 May 1888
2 Apr 1891   **From 250 EF**

	Specimen	4 Mar 1886		n/k	
		2 Apr 1891		25	**From 350 EF**

UB 56a Specimen 1891

UB 56b	£100	*Printer:* **Perkins, Bacon & Co Ld London**					
		1 Feb 1895	B 1/001	-	15/100	1,500	
		5 Mar 1897	B 16/001	-	35/100	2,000	
		24 Oct 1900	B 36/001	-	55/100	2,000	
		18 Feb 1903	B 56/001	-	83/100	2,800	**RARE**

The following **Proof** notes have been recorded:
1 Feb 1895   5 Mar 1897   24 Oct 1900   18 Feb 1903   **From 250 EF**

FOURTH GENERAL ISSUE – 1905 *to* 1920

First Waterlow Issue

In 1904 a dispute arose among the directors of **Perkins Bacon** and pending a settlement a receiver was appointed. The bank was concerned about the security of supply of new notes and approached **Waterlow & Sons Ltd** to seek estimates to replace their whole note issue. Waterlows were critical of the quality of the engraving on the Perkins notes (a fully justified criticism as a brief examination will confirm) and were quickly appointed to engrave and print a new series to the same overall design. Waterlow's notes are indeed of a noticeably higher quality than those they replaced and can be considered very handsome designs. The reverses are now much more elaborate and feature numerals representing the denomination of the note.

All £1 notes carry the printed signature of the Accountant but are still handsigned on behalf of the Cashier. Waterlow's usual positional plate letters are to be found in the extreme lower left corner of the front and just outside the main design of the reverse. All notes are printed on watermarked paper. Dates, prefixes, serial ranges and numbers printed are all taken from the Bank's note registers. The book numbers (the upper ones of the fractional serials) do not have initial zeroes while the sequential (lower) numbers do.

Archive Material – Printers' Remainders

A large number of proofs, stage proofs, part completed notes, sheets of printed notes and other items from the Waterlow archives have survived. These remainders are not listed separately but do appear regularly on the market. Much of the material has ink annotations and multiple punch hole cancellations and is generally valued below that of bank specimens (distinguished by none or few punch holes and a single SPECIMEN stamp). The archive material covers the period 1905 to 1954.

In 1904 Bradbury Wilkinson prepared an essay, believed to be unsolicited, of a £1 note with a completely different and much more ornate design. Sadly, only a black and white photograph image of it survives.

Bradbury Wilkinson Photographic Essay c.1904

UB 57a	£1	**J R Wood** Printed signature Acco.^t	**Handsigned** p Cashier			
		6 Apr 1905	A 1/001	-	400/1000	400,000
		27 Mar 1906	A 401/001	-	800/1000	400,000
		1 May 1907	A 801/001	-	1000/1000	200,000
		2 Oct 1907	B 1/001	-	100/1000	100,000	**From 900 F**

UB 57a

| | **Specimen** 6 Apr 1905 | | | 25 | **From 250 EF** |

UB 57b	£1	**G H Moritz** Printed signature Acco.^t	**Handsigned** p Cashier			
		2 Jan 1908	B 101/001	-	550/1000	550,000
		28 Sep 1909	B 551/001	-	750/1000	200,000	**From 900 F**

UB 57b

UB 57c	£1	John Alexander Printed signature Acco! Handsigned p Cashier				F	VF
		12 Feb 1910	B 751/001	-	1000/1000	250,000	
		9 Sep 1910	C 1/001	-	450/1000	450,000	
		12 Apr 1912	C 451/001	-	1000/1000	550,000	
		26 Aug 1913	D 1/001	-	400/1000	400,000	350	600

UB 57c 1913

UB 57d	£1	J F McCrindle Printed signature Acco! Handsigned p Cashier					
		Roman prefix					
		3 Aug 1914	D 401/001	-	600/1000	200,000	
		24 Dec 1914	D 601/001	-	1000/1000	400,000	
		8 Nov 1915	E 1/001	-	400/1000	400,000	
		25 Jul 1916	E 401/001	-	700/1000	300,000	
		30 Mar 1917	E 701/001	-	1000/1000	300,000	
		Gothic prefix					
		4 Oct 1917	𝔉 1/001	-	100/1000	100,000	
		4 Apr 1918	𝔉 101/001	-	700/1000	600,000	
		28 Feb 1919	𝔉 701/001	-	1000/1000	300,000	
		20 Jun 1919	𝔊 1/001	-	500/1000	500,000	
		7 Jul 1920	𝔊 501/001	-	1000/1000	500,000	
		Roman prefix					
		10 Dec 1920	H 1/001	-	094/1000	94,000	250	550

UB 57d Roman prefix

UB 57d Gothic 𝔊 prefix   1000 serial

UB 58	£5	Blue Red FIVE	Handsigned	p Cashier & p Acco!			F	VF
		25 Feb 1905	A 1/001	-	360/200	72,000		
		6 Oct 1909	A 361/001	-	650/200	58,000		
		17 Sep 1912	A 651/001	-	800/200	30,000		
		1 Aug 1914	A 801/001	-	1000/200	40,000		
		14 Jul 1916	B 1/001	-	140/200	28,000		
		3 Oct 1917	B 141/001	-	190/200	10,000		
		29 Mar 1918	B 191/001	-	270/200	16,000		
		20 Sep 1918	B 271/001	-	780/200	102,000		
		16 Jan 1920	B 781/001	-	1000/200	44,000		
		18 Aug 1920	C 1/001	-	250/200	50,000	500	1000
		Specimen 25 Feb 1905				25	From 300 EF	

UB 59	£10	Blue Red TEN	Handsigned	p Cashier & p Acco!				
		4 Apr 1905	A 1/001	-	35/200	7,000		
		15 Oct 1913	A 36/001	-	50/200	3,000		
		23 Mar 1917	A 51/001	-	65/200	3,000		
		28 Feb 1918	A 66/001	-	100/200	7,000		
		6 Aug 1920	A 101/001	-	120/200	4,000		RARE
		Specimen 4 Apr 1905				25	From 300 EF	

UB 59 Specimen 1905

UB 60	£20	Blue Red TWENTY Handsigned p Cashier & p Acco!			
		31 Mar 1905	A 1/001 - 100/200	20,000	
		8 Oct 1913	A 101/001 - 120/200	4,000	
		3 Nov 1915	A 121/001 - 150/200	6,000	
		20 Sep 1917	A 151/001 - 165/200	3,000	
		3 Apr 1918	A 166/001 - 180/200	3,000	
		26 Aug 1918	A 181/001 - 230/200	10,000	
		14 Jun 1920	A 231/001 - 250/200	4,000	**From 1500 F**

UB 60 £20 1918

Specimen 31 Mar 1905   25   **From 300 EF**

UB 60 Reverse

UB 61	£100	Blue Red **£100 Handsigned** Cashier & Acco!				
		27 Mar 1906	A 1/001 - 40/100	4,000		
		4 Nov 1913	A 41/001 - 50/100	1,000		
		9 Nov 1915	A 51/001 - 60/100	1,000		
		2 Apr 1919	A 61/001 - 80/100	2,000		**RARE**
	Specimen 7 Apr 1905 27 Mar 1906			25 *each*		**From 400 EF**

UB 61 Specimen 1905

FIFTH GENERAL ISSUE – 1921 *to* 1949

Second Waterlow Issue Sunburst added

In 1921 it was decided to provide greater protection against forgery by adding – on the recommendation of Waterlows themselves – an overlay of brilliant red and yellow in the form of a 'sunburst'. The underlying designs and the reverses are unchanged. The resulting notes are spectacular and deservedly very popular with collectors.

The £1 note carries two printed signatures, that of the Cashier lithographed rather than engraved on the plate. This is the final Size A (~ 160 x 125mm) square note printing which remained in circulation for a relatively limited period. It is believed that very few of the B prefix notes were actually issued. The notes were printed on sheets of eight with positional plate letters indicating the note's place on the plate, as before. The bank's full note registers have not been located but all information available is set out below. The book numbers on denominations of £5 and above again do not use the initial zeroes.

UB 62	£1	**Norman Hird** General Manager			**F**	**VF**
		J F McCrindle Cashier Printed signatures				
		1 Oct 1921	A 000001 - 974000	974,000	**400**	**800**
		2 Nov 1923	B 000001 - 226000	226,000	**450**	**900**

UB 62 Last

Specimen 1 Oct 1921 A 000000   25   From 350 EF

In 1924 the square £1 note was replaced by the smaller Size B note (~ 155 x 85mm) which remained the size of all the bank's £1 notes until the merger with the Bank of Scotland in 1955. The size reduction necessitated a design change but the bank arms and equestrian statues are retained and the result is still attractive. The reverse was also redesigned and fills more of the available space. The notes were printed on sheets of sixteen with positional plate letters as before. The General Manager's signature is engraved on the plate while the second signature was initially lithographed. Prefixes J, L, N, Q and U were not used.

UB 63a	£1	**Norman Hird** Printed signature General Manager				F	VF	EF
		J F McCrindle Lithographed signature Cashier						
		2 Jun 1924	A 000001 - 988000	988,000				
		J F McCrindle Engraved on the plate						
		4 Jan 1926	B 000001 - 1000000	1,000,000				
		3 Oct 1927	C 000001 - 1000000	1,000,000		60	120	250

UB 63a Lithographed signature of McCrindle

UB 63a Engraved signature of McCrindle

UB 63 Reverse

Waterlow Colour Trial Black & Green 2 Jun 1924 A **From 300 EF**

UB 63a Colour Trial

Specimen 2 Jun 1924   25   **From 200 EF**

UB 63b	£1	**Norman Hird** General Manager					F	VF	EF
		J F McCrindle Chief Accountant Printed signatures							
		2 Jan 1929	D 000001	-	1000000	1,000,000			
		2 Apr 1930	E 000001	-	1000000	1,000,000			
		5 Dec 1931	F 000001	-	1000000	1,000,000	55	110	220

UB 63b J F McCrindle now Chief Accountant

Waterlow Colour Trial Black & Green 2 Apr 1930 E   **From 300 EF**

UB 63c	£1	**Norman Hird** General Manager							
		John Wink Chief Accountant Printed signatures							
		1 Jun 1933	G 000001	-	750000	750,000	60	120	250

UB 63c G high serial last

A revised numbering system was introduced part way through the 1933 G prefix notes. The prefix is now letter over number with the number changing every 25,000 notes.

UB 63d	£1	Fractional prefix					F	VF	EF
		1 Jun 1933 G/31 750001	-	G/40 1000000	250,000				
		5 Oct 1934 H/1 000001	-	H/40 1000000	1,000,000				
		31 Mar 1936 I/1 000001	-	I/40 1000000	1,000,000		**20**	**50**	**90**

UB 63d G First date 1933

UB 63e	£1	**Norman Hird** General Manager							
		M J Wilson Cashier Printed signatures							
		12 Feb 1937 K/1 000001	-	K/40 1000000	1,000,000				
		31 May 1938 M/1 000001	-	M/40 1000000	1,000,000				
		10 Jan 1939 O/1 000001	-	O/40 1000000	1,000,000				
		1 Aug 1940 P/1 000001	-	P/40 1000000	1,000,000				
		14 Jan 1942 R/1 000001	-	R/40 1000000	1,000,000				
		30 Nov 1942 S/1 000001	-	S/40 1000000	1,000,000				
		10 Apr 1944 T/1 000001	-	T/40 1000000	1,000,000				
		28 Sep 1945 V/1 000001	-	V/30 750000	750,000		**20**	**50**	**90**

UB 63e First date 1937

UB 63f	£1	**J A Morrison** General Manager			F	VF	EF
		M J Wilson Cashier Printed signatures					
		20 Mar 1946 V/31 750001 - V/40 1000000	250,000				
		31 Jul 1947 W/1 000001 - W/40 1000000	1,000,000				
		1 Jun 1948 X/1 000001 - X/20 500000	500,000		20	50	90

UB 63f First date 1946

UB 63f Last date 1948

£5 notes were printed on plates of four notes and numbered in books of 200. Previous catalogues have referred to £5 notes dated 5 April 1921 and 4 May 1923 but these dates have never been seen, even in proof form. The evidence in the note registers is quite clear that the first note of this type is dated 4 August 1923. It has also been suggested the first notes had been handsigned on behalf of the Cashier but again there is no evidence for this. The signature of the Cashier was lithographed on UB 64a.

UB 64a	£5	**Norman Hird** Printed signature General Manager					
		J F McCrindle Lithographed signature Cashier					
		4 Aug 1923 A 1/001 - 750/200	150,000				
		5 Apr 1926 A 751/001 - 1000/200	50,000				
		15 Jan 1927 B 1/001 - 150/200	30,000		200	500	-

Specimen 4 Aug 1923 *reported not confirmed*

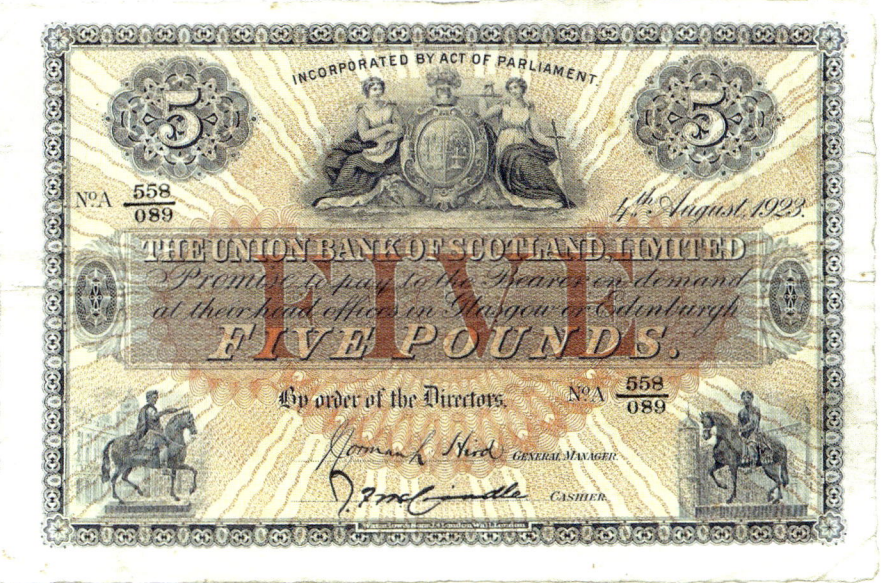

UB 64a First date 1928

UB 64b	£5	Norman Hird General Manager J F McCrindle Chief Accountant Printed signatures					F	VF
		6 Jul 1928	B 151/001	-	350/200	40,000		
		5 Mar 1930	B 351/001	-	550/200	40,000		
		1 Jun 1931	B 551/001	-	750/200	40,000		
		3 Oct 1931	B 751/001	-	950/200	40,000		
		4 May 1932	B 951/001	-	1000/200	10,000	200	500

UB 64b £5 First date 1928

UB 64c	£5	**Norman Hird** General Manager **John Wink** Chief Accountant Printed signatures			**F**	**VF**	**EF**
		2 Feb 1933 C 1/001 - 150/200	30,000				
		15 Dec 1933 C 151/001 - 250/200	20,000				
		3 Sep 1934 C 251/001 - 450/200	40,000				
		1 Nov 1935 C 451/001 - 650/200	40,000				
		18 May 1936 C 651/001 - 800/200	30,000		**200**	**450**	**-**

UB 64c Fractional serials

From August 1937 the serials are in-line rather than fractional, though the book system is still used. Prefix F not used.

UB 64d	£5	**Norman Hird** General Manager **M J Wilson** Cashier Printed signatures					
		18 Aug 1937 C 801/001 - 1000/200	40,000				
		31 May 1938 D 1/001 - 150/200	30,000				
		10 Jul 1939 D 151/001 - 350/200	40,000				
		24 Jun 1940 D 351/001 - 550/200	40,000				
		29 Sep 1941 D 551/001 - 750/200	40,000				
		30 Apr 1942 D 751/001 - 1000/200	50,000				
		4 Aug 1942 E 1/001 - 150/200	30,000				
		20 Oct 1942 E 151/001 - 350/200	40,000				
		30 Jan 1943 E 351/001 - 550/200	40,000				
		25 May 1943 E 551/001 - 750/200	40,000				
		5 Nov 1943 E 751/001 - 950/200	40,000				
		24 Jul 1944 E 951/001 - 1000/200	10,000				
		31 Aug 1944 G 1/001 - 200/200	40,000		**100**	**280**	**500**

UB 64d In-line serials

UB 64e	£5	John A Morrison General Manager M J Wilson Cashier Printed signatures				F	VF	EF
		12 Sep 1946	G 201/001	-	450/200	50,000		
		31 Mar 1947	G 451/001	-	1000/200	110,000		
		30 Jun 1947	H 1/001	-	300/200	60,000		
		3 May 1949	H 301/001	-	838/100	107,500	**100**	**280**	**500**

UB 64e £5

The £10 note of this issue is the last of this unpopular denomination. The bank decided in March 1937 that they were to be discontinued when remaining supplies ran out. The signature of the Cashier is lithographed on the 1923 notes.

| UB 65a | £10 | **Norman Hird** Printed signature General Manager
J F McCrindle Lithographed signature Cashier
3 Aug 1923   A   1/001   -   55/200 | 11,000 | **RARE** |

UB 65a £10

| | | Specimen 3 Aug 1923 | 25 | **From 500 EF** |

| UB 65b | £10 | **Norman Hird** General Manager
J F McCrindle Chief Accountant Printed signatures
4 Jul 1928   A   56/001   -   75/200 | 4,000 | **RARE** |

| UB 65c | £10 | **Norman Hird** General Manager
John Wink Chief Accountant Printed signatures
8 Dec 1933   A   76/001   -   85/200
8 Jul 1935   A   86/001   -   95/200 | 2,000
2,000 | **F   VF**
850 2000 |

UB 65c £10 1935

£20 notes were handsigned until 1942 when rising issue numbers dictated that signatures were to be printed.

UB 66a	£20	**Handsigned** p General Manager & p Cashier			
		2 Aug 1923 A 1/001 - 90/200		18,000	**From 600 F**
		Specimen 2 Aug 1923		25	**From 500 EF**

UB 66 Reverse

UB 66b	£20	**Handsigned** p General Manager & p Chief Accountant					
		3 Jul 1928	A 91/001	-	130/200	8,000	
		2 Aug 1932	A 131/001	-	155/200	5,000	
		5 Sep 1933	A 156/001	-	180/200	5,000	
		2 Oct 1934	A 181/001	-	190/200	2,000	
		14 Aug 1935	A 191/001	-	215/200	5,000	**From 500 F**

UB 66b £20 1928

UB 66c	£20	**Handsigned** p General Manager & p Cashier					F	VF
		Fractional serials						
		31 May 1937	A 216/001	-	240/200	5,000		
		In-line serials						
		30 Nov 1938	A 241/001	-	250/200	2,000		
		3 Jan 1939	B 1/001	-	15/200	3,000		
		1 Jun 1940	B 16/001	-	40/200	5,000		
		2 Jan 1942	B 41/001	-	65/200	5,000	400	750

UB 66c 1937 Fractional serials

UB 66d	£20	**Norman Hird** General Manager **M J Wilson** Cashier Printed signatures				**F**	**VF**	**EF**
		30 Apr 1942	B 66/001	-	90/200	5,000		
		1 Feb 1943	B 91/001	-	115/200	5,000		
		10 Jul 1944	B 116/001	-	140/200	5,000	**250**	**500**	**950**

UB 66d 1944 In-line serials

UB 66e	£20	**John A Morrison** General Manager				F	VF	EF
		M J Wilson Cashier Printed signatures						
		2 Dec 1946	B 141/001	-	165/200	5,000		
		1 Sep 1947	B 166/001	-	215/200	10,000	**250**	**500**	**950**

UB 66e Last date 1947

The £100 notes of this series represent the culmination of this exuberant design. All but the 1947 issue were handsigned and issued examples are rare, especially of the pre-war years. Book sizes are 100 notes befitting the very low issue numbers and high face value. Fractional serials until 1936.

UB 67a	£100	**Handsigned** p General Manager & p Cashier					
		1 Aug 1923	A	1/001	-	20/100	2,000	**RARE**

UB 67b	£100	**Handsigned** p General Manager & p Chief Accountant					
		30 Jun 1928	A	21/001	-	30/100	1,000	
		16 Apr 1931	A	31/200	-	40/100	1,000	
		1 Dec 1933	A	41/001	-	50/100	1,000	
		20 May 1936	A	51/001	-	60/100	1,000	**RARE**

UB 67b Fractional serials

UB 67c	£100	**Handsigned**	p General Manager & p Cashier	**In-line serials**		
	1 Mar 1939	A 61/001	-	70/100	1,000	
	2 Jan 1942	A 71/001	-	80/100	1,000	**From 2500 F**

UB 67c In-line serials

Specimen undated   25   **From 750 EF**

					F	VF	EF
UB 67d	**£100**	**John A Morrison** General Manager					
		M J Wilson Cashier Printed signatures					
		18 Feb 1947 A 81/001 - 90/100		1,000	**800**	**1800**	**3500**

UB 67d In-line serials 1947

UB 67 Reverse

SIXTH GENERAL ISSUE – 1949 *to* 1954

Third Waterlow Issue

To coincide with the granting of a new Coat of Arms to the bank in 1949 by the Lord Lyon King of Arms, the ultimate heraldic authority in Scotland, the bank commissioned a new series of banknotes from **Waterlow & Sons Limited, London**. The new design featured the Coat of Arms and the bank had hoped that it would be shown on the notes in its full glorious colours of red, blue, green, gold and silver. Unfortunately Waterlow had to confess that this would not be possible due to a number of factors – the banknote paper was not suitable for the type of ink used in multicolour intaglio printing and the need for exact alignment, or 'registration', on the reduced scale required would be impossible to achieve in the volumes needed, no matter (they said) who was printing the notes. The bank therefore opted for a plain blue background with no underlying tint.

As the £10 had been discontinued there are only four denominations in the Union Bank's final issue before it merged with the Bank of Scotland in 1955. The higher denominations are reduced to Size X (~ 185 x 105mm) and the positional plate letters are again to be found on the notes. The book numbers now include initial zeroes.

Sir William Watson, who signed the final issues of the £1, £5 and £100 notes, was already (and remained) Treasurer of the Bank of Scotland when he was appointed General Manager of the Union Bank, this appointment being made to facilitate the merger between the two banks. He therefore joins the select band of bank officials who have signed the notes of more than one bank. He retired in 1966.

UB 68a	£1	John A Morrison General Manager				F	VF	EF
		1 Mar 1949	A/1 000001 - A/40 1000000	1,000,000				
		17 Oct 1949	B/1 000001 - B/40 1000000	1,000,000				
		3 Jul 1950	C/1 000001 - C/40 1000000	1,000,000				
		2 Aug 1951	D/1 000001 - D/40 1000000	1,000,000				
		7 Apr 1952	E/1 000001 - E/40 1000000	1,000,000				
		8 Dec 1952	F/1 000001 - F/40 1000000	1,000,000				
		1 Sep 1953	G/1 000001 - G/40 1000000	1,000,000		10	40	90

UB 68a First date

Specimen 2 Aug 1951   25   **From 250 EF**

UB 68 Reverse

UB 68b	£1	Sir William Watson General Manager			F	VF	EF
		1 Jun 1954 H/1 000001 - H/30 750000		750,000	**15**	**60**	**160**

UB 68b £1

UB 69a	£5	**John A Morrison** General Manager					F	VF	EF
		17 Jul 1950	A 001/001	-	500/200	100,000			
		5 Jun 1951	A 501/001	-	1000/200	100,000			
		5 Feb 1952	B 001/001	-	500/200	100,000			
		3 Nov 1952	B 501/001	-	1000/200	100,000			
		5 Jan 1953	C 001/001	-	500/200	100,000			
		1 Oct 1953	C 501/001	-	1000/200	100,000	**40**	**110**	**250**

UB 69a £5

		Specimen 5 Jun 1951					25	**From 300 EF**

UB 69b	£5	**Sir William Watson** General Manager							
		2 Apr 1954	D 001/001	-	500/200	100,000	**80**	**160**	**400**

UB 69b £5

UB 70	£20	**John A Morrison** General Manager				F	VF	EF
		1 Sep 1950	A 001/001	-	050/200	10,000		
		19 Jun 1951	A 051/001	-	100/200	10,000		
		6 May 1952	A 101/001	-	150/200	10,000		
		1 May 1953	A 151/001	-	198/100	9,500	**100**	**220**	**500**

UB 70 £20 First date

	Specimen 1 Sep 1950		25	**From 350 EF**

UB 70 Reverse

						F	VF	EF
UB 71a	£100	John A Morrison General Manager						
		9 Oct 1950	A 001/001 - 010/1000	1,000				
		10 Mar 1952	A 011/001 - 020/1000	1,000		**700**	**1500**	**3000**

UB 71a £100

Specimen 9 Oct 1950	25	**From 500 EF**

The final issue of the £100 note is very scarce and it is possible not all of the 1,000 notes printed were actually issued, although they were all taken into cash. As few as six may have survived.

UB 71b	£100	Sir William Watson General Manager					
		1 Oct 1954	A 021/001 - 030/1000	1,000	**1500**	**3000**	-

UB 71b £100

NOTES OUTSTANDING IN 1933

The Union Bank kept records of outstanding unredeemed notes until 1933. A list of these notes covering issues from 1903 to 1933 is given below. Inevitably notes outstanding in the years close to 1933 will be far higher than is likely to be the case today. The list should nevertheless be of interest to collectors.

Denomination	First date of prefix	Prefix	Outstanding in 1933
£1 'Square'	10 Mar 1903	H	1,987
	6 Apr 1905	A	2,345
	2 Jan 1908	B	3,027
	9 Sep 1910	C	6,778
	26 Aug 1913	D	9,302
	8 Nov 1915	E	12,756
	4 Oct 1917	F	10,518
	20 Jun 1919	G	11,196
	10 Dec 1920	H	1,248
	1 Oct 1921	A	14,985
	2 Oct 1923	B	3,077
£1 B size	2 Jun 1924	A	41,271
	4 Jan 1926	B	61,591
	3 Oct 1927	C	151,678
	2 Jan 1929	D	271,977
	2 Apr 1930	E	302,971
	5 Dec 1931	F	542,965
	1 Jun 1933	G	649,996
£5	11 Feb 1905	A	3,746
	14 Jul 1916	B	6,592
	18 Aug 1920	C	2,760
	5 Apr 1921	A	32,337
	15 Jan 1927	B	132,619
£10	4 Apr 1905	A	614
	3 Aug 1923	A	9,151
£20	31 Mar 1905	A	1,670
	2 Aug 1923	A	23,011
£100	7 Apr 1905	A	155
	1 Aug 1923	A	2,575

Bank of Scotland – Other Constituent Banks

This chapter covers the numerous smaller banks which directly or indirectly became constituents of the Bank of Scotland. All lost their independence in the 19th century and all were regional operators of varying significance although the history of many of these banks stretches back into the 18th century. It will be seen that nearly all these banks came into the Bank of Scotland group via the Union Bank, whose remarkable sequence of acquisitions in the first twenty years of its life swept up many old-established banks.

BANKING COMPANY IN ABERDEEN – 1767 *to* 1849

Aberdeen Banking Company (2)

Not to be confused with Aberdeen's first bank, its short-lived predecessor the Banking Company *of* Aberdeen, the Banking Company *in* Aberdeen was formed in 1767 at a time when there was no local bank in the town. The bank was sometimes also referred to as the Aberdeen Banking Company but this name does not appear on the notes. The founding of the new bank was prompted by the lack of local sources of credit and it mustered no fewer than 109 partners and a substantial £72,000 capital at the outset. After a year it had already put £43,000 of notes into circulation and it fast became a staple of commercial life in the city. A turf war developed, however. The new bank sought quite understandably to establish a monopoly position in the northeast but one of the more aggressive Glasgow banks, the Thistle Bank, felt the need to challenge this by appointing agents in the region whose job it was to spread the issue of their notes at the expense of the Aberdeen bank's own note circulation. The familiar tactic of gathering quantities of notes and making a sudden demand for payment was used. The Banking Company retaliated in kind by appointing their own 'note-pickers' but the dispute rumbled on from 1767 until at least 1770 when some sort of compromise appears to have been reached.

The bank continued to prosper in the absence of a local competitor but even the arrival in 1778 of the Aberdeen Commercial Banking Company failed to dent progress. The two banking partnerships co-existed peacefully until 1825 when they were joined by the first local joint stock bank, the Aberdeen Town & County Bank. Initially, nothing seemed to change. They continued to trade profitably but the end came, eventually. The Banking Company was absorbed by the Union Bank of Scotland in 1849 after falling into a dangerously weakened state, having approached the National Bank in 1844 to no avail. Its substance had been eroded by numerous bad debts, including that of Banner Mill, a large local business which had got into difficulties. The bank took possession of the mill but was unable to sell it or operate it profitably. The large unproductive asset weighed heavily on its balance sheet. When the Union Bank made their offer of £1 10s per share, well below the bank's apparent book value, the partners seized it gratefully. Its Authorised Circulation was £88,467.

First Issue 1767 *to* 1848

A little information on the bank's note issues has been found in the archives of the Bank of Scotland and details are set out below. The first notes issued in 1767 were for £1 and £5 and signed by the Cashier Robert Sandilands and two directors. They were printed by Thomas Innes of Edinburgh on paper made at Balfours Mill, Colinton. The earliest known survivor is a £1 note from the 1773 issue when notes for £10 and £20 were added. Engraving of the 1773 and 1775 notes was by **Andrew Bell** of Edinburgh (no imprint). All pre-1800 notes are rare. £1 notes of the 1820s are seen but almost always as forgeries, lacking the bank's distinctive watermark. All the notes up to the final issue of 1849 were simple designs which surely accounts for the attention paid to them by forgers. Embossed revenue stamps appear from 1783 on notes for 1 Guinea or more. From 1799 stamp duty also became payable on £1 and 5s notes.

BC 1a	£1	**Arms of Aberdeen with One Pound & Sterling either side** Payee inserted by hand printed date uniface		
		1 May 1767	103,000	
		1 May 1773	155,000	**RARE**
		Forgery 1773		**From 200 F**
BC 1b	£1	**One Pound & Sterling in Gothic script** printed date uniface *Engraved by:* **M Ashby, London** Payee inserted by hand		
		2 May 1781	50,000	
		2 May 1786	80,000	
		2 Dec 1799	2,500	
		10 Oct 1805	n/k	**RARE**
		Forgery 1805		**From 200 F**
BC 1c	£1	**Similar to BC 1b** *Engraved by:* **M Ashby, London** Dated by hand uniface Congreve		
		1824 to 1825		**From 2000 F**
		Forgery 1819 to 1825		**From 200 F**
		Specimen undated (1808)		**From 500 EF**

BC 1c Unissued note prepared 1808 for Edinburgh Stamp Office

Bank of Scotland - Other Constituent Banks

BC 2 **1gn** **Similar to BC 1b One Guinea to right of arms**
Designed by: **J McNaughton** *Engraved by:* **Kirkwood & Son**
Payee inserted by hand
    1 May 1797   40,000   **RARE**

Specimen 1 May 1797 plate A   **From 500 EF**

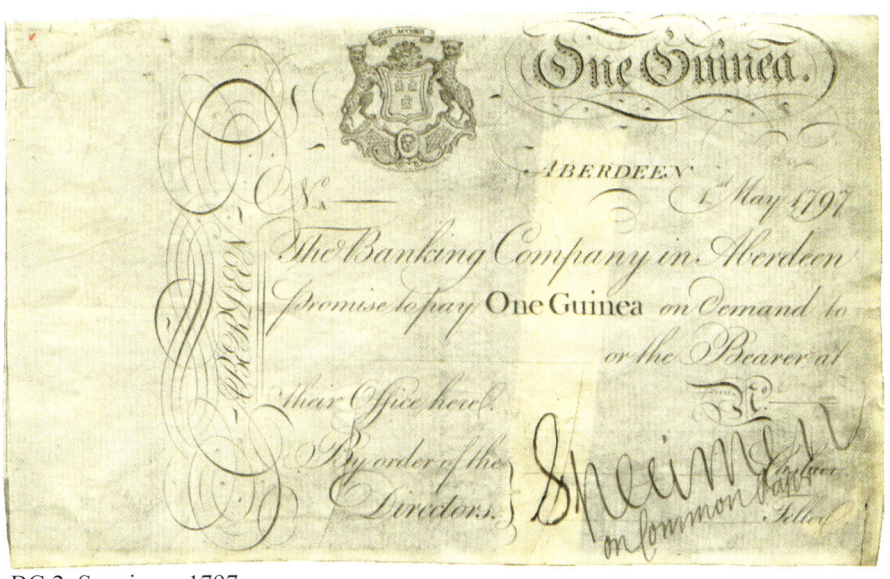

BC 2 Specimen 1797

BC 3 **£5** **Similar to BC 1b** Payee inserted by hand printed date
Designed by: **Tomkins** *Engraved by:* **Ashby** (no imprint)
    1 May 1767   20,000
    1 May 1773   14,000
    1 Aug 1783   7,600
    1 Aug 1788   6,400
    6 Jul 1797   10,000
    1 Aug 1801   n/k
    10 Oct 1805   n/k   **RARE**

Proof / Colour Trial Red 6 Jul 1797   **RARE**

Specimen 1 Aug 1783 6 Jul 1797   **From 600 EF**

BC 3 Specimen 1797

BC 4　　　**£10**　　**Similar to BC 1b**　Payee inserted by hand　printed date
　　　　　　　　　Designed by: **Tomkins**　*Engraved by:* **Ashby** (no imprint)
　　　　　　　　　　1 May 1773　　　　　　　　　　　　　　　　　　2,200

　　　　　　　　　Specimen　1 May 1773　　　　　　　　　　　**From 600 EF**

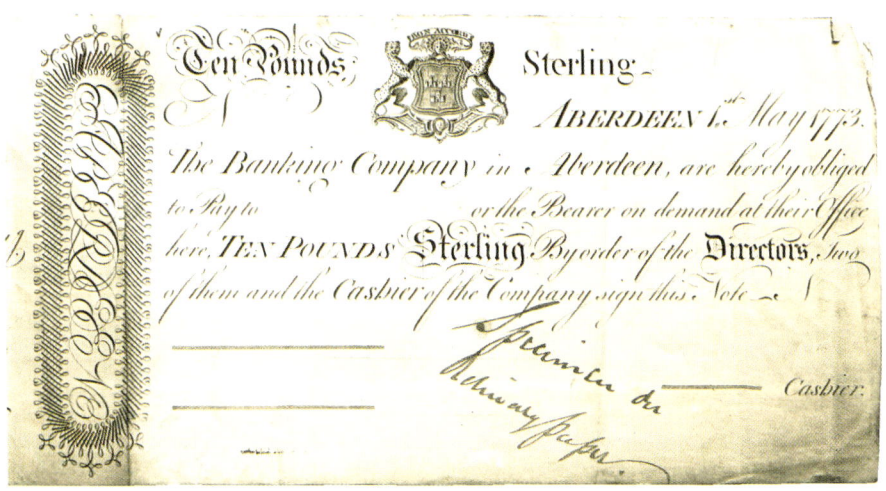

BC 4 Specimen 1773

BC 5a　　**£20**　　**Similar to BC 1b**　Payee inserted by hand
　　　　　　　　　Twenty Pounds to left of arms　printed date
　　　　　　　　　Designed by: **Tomkins**　*Engraved by:* **Ashby** (with imprint)
　　　　　　　　　　1 May 1773　　　　　　　　　　　　　　　　　　600
　　　　　　　　　　1 May 1786　　　　　　　　　　　　　　　　　1,400

　　　　　　　　　Unissued　1 May 1786　　　　　　　　　　**From 750 EF**

BC 5b   £20   Similar to BC 1b £20 to left of arms
             1 Aug 1797   3,000

             Unissued 6 Jul 1797 1 Aug 1797   From 750 EF

BC 5b Unissued 1797

             Specimen 1 Aug 1797   From 750 EF

BC 5c   £20   Similar to BC 1b Printed in Red
             1 Aug 1801   n/k
             20 Dec 1805   n/k

             Unissued 1 Aug 1801   From 1000 EF

BC 6 Aberdeen City Arms with motto Bon Accord

In 1799 a 5 Shillings note was added to the range. It circulated for only a few years and was issued in response to the widespread shortage of small change during the Napoleonic Wars.

BC 6   **5s**   **Aberdeen arms upper left Pay A Morrice**
Designed by: **G Paton** *Engraved by:* **Kirkwood & Son**
Watermarked paper printed date 135 x 110mm
   2 Sep 1799   n/k   **From 1000 F**

   Unissued   **From 800 EF**

BC 6 1799

Second Issue 1849 *to* 1855

The second and final issue was a very different affair. **W H Lizars** was entrusted with the engraving and printing and the results show what a step change had taken place once steel plate engraving – and artistic endeavour – were brought to bear. All notes carry the names of the six constituent banks of the Union Bank of Scotland in their borders, with the Union Bank itself across the top. The name of the Banking Company in Aberdeen dominates the centre of the note, in small text below the caption: 'ESTABLISHED IN 1767 / INCORPORATED WITH THE UNION BANK OF SCOTLAND IN 1849'. Each design comprises three vignettes and all notes are signed by the Teller and Cashier. These notes continued to be issued until 1855. The archives of the Royal Bank hold an artist's essay of a £1 note, probably prepared in the 1840s by Lizars though it cannot be attributed with certainty.

BC 7   **£1**   **Vignette of Victoria supported by Agriculture & Science**
Dated by hand printed serials
   3 May 1852   5/282   -   10/18
   1 May 1855   73/217   -   92/441   **From 2000 F**

   Proof undated   **From 500 EF**

BC 7 1852

BC 8   £5   Victoria supported by Plenty & Justice

   Proof undated   **From 500 EF**

BC 8 Proof

BC 9   **£20**   **Victoria supported by Commerce & Learning**

Proof undated   **From 500 EF**

BC 9 Proof

CENTRAL BANK OF SCOTLAND – 1834 *to* 1868

This Perth-based bank opened its doors on 1st May 1834 with paid up capital of £78,125 subscribed by 405 shareholders. It was the last remaining independent bank in Perth when it was acquired by the Bank of Scotland in 1868. Perhaps its most lasting legacy is its fine Grade 1 listed head office building in St John Street in the city centre (now a kitchenware shop). By 1841 branches had been opened in Aberfeldy, Auchterarder, Crieff, Dunkeld, Killin, Newburgh and Pitlochry. Its record was not unblemished and despite financial support from the Bank of Scotland it endured a crisis in 1864 which required that bank to come to its rescue by acquiring several of its branches in Perthshire. The Bank of Scotland assumed full control in 1868 but some shareholders declined to sell their interest and retained nominal independence until 1880 when they were finally bought out. The bank's liabilities had totalled £51,525 in 1868 and these shareholders had managed to reduce this by half in the ensuing twelve years. Authorised Circulation in 1845 was £42,933.

From the outset the Central Bank's notes were designed and engraved by **W H Lizars**. Officials were despatched to Edinburgh to negotiate with engravers and Lizars was chosen ahead of Kirkwood & Son and two others. After Lizars' death in 1859 the contract was taken over by **W & A K Johnston** who retained his designs. The notes are beautiful and artistic creations which would grace any collection. Most will be seen as proofs as surviving issued notes are rare – only issued £1 notes have been observed though a specimen set of numbered but unissued notes is to be found in Lloyds' archives. These notes had been framed and put on display in the Bank of Scotland's boardroom. From the few records available it can be confirmed that notes of £1, £5, £10 and £20 were issued from the outset. All notes were issued in the name of 'The Governor and Company of the

Central Bank of Scotland'. The final issues of all the notes had a coloured central value panel but it is not clear when this was first added to the notes. Around 1857 all notes were amended by the addition of the words 'PURSUANT TO ACT OF PARLIAMENT' to reflect the change of law in 1853 relating to stamp duty on banknotes.

Total issuance of all £1 notes from 1st May 1834 to 1st November 1865 was ~ 235,000 with the bank adopting the usual Scottish fractional numbering system. A curious and apparently random sequence of prefix letters was used. Notes were issued in books of 300 notes each. All £1 notes signed by the Accountant and Manager. Some proof notes stamped 'CANCELLED'.

CE 1	£1	Black Single vignette of Perth No borders uniface Congreve

Printer: **W H Lizars** Numbered & dated by hand
1840 to 1844   **From 1750 F**

Proof undated   **From 450 EF**

CE 1 Proof

The £1 note was redesigned in 1848. An artist's essay is known with the bank's title on a single line. It is not known at which point printed dates were introduced.

CE 2a	£1	Black Vignette of Perth Borders Numbered & dated by hand

Vignettes of Agriculture & Commerce *Printer:* **W H Lizars**

Proof undated   **From 450 EF**

CE 2b	£1	Black Blue ONE panel *Printer:* W H Lizars

Additional text: 'PURSUANT TO ACT OF PARLIAMENT'

Proof undated   **From 450 EF**

CE 2c	£1	**Similar to CE 2b** *Printer:* **W & A K Johnston** printed date Additional text: 'PURSUANT TO ACT OF PARLIAMENT' 1 Nov 1865 N	**From 1750 F**
		Proof 11 Nov 1863 1 Nov 1865	**From 450 EF**
		Proof undated amended Blue ONE panel	**From 750 EF**

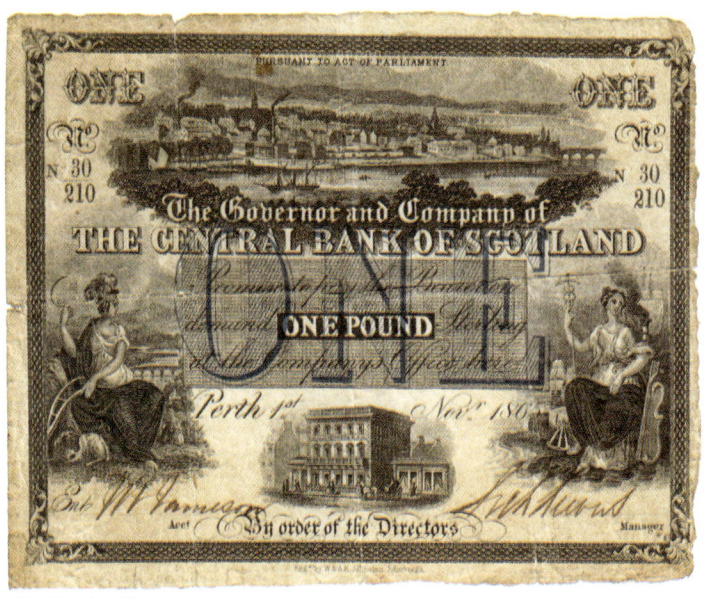

CE 2c 1865

Total issuance of all £5 notes from 1st May 1834 to 12th November 1866 was ~ 18,600 in books of 200 each. The only £5 note to survive in issued format carries the final date and is printed in blue with a red FIVE panel. The earlier issued notes were probably printed in black only.

CE 3a	£5	**Black** *Printer:* **W H Lizars** Numbered & dated by hand **Vignette of Perth across the Tay with Scotia and Plenty**	
		Proof undated	**From 500 EF**
CE 3b	£5	**Similar to CE 3a** Numbered & dated by hand *Printer:* **W H Lizars** Additional text: 'PURSUANT TO ACT OF PARLIAMENT'	
		Proof undated	**From 500 EF**
CE 3c	£5	**Blue Red FIVE** Printed prefix/serials printed date Additional text: 'PURSUANT TO ACT OF PARLIAMENT' *Printer:* **W & A K Johnston**	
		Unissued 12 Nov 1866	**RARE**
		Proof Black undated 12 Nov 1866	**From 500 EF**

CE 3c Unissued

Issue numbers of the £10 note were so low at ~ 2,100 that it does not appear as though any were prepared with the W & A K Johnston imprint. It is not known at which point the blue TEN was added to the note. The notes were issued between 1st May 1834 and 3rd June 1867.

CE 4a	£10	Black Similar to CE 3a Numbered & dated by hand	
		Printer: **W H Lizars**	
		Proof undated	From 500 EF

CE 4a Proof

CE 4b	**£10**	**Black Blue TEN** Printed prefix/serials Dated by hand Additional text: 'PURSUANT TO ACT OF PARLIAMENT' *Printer:* **W H Lizars**

                Unissued undated   **RARE**

                Proof undated (no blue TEN)   **From 500 EF**

Issue numbers of the £20 note were also low at ~ 4,400 but the printers' imprint was nevertheless amended from that of W H Lizars to W & A K Johnston on the final issues. £20 notes were issued between 1st May 1834 and 11th May 1867.

CE 5a	**£20**	**Black Similar to CE 3a but with Lion added** *Printer:* **W H Lizars** Numbered & dated by hand

                Proof undated   **From 600 EF**

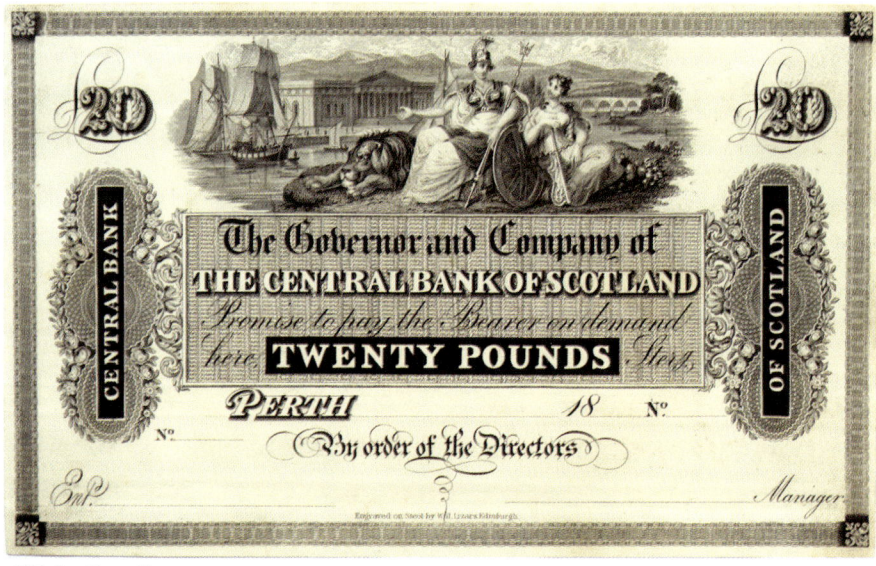

CE 5a Proof

CE 5b	**£20**	**Blue Red TWENTY** Printed prefix/serials Dated by hand Additional text: 'PURSUANT TO ACT OF PARLIAMENT' *Printer:* **W & A K Johnston**

                Unissued undated   **RARE**

                Proof undated (no red TWENTY)   **From 600 EF**

CE 5b Unissued

SIR WILLIAM FORBES, JAMES HUNTER & COMPANY – 1773 *to* 1838

This long-lived Edinburgh private bank was the most famous and eminent of Scotland's private banking partnerships. While 1st January 1773 was the formal date of establishment of Forbes Hunter & Co, the firm's origins go back possibly as far as 1675 when a trading firm was started by Patrick Coutts, a timber merchant originally from Montrose who moved to Edinburgh around 1696. In 1723 a successor firm was founded by his son John Coutts who became an eminent businessman in Edinburgh and was Lord Provost in 1748-1749. John Coutts & Co began life as corn dealers and discounters of bills of exchange. After John's death in 1750 the partnership was taken over by his four sons, Patrick, John, James and Thomas, who also set up a corn trading and banking firm in London. This firm was the predecessor of the famous London private bank Coutts & Co, bankers to the Royal Family as well as many establishment figures. From at least 1763 the Edinburgh firm was concentrating on the classic business of banking: taking deposits, discounting bills and financing domestic and foreign trade, but not, as yet, issuing banknotes. A disagreement between the partners resulted in the separation of the London and Edinburgh firms and the formation of Forbes Hunter in 1773. William (later Sir William) Forbes had been first an apprentice and later a partner in all but name to the Edinburgh firm while James Hunter had also risen from an apprenticeship.

Once the new partnership of Forbes Hunter & Co was established in 1773 it continued to concentrate purely on banking, though it did not commence note issuance until 1782 (prior to then they had issued notes of the Royal Bank of Scotland). By the end of that year total issuance had reached £82,750. Hunter died in 1787 but Sir William Forbes continued to lead the firm with great distinction until his own death in 1806. He acted as an informal financial adviser to the government and became a respected philanthropist and establishment figure in Edinburgh. Forbes Hunter acted as Edinburgh agents for at least seven provincial banks and opened branches in somewhat unlikely locations: Inverary, Johnstone, Lerwick and Stranraer.

Forbes Hunter was about the same size as the Glasgow Union Banking Company when the two banks agreed to merge in 1838, at least as measured by their note issues: in April 1838 both had around £300,000 of notes outstanding. The merger was only completed when the Union Bank of Scotland was formed in May 1843 as it had been agreed that Forbes Hunter would continue to operate under its own name. There were two reasons why this leading and highly respected firm decided to give up its independence; the first was that they had been hurt by the banking crisis of 1836/37 which had thinned the ranks of the remaining small private banks; the second and more fundamental one was that they had felt the winds of change. Banking in 19th century industrial Britain required substantial capital and private banks no longer had the necessary scale. They were being marginalised by the new joint stock banks with their access to the stock markets and large deposit bases. The former partners of Forbes Hunter did however become directors in the Union Bank's second Head Office in Edinburgh.

Notes issued by Forbes Hunter have survived in reasonable number, though examples dated later than 1825 are hard to find. There are two note issues, the first designed by Butterworth and engraved by **Robert Kirkwood** (later **Kirkwood & Son**) and the second engraved by **W H Lizars**. Remnants of the note registers have been located and details summarised in the listing. The first notes issued were for 1 Guinea, £5 and £20 in early 1782 despite the printed date on the first 1 Guinea and £5 notes of 1st July 1781. Notes with this date were quickly replaced by ones dated 5th March 1782 when it was realised the former date was a Sunday, thus casting doubts on their validity. The designs remained essentially unchanged until Lizars was invited to engrave new notes on steel plate around 1825. All issued notes examined contain a watermark, while the forgeries do not.

First Issue

The first £1 notes were dated 1st January 1798. 705,000 notes were issued between 1798 and 1824 with 2,074 recorded as outstanding in 1845.

FH 1a	**£1**	Vignette of Parliament Close, **TWENTY / SHILLINGS** either side **Pay Lewis Hay** Impressed revenue stamp uniface *Reported not confirmed*		
FH 1b	**£1**	Similar to FH 1a **Pay Patrick Maxton** Impressed revenue stamp uniface printed date		
		2 Sep 1805	plate M	**From 1500 F**

FH 1b 1805

FH 1c   £1   **Similar to FH 1a Pay Patrick Sanderson** printed dates
Impressed revenue stamp uniface
   3 Nov 1808   plate S
   12 Oct 1813   plate C   **From 1500 F**

Proof undated plate A B
   3 Nov 1808 printed date plate U   **From 500 EF**

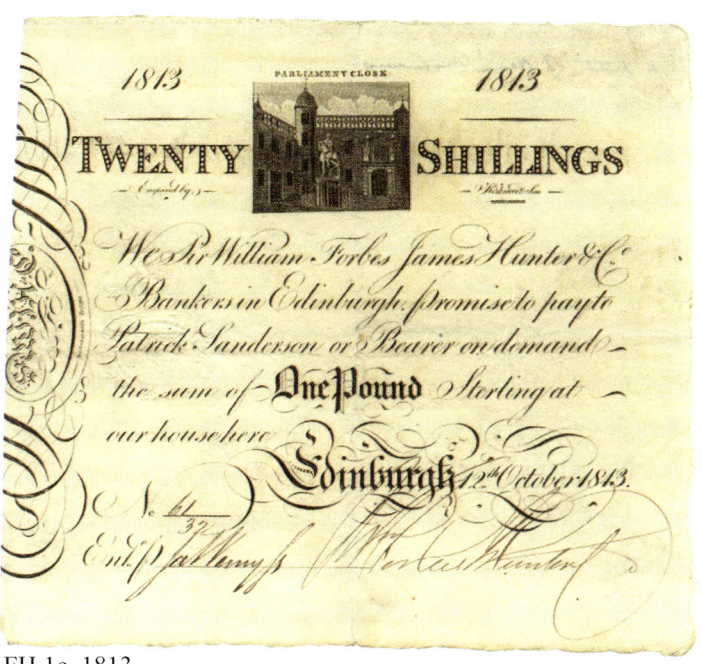

FH 1c 1813

FH 2a	£1	**ONE & POUND either side of re-shaped vignette** **Pay Robert Borrowman** Impressed revenue stamp Dated by hand uniface		
		1818 to 1821	plate A	**From 750 F**
		Forgery 1820 to 1821 plate A		**From 150 F**
		Proof undated plate A B		**From 350 EF**

FH 2a 1818

FH 2b	£1	**Similar to FH 2a Pay Robert Borrowman** Congreve		
		1822 to 1823	plate A	**From 750 F**
		Forgery 1822 to 1826 plate A		**From 150 F**

The first 1 Guinea notes were dated 5th March 1782. 770,600 notes (not including 36,000 dated 1st July 1781 which were all withdrawn and destroyed) were issued between 1782 and 1820 with 1,133 recorded as outstanding in 1845.

FH 3a	**1gn**	**Pay Lewis Hay Oval vignette of Parliament Close** uniface **ONE GUINEA in gothic script to right** printed date 5 Mar 1782	**RARE**
		Proof 5 Mar 1782	**From 750 EF**

FH 3b	**1gn**	**Similar to FH 3a** Payee Patrick Maxton inserted by hand printed date 1 Jan 1789	plate C E	**From 2000 F**
		Forgery		**From 150 F**

FH 3b 1789

FH 3c	**1gn**	**Similar to FH 3a Pay Patrick Maxton** printed printed date 2 Sep 1805	plate E	**From 1500 F**

FH 3d	1gn	Similar to FH 3a **Pay Patrick Sanderson** printed date 3 Nov 1808		From 1500 F
		Proof 3 Nov 1808 plate I		From 350 EF

FH 4a	1gn	**ONE in small Roman capitals Amended vignette** **Pay Robert Borrowman** *Designed by:* **Forrester** *Engraved by:* **Kirkwood** Impressed revenue stamp Dated by hand 1820 to 1821	plate A B C D	From 500 F
		Forgery 1820 to 1821 plate B D		From 150 F

FH 4a 1820

FH 4b	1gn	Similar to FH 4a **Pay Robert Borrowman** Congreve 1822 to 1824	plate A B C D	From 500 F
		Forgery 1822 to 1824 plate B D		From 150 F

The first £5 notes were dated 5th March 1782. 203,200 notes (not including 6,000 dated 1st July 1781 which were all burnt before issue) were issued between 1782 and 1824 with 186 recorded as outstanding in 1845.

FH 5　£5　**Oval vignette of Parliament Close Black Pay Lewis Hay**
　　　　　　Five Pounds in large gothic to right printed date uniface
　　　　　　Impressed revenue stamp
　　　　　　　1 Jul 1781
　　　　　　　1 Mar 1782　　　　　　　　　　　　　　　　　　　　　　　**RARE**

FH 6　£5　**Oval vignette & Five Pounds in Red Pay Patrick Sanderson**
　　　　　　Impressed revenue stamp printed date uniface
　　　　　　　2 Jan 1815　　　　　　　　　　　　　　　　　　　　　　　**RARE**

　　　　　　Specimen undated　　　　　　　　　　　　　　　　**From 1000 EF**

FH 6 1815

Board minutes of the Union Bank in Edinburgh confirm that no Forbes, Hunter & Co notes were to be issued after October 1845 and that outstanding notes were to be withdrawn and destroyed along with all unissued notes. The destruction of the plates was also ordered. Notes in circulation were still being withdrawn as late as March 1858. The minutes also confirm that Forbes Hunter notes for £10, £20 and £100 had been issued but these denominations have not been seen so design details cannot be confirmed. It has been assumed here that they would have been similar to the first issues engraved by Kirkwood & Son.

The first £10 notes were dated 1st January 1800. 19,200 notes were issued between 1800 and 1820 with just 4 recorded as outstanding in 1845.

FH 7   £10   *Confirmed issued, not seen*

The first £20 notes were dated 5th March 1782. 61,500 notes were issued between 1782 and 1819 with just 9 recorded as outstanding in 1845.

FH 8   £20   *Confirmed issued, not seen*

The first £100 notes were dated 1st May 1820. 1,200 notes were issued between 1820 and 1821. None believed outstanding.

FH 9   £100   *Confirmed issued, not seen*

Second Issue

New designs prepared by **W H Lizars** around 1825 are radically different, being complex and finely engraved steel plate engravings. Only £1 and 1 Guinea notes have been seen but other denominations may also have been prepared. Only a very few issued Lizars £1 notes have survived even though they were being issued for at least twenty years and circulated for even longer. No issued 1 Guinea notes have been seen.

FH 10   £1   **Pay Robert Borrowman Elaborate machinework panels**
                    Vignette of Charles II on horseback in Parliament Square
                    Congreve
                    1835   **RARE**

                    Proof undated   **From 500 EF**

FH 10 Proof

FH 11   1gn   Pay Robert Borrowman Vignette of equestrian statue
                Elaborate machinework panels

         Proof undated   **From 500 EF**

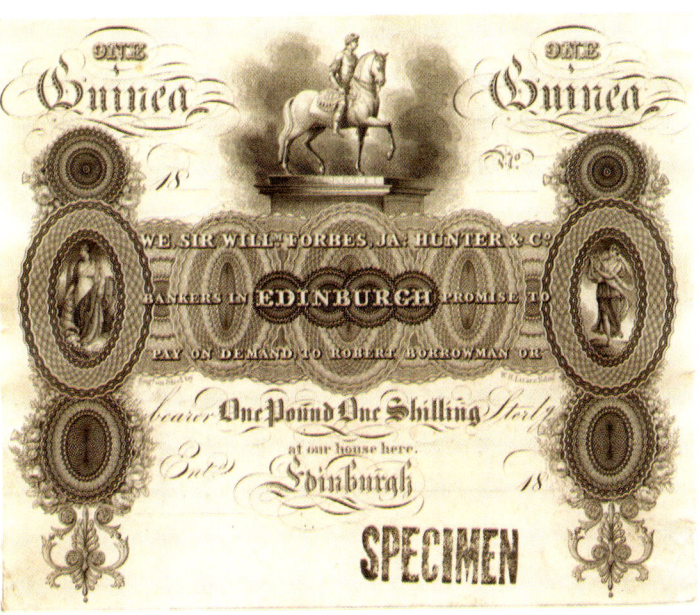

FH 11 Proof, stamped SPECIMEN

GLASGOW BANK COMPANY – 1809 *to* 1836

Dennistoun, Nicholson Inglis & Co

Established in 1809 by James Dennistoun of Golfhill, Samuel Nicholson and fifteen other partners as a private banking partnership. Some of these were partners in the London private bank Ransom, Morland & Co while others were from Dundee where they had been instrumental in forming the Dundee New Bank. The bank grew rapidly and overtook its older Glasgow rivals. Its note circulation was extensive from the beginning, rising from £89,847 in June 1811 to £153,920 by 1819, the largest of the early Glasgow banks. Paid up capital was in the region of £100,000. It merged with the Ship Bank of Carrick, Brown & Co in 1836 to form the Glasgow & Ship Bank Company. Apart from an unissued 1 Guinea note only £1 notes have been recorded but higher denominations are likely to have been issued. Some notes annotated as forgeries seem to have been produced from genuine plates so quite possibly just the signatures were forged. They also issued counterstamped dollar coins for 5 Shillings around 1810.

GB 1	£1	Black Small monogram panel top centre uniface			
		GLASGOW BANK panel to left *Engraved by:* **James Haldane**			
		1809 to 1824		plate A B C D	From **500 F**
		Unissued plate A			From **400 EF**
		Forgery 1819 to 1826			From **150 F**

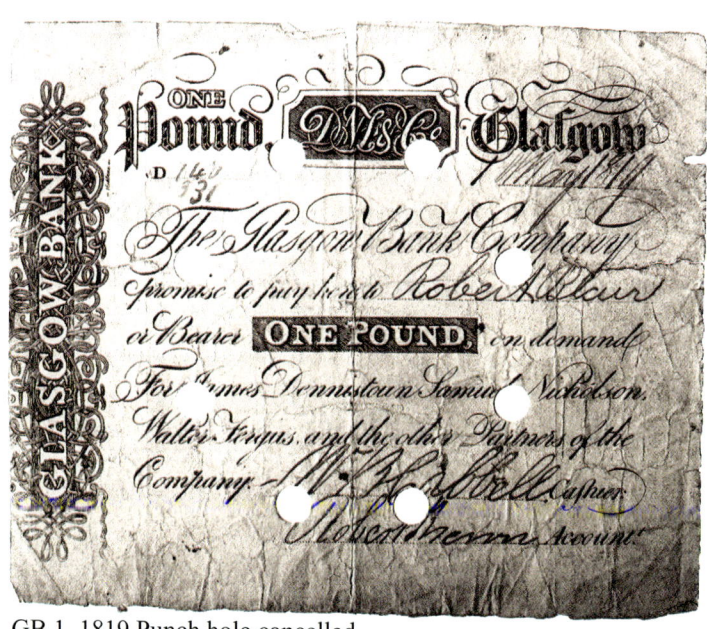

GB 1 1819 Punch hole cancelled

GB 2	1gn	Similar to GB 1 Monogram upper left uniface **GLASGOW BANK panel to left**

                    Unissued plate B   **From 500 EF**

In 1830 a new design was prepared using steel plate engraving and incorporating a border in an unusual shade of brown. A number of these notes have been seen inscribed 'Forgery' but it may only be the signatures which have been forged as the quality of the engraving appears very similar to genuine notes.

GB 3	£1	**Black Brown border Glasgow Arms in wreath upper centre** **Pay James Ewing** *Engraved by:* **James Haldane** Congreve 1830 **From 400 F** Forgery 1830 **From 200 F**

GB 3 1830

| GB 4 | £1 | **Similar to GB 3 Central blue security panel** Congreve
Engraved by: **James Haldane**
1830 | **From 700 F** |

A final design was prepared in 1836 by Perkins & Bacon but has been seen only as a proof.

GB 5	£1	**Ornate design Glasgow Arms upper centre flanked by ONE panels Britannia left** *Printer:* **Perkins & Bacon**	
		Proof year printed as 183	**From 500 EF**

GB 5 Proof Ornate design

GLASGOW & SHIP BANK COMPANY – 1836 *to* 1843

This bank was initially established in 1836 as a private bank arising from a merger of the Ship Bank of Carrick, Brown & Co (who contributed four partners to the new bank) and the Glasgow Bank Company (another 24 partners). The partners debated conversion to a joint stock bank but this had not happened by the time the offer to acquire it had come in from the newly established Union Bank of Scotland in 1843. The bank traded very profitably throughout its short life and the Union Bank took over its head office to use as its own. The bank's only surviving notes were engraved by **Perkins & Bacon** using ornate designs closely based on the final £1 note prepared by Perkins for the Glasgow Bank Company. Only proofs have been recorded and no issued notes are known to have survived.

GS 1	£1	Ornate design Glasgow arms upper centre flanked by ONE panels Ship left *Printer:* **Perkins, Bacon & Petch**

Proof year printed as 183   **From 500 EF**

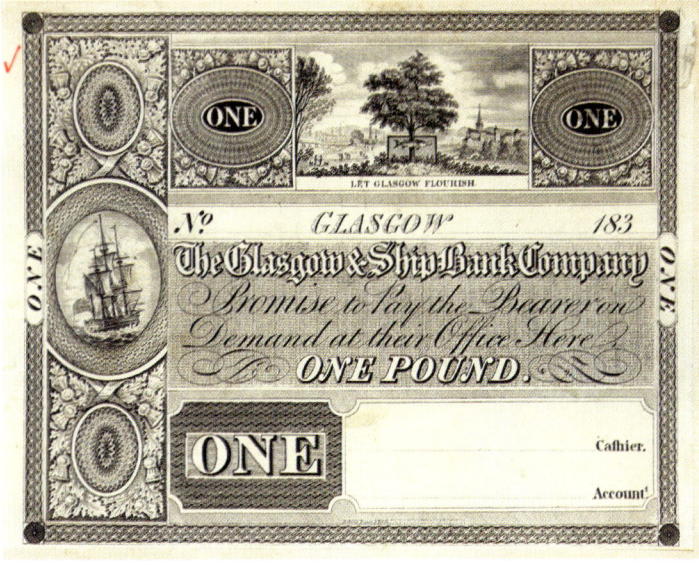

GS 1 Proof

GS 2	£5	Similar to GS 1

Proof undated   **From 500 EF**

GS 3	£20	Similar to GS 1

Proof undated   **From 500 EF**

GS 4	£100	Similar to GS 1 *Printer:* **Perkins & Bacon**

Proof undated   **From 600 EF**

GLASGOW UNION BANKING COMPANY – 1830 *to* 1843

The Glasgow Union Banking Company was established as a joint stock bank and opened for business in May 1830 as a response by Glaswegian businessmen to the dominance of the Edinburgh banks and out of frustration that the three local private banks, the Glasgow Bank Company, the Ship Bank and the Thistle Bank were too small to compete. The bank's first location was in Post Office Court, off Trongate. The 18 original promoters invited subscriptions and in total some 488 shareholders contributed an initial £350,000 paid-in capital. Over 80% were based in the Glasgow area, representing mainly merchant and manufacturing interests. Authorised capital was set at £2,000,000. A profit of £8,779 was achieved in the bank's first year and by 1836 the bank had total assets of over £6,000,000 and had opened 13 offices, including two in the English towns of Carlisle and Penrith. In 1835 they made the first of a number of unsuccessful applications for a Royal Charter. The bank made three acquisitions, the Thistle Bank in June 1836, the Edinburgh private bank of Sir William Forbes, James Hunter & Co in April 1838 and finally the Paisley Union Bank in June 1838. In 1843 the bank was re-established as the Union Bank of Scotland.

One of the Glasgow Union's shareholders was **W H Lizars**, the Edinburgh-based engraver and printer who designed and engraved all but the £100 note of the bank's note issues. The £100 note was engraved by **Joseph Swan** of Glasgow, perhaps Lizars's greatest rival for the crown of Scotland's finest banknote engraver.

Some fragments of the note registers have survived, confirming that at least 387,000 £1 notes were issued between 1830 and 1841 in 774 books of 500 notes each. Issue numbers of higher denominations were much lower: 34,600 £5 notes in 173 books of 200 notes each; 7,200 £20 notes in 36 books of 200 notes each; and 1,350 £100 notes in five books of uneven sizes. Intriguingly, the records indicate that specimens in red and blue of the £5 and £20 notes were prepared. These have never been seen. Very few issued notes have survived, the sole £1 and £5 notes recorded being located in Lloyds Bank's archives.

GU 1	£1	Vignette of equestrian statue of William of Orange in Trongate **Central vignette of George IV** Congreve *Printer:* **W H Lizars** Dated & numbered by hand		
		1830 to 1841	plate A	**RARE**
		Proof undated plate A		From 500 EF

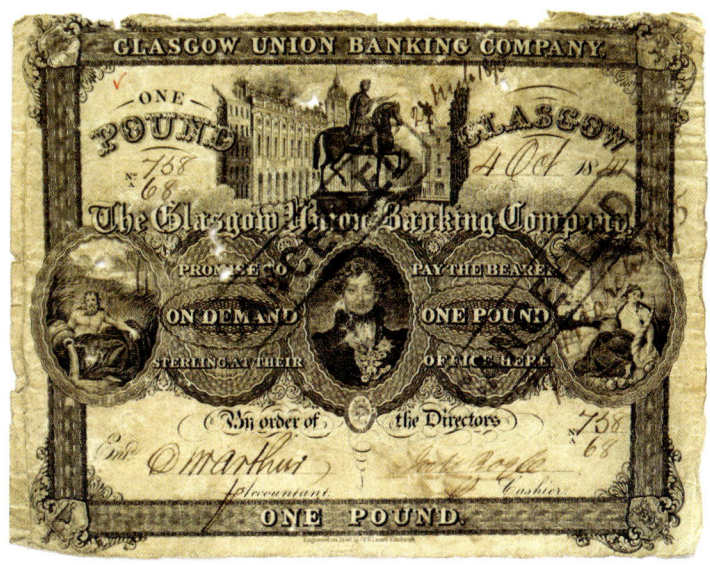

GU 1 Issued, two CANCELLED stamps

GU 2	£5	**Vignette of William of Orange Two allegorical vignettes** Congreve
		Printer: **W H Lizars** Dated & numbered by hand uniface
		1841 plate A **RARE**

        Proof undated plate A   **From 600 EF**

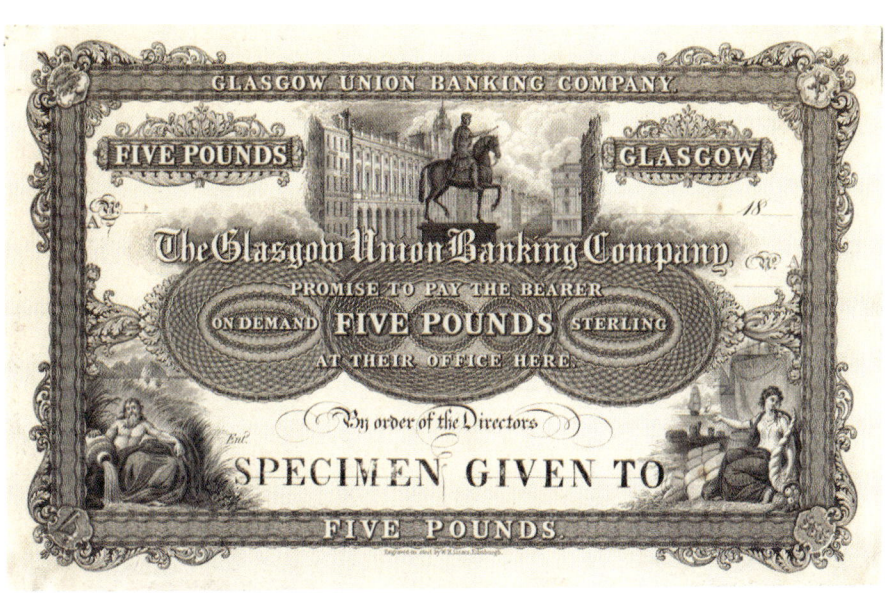

GU 2 Proof, overprinted SPECIMEN GIVEN TO

GU 3   £20   **Vignette of William of Orange Central vignette of George IV** uniface
        Printer: **W H Lizars** Dated & numbered by hand

        Proof undated plate A   From 600 EF

GU 4   £100   **Vignette of William of Orange Two allegorical vignettes**
        Printer: **Joseph Swan** Dated & numbered by hand uniface

        Proof undated   From 850 EF

GU 4 Proof, hand-written specimen

HUNTERS & COMPANY – 1773 *to* 1843

Founded in Ayr in 1773 by James Hunter, the former Cashier of the ill-fated Douglas, Heron & Co (known as the Air Bank) with capital of £10,000. Other partners included James's brother Robert and his son-in-law William Wood. A second James Hunter, also a partner in Forbes, Hunter & Co, was an undisclosed partner but he withdrew when his position became known due to a concern that his association with the Ayr-based bank would reflect badly on Forbes, Hunter & Co. The lingering effects of the collapse of Douglas, Heron & Co were at the root of this. When the founding partner James Hunter died he was replaced by James Ballantine, a friend of the famous poet Robert Burns. Hunters & Co was a well-managed bank with a note circulation of £42,000 by 1777. In 1821 it acquired the Kilmarnock Bank and eventually operated seven branches in Ayrshire. A disagreement with Quintin Kennedy, brought in after the acquisition to manage the Kilmarnock office, resulted in Kennedy leaving to found the Ayrshire Bank in direct competition. Hunters & Co were taken over by the Union Bank of Scotland in 1843 after beginning to struggle against the growing competition of the joint stock banks. Few notes have survived and those of the first issue are especially rare.

HU 1 £1 *Design unconfirmed*
(1773)

HU 2 1gn **Vignette of George III upper left**
Image of contemporary Guinea coin lower left
1781 **RARE**

Forgery 1781 From 300 F

HU 2 1781

HU 3 £5 Similar to HU 2

By 1828 a £1 note with improved engraving in dual colours had been prepared by **Kirkwood & Son**. The elaborate left hand panel of thistle motifs with a charming allegorical vignette and the promissory text were both in black, but a vivid brick red panel was added curving over a similarly coloured vignette of a contemporary gold sovereign (equal to £1) with the George and the Dragon design.

HU 4	**£1**	**Black & Red** Congreve		
		Designed by: **Taylor** *Engraved by:* **Kirkwood & Son**		
		1829 to 1839	plate E F	**From 2000 F**
		1839 (red portion printed, text completed by hand)		**From 1500 VF**
		Specimen undated plate F		**From 750 EF**

HU 4 1829

Other denominations may have been issued.

KILMARNOCK BANKING COMPANY – 1802 *to* 1821

Established on 10th June 1802, this small operation had a fairly successful but strictly local business. The partners were James and Mungo Fairlie, Patrick Ballantine, George Douglas and William Parker, all local businessmen and landowners. William Parker was Cashier and Manager. In October 1821 the bank was absorbed by Hunters & Co of Ayr who agreed to open a branch in the town as a result. Very few notes have survived.

KB 1	1gn	**Arms of Kilmarnock flanked by One Guinea / Kilmarnock**

Designed by: **J Sanderson** *Engraved by:* **Kirkwood & Son**
1806 to 1808   plate A B D   **RARE**

KB 1 1808

KB 2 2gn **Arms of Kilmarnock flanked by TWO / GUINEAS**
Designed by: **J Sanderson** *Engraved by:* **Kirkwood & Son**

Part Issued undated plate A   **RARE**

KB 2 Part Issued

Other denominations may have been issued.

PAISLEY BANKING COMPANY – 1783 to 1837

This private banking partnership opened for business on 1st October 1783 and went on to establish branches in Alloa, Dundee, Glasgow, Irvine and Stranraer. There were nine partners at the outset including two local landowners, four local merchants and two from Glasgow. One partner, Andrew Thomson, was also a partner of Glasgow's Ship Bank and went on to found his own private bank of Andrew, George & Andrew Thomson. A fierce rivalry developed between the Paisley Banking Company and the Paisley Union Bank after the latter was founded in 1788. As was often the case, this took the form of 'note-picking', i.e. collecting notes of the opposing bank and presenting them in bulk in the hope of causing financial difficulties. The Paisley Banking Company ceased trading in November 1837 and its business was transferred to the British Linen Company. According to remnants of the note registers found in Lloyds' archives, the bank was unique in Scotland for having issued notes payable in Dublin. Unfortunately none of the 1,600 notes issued appear to have survived. The bank issued 1 Guinea, £5 and £20 notes from the outset in books of 400 notes each. A £1 note was added to the range in 1821, also issued in books of 400.

PA 1a 1gn **Arms of Paisley flanked by One Guinea & Paisley** printed dates
Designed by: **Butterworth** *Engraved by:* **Robert Kirkwood**
3 Jul 1783   plate A B E F G H I (all dates)   826,400 (all dates)
3 Oct 1785
24 Nov 1788
19 Oct 1795   **From 1500 F**

PA 1a 1785

PA 1b 1gn **Same as PA1b Embossed revenue stamp** printed dates
1 Jul 1799 onwards   plate E F G H   213,200   **From 1500 F**

PA 2 1gn **Same as PA1b Payable in Dublin** printed date
24 Nov 1788   1,600

PA 3a	1gn	**One Guinea flanked by oval vignette of Bishop Schaw** **Coats of Arms of the Stewards, Hamiltons & Shaws down left side** **Pay Alexander Wilson Oval panel for serials** uniface *Designed by:* **Butterworth** *Engraved by:* **Robert Kirkwood** Embossed revenue stamp 1806 to 1822	269,600	**From 800 F**
PA 3b	1gn	Same as PA 3a Large Congreve 1822 to 1828	36,000	**From 800 F**
		Forgery 1826		**From 100 F**

PA 3b Probable forgery 1826

£5 notes were issued throughout the bank's life. An embossed revenue stamp was added after 1800 and a large Congreve revenue stamp applied on the reverse after 1822.

PA 4	£5	**Coats of Arms of the Stewards, Hamiltons & Shaws down left side** **PAISLEY BANK & £5 FIVE POUNDS between oval panels** 1820	72,600 *(1783 to 1836)*	**RARE**

£20 notes were issued throughout the bank's life but none appear to have survived.

PA 5   **£20**   **1783 to 1835**   22,800 (all dates)
                        Believed similar, not seen

A £1 note was first issued in 1821, initially with an embossed revenue stamp but with a Congreve stamp from 1822. The notes were engraved and printed by Robert Kirkwood and carry his imprint.

PA 6a   **£1**   **Coats of Arms of the Stewards, Hamiltons & Shaws down left side**
                        Oval vignette of Bishop Schaw flanked by ONE / POUND
                        Pay Alexander Wilson Embossed revenue stamp
                        1821 to 1822   plate A   110,000 *(1821 to 1836)*   **From 500 F**

                        Forgery 1821 to 1822   **From 100 F**

PA 6b   **£1**   **Similar to PA 6a** Congreve
                        1822 to 1823   plate A   **From 750 F**

                        Forgery 1822 to 1823   **From 150 F**

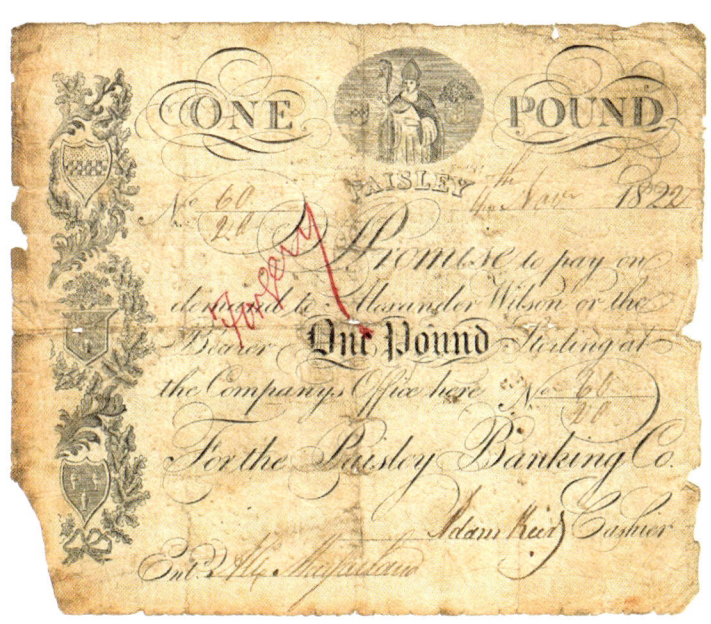

PA 6a 1822 Forgery

A very attractive £1 note engraved on steel plate by **W H Lizars** after 1828 has been seen in proof form. It is not known if this note was ever issued.

PA 7   £1   **Central vignette of abbey building Machinework central panel**
Vignettes of allegorical female left & Bishop Schaw right
Pay John Peden *Engraved by:* **W H Lizars**

Proof undated   **From 500 EF**

PA 7 Proof overprinted SPECIMEN GIVEN TO

PAISLEY UNION BANKING COMPANY – 1788 *to* 1838

The Union Bank Company

Commenced business on 9th September 1788 with capital of £10,000 subscribed by ten partners who were mostly Paisley merchants seeking to establish a competitor to the Paisley Banking Company which had opened for business five years earlier. The bank opened several branches across Scotland and another four in England, in Berwick, Carlisle, Penrith and Wigton, but all apart from Berwick had been closed by 1810. The two Paisley banks competed fiercely. The bank's Edinburgh agents were Forbes, Hunter & Co who also provided the bank with a £5,000 line of credit. In July 1811 the Paisley Union's Glasgow branch in Ingram Street was the scene of a famous robbery when some £50,000 was stolen, although about £14,000 was later recovered. A reward of 500 Guineas was posted, a huge sum in those days, but never paid out. A delightful account can be found in Peter Mackenzie's '*Old Reminiscences of Glasgow and the West of Scotland*' (vol. 1, 1865), itself based in part on a florid account of the life and trial of James Mackoull (Moffat) written in 1822.

The bank's circulation was £59,750 in 1789 and continued to rise strongly, reaching £108,332 by 1836 due to the assiduous distribution of its notes at cattle markets across Scotland. The bank nevertheless went into decline after 1820 and was finally acquired by the Glasgow Union Banking Company in 1838 after further setbacks. All notes were designed and engraved by **Kirkwood & Son**. The bank's name is abbreviated to 'The Union Bank Company' on the notes.

PU 1	£1	**Oval vignette of spinning wheel with Roses & Thistles upper left** **ONE POUND upper right** Congreve		
		1827 to 1828	plate A	**From 1250 F**
		Forgery 1827		**From 150 F**

PU 1 1828

PU 2 **1gn** **Central vignette flanked by ONE GUINEA / PAISLEY**
printed date
1 May 1788

From 1250 F

PU 2 1788

PU 3 **1gn** **Oval vignette of spinning wheel with Roses & Thistles,** flanked by **ONE GUINEA / PAISLEY** in Roman capitals
1804 to 1806   plate C

From 1000 F

PU 3 1806

PU 4 **1gn** **Oval vignette of spinning wheel with Roses & Thistles**
One / Guinea to the left **£1.1 / PAISLEY** to the right
1822   plate D   **From 1000 F**

PU 4 1822

PU 5 **£5** **Similar vignette to PU 4** *Engraved by:* **Kirkwood & Sons**

Proof / Unissued undated (c.1808)   **From 600 VF**

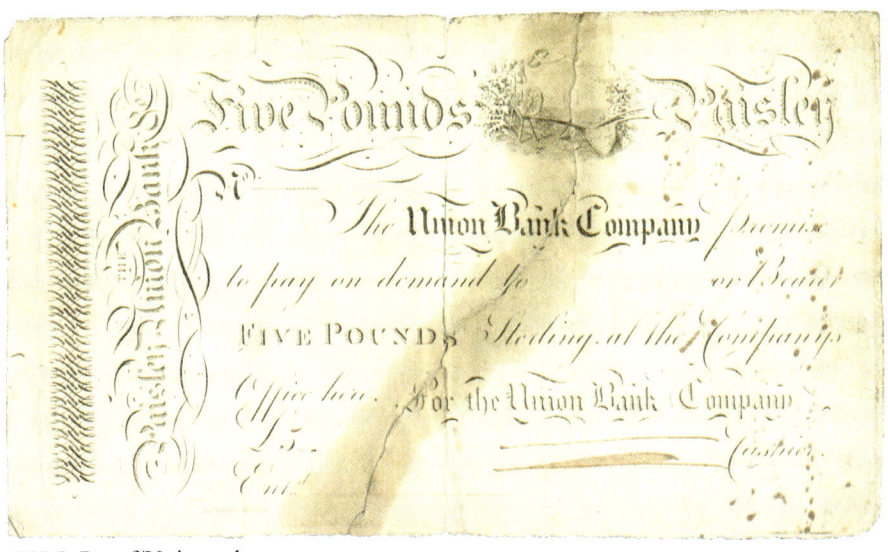

PU 5 Proof/Unissued

PU 6 **£20** *Confirmed issued, not seen*
(Numerous £20 notes feature in the story of the robbery)

PERTH BANKING COMPANY – 1787 *to* 1857

This bank was formed to take over the business of the preceding Perth United Company. It was organised as a co-partnery with initial capital of £34,000 contributed by 99 shareholders and began trading on 7th May 1787. Thirteen of the 99 partners were elected as directors. The bank was as successful as its predecessor and traded profitably throughout its life. By agreement it redeemed the notes of its predecessor paying face value less 7½% to allow for lost or destroyed notes. The redemption process took nearly twenty years. In the custom of the time its co-partnership agreement expired after 21 years though this was renewed in 1808 and again in 1829 and 1850. Branches were opened in several local towns. The bank was approached by the Union Bank of Scotland in 1857 with an attractive all-share offer to acquire the bank and the directors quickly accepted. They realised that the days of the smaller provincial banks, even those which had operated profitably and prudently, were numbered. Authorised Circulation in 1845 was £38,656 though earlier in its life total notes in issue had been somewhat higher, reaching £83,200 in 1808 when the second partnership had commenced operation.

The first note issues appeared in 1787 when just two denominations were issued, this confirmed by surviving directors' minutes. All the early notes featured the town's Seal, a double-headed eagle and shield with the motto 'PRO REGE, LEGE ET GREGE' (for the King, Law and People). The initial printings of the 1 Guinea note totalled 240 books of 500 notes each (from two copper plates: A and B, C and D) while those of the £5 note totalled a mere eight books of 500 notes each. The two 1 Guinea plates were reworked several times due to wear and were replaced in 1795 by a plate lettered E and F, with no change of design (or date). All early notes were engraved by **Kirkwood & Son** on paper provided first by William Cadell of Auchendinny Mill and later by William Simpson of Polton Mill. A revenue stamp was applied to notes from 1791 even if dated earlier.

PB 1a 1gn Black **Arms of Perth No revenue stamp** printed date
Numbered by hand
7 May 1787   plate A B C D   **From 1500 F**

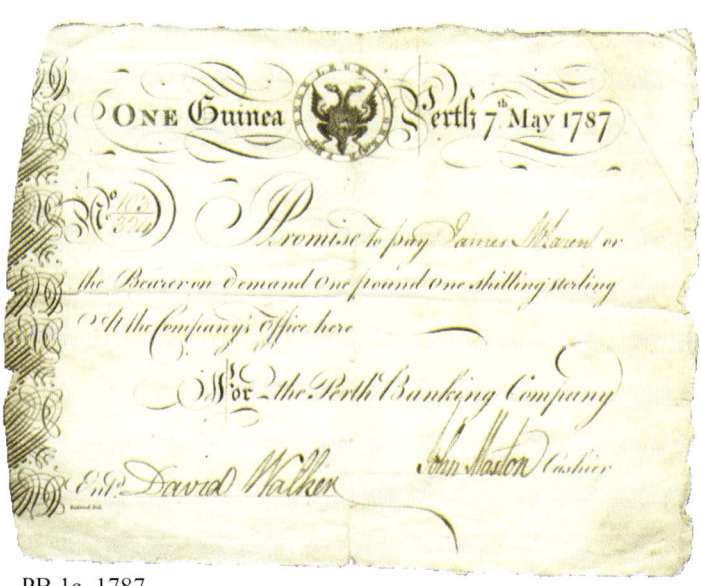

PB 1a 1787

PB 1b   **1gn**   **Similar to PB 1a** Embossed revenue stamp printed date
                7 May 1787   plate E F
                1 Jan 1800   **From 1500 F**

PB 1c   **1gn**   **Similar to PB 1a/b** Embossed revenue stamp
                Dated & numbered by hand
                1812 to 1818   plate H I   **From 1000 F**

                Forgery 1812   **From 150 F**

PB 1c 1818

PB 2   **£5**   *Believed similar, not seen*

In 1798 the bank, in common with several other banks in Scotland, issued small format notes for 5 Shillings. The first printing was of 146 books of 200 notes each. Forgeries soon turned up and the bank's minutes reveal that the forgery had been carried out by a clerk who had previously worked for Kirkwood & Son. A reward of £100 for his arrest was advertised in the Edinburgh and Glasgow newspapers.

PB 3	**5s**	**Black Arms of Perth** printed date 140 x 100mm		
		1 Jan 1798	plate A B C D	**From 750 F**
		Forgery		**From 150 F**

PB 3 1798

In 1802 it was decided to issue three books of £10 notes and one book of £20 notes, the designs to follow that of the £5 note. The £10 was to be printed in red and the £20 in blue. None of these notes have been seen. The first recorded £1 note was for 'Twenty Shillings' and issued in 1806. The initial print run was 100 books of 500 notes each. The notes were designed by G Paton and engraved by **Kirkwood & Son**.

PB 4	**£1**	**Perth arms upper left Embossed revenue stamp**		
		TWENTY SHILLINGS in Roman capitals to the right		
		Dated & numbered by hand Watermarked paper		
		1806 to 1812	plate C F	**From 1000 F**

PB 4 1806

Unissued undated plate H   **From 600 EF**

Forgery 1812   **From 150 F**

PB 4 Unissued

PB 5	**£10**	**Printed in Red**
		Believed similar to £5 note, not seen

PB 6	**£20**	**Printed in Blue**
		Believed similar to £5 note, not seen

In 1820 a bold decision was taken to have the £1 note printed in three colours, black, red and blue. As the bank had been troubled by forgeries prior to this it seems the decision was prompted by the need to combat this persistent problem. The engraving was again done by **Kirkwood & Son**. This design appears to have been printed in three colours for only a short time as a similar note printed wholly in black appears from 1823. The establishing of the third partnership in 1829 confirmed that notes for £1, 1 Guinea, £5, £10 and £20 were issued in that year. It is assumed the designs remained unchanged. Banknote paper is now supplied by Alex Cowan & Sons. Surviving copies of correspondence suggest that by 1830 the bank was getting tired of slow work by Kirkwood & Son but surviving notes confirm they were still printing the bank's £1 notes in 1838.

PB 7	**£1**	**Arms of Perth in blue, left hand panel in red Promissory text in black**
		Twenty Shillings in gothic script Embossed revenue stamp
		Payee inserted by hand Dated & numbered by hand
		1820 plate F **RARE**

PB 7 1820

PB 8a	£1	**Similar to PB 7 Black only** Payee inserted by hand Congreve		
		1823 to 1838	plate E G	**From 1000 F**
		Forgery 1823 to 1835		**From 100 F**

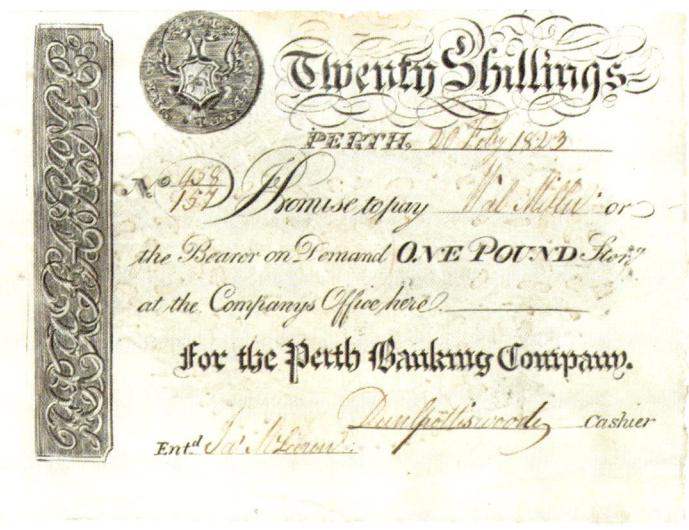

PB 8a Forgery

PB 8b	£1	**Similar to PB 7 Pay Walter Miller** (printed) Congreve		
		1835 to 1838	plate E G	**From 1000 F**
		Forgery 1823 to 1835		**From 100 F**

By 1850 (and possibly earlier) the printing and engraving contract had been taken over by the renowned engraver **W H Lizars** whose designs are amongst his finest work for Scottish banks. Proofs have survived to enable collectors to enjoy these beautiful works of art. In 1856 the bank was incorporated under the Companies Act so additional text was added: PURSUANT TO ACT OF PARLIAMENT / 16-17 VICT. CAP. 65

PB 9a	£1	**Arms of Perth with city views behind** reverse in blue		
		Vignettes of Victoria & Albert standing		
		Printed prefix & serials Signed & dated by hand		
		1853	plate H	**From 1500 F**
		Proof undated uniface plate H		**From 400 EF**

PB 9b   **£1**   **Additional text:** 'PURSUANT TO ACT …' reverse in blue
            1856   I   **From 1500 F**

PB 9b 1856 Punch hole cancelled

Proof undated uniface plate I   **From 400 EF**

Colour Trial Blue plate I   **From 1000 EF**

PB 9b Colour Trial

PB 10a £5 Similar to PB 9b Victoria & Albert on horseback

        Proof year printed as 185 uniface plate C   From 500 EF

PB 10a Proof, hand-written 'Specimen'

PB 10b £5 Additional text: 'PURSUANT TO ACT ... '

        Proof undated uniface plate C   From 500 EF

PB 11a £20 Similar to PB 10b ¾ length portraits of Victoria & Albert

        Proof year printed as 185 uniface plate B   From 500 EF

PB 11a Proof

PB 11b   £20   Additional text: 'PURSUANT TO ACT … '

   Proof undated uniface plate B   From 500 EF

In 1857 the bank's final issues were overprinted with '**UNION BANK OF SCOTLAND**' above the upper border and in one case also below the lower one. The only examples seen are unissued notes in Lloyds' archives.

PB 12   £1   Overprinted: '**UNION BANK OF SCOTLAND**'

   Unissued undated uniface plate I

PB 12 Unissued

PB 13   £5   Overprinted: '**UNION BANK OF SCOTLAND**'

   Unissued undated uniface plate C

PB 14   £20   Overprinted: '**UNION BANK OF SCOTLAND**'

   Unissued undated uniface plate B

PERTH UNITED COMPANY – 1766 *to* 1787
or
PERTH UNITED BANKING COMPANY

The Perth United Company was created as a co-partnery from a merger of six very small local 'banks', all probably with just one or two partners who may well have been local traders issuing small notes for the convenience of their customers. All these small banks were said to have issued low denomination notes with an option clause allowing payment to be delayed for a fixed period (usually six months) at the option of the issuer. Only one of these notes is known to have survived, a 5s note of the Banking Company of McKeith Rintoul & Co (in the National Museum of Scotland). The option clause is to pay not in cash but in Edinburgh notes. The precise denominations of the other notes are unrecorded. The six banks were listed by R S Rait in his 1930 history of the Union Bank of Scotland as follows:

Trading name	Partnership	Founded	Main feature on notes
The Perth Banking Company	John Stewart & Co	1763	Arms of city of Perth
The Tannerie Banking Company	Stewart Buchanan & Co	1764	Oak tree
The Banking Company	Wedderspoon & Co	1764	Crowned thistle
The Banking Company	McKeith Rintoul & Co	1764	King's portrait
The Craigie Banking Company	John Ramsay & Co	1764	Sheaf of grain
The Banking Company	John Bruce	1764	Bruce family crest & motto

PE 1   5s   King's portrait *Issuer:* **McKeith Rintoul & Co**   14 Jul 1764   **RARE**

PE 1 1764 by McKeith Rintoul

The Perth United Company began business on 6th May 1766 with capital of £8,000. Its founding was prompted by the 1765 Bank Act which prohibited the issue of small notes and notes containing the option clause. One of the original partners was George Dempster who was also the founding partner of the Dundee Banking Company in 1763. Agencies were set up in the main cities but the partnership contract was for a fixed period of 21 years, a frequent feature of business undertakings in those days. Consequently voluntary liquidation took place in 1787. Circulation had reached a substantial £83,200 by 1787 but few notes were still unaccounted for by 1793. Very few notes have survived as nearly all were redeemed from 1789 onwards by the successor firm, the Perth Banking Company. According to surviving records of that bank £2,549 worth of £1 and £5 notes were retired and burnt in 1790 and small numbers continue to be dealt with in this way at least until October 1802 when plates of the United Company's notes for £1 and £5 were melted down. There is no record of notes for 1 Guinea having been issued though Douglas does record this denomination.

PE 2   £1   **Vignette of Perth arms** Dated & numbered by hand

PE 3   1gn   Reported by Douglas
              Not seen

PE 4   £5   **Similar to PE 2**

The Banknote Society of Scotland

Since 1994 the Banknote Society of Scotland has been holding well attended meetings in Edinburgh of which there are currently four per annum.

Worldwide membership currently stands at seventy with about twenty members attending each meeting rising closer to thirty for our September AGM and premium free auction usually consisting of 250+ lots.

The Society's highly acclaimed e-magazine Banknote Buzz has been published online every three months since April 2015 and all new members are emailed all back issues.

To receive a sample copy of Banknote Buzz and an application form please email:
bnss2006@ntlworld.com

The authors and the publisher of Paper Money of Scotland are long time members and becoming a member will greatly increase your enjoyment of collecting.

Annual membership currently costs a very reasonable ten pounds, Scottish or English, or the equivalent in a foreign currency.

SHIP BANK – 1750 *to* 1836

Dunlop, Houston & Company – 1750 *to* 1775
Moores, Carrick & Company – 1775 *to* 1789
Carrick, Brown & Company – 1789 *to* 1836

Founded in 1749 and opened its doors in January 1750, the first bank to be established in Glasgow. The founding partners were wealthy 'tobacco lords' who had made their money from building up and dominating the tobacco import trade which contributed so much to Glasgow's rise to become the 'Second City of the British Empire'. The six founding partners were Colin Dunlop of Carmyle, Alexander Houston of Jordanhill, Andrew Buchanan of Drumpellier, Allan Dreghorn of Ruchill, Robert Dunlop and William McDowall of Castle Semple. The name Ship Bank was not formally part of the trading name but the partners chose to use the symbol of a ship in full sail on all their notes, bills of exchange and other documents in a deliberate attempt to establish a clear visual identity for the new firm. Unusually, the partners deposited a joint and several bond with the municipal authorities as cover for payment of their notes, although this was hardly necessary given their prominence and wealth. It was however obviously prudent and a valuable reassurance to those who might accept the notes. The bank was profitable from the start, with a net profit of £2,163 in 1752 rising to £12,900 in 1761. Note circulation in that year was £82,331.

The partnership agreement was drawn up for a fixed term of 25 years and in 1775 a new firm was established to take over its business. The original partners all retired and the new firm was renamed as Moores, Carrick & Co with eight partners in all. The senior partner was George Moore who resided on the Isle of Man. Robert Carrick was the most visible and eminent partner and remained a leading light in the firm for almost fifty years until dying in his home above the bank in 1821. Further changes of partner took place and the firm's name changed to Carrick, Brown & Co in 1789, all the while continuing to trade as the Ship Bank. The early success of the bank and its strong connections to the local business community ensured it survived and prospered – and was able to repel the advances of the Edinburgh banks seeking to head off the Glasgow challenge. In the end, however, despite continuing to grow and trade profitably the partners of the time felt that the new world of joint stock banks was overtaking them so they agreed a merger with the Glasgow Bank Company in 1836 to form the Glasgow & Ship Bank.

Colin Dunlop, Alexander Houston & Company Partnership name

A surprising number of notes from the period 1750 to 1765 have survived. All these notes were signed by Colin Dunlop and Alexander Houston as well as the named official appointed to issue the notes.

SH 1	£1	**One Pound Sterling heading in Gothic script** No vignette Promissory text starts: 'I, Arthur Robertson, Merchant …' 1750	**From 2500 F**

SH 2	£1	**Vignette of ship sailing west** **£12 Scots above Glasgow in gothic script** Promissory text starts: 'I James Simson, Cashier …' 1753 to 1754	**From 2500 F**

SH 2 1754

SH 3   £1   **Vignette of ship sailing east Six months Option clause**
              Denomination inserted by hand
              Promissory text starts: 'I, Alexander Morson Cashier …'
              1759 to 1760

                                                                    From 2500 F

SH 3 1759 Six months Option clause

SH 4	**£1**	**Vignette of ship sailing west** **£12 Scots above Glasgow in gothic script** Promissory text starts: 'I Alexander Morson, Cashier …' 1765

From 2500 F

SH 4 1765

SH 5	**£1**	**Vignette of ship sailing east George Oswald to sign** **ONE POUND STERLING to right** Promissory text starts: 'I Alexander Morson, Cashier …' 1766

From 2500 F

SH 6	**£5**	**Vignette of ship sailing east Glasgow upper right** **Six months Option clause** Promissory text starts: 'I, James Simson, Cashier …' 1756

RARE

SH 7	£5	Vignette of ship sailing east Five Pounds Ster upper centre

Promissory text starts: 'I Alexander Morson, Cashier …'
1765   From 3000 F

SH 7 1765

Moores, Carrick & Company Partnership name

No notes issued by this partnership have been seen though they were undoubtedly issued.

Carrick, Brown & Company Partnership name

SH 8	£1	Ship vignette upper left Blue TWENTY SHILLINGS panel top centre

Blue left hand panel SHIP BANK OF GLASGOW
Printer: **Kirkwood & Son** Congreve
1823 to 1829   plate D   From 1500 F

Forgery 1829   From 250 F

SH 8 1829

SH 9	£1	Bank building with ship vignettes either side

Neptune & Britannia vignette below uniface
Blue panel top centre TWENTY SHILLINGS Blue left hand panel
Engraved on steel plate by: **Joseph Swan**

1834 to 1835   plate A   **From 1500 F**

Proof undated all Black   **From 400 EF**

SH 9 1835

SH 10a **1gn** Ship vignette top centre One Guinea in blue to left
Blue left hand panel SHIP BANK OF GLASGOW
Printer: **Kirkwood & Son** printed date
1 Jan 1790   **RARE**

SH 10a 1790

SH 10b **1gn** **Similar to SH 10a** Dated by hand Congreve
1823   plate B   **From 1500 F**

Forgery 1813 uniface   **From 250 F**

Notes of £5 or above have not been seen but may have been issued.

THISTLE BANK – 1761 *to* 1836

Maxwell, Ritchie & Company – 1761 *to* 1798
The Thistle Bank – 1798 *to* 1836

The Thistle Bank of Sir Walter Maxwell of Pollok, James Ritchie of Busbie, John Glassford of Dougalston (also a partner of the Glasgow Arms Bank), William Mure, John McCall and John Campbell, all wealthy Glasgow tobacco merchants and landowners, was founded in 1761. Sir Walter Maxwell was quickly succeeded by Sir John and then Sir James Maxwell whose name appears on the earliest surviving notes. Nominal paid-in capital was only £7,000 but given the partners' wealth and evident standing, this did not prove inadequate. The thistle symbol was adopted and quickly established the 'Aristocratic Bank', as it was sometimes known, in the public's eye. It expanded rapidly, financing itself with an aggressive campaign of note issuance throughout Scotland. Within two years notes in circulation totalled £64,000. After the late 1790s the bank appeared to decline and it finally ran out of steam in 1836 after trading for over 70 years, being acquired by the Glasgow Union Banking Company. By then net assets totalled a modest £5,000. From the few surviving notes the bank appears to have traded as the Thistle Bank Company from 1798 and possibly earlier. Countermarked Spanish silver dollar coins in the name of the Thistle Bank were issued around this time. Extracts from some early ledgers have been located and record the burning of retired notes for a number of denominations including several not so far seen.

Denomination	Dates
5s	1797 *to* 1799
10s	1762 *to* 1763
£1	1761 *to* 1816
1gn	1805 *to* 1815
£5	1762 *to* 1816
£20	1770 *to* 1817
£50	1797
£100	1797

Thistle Vignette

Maxwell Ritchie & Company Partnership name

TH 1   10s   *Not seen*

TH 2   **£1**   **Thistle vignette top centre flanked by One Pound & Sterling**
Promissory text starts: 'I, David Fleming, Cashier…'
1765   **RARE**

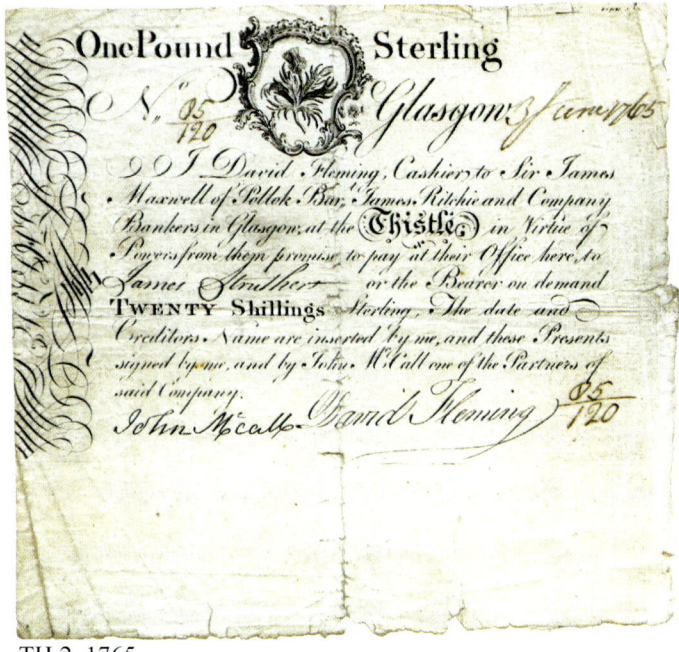

TH 2 1765

TH 3   **£1**   **Blue Thistle vignette top centre Blue panel left**
Dated & numbered by hand
1770   **RARE**

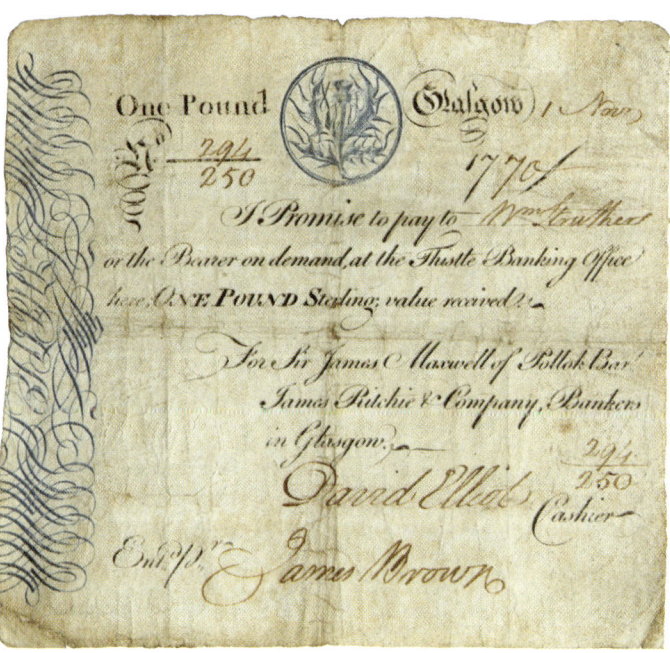

TH 3 1770

TH 4	£5	*Not seen*

TH 5	£20	*Not seen*

TH 6	£50	*Not seen*

TH 7	£100	*Not seen*

The Thistle Bank Company Partnership name

The first notes recorded in the Thistle Bank's name are 5 Shilling notes issued in 1798 after the law was changed to allow 'small notes' to be issued in a time of shortage of coin.

TH 8a 5s **Left hand panel of thistles Five Shillings in Gothic upper right**
Engraved by: **James Lumsden & Son** printed date 125 x 100mm
10 Jan 1798   plate B D   **From 1500 F**

Forgery   **From 350 F**

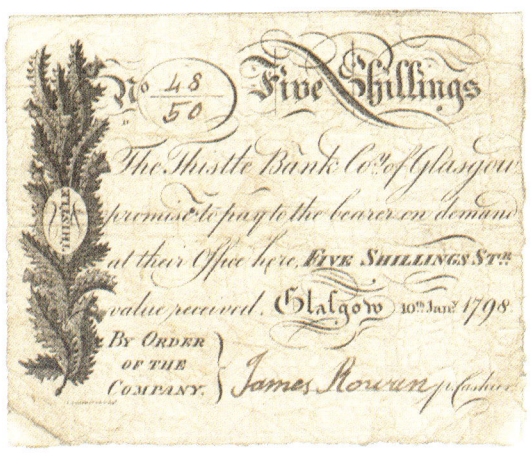

TH 8a 1798

TH 8b 5s **Similar to TH 8a Blue oval thistle stamp upper centre**
printed date
10 Jan 1798   plate B D F   **From 1500 F**

TH 8c 5s **Similar to TH 8a Blue oval thistle stamp upper centre**
Engraved by: **Kirkwood & Son** printed date
2 Dec 1799   plate F   **From 1500 F**

Forgery   **From 350 F**

TH 9	£1	**Thistle vignette flanked by One Pound & £1 Glasgow** *Designed by:* **Menzies** *Engraved by:* **Kirkwood & Son** 1813	**RARE**
		Forgery 1813	From 350 F

TH 10	1gn	**Thistle vignette flanked by One & Guinea** *Designed by:* **G Paton** *Engraved by:* **Kirkwood & Son** 1813	**RARE**
		Forgery 1813	From 350 F

TH 11	1gn	**One Guinea curved over vignette of thistles** **Thistle panel down left hand side Pay John Kemp** *Designed & Engraved by:* **Kirkwood & Son** 1820 plate C	**RARE**

TH 11 1820 Punch hole cancelled

TH 12	£5	**Thistles top centre Ornate column of thistles on left**	
		Proof undated	From 500 EF

TH 13	£20	**Thistles top centre, oval value panels to left & right** **Ornate column of thistles on left**	
		Proof undated	From 500 EF

Clydesdale Bank

Clydesdale Banking Company 1838 *to* **1882**
Clydesdale Bank Limited 1882 *to* **1949**
Clydesdale & North of Scotland Bank Limited 1950 *to* **1963**
Clydesdale Bank Limited 1963 *to* **1981**
Clydesdale Bank PLC 1981 *to* **date**

The Clydesdale Banking Company was established in 1838 by James Lumsden, an influential Glasgow businessman who had joined his father's printing and engraving firm in 1799 which he expanded and developed after his father's death in 1821. He also founded the Glasgow Savings Bank in 1836. The Clydesdale was one of eight joint stock banks started in Glasgow in the 1830s and 1840s but is the only one to survive through to the present day. Prior to the joint stock bank boom there had been just three private banks in Glasgow, the Ship Bank, the Thistle Bank and the Glasgow Banking Company. None was well capitalised and all three ended up as part of the Union Bank of Scotland, in essence driven out of business by the rise of the new, better capitalised, joint stock banks.

Unfortunately, two of the Clydesdale's joint stock bank rivals in Glasgow failed, the Western Bank of Scotland in 1857 and the City of Glasgow Bank in 1878. These debacles proved a major setback to Glasgow's efforts to counter the dominance of the Edinburgh-based banks but the Clydesdale was well enough managed to be able to overcome these difficulties and to survive and prosper into the current era. It made several acquisitions over the years including the Greenock Union Bank, the Edinburgh & Glasgow Bank and the Eastern Bank of Scotland. By 1873 the bank had 71 branches and in the same year almost agreed to merge with the Bank of Scotland, the deal failing at a late stage due to personality clashes between the directors of the two banks. Its Authorised Circulation under the 1845 Act was £104,028, a figure which had risen to £498,773 by 1950 thanks to its acquisitions. In 2015 average circulation was £2bn, the highest of the three Scottish issuers.

The branch network was extended into England in 1874 when three branches were opened in Cumberland. This caused protests from the English banks and in the end it was agreed the Clydesdale would not open any more branches south of the border, with the exception of an office in London. The bank adopted limited liability in 1882 and in 1919 was acquired by the London-based Midland Bank, who in 1923 also acquired the North of Scotland Bank. The two banks were finally merged in 1950 under the title Clydesdale and North of Scotland Bank but in 1963 the combined group reverted to its earlier name. In 1987 Midland sold the Clydesdale to National Australia Bank (NAB) under whose ownership the bank continued to operate with a degree of independence. NAB demerged and floated the Clydesdale (together with what is now its subsidiary, the Yorkshire Bank) in February 2016 as part of the London-listed CYBG Group.

The note issue records of the Clydesdale Bank have survived in part but there are still some uncertainties about the pre-1882 issues despite the survival of some useful material in the archives (including a 'Dead Utterings' ledger containing details of counterfeit and mutilated notes paid in). The first notes issued by the bank in 1838 were engraved by W & A K Johnston but by 1858 all the notes carried the imprint of Hugh Wilson, an engraver who had started his career working for James Lumsden and bought his engraving and copperplate printing business in 1821. Hugh Wilson's 1858 design of the £1 note (engraved on steel plate) lasted until 1949 despite various modifications including a size reduction. There was a brief interruption in the 1870s when Thomas De La Rue was contracted to supply £1 notes, that printer's first such contract in Scotland.

In 1882 responsibility for all the note issues passed to E (Ebenezer) Bacon & Son, London, although they soon lost the contract for £1 notes to W & A K Johnston. The bank's notes were printed in the Stationery Department of its head office in St. Vincent Place, Glasgow from 1874 until 1949, a practice which had by then long died out at other Scottish banks. Notes from the period 1882 to 1949 were printed on poor quality paper so that the slightest wear caused the paper to deteriorate. Attempts to clean or press these notes tend only to highlight weaknesses in the paper especially where there is wear on the folds. By contrast the note issues of the newly merged Clydesdale & North of Scotland Bank from 1950 onwards were better engraved and printed to a much higher standard and on higher quality paper. They were produced by Thomas De La Rue, who had already been printing the North of Scotland's notes and have been responsible for all the Clydesdale's notes ever since. In 2015 the Clydesdale became the first bank in Scotland to issue polymer notes.

The Clydesdale began by using the traditional fractional system of book numbers over sequential numbers but this did not last and the series from 1882 to 1949 is notable for its use of serial numbers with several initial zeroes on its higher value notes even where the numbers printed per prefix were very low. After 1950 the North of Scotland Bank's practice was adopted of printing £1,000,000 worth of notes for each prefix, at least until the mid-1990s, i.e. there were 200,000 £5 notes per prefix, 100,000 £10 notes, 50,000 £20 notes and 10,000 £100 notes. There are occasional minor gaps in the issue records from 1971 onwards and listings rely on a combination of firm sightings, a review of De La Rue archival specimens and some educated guesswork.

CL 1 First day of issue 7th May 1838

FIRST ISSUE – 1838 *to* c.1847

Heading: CLYDESDALE BANKING COMPANY

All notes engraved on steel plate and printed by **W & A K Johnston, Edinburgh**. Each design features Glasgow's Coat of Arms upper centre flanked by value panels. To the left is an elaborate vertical panel with a CBCo monogram of varying design on the different denominations. The bank's name is displayed prominently across the centre of the note in bold Gothic script. On the £1 note the garter around the Coat of Arms contains the words 'Joint Stock Company'. £1 notes have a light blue underlay with an outline CBCo monogram. Serial numbers and dates are inserted by hand. The earliest £1 notes are dated 7th May 1838, the day the bank opened for business. The bank's archives contain ink sketches of proposed designs for the £1 note apparently drawn by James Lumsden himself in 1838. No £10 note was issued, contrary to Douglas. All notes uniface.

CL 1	£1	**Black Light Blue underlay** Congreve **Handsigned** p Manager & p Accountant 7 May 1838 14/355 - 32/92 plate A B	**From 3000 F**
		Proof undated without Blue underlay plate B	**From 500 EF**
		Unissued undated plate A	**From 800 VF**
CL 2	£5	**Similar to CL 1 Handsigned** Accountant & Manager	
		Proof undated with Blue underlay undated without Blue underlay	**From 800 EF** **From 500 EF**

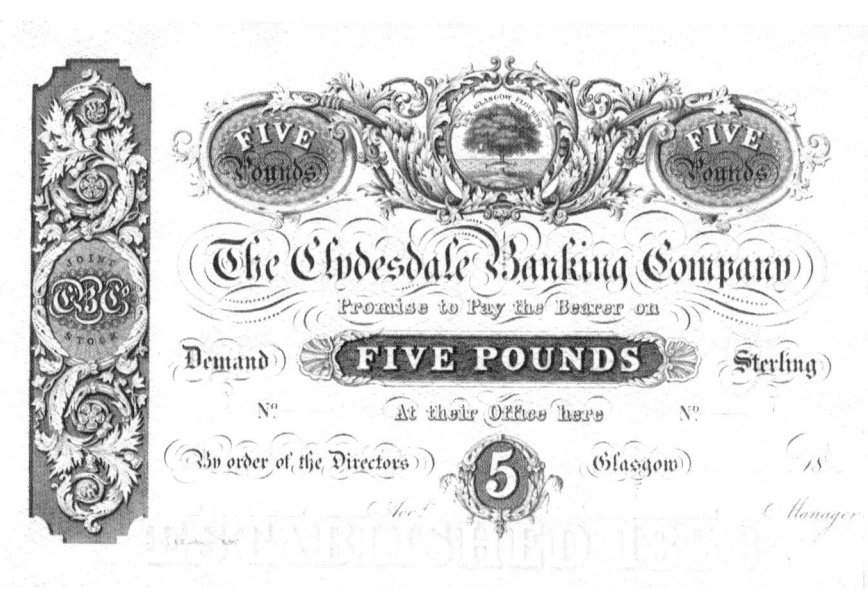

CL 2 Proof with Blue underlay

CL 3   £20   **Similar to CL 1 no imprint**

Proof undated with Blue underlay	**From 800 EF**
undated without Blue underlay	**From 500 EF**

CL 3 Proof with Blue underlay

CL 4   £100   **Similar to CL 3 but with printed borders**

Proof undated without Blue underlay	**From 1000 EF**

CL 4 Proof without Blue underlay

SECOND ISSUE – c.1847 *to* 1882

Hugh Wilson designs

By the late 1840s a revised £1 note had been issued, engraved by **Hugh Wilson**. It is not clear if work on other denominations had also been taken over by him at this stage. His first £1 note is very similar to the preceding Johnston design although the light blue underlay has been dispensed with, the bank's title is now in Roman capitals and the text in the garter round the vignette is now the city's motto 'LET GLASGOW FLOURISH'. An undated proof of this design by W & A K Johnston suggests maybe the two competed to produce the revised note but Wilson won. In any event it is not clear whose original design this was. All notes uniface.

CL 5	**£1**	**Black Handsigned** p Accountant & p Manager Congreve			
		Dated & numbered by hand uniface			
		1 Mar 1847 18/96		plate F	**RARE**

CL 5 1847

Proof undated by W & A K Johnston plate C **From 500 EF**

By 1858 **Hugh Wilson** had clearly become the sole designer and engraver of the Clydesdale's notes. His revised £1 note design first seen in 1858 was to last, with many modifications, until 1949, a remarkable testament to his design skills and the bank's conservatism. The higher values were modified only slightly from Johnston's originals and they too continued little changed until 1949 despite undergoing several further amendments.

The £1 note now has three prominent vignettes, Glasgow's Coat of Arms again taking prime position supported by three allegorical females representing Commerce, Industry and the Arts. Two additional vignettes appear to the lower left and right, also featuring allegorical females. The upper and lower borders now include the text 'ISSUED PURSUANT TO ACT OF PARLIAMENT / 16 & 17 VICTORIA CAP 63', this 1853 Act regulating the payment of stamp duties by the banks on their note issues. The first version of this note has a striking red overlay covering the whole of the note with the bank's name outlined in white and two small oval value panels upper left and right in a more vivid shade of red. A series of colour trials by Wilson used a modified design with the bank's name in Roman capitals rather than the Gothic script otherwise used.

In 1871 when De La Rue was negotiating to supply new £1 notes, the bank sent them a full set of specimens dated between 1865 and 1868. These survive in the British Library.

When the bank's new head office was opened in 1874 a Printing Department was established to print both banknotes and other stationery. This practice continued until 1949.

CL 6a　　£1　　**Bank name in Gothic script　Black with Red overlay**
　　　　　　　　Handsigned　p Accountant & p Manager　Dated by hand　uniface
　　　　　　　　16 Apr 1858　　D/H
　　　　　　　　14 Jun 1858　　E/G　-　G/R　　　　　　　　　　　　　　　**RARE**

CL 6a 1858

CL 6b　　£1　　**Similar to CL 6a**　printed date
　　　　　　　　13 Feb 1863　　E/B
　　　　　　　　20 Apr 1863　　E/M　-　F/C　　　　　　　　　　　　　　　**RARE**

CL 7   £1   **Similar to CL 6a Bank's name & ONE POUND outlined in Red**
              No red overlay
              16 Nov 1864   T 810   **RARE**

CL 7 1864

Essay 16 Mar 1864 no outline ONE POUND   **From 750 EF**

CL 7 Essay 1864

Specimen 16 May 1866   **From 1000 EF**

Colour Trials Red - Light Green - Blue
undated bank name in Roman capitals

RARE

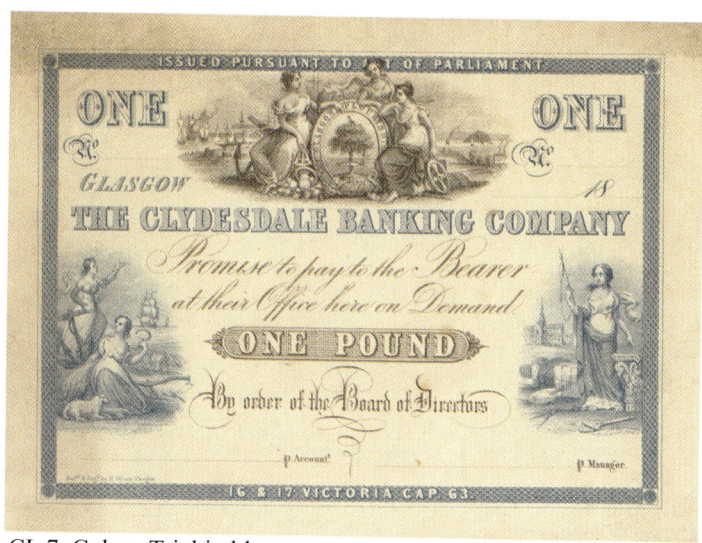

CL 7 Colour Trial in blue

CL 8   **£1**   **Similar to CL 7 but Act now 19 & 20 Victoria Cap 47**
Duncan Dewar Printed signature Accountant **Handsigned** p Manager
Printed date lower centre
30 Jan 1878   № 0084640

RARE

CL 8 1878

Proof Black year printed as 186

From 500 EF

The basic plates of the higher value notes were essentially unchanged and the bank probably handed over the Johnstons' plates to Wilson, probably in 1865. The blue underlay has however been replaced by red value panels and the bank's name is now superimposed in red. The reference to the Act of Parliament, 16 & 17 Victoria Cap 63, is printed vertically next to the left hand panel and appears only on the £5 note. A surviving note register records a total of 156,000 £5 notes being issued on 20 dates between 19 Feb 1868 and 12 Feb 1879. These used the prefix letters B/V to H/Z with 1,000 notes per prefix. No issued £5 notes are known to have survived.

CL 9	**£5**	**Black Value panels in Red Bank's name outlined in Red**

        Specimen 4 Sep 1865 no prefix/serials   **From 600 EF**

CL 9 Specimen

A surviving note register records a total of 50,000 £20 notes being issued on 15 dates between 28 Feb 1866 and 1 Sep 1876. These used the prefix letters S to Z, then A/A to B/R with 1,000 notes per prefix. No issued £20 notes are known to have survived.

CL 10	**£20**	**Similar to CL 9 but no reference to Act of Parliament** *Printer:* **W & A K Johnston**

        Specimen 4 Sep 1865 no prefix/serials   **From 750 EF**

CL 10 Specimen

The £100 note was printed in blue and had a large central oval value panel in red. A single issued survivor with the H Wilson imprint is in the bank's archives while a similar specimen note was prepared by W & A K Johnston. A surviving note register records a total of 30,000 £100 notes being issued on five dates between 17 Apr 1867 and 6 Dec 1871. These used the prefix letters T to W, then A to Z with 1,000 notes per prefix.

CL 11   **£100 Blue Red oval central panel no reference to Act of Parliament**
           Printer: **H Wilson** uniface
              7 Jun 1871   S 166   **RARE**

CL 11 1871 Imprint of H. Wilson

Specimen 16 Sep 1868 with/without imprint of W & AK Johnston **From 2500 EF**

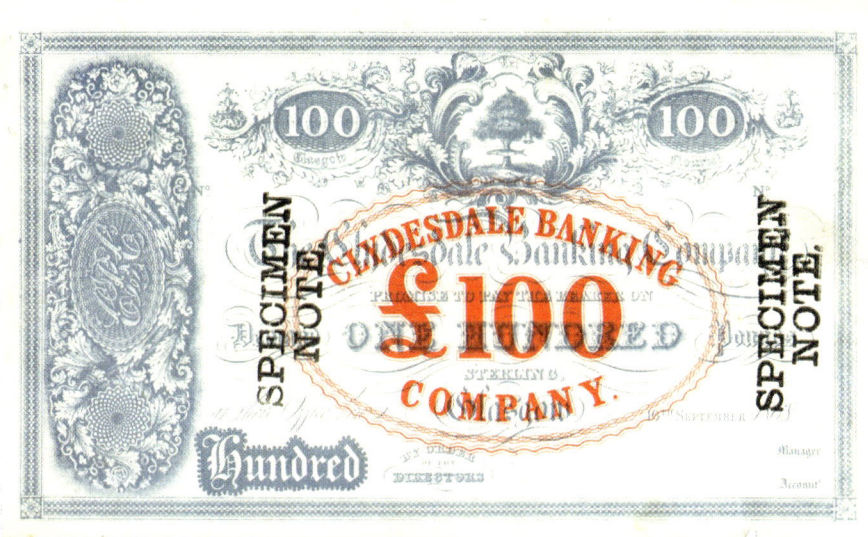

CL 11 Specimen 1868 with W & AK Johnston imprint

DE LA RUE ISSUE – 1871 *to* 1878

£1 Purple & Green

In a radical departure from the established designs the Clydesdale decided in 1871 to appoint Thomas De La Rue & Co to engrave and print a series of £1 notes. The chosen design was very different in both style and colours and according to the bank's archives De La Rue were given a seven year contract in January 1871 to print 1,500,000 notes at a cost of 46 shillings (£2 6s) per 1,000 notes (though most of the order was charged at 49s or £2 9s per 1,000). The cost, according to a surviving letter from De La Rue to the bank, included printing the notes '*on suitable watermark paper in two colours from surface plates and to be overprinted with an invisible ink to prevent the transfer of the design*'. The letter goes on to ask if the head of Adam Smith was to be adopted – a decision the bank finally took 100 years later in 1981 when they introduced their £50 note. A series of trials, essays, stage proofs and specimens of this design have survived in the British Library.

The note's design is unconventional with two small classical heads to the lower left and right but the overall effect is enhanced by very intricate border designs and other ornamentation. The note was printed from two basic plates with the printed signature of the Accountant, the serial numbers and the date all added separately. No other denominations were involved and after 1878 the contract reverted to the Hugh Wilson designs in use prior to 1871. These notes were printed by De La Rue and not in the bank itself. To date just seven issued notes are known to have survived.

CL 12	**£1**	**Purple & Green** uniface			
		D Ferguson Printed signature Accountant **Handsigned** p Manager			
		28 Feb 1872	№ 0052510	-	0424111
		4 Mar 1874	№ 0559118	-	0887131
		9 Feb 1876	№ 1226444		**From 3000 F**

CL 12 1874

Essay 1 Jan 1871	**From 1500 EF**
Proof undated	**From 1500 EF**
Specimen undated 1 Jan 1872	**From 2000 EF**

THIRD ISSUE – 1882 *to* 1921

Heading: THE CLYDESDALE BANK LIMITED

The bank adopted limited liability in 1882 and its name was amended accordingly. All its notes continued to be printed in the head office Printing Dept. Despite this the engravers' name was displayed on the notes. The contract was initially awarded to **E Bacon & Son Bank Note Machinagraphists London NW** but the £1 note engraving was taken over by **W & A K Johnston** in 1891. Designs were unchanged apart from the bank's name change and the dropping of the reference to the Act of Parliament. A full record of the bank's note issues from 1882 to 1972 has survived but the original note registers can no longer be located. The information in this section is therefore based on *20th Century Scottish Banknotes Vol III* by Trevor Jones (with additions and corrections). Prefixes where used, serial numbers and numbers printed per date are listed. All notes uniface.

Bradbury Wilkinson submitted an interesting and unusual essay dated 28th May 1904. This retained certain elements of the Wilson/Johnston design but with two charming female portraits as the secondary vignettes. Sadly only a black and white photograph of it has survived.

CL 13   **£1**   **Black bank's name & value panels in Red** uniface
Duncan Dewar Printed signature Accountant **Handsigned** p General Manager
Serial numbers with no prefix
Imprint: **E Bacon & Son Bank Note Machinagraphists London NW**

4 Jul 1882	№ 0800001	-	1200000	400,000
1 Mar 1884	№ 1200001	-	1600000	400,000
5 Aug 1885	№ 1600001	-	2000000	400,000
7 May 1888	№ 2000001	-	2400000	400,000
4 Dec 1889	№ 2400001	-	2800000	400,000

From 1500 F

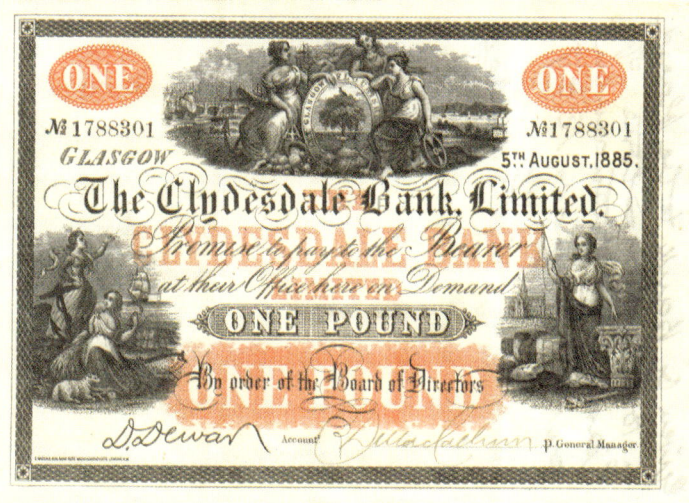

CL 13 1885, placed under the foundation stone of the Glasgow Athenaeum in 1887

Colour Trials undated Black/Blue panels - Blue/Red panels   **From 750 EF**

Specimen undated 4 Jul 1882   **From 750 EF**

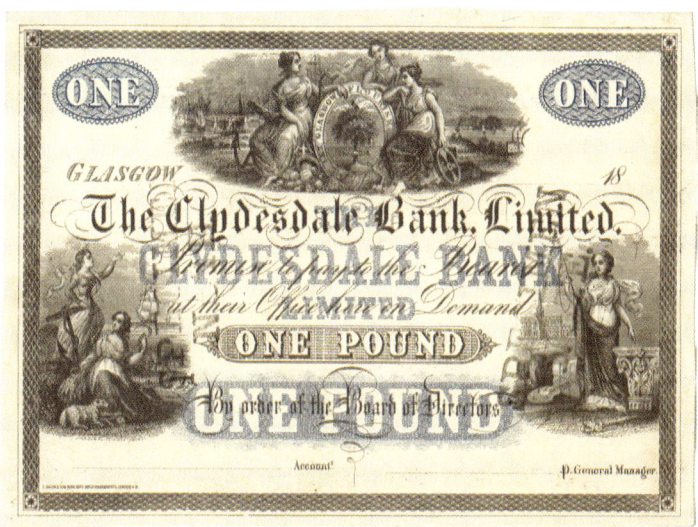

CL 13 Colour Trial in black with blue panels

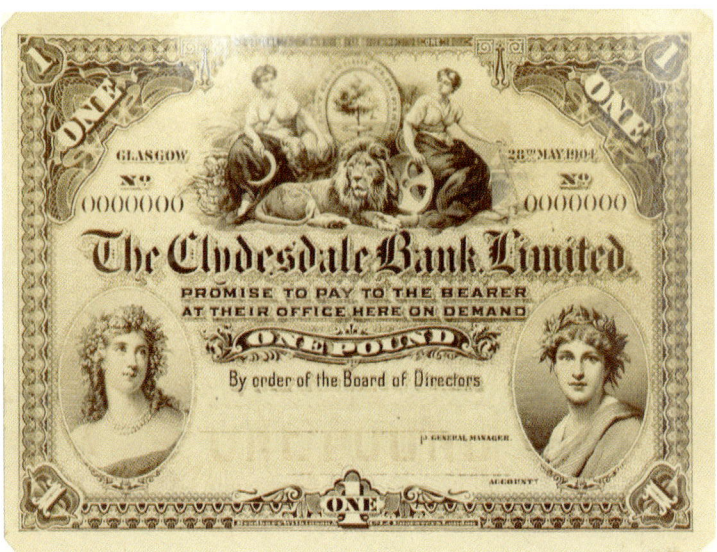

Photographic copy of Bradbury Wilkinson essay 1904

						F	VF	EF
CL 14a	£1	Similar to CL 13 *Imprint:* **W & A K Johnston**						
		Duncan Dewar Printed signature Accountant						
		Handsigned p Gen Manager						
		29 Jul 1891	№ 2800001	-	3200000	400,000		
		25 Jan 1893	№ 3200001	-	3600000	400,000		
		17 Oct 1894	№ 3600001	-	4000000	400,000		
		26 Feb 1896	№ 4000001	-	4400000	400,000		
		13 Oct 1897	№ 4400001	-	4800000	400,000		
		15 Feb 1899	№ 4800001	-	5200000	400,000		
		7 Mar 1900	№ 5200001	-	5600000	400,000	800	1500	-
		5 Jun 1901	№ 5600001	-	6000000	400,000		
		28 May 1902	№ 6000001	-	6400000	400,000		
		4 Nov 1903	№ 6400001	-	6600000	200,000		
		1 Jun 1904	№ 6600001	-	6800000	200,000		
		8 Feb 1905	№ 6800001	-	7200000	400,000		
		11 Apr 1906	№ 7200001	-	7600000	400,000		
		19 Jun 1907	№ 7600001	-	8000000	400,000		
		21 Oct 1908	№ 8000001	-	8400000	400,000		
		15 Sep 1909	№ 8400001	-	8800000	400,000		
		29 Jun 1910	№ 8800001	-	9200000	400,000		
		8 Nov 1911	№ 9200001	-	9600000	400,000		
		30 Oct 1912	№ 9600001	-	10000000	400,000	350	750	-
		Colour Trials undated Black/Brown panels - Blue/Red panels				From 750 EF		
		Specimen undated 29 Jul 1891 26 Feb 1896 no prefix/serials				From 750 EF		

CL 14b	£1	Similar to CL 14a Prefix A					F	VF	EF
		8 Oct 1913	A 0000001	-	0400000	400,000			
		5 Aug 1914	A 0400001	-	0800000	400,000			
		4 Nov 1914	A 0800001	-	1200000	400,000			
		6 Oct 1915	A 1200001	-	1600000	400,000			
		19 Apr 1916	A 1600001	-	2400000	800,000			
		10 Oct 1917	A 2400001	-	3200000	800,000			
		9 Oct 1918	A 3200001	-	4000000	800,000			
		7 Jan 1920	A 4000001	-	4800000	800,000	300	650	-

CL 14b 1914

Specimen 4 Nov 1914 A   **From 500 EF**

A final issue of this £1 note took place in 1921 with the hand signature now on behalf of the Joint General Managers. This reflected the appointments of Frederick Tod and David Young to this position in 1920. Tod retired in 1922 leaving Young as sole General Manager, a position he held until 1931.

						F	VF	EF
CL 14c	**£1**	**Similar to CL 14b Handsigned** p Joint General Managers						
		9 Feb 1921	A 4800001 - 5200000		400,000	**350**	**750**	-

CL 14c 1921

The £5 design is essentially unchanged from the Hugh Wilson notes of 1865 onwards. This series is noted for the several initial zeroes in the seven digit serial number despite the number per prefix not exceeding 1,000. All letters except I were used in the prefix sequences.

CL 15	**£5**	**Black, bank's name and value panels in red** uniface				
		Duncan Dewar Printed signature Accountant **Handsigned** p General Manager				
		Imprint: **E Bacon & Son Bank Note Machinagraphists London NW**				
		4 Jul 1882	K/Q	-	L/K	20,000
		11 Jul 1883	L/L	-	L/S	8,000
		16 Jan 1884	L/T	-	M/E	12,000
		2 Jun 1884	M/F	-	M/N	8,000
		11 Feb 1885	M/O	-	M/X	10,000
		29 Jun 1885	M/Y	-	N/F	8,000
		20 Jan 1886	N/G	-	N/M	6,000
		26 May 1886	N/N	-	N/U	8,000
		19 Jan 1887	N/V	-	O/C	8,000
		8 Jun 1887	O/D	-	O/J	6,000
		7 May 1888	O/K	-	O/X	14,000
		28 Nov 1888	O/Y	-	P/F	8,000
		12 Jun 1889	P/G	-	P/O	8,000
		4 Dec 1889	P/P	-	P/W	8,000
		28 May 1890	P/X	-	Q/E	8,000	**RARE**

CL 15	£5	*Cont*					
		31 Dec 1890	Q/F	-	Q/N	8,000	
		10 Jun 1891	Q/O	-	Q/V	8,000	
		16 Dec 1891	Q/W	-	Q/Z	4,000	
		15 Jun 1892	R/A	-	R/F	6,000	
		23 Nov 1892	R/G	-	R/O	8,000	
		24 May 1893	R/P	-	R/W	8,000	
		17 Jan 1894	R/X	-	S/E	8,000	
		27 Jun 1894	S/F	-	S/N	8,000	
		16 Jan 1895	S/O	-	S/V	8,000	
		26 Jun 1895	S/W	-	T/D	8,000	
		22 Jan 1896	T/E	-	T/M	8,000	
		9 Jun 1897	T/N	-	T/U	8,000	
		16 Feb 1898	T/V	-	U/C	8,000	
		22 Jun 1898	U/D	-	U/L	8,000	
		15 Feb 1899	U/M	-	U/T		
			U/X			9,000	
		5 Jul 1899	U/U	-	U/W		
			U/Y	-	V/B	7,000	
		20 Sep 1899	V/C	-	V/L	9,000	
		14 Jun 1900	V/M	-	V/S	7,000	**From 1200 F**
		13 Feb 1901	V/T	-	W/A	8,000	
		19 Jun 1901	W/B	-	W/J	8,000	
		12 Feb 1902	W/K	-	W/R	8,000	
		2 Apr 1902	W/S	-	W/Z	8,000	
		18 Feb 1903	X/A	-	X/Q	16,000	
		24 Feb 1904	X/R	-	Y/G	16,000	
		8 Feb 1905	Y/H	-	Y/X	16,000	
		11 Jul 1906	Y/Y	-	Z/O	16,000	
		29 Jan 1908	Z/P	-	A^2/E	16,000	
		15 Sep 1909	A^2/F	-	A^2/V	16,000	
		29 Jun 1910	A^2/W	-	B^2/M	16,000	
		29 Mar 1911	B^2/N	-	C^2/C	16,000	
		27 Mar 1912	C^2/D	-	C^2/T	16,000	
		5 Mar 1913	C^2/U	-	D^2/K	16,000	
		25 Mar 1914	D^2/L	-	E^2/A	16,000	
		5 Aug 1914	E^2/B	-	E^2/V	20,000	
		10 May 1916	E^2/W	-	F^2/M	16,000	
		15 Nov 1916	F^2/N	-	G^2/C	16,000	
		10 Oct 1917	G^2/D	-	H^2/K	32,000	
		8 Apr 1918	H^2/L	-	J^2/R	32,000	
		9 Dec 1918	J^2/S	-	K^2/H	16,000	
		9 Apr 1919	K^2/J	-	L^2/P	32,000	
		16 Jun 1919	L^2/Q	-	M^2/F	16,000	
		7 Jan 1920	M^2/G	-	M^2/W	16,000	
		12 May 1920	M^2/X	-	O^2/D	32,000	
		9 Jun 1920	O^2/E	-	P^2/L	32,000	
		9 Feb 1921	P^2/M	-	Q^2/B	16,000	**From 900 F**

CL 15 1917

Specimen 4 Jul 1882 L/H L/K
5 Aug 1914 E²/B E²/C E²/D E²/E   **From 1200 EF**

CL 15 Specimen 1882

The £20 design is essentially unchanged from the Hugh Wilson notes of 1865 onwards. This series also uses several initial zeroes in the seven digit serial number despite the number per prefix not exceeding 500. All letters except I were used in the prefix sequences.

CL 16   **£20**   **Black bank's name & value panels in Red** uniface
Duncan Dewar Printed signature Accountant **Handsigned** p General Manager
Imprint: **E Bacon & Son Bank Note Machinagraphists London NW**

Date	From		To	Quantity	Notes
4 Jul 1882	D/Q	-	D/Z	5,000	
11 Jul 1883	E/A	-	E/D	2,000	
16 Jan 1884	E/E	-	E/K	3,000	
2 Jun 1884	E/L	-	E/O	2,000	
11 Feb 1885	E/P	-	E/S	2,000	
29 Jun 1885	E/T	-	E/W	2,000	
20 Jan 1886	E/X	-	E/Z	1,500	
26 May 1886	F/A	-	F/D	2,000	
19 Jan 1887	F/E	-	F/G	1,500	
8 Jun 1887	F/H	-	F/J	1,000	
7 May 1888	F/K	-	F/O	2,500	
28 Nov 1888	F/P	-	F/S	2,000	
12 Jun 1889	F/T	-	F/W	2,000	
4 Dec 1889	F/X	-	G/A	2,000	
28 May 1890	G/B	-	G/E	2,000	
31 Dec 1890	G/F	-	G/J	2,000	
10 Jun 1891	G/K	-	G/N	2,000	
16 Dec 1891	G/O	-	G/R	2,000	
15 Jun 1892	G/S	-	G/T	1,000	
23 Nov 1892	G/U	-	G/X	2,000	
24 May 1893	G/Y	-	H/B	2,000	
17 Jan 1894	H/C	-	H/F	2,000	
27 Jun 1894	H/G	-	H/K	2,000	
16 Jan 1895	H/L	-	H/O	2,000	
26 Jun 1895	H/P	-	H/S	2,000	
22 Jan 1896	H/T	-	H/W	2,000	
9 Jun 1897	H/X	-	J/A	2,000	
16 Feb 1898	J/B	-	J/E	2,000	
22 Jun 1898	J/F	-	J/J	2,000	
5 Jul 1899	J/K	-	J/N	2,000	
20 Sep 1899	J/O	-	J/R	2,000	
14 Jun 1900	J/S	-	J/V	2,000	**RARE**
13 Feb 1901	J/W	-	J/Z	2,000	
19 Jun 1901	K/A	-	K/D	2,000	
2 Apr 1902	K/E	-	K/H	2,000	
18 Feb 1903	K/J	-	K/Q	4,000	
24 Feb 1904	K/R	-	K/Y	4,000	
8 Feb 1905	K/Z	-	L/G	4,000	
11 Jul 1906	L/H	-	L/P	4,000	
29 Jan 1908	L/Q	-	L/X	4,000	
15 Sep 1909	L/Y	-	M/B	2,000	
29 Jun 1910	M/C	-	M/K	4,000	
29 Mar 1911	M/L	-	M/O	2,000	
27 Mar 1912	M/P	-	M/S	2,000	
5 Mar 1913	M/T	-	N/A	4,000	
25 Mar 1914	N/B	-	N/E	2,000	
5 Aug 1914	N/F	-	N/U	7,500	
8 Apr 1918	N/V	-	O/C	4,000	
9 Dec 1918	O/D	-	O/L	4,000	
16 Jun 1919	O/M	-	O/T	4,000	
9 Jun 1920	O/U	-	P/B	4,000	**From 1500 F**

CL 16 1918

Specimen 4 Jul 1882 D/U D/W D/X
5 Aug 1914 N/F N/G N/H N/J   **From 1500 EF**

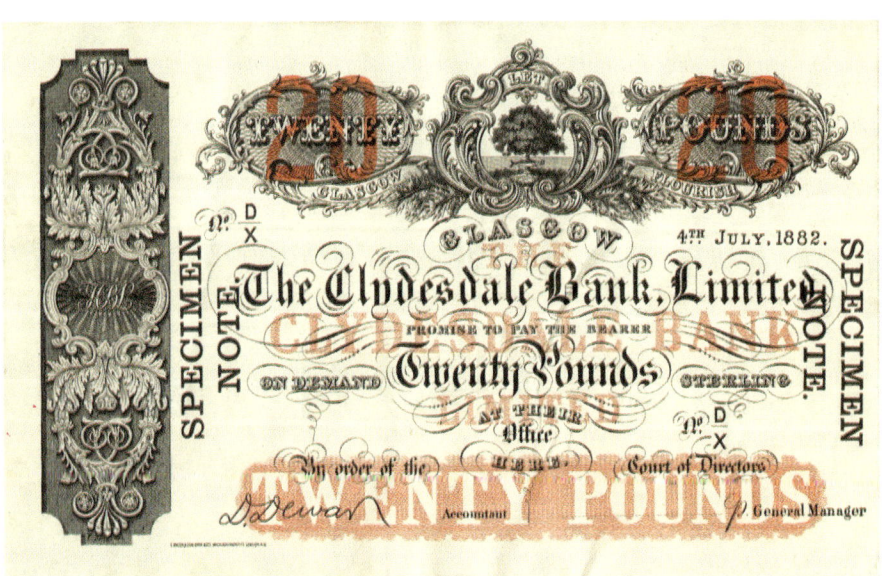

CL 16 Specimen 1882

The £100 design is essentially unchanged from the Hugh Wilson notes of 1865 onwards but the central oval panel is discontinued. No issued notes are known to have survived but a few specimens and proofs have been recorded. It is believed seven digit serial numbers were used despite the number per prefix not exceeding 500. All letters except I were used in the prefix sequences.

CL 17 £100 **Blue bank's name & value panels in Red** uniface
Duncan Dewar Printed signature Accountant **Handsigned** Asst Manager
Imprint: **E Bacon & Son Bank Note Machinagraphists London NW**

16 Jan 1884	B/K	-	B/S	4,500	
26 May 1886	B/T	-	C/A	4,000	
12 Jun 1889	C/B	-	C/L	5,000	
24 May 1893	C/M	-	C/V	5,000	
9 Jun 1897	C/W	-	D/F	5,000	
19 Jun 1901	D/G	-	D/Q	5,000	
8 Feb 1905	D/R	-	E/A	5,000	
26 Jan 1910	E/B	-	E/L	5,000	
5 Aug 1914	E/M	-	E/V	5,000	**RARE**

Proof undated black to be signed Manager & Accountant   **From 1000 EF**

CL 17 Proof undated

Specimen 16 Jan 1884 B/O 5 Aug 1914 E/M E/N E/O E/P   **From 2500 EF**

CL 17 Specimen 1884

FOURTH ISSUE – 1921 *to* 1949

Blue with Red underlay blue reverse

The basics of previous designs are retained but a blue reverse featuring the arms of the City of Glasgow in a field of machinework patterns is added to the notes. The higher denominations were engraved by **E Bacon & Son Bank Note Machinagraphists London NW**, as before, and carried their imprint until 1937/8. There is no imprint on the £1 notes but it is believed that W & A K Johnston continued to engrave the plates where a number of detail changes were made. The paper for all the notes was made by W S Hodgkinson & Co, probably from 1921 onwards, while the notes continued to be printed by the bank's Printing Dept. All notes now carry printed signatures. No £1 notes dated 27th October 1926 have been sighted and it is possible notes of this date were not issued.

CL 18a	£1	Blue bank's name & value panels in Red			F	VF	EF
		Red sunburst underlay					
		Alexander Swanson Cashier **John D Dewar** Accountant					
		4 Jan 1922 A 0000001 - 0400000		400,000			
		14 Jun 1922 A 0400001 - 0800000		400,000	280	550	-

CL 18a First date 4th January 1922

Colour Trial 7 Jan 1921 Black/Red
   Duncan Dewar printed signature Accountant   **RARE**

Specimen 4 Jan 1922   From 550 EF

CL 18b	£1	Alexander Swanson Cashier	Robert Young Accountant		F	VF	EF
		14 Mar 1923	A 0800001 - 1200000	400,000			
		26 Sep 1923	A 1200001 - 1600000	400,000			
		21 May 1924	A 1600001 - 2000000	400,000			
		21 Jan 1925	A 2000001 - 2400000	400,000			
		30 Sep 1925	A 2400001 - 2800000	400,000			
		30 Mar 1926	A 2800001 - 3200000	400,000			
		27 Oct 1926	A 3200001 - 3800000	600,000	220	450	-

CL 18b 1925

In 1927 the Clydesdale decided to follow the lead of other Scottish banks and reduce the size of their £1 note to that of the newly issued Bank of England £1 notes. They reached their decision only after calculating that they could recoup the initial cost of £1,294 for preparation of the new notes through annual savings in paper of about £300. The design was essentially unchanged but the design elements now had to be squeezed into a smaller space and the overall effect suffered accordingly as did the quality of the engraving.

							F	VF	EF
CL 19a	**£1**	**Alexander Swanson** Cashier **Robert Young** Accountant							
		152 x 85mm							
		3 Jan 1927	A 0000001	-	0400000	400,000			
		23 Feb 1927	A 0400001	-	0800000	400,000			
		11 May 1927	A 0800001	-	1200000	400,000			
		16 Nov 1927	A 1200001	-	1600000	400,000			
		8 Feb 1928	A 1600001	-	2000000	400,000			
		4 Jul 1928	A 2000001	-	2400000	400,000			
		9 Jan 1929	A 2400001	-	2800000	400,000			
		10 Apr 1929	A 2800001	-	3200000	400,000			
		4 Sep 1929	A 3200001	-	3600000	400,000			
		5 Mar 1930	A 3600001	-	4000000	400,000			
		11 Jun 1930	A 4000001	-	4400000	400,000			
		17 Dec 1930	A 4400001	-	4800000	400,000			
		15 Apr 1931	A 4800001	-	5200000	400,000			
		7 Oct 1931	A 5200001	-	5600000	400,000	**45**	**100**	**250**

CL 19a First date

							F	VF	EF
CL 19b	£1	**Andrew Mitchell** General Manager							
		Robert Young Accountant & Cashier							
		Date in small serif capitals							
		2 Mar 1932	A 5600001	-	6000000	400,000			
		3 Aug 1932	A 6000001	-	6400000	400,000			
		7 Dec 1932	A 6400001	-	6800000	400,000			
		12 Apr 1933	A 6800001	-	7200000	400,000			
		1 Nov 1933	A 7200001	-	7600000	400,000			
		25 Apr 1934	A 7600001	-	8000000	400,000			
		8 Aug 1934	A 8000001	-	8400000	400,000			
		23 Jan 1935	A 8400001	-	8800000	400,000			
		24 Apr 1935	A 8800001	-	9200000	400,000			
		16 Oct 1935	A 9200001	-	9600000	400,000			
		12 Feb 1936	A 9600001	-	10000000	400,000			
		20 May 1936	B 0000001	-	0400000	400,000			
		30 Sep 1936	B 0400001	-	0800000	400,000			
		17 Mar 1937	B 0800001	-	1200000	400,000			
		30 Jun 1937	B 1200001	-	1600000	400,000			
		27 Oct 1937	B 1600001	-	2000000	400,000			
		6 Apr 1938	B 2000001	-	2400000	400,000			
		31 Aug 1938	B 2400001	-	2800000	400,000			
		11 Jan 1939	B 2800001	-	3200000	400,000			
		19 Apr 1939	B 3200001	-	3600000	400,000			
		23 Aug 1939	B 3600001	-	4000000	400,000			
		22 Nov 1939	B 4000001	-	4400000	400,000			
		17 Apr 1940	B 4400001	-	4800000	400,000			
		17 Jul 1940	B 4800001	-	5200000	400,000			
		20 Nov 1940	B 5200001	-	5600000	400,000			
		19 Mar 1941	B 5600001	-	6000000	400,000			
		23 Jul 1941	B 6000001	-	6400000	400,000			
		5 Nov 1941	B 6400001	-	6800000	400,000	**35**	**90**	**200**

CL 19b First date of B prefix

CL 19c £1 **Andrew Mitchell** General Manager
Robert Young Accountant & Cashier
Date in small sans serif capitals

			F	VF	EF
25 Feb 1942	B 6800001 - 7200000	400,000			
1 Jul 1942	B 7200001 - 7600000	400,000			
24 Feb 1943	B 7600001 - 8000000	400,000			
28 Jul 1943	B 8000001 - 8400000	400,000			
12 Apr 1944	B 8400001 - 8800000	400,000			
15 Nov 1944	B 8800001 - 9200000	400,000	35	90	200

CL 19c Date in small sans serif capitals

CL 19d £1 **Andrew Mitchell** General Manager
Robert Young Accountant & Cashier
Date in heavy sans serif capitals

			F	VF	EF
4 Apr 1945	B 9200001 - 9600000	400,000			
24 Oct 1945	B 9600001 - 10000000	400,000	35	90	200

CL 19d Date in heavy sans serif capitals

CL 19e   £1   **Andrew Mitchell** General Manager   F   VF   EF
John W Pairman Accountant & Cashier
Large prefix C Date in heavy sans serif capitals

1 May 1946	C 0000001	-	0400000	400,000	**45 120 250**

CL 19e Large prefix C

CL 19f   £1   **John J Campbell** General Manager
John W Pairman Chief Accountant & Cashier
Large prefix C Date in heavy sans serif capitals

20 Nov 1946	C 0400001	-	0800000	400,000	
19 Mar 1947	C 0800001	-	1200000	400,000	
3 Sep 1947	C 1200001	-	1600000	400,000	**25 70 160**

CL 19f Large prefix C

CL 19g   £1   **John J Campbell** General Manager
R R Houston Chief Accountant & Cashier
Small prefix C Date in heavy sans serif capitals

7 Apr 1948	C 1600001	-	2000000	400,000	
26 May 1948	C 2000001	-	2400000	400,000	
27 Oct 1948	C 2400001	-	2800000	400,000	
12 Jan 1949	C 2800001	-	3200000	400,000	
13 Jul 1949	C 3200001	-	3600000	400,000	
14 Dec 1949	C 3600001	-	4400000	800,000	**25 60 140**

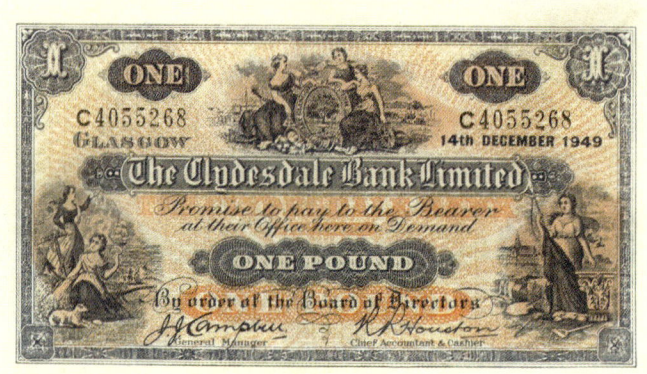

CL 19g Small prefix C Last date

Specimen 14 Dec 1949 punch hole cancelled
stamped CANCELLED   **From 200 EF**

The key change to the £5 note was to print the basic plate in blue rather than black. The red value panels and bank name remained unchanged while a blue reverse was added. The seven digit serial numbers again feature several initial zeroes despite the number per prefix not exceeding 1,000 up to January 1923, thereafter 5,000 per prefix. All letters except I were used in the prefix sequences.

CL 20a	£5	**Blue bank's name & value panels in Red** blue reverse				**F**	**VF**	**EF**
		Alexander Swanson Cashier **John D Dewar** Accountant						
		Imprint: **E Bacon & Son Bank Note Machinagraphists London NW**						
		Date in small serif capitals						
		15 Feb 1922	Q²/C	-	Q²/S	16,000		
		14 Jun 1922	Q²/T	-	R²/J	16,000	**600**	**1200**	-

CL 20a First date

Specimen 15 Feb 1922 prefix Q²/C Q²/D Q²/E Q²/F   **From 500 EF**

								F	VF	EF
CL 20b	£5	**Alexander Swanson** Cashier		**Robert Young** Accountant						
		31 Jan 1923	R^2/K	-	R^2/Z	16,000				
		2 May 1923	S^2/A	-	S^2/D	20,000				
		19 Dec 1923	S^2/E	-	S^2/H	20,000				
		18 Jun 1924	S^2/J	-	S^2/M	20,000				
		1 Apr 1925	S^2/N	-	S^2/Q	20,000				
		16 Dec 1925	S^2/R	-	S^2/U	20,000				
		31 May 1926	S^2/V	-	S^2/Y	20,000				
		3 Jan 1927	S^2/Z	-	T^2/C	20,000				
		10 Aug 1927	T^2/D	-	T^2/G	20,000				
		18 Apr 1928	T^2/H	-	T^2/L	20,000				
		24 Oct 1928	T^2/M	-	T^2/P	20,000				
		10 Apr 1929	T^2/Q	-	T^2/T	20,000				
		13 Jan 1930	T^2/U	-	T^2/X	20,000				
		11 Jun 1930	T^2/Y	-	U^2/B	20,000				
		19 Nov 1930	U^2/C	-	U^2/F	20,000				
		3 Jun 1931	U^2/G	-	U^2/K	20,000				
		9 Dec 1931	U^2/L	-	U^2/O	20,000		250	500	-

CL 20b 1923

								F	VF	EF
CL 20c	£5	**Andrew Mitchell** General Manager								
		Robert Young Accountant & Cashier								
		16 Nov 1932	U^2/P	-	U^2/S	20,000				
		12 Jul 1933	U^2/T	-	U^2/W	20,000				
		10 Jan 1934	U^2/X	-	V^2/A	20,000				
		5 Dec 1934	V^2/B	-	V^2/J	40,000				
		19 Jun 1935	V^2/K	-	V^2/R	40,000				
		8 Jul 1936	V^2/S	-	V^2/V	20,000				
		10 May 1937	V^2/W	-	V^2/Z	20,000				
		30 Jun 1937	W^2/A	-	W^2/D	20,000				
		27 Oct 1937	W^2/E	-	W^2/H	20,000		220	450	-

CL 20c Last date, final prefix

CL 20d	£5	**Andrew Mitchell** General Manager **Robert Young** Accountant & Cashier **No printers' imprint**				F	VF	EF
		25 May 1938	W^2/J	-	W^2/Q	40,000		
		14 Jun 1939	W^2/R	-	W^2/Y	40,000		
		8 Nov 1939	W^2/Z	-	X^2/C	20,000		
		15 May 1940	X^2/D	-	X^2/L	40,000		
		26 Jun 1940	X^2/M	-	X^2/T	40,000		
		5 Feb 1941	X^2/U	-	Y^2/B	40,000		
		2 Jul 1941	Y^2/C	-	Y^2/K	40,000		
		15 Oct 1941	Y^2/L	-	Y^2/O	20,000	150	300	650

CL 20d 1939

								F	VF	EF
CL 20e	**£5**	**Andrew Mitchell** General Manager								
		Robert Young Accountant & Cashier								
		Date in small sans serif capitals								
			3 Jun 1942	Y^2/P	-	Y^2/W	40,000			
			15 Jul 1942	Y^2/X	-	Z^2/E	40,000			
			13 Jan 1943	Z^2/F	-	Z^2/N	40,000			
			21 Apr 1943	Z^2/O	-	Z^2/V	40,000			
			5 May 1943	Z^2/W	-	A^3/M	80,000			
			17 Nov 1943	A^3/N	-	B^3/C	80,000			
			16 Feb 1944	B^3/D	-	B^3/T	80,000			
			5 Jul 1944	B^3/U	-	C^3/K	80,000	150	300	650

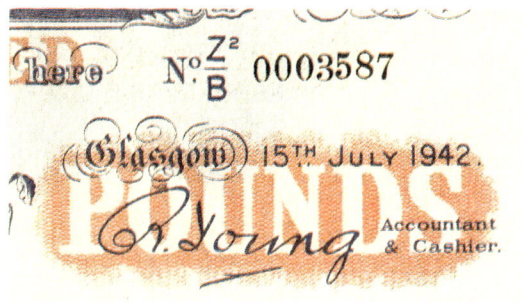

CL 20e Detail

Forgery 5 Jul 1944   From 80 VF

							F	VF	EF
CL 20f	**£5**	**Andrew Mitchell** General Manager							
		Robert Young Accountant & Cashier							
		Date in heavy sans serif capitals							
		24 Oct 1945	C^3/L	-	D^3/A	80,000	150	300	650

CL 20f Detail

						F	VF	EF
CL 20g	£5	**John J Campbell** General Manager **John W Pairman** Accountant & Cashier **Date in heavy sans serif capitals**						
		10 Jul 1946	D³/B	-	D³/R	80,000	**150**	**300**	**650**

CL 20g Last date, last prefix

Specimen 10 Jul 1946 D³/H perforated CANCELLED   **From 350 EF**

After a spate of wartime forgeries an additional security device was added to the £5 notes in the form of a light blue underlay. A new prefix system was also introduced (not using the letter I as before) but the design was otherwise unchanged. As before 5,000 notes per prefix were printed.

						F	VF	EF
CL 21a	£5	**John J Campbell** General Manager **John W Pairman** Chief Accountant & Cashier						
		3 Mar 1948	AA	-	AQ	80,000	**180**	**380**	**750**

CL 21a First date / prefix

Specimen undated no prefix   **From 500 EF**

CL 21b	£5	John J Campbell General Manager R R Houston Chief Accountant & Cashier		F	VF	EF
		12 Jan 1949 AR - AZ BA - BG	80,000	180	380	750

CL 21b 1949

Specimen 12 Jan 1949 BE perforated CANCELLED   **From 350 EF**

As with the £5 note, the key change to the £20 note was to print the basic plate in blue rather than black. The red value panels and bank name remained unchanged. A blue reverse was added. The seven digit serial numbers again feature several initial zeroes despite the number per prefix ranging only from 500 to 1,000. All letters except I were used in the prefix sequences.

CL 22a   **£20**   **Blue bank's name & value panels in Red** blue reverse
             Alexander Swanson Cashier **John D Dewar** Accountant
             Imprint: **E Bacon & Son Bank Note Machinagraphists London NW**
             Date in small serif capitals

15 Feb 1922	P/C	-	P/K	4,000
14 Jun 1922	P/L	-	P/S	4,000

From 1400 F

CL 22a 1922

Specimen   15 Feb 1922 P/C P/D P/E P/F   **From 500 EF**

CL 22b   **£20**   **Alexander Swanson** Cashier **Robert Young** Accountant   **F   VF   EF**

31 Jan 1923	P/T	-	Q/A	4,000			
2 May 1923	Q/B	-	Q/E	4,000			
18 Jun 1924	Q/F	-	Q/J	4,000			
10 Apr 1929	Q/K	-	Q/N	4,000			
11 Jun 1930	Q/O	-	Q/R	4,000			
19 Nov 1930	Q/S	-	Q/V	4,000			
3 Jun 1931	Q/W	-	Q/Z	4,000	500	1000	-

CL 22b 1924

CL 22c	£20	**Andrew Mitchell** General Manager **Robert Young** Accountant & Cashier					F	VF	EF
		16 Nov 1932	R/A	-	R/D	4,000			
		12 Jul 1933	R/E	-	R/H	4,000			
		10 Jan 1934	R/J	-	R/M	4,000	400	800	-

CL 22c Last date

CL 22d	£20	**Andrew Mitchell** General Manager **Robert Young** Accountant & Cashier **No printers' imprint Date in small serif capitals**					F	VF	EF
		24 Nov 1937	R/N	-	R/Q	4,000			
		23 Nov 1938	R/R	-	R/U	4,000			
		14 Jun 1939	R/V	-	R/Y	4,000			
		8 Nov 1939	R/Z	-	S/C	4,000			
		25 Sep 1940	S/D	-	S/L	8,000			
		15 Oct 1941	S/M	-	S/T	8,000	400	800	-

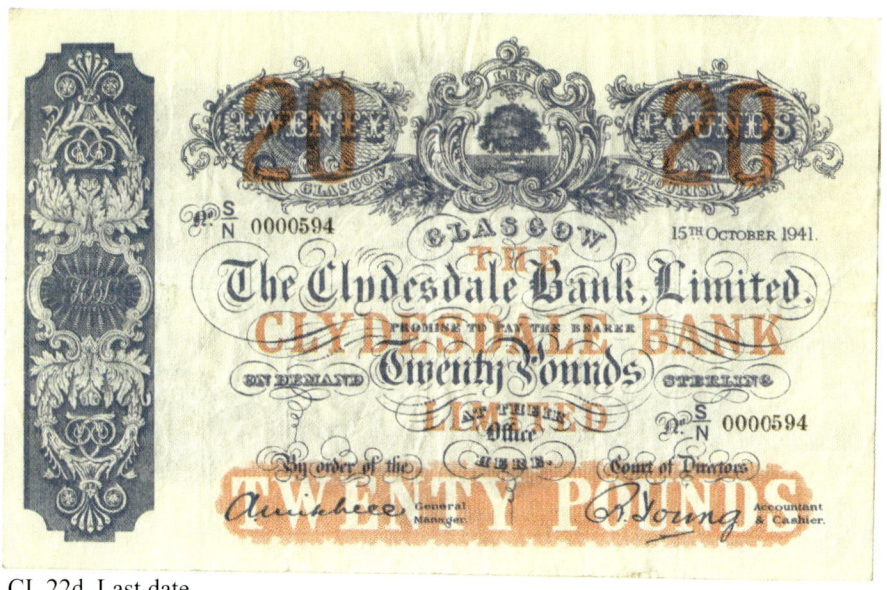

CL 22d Last date

Unissued undated punch holes stamped CANCELLED   From 500 EF

CL 22e	£20	**Andrew Mitchell** General Manager **Robert Young** Accountant & Cashier **Date in small sans serif capitals**							
		4 Nov 1942	S/U	-	T/B	8,000			
		13 Jan 1943	T/C	-	T/K	8,000			
		5 Jul 1944	T/L	-	T/S	8,000			
		15 Nov 1944	T/T	-	U/A	4,000	300	600	1400

CL 22e Last date

CL 22f	£20	John J Campbell General Manager John W Pairman Chief Accountant & Cashier Date in heavy sans serif capitals				F	VF	EF
		4 Jun 1947	U/B	-	U/J	8,000	300	600	1400

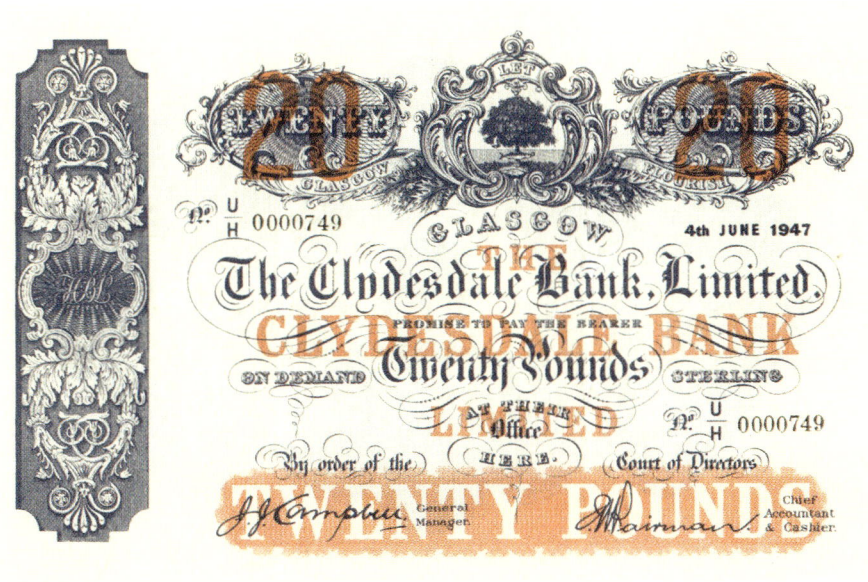

CL 22f

The only change to the £100 note was to add a blue reverse. Both signatures are now printed. The seven digit serial numbers again feature several initial zeroes despite only 500 notes per prefix being printed. All letters except I were used in the prefix sequences. The earliest issued note seen is dated 1931.

CL 23a	**£100**	**Blue bank's name & value panels in Red blue reverse** **Alexander Swanson** Cashier **John D Dewar** Accountant *Imprint:* **E Bacon & Son Bank Note Machinagraphists London NW** **Date in small serif capitals**	
		15 Feb 1922 E/W - F/A 2,500	**RARE**
		Specimen 15 Feb 1922 E/W E/X E/Y E/Z	**From 1200 EF**

CL 23a Specimen

CL 23b	**£100**	**Alexander Swanson** Cashier **Robert Young** Accountant	
		16 Dec 1925 F/B - F/F 2,500	
		3 Jun 1931 F/G - F/L 2,500	**RARE**

CL 23c	**£100**	**Andrew Mitchell** General Manager **Robert Young** Accountant & Cashier	
		19 Jun 1935 F/M - F/Q 2,500	**From 2500 F**

CL 23d	£100	**Andrew Mitchell** General Manager				F	VF	EF
		Robert Young Accountant & Cashier						
		No printers' imprint Date in small sans serif capitals						
		23 Nov 1938	F/R - F/V		2,500			
		4 Nov 1942	F/W - F/Z		2,000			
		3 Feb 1943	G/A - G/D		2,000	**1400**	**3000**	-

CL 23d Final prefix Last date

CL 23e	£100	**John J Campbell** General Manager						
		John W Pairman Chief Accountant & Cashier						
		Date in heavy sans serif capitals						
		26 Mar 1947	G/E - G/H		2,000	**1400**	**3000**	-

CL 23e First prefix

CL 23 £100 Common reverse 1922 to 1947

FIFTH ISSUE – 1950 *to* 1960

Heading: CLYDESDALE & NORTH OF SCOTLAND BANK LIMITED

Following the merger in 1950 of Clydesdale Bank and North of Scotland Bank, both owned by the London-based Midland Bank, a new series of notes was prepared. **Thomas De La Rue & Co Limited** was chosen to design and engrave the notes in recognition of the success of their work for the North Bank. They have produced the Clydesdale's notes ever since. The notes of this issue were the first in Scotland to incorporate a metal security thread and again have been lauded for their design quality. The £1 note carries the bank's coat of arms (granted in 1948) upper centre on the obverse of the note while the arms are the dominant feature of the common reverse of the higher denomination notes. The Latin motto 'FIDE ET INDUSTRIA LITORE AD LITUS' translates as 'By Faith and Diligence (i.e. Industry), from One Shore to the Other'. Some superb art work (seen also in presentation albums) has survived of De La Rue essays for the new series, dated either 1st July 1949 or 1st January 1950. Bradbury Wilkinson also prepared and submitted essays, all dated 27th October 1950, but seen only in photographic form, and further De La Rue £1 essays dated 1950 and 1960 have also come on to the market.

Both official bank specimens and De La Rue archival specimens have survived in some number. Unless otherwise stated all specimens have 000000 serials.

The North Bank's practice of printing £1,000,000 of notes per prefix was adopted, i.e. 200,000 notes per prefix for the £5, 50,000 per prefix for the £20 (prefix A excepted) and 10,000 for the £100 note. The higher value notes were reduced in size to conform to the sizes used in the final North Bank series. Prefix letters I and O were not used.

The appearance of darker red (mulberry) prefixes, serials and date on the £1, £5 and £20 notes in the mid to late 1950s can probably be ascribed to production difficulties at De La Rue. Many shades from light red through to dark plum have been seen, and variations have even been seen on consecutively numbered notes.

							VF	EF	UNC
CL 24a	£1	Blue vignettes of Clyde shipping & farming							
		Highland river scene reverse 152 x 85mm							
		John J Campbell General Manager							
		1 Nov 1950	A	-	C	3,000,000			
		1 Mar 1952	D	-	F	3,000,000			
		1 Mar 1954	G	-	J	3,000,000			
		1 Jun 1955	K	-	M	3,000,000	35	70	170

CL 24a First date / prefix

Specimen 1 Nov 1950 A From 250 UNC

De La Rue Specimen 1 Nov 1950 A 1 Mar 1954 J
1 Jun 1955 M From 180 UNC

CL 24b	£1	Fractional prefixes introduced							
		1 Nov 1956	A/N	-	A/Q	3,000,000	35	90	170

CL 24b First fractional prefix

					VF	EF	UNC
CL 24c	£1	Mulberry prefix/serials on CL 24b			35	90	170

					VF	EF	UNC
CL 24d	£1	Robert D Fairbairn General Manager					
		1 May 1958	A/R - A/T	3,000,000			
		1 Nov 1960	A/U	500,000	35	90	170

CL 24d Last date / prefix

Specimen 1 May 1958 A/R — From 250 UNC

De La Rue Specimen 1 May 1958 A/R 1 Nov 1960 A/U — From 180 UNC

			VF	EF	UNC
CL 24e	£1	Mulberry prefix/serials on CL 24d	35	90	170

CL 24 Common reverse

								VF	EF	UNC
CL 25a	£5	Purple Vignettes of King's College Aberdeen & Glasgow Cathedral								
		John J Campbell General Manager								
		Bank arms reverse 180 x 100mm								
			2 May 1951	A	-	B	400,000			
			2 May 1952	C	-	D	400,000			
			2 Mar 1953	E	-	F	400,000			
			2 Sep 1953	G	-	K	800,000			
			1 Jun 1955	L	-	P	800,000	60	180	320

CL 25 Common reverse

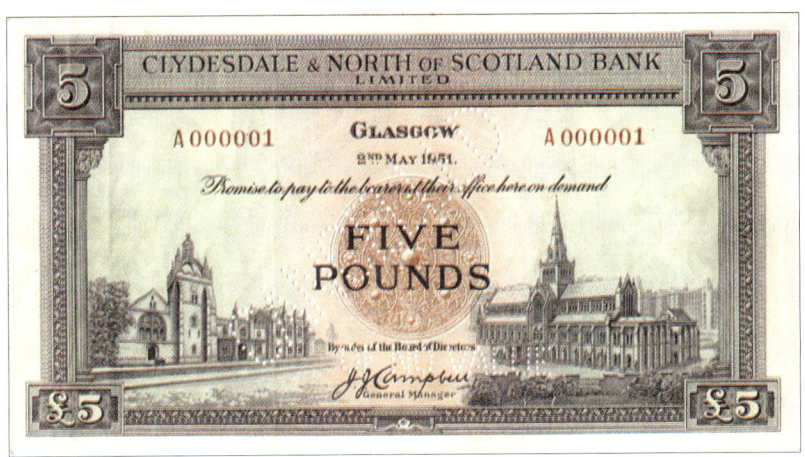

CL 25a Serial 1 note, perforated CANCELLED / OF NO VALUE

Specimen 2 May 1951 A From 300 UNC

De La Rue Specimen 2 May 1951 A B 2 Mar 1953 F
2 Sep 1953 H From 240 UNC

510 *Paper Money of Scotland*

CL 25b	£5	Fractional prefixes introduced				VF	EF	UNC
		1 Nov 1956	A/Q - A/T	800,000				
		1 Feb 1958	A/U - A/X	800,000		60	180	320

De La Rue Specimen 1 Feb 1958 A/U   From 280 UNC

CL 25c	£5	Mulberry prefix/serials on CL 25b	60	180	320

CL 25c Mulberry prefix/serials

CL 25d	£5	**Robert D Fairbairn** General Manager			VF	EF	UNC
		1 Mar 1960 A/Y - A/Z A/A - A/B	800,000		60	180	320

CL 25e	£5	Mulberry prefix/serials on CL 25d	60	180	320

CL 25e Mulberry prefix/serials

							VF	EF	UNC
CL 26a	£20	Green **Similar to £5** 180 x 100mm							
		John J Campbell General Manager							
		2 May 1951	A 000001	-	050000	50,000			
		1 Jun 1955	A 050001	-	100000	50,000			
		1 Feb 1958	B 000001	-	050000	50,000	120	300	550

CL 26a First date / prefix

	Specimen 2 May 1951 A		From 350 UNC
	De La Rue Specimen 2 May 1951 A 1 Jun 1955 A		
	1 Feb 1958 B		From 320 UNC

				VF	EF	UNC
CL 26b	£20	**Mulberry prefix/serials on CL 26a**		110	250	500
CL 26c	£20	**Robert D Fairbairn** General Manager				
		1 Dec 1960 C 000001 - 050000	50,000			
		1 Jul 1961 D 000001 - 050000	50,000			
		1 Aug 1962 E 000001 - 050000	50,000	110	250	500

SCOTTISH UNC

A reminder to collectors that early Scottish 'Square' £1 notes and higher value 'Horse Blankets' will often be found with folds even if otherwise unused. The reason for this is the engrained habit of Scottish bank tellers of folding their notes at least once to fit them into their tills. Horse Blankets will often be found with two vertical folds, one third in on each side, while Squares will usually have a single vertical fold. As a result the top grade for a Scottish note is sometimes referred to as 'Scottish UNC', in reality this being between EF and AUNC depending on how heavy the folds are. Do not be put off buying this grade in the hope that a better one will come along as it is unlikely truly uncirculated notes exist.

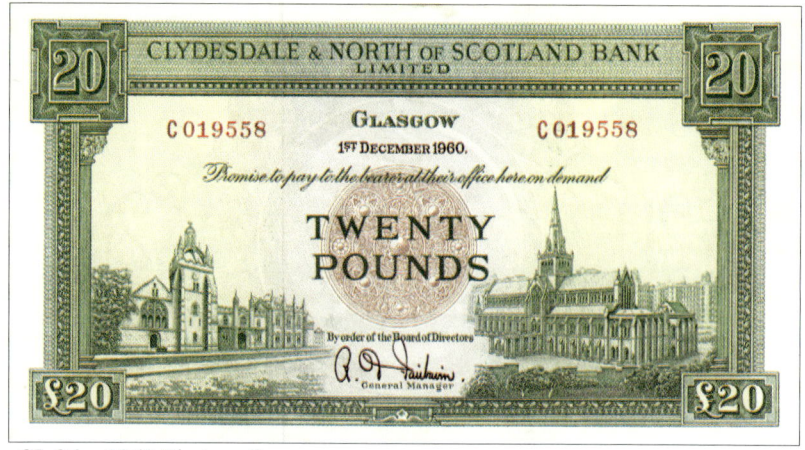

CL 26c 1960 First prefix

				VF	EF	UNC
	Specimen 1 Jul 1961 D				From 320	UNC
	De La Rue Specimen 1 Jul 1961 D				From 280	UNC
CL 26d	£20	Mulberry prefix/serials on CL 26c		110	250	500

CL 27a	£100	Blue Similar to £5 Black prefix/serials 180 x 100mm John J Campbell General Manager				
		2 May 1951 A 000001 - 005000	5,000	900	1750	-

CL 27a 1951

	Specimen 2 May 1951 A	From 520 UNC
	De La Rue Specimen 2 May 1951 A	From 450 UNC

CL 27b	£100	Robert D Fairbairn General Manager				
		1 Dec 1960 A 005001 - 010000	5,000	1000	2000	-

SIXTH ISSUE – 1961 to 1963

CELTIC DESIGN

Heading: CLYDESDALE & NORTH OF SCOTLAND BANK LIMITED

A new design was introduced in 1961 when both the £1 and £5 notes were again reduced in size. The shared obverse design features the bank's arms to the right set in an attractive modern interpretation of traditional Celtic patterns. The prefix and serials as well as the date were separately lithographed in black. Prefix I not used. 1,000,000 £1 and 200,000 £5 notes per prefix printed, except final £1 prefix B/H.

A number of composite essays by De La Rue have come on to the market indicating that work on this new series started in 1960. These comprised a £5 note in purple, a £10 in mauve-purple, a £20 in green and a £100 in blue. A reverse essay of a £20 note has also been recorded, depicting the same view of King's College as seen on the reverse of the issued £5 note. An essay of a £1 note in the new reduced size but essentially keeping to the previous design has also come on to the market.

In the early 1960s the first trials of magnetic encoding were carried out. These were undertaken by Crosfield Electronics who were developing note sorting machinery to handle the laborious work of the daily note exchange. A specimen £5 note has been recorded with trial magnetic codes on the centre left and centre right edges of the obverse. All specimens have 000000 serials unless indicated.

CL 28	£1	Green Clyde shipping scene reverse 152 x 72mm				VF	EF	UNC
		Robert D Fairbairn General Manager						
		1 Mar 1961	B/A	-	B/C	3,000,000		
		2 May 1962	B/D	-	B/F	3,000,000		
		1 Feb 1963	B/G	-	B/H 500000	1,500,000	10	35	70

CL 28 First prefix serial 3

Specimen 1 Mar 1961 B/A 2 May 1962 B/D   From **220** UNC

De La Rue Specimen 1 Mar 1961 B/A 2 May 1962 B/D
                        1 Feb 1963 B/G   From **180** UNC

CL 29	£5	Dark Blue King's College Aberdeen reverse 140 x 84mm		VF	EF	UNC
		Robert D Fairbairn General Manager				
		20 Sep 1961 B/A - B/D	800,000			
		1 Jun 1962 B/E - B/H	800,000			
		1 Feb 1963 B/J - B/M	800,000	20	110	200

Specimen 20 Sep 1961 B/A 1 Feb 1963 B/J   From 250 UNC

De La Rue Specimen 20 Sep 1961 B/A 1 Jun 1962 B/E
                                  1 Feb 1963 B/J   From 220 UNC

De La Rue Specimen with **Trial Encoding** 20 Sep 1961 B/A   From 300 UNC

CL 29 First date / prefix

CL 29 De La Rue Specimen with Trial Encoding

£10 Essay 1961

£20 Essay 1960

SEVENTH ISSUE – 1963 *to* 1969

CELTIC DESIGN

Heading: CLYDESDALE BANK LIMITED

In 1963 the bank decided to shorten its name and this of course required the existing notes to be modified. A year later the £1 and £5 notes were joined by the first £10 note to be issued by the bank. A new £20 note was issued the same year and a new £100 note was issued in 1965. The unchanged obverse designs were also used on the new denominations but each one had a different predominant colour and a different reverse. Prefix letter I not used. 1,000,000 £1 and 200,000 £5 notes per prefix were printed, except where stated. The same pattern of £1,000,000 worth of notes was followed for the £10 (100,000 per prefix), £20 (50,000) and £100 notes (10,000). Essays and artwork of all denominations have been released from the De La Rue archives. All specimens have 000000 serials unless indicated.

After the earlier trials, magnetic sorting codes were finally added to the £1 and £5 notes in 1967 following long delays caused by technical difficulties with the Crosfield sorting machines. In each case the codes were added part way through a single date run.

CL 30a   **£1**   Green Clyde shipping scene reverse   VF   EF   UNC
Robert D Fairbairn General Manager

	2 Sep 1963	C/A	-	C/C	3,000,000			
	1 Feb 1965	C/D	-	C/F	3,000,000			
	30 Mar 1966	C/G	-	C/J	3,000,000			
	3 Apr 1967	C/K			1,000,000	10	30	60

Specimen 2 Sep 1963 C/A 1 Feb 1965 C/D
 30 Mar 1966 C/G 3 Apr 1967 C/K   **From 180 UNC**

De La Rue Specimen 2 Sep 1963 C/A 1 Feb 1965 C/D
 30 Mar 1966 C/G 3 Apr 1967 C/K   **From 140 UNC**

CL 30a First prefix low serial

Clydesdale Bank 517

							VF	EF	UNC
CL 30b	£1	**Magnetic Sorting Codes on reverse**							
		Robert D Fairbairn General Manager							
		3 Apr 1967	C/L	-	C/M	2,000,000			
		1 Oct 1968	C/N	-	C/P	3,000,000			
		1 Sep 1969	C/Q	-	C/T	4,000,000			
			C/U to 500000			500,000	10	30	55

Specimen 1 Sep 1969 C/Q 1 Sep 1969 C/T **From 160 UNC**

De La Rue Specimen 1 Oct 1968 C/N 1 Sep 1969 C/Q C/T **From 120 UNC**

CL 30b First prefix

CL 30b Encoded reverse

							VF	EF	UNC
CL 31a	£5	**Dark blue King's College Aberdeen reverse**							
		Robert D Fairbairn General Manager							
		2 Sep 1963	C/A	-	C/E	1,000,000			
		1 Mar 1965	C/F	-	C/K	1,000,000			
		18 Apr 1966	C/L	-	C/P	1,000,000			
		1 May 1967	C/Q	-	C/R	400,000	25	60	140

De La Rue Essay with Trial Encoding 20 Sep 1961 B/A **From 300 UNC**

Specimen 2 Sep 1963 C/A 1 Mar 1965 C/F
18 Apr 1966 C/L 1 May 1967 C/Q **From 280 UNC**

De La Rue Specimen 2 Sep 1963 C/A 1 Mar 1965 C/F
                       18 Apr 1966 C/L 1 May 1967 C/Q   **From 220 UNC**

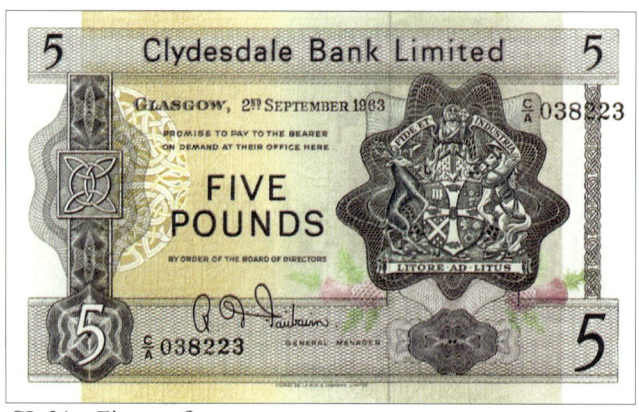

CL 31a First prefix

CL 31b	£5	Magnetic Sorting Codes on reverse				VF	EF	UNC
		Robert D Fairbairn General Manager						
		1 May 1967	C/S	-	C/U	600,000		
		1 Nov 1968	C/V	-	C/Z	1,000,000		
		1 Sep 1969	C/AA	-	C/GG	1,400,000	**25**	**60**	**130**

Specimen 1 Nov 1968 C/V 1 Sep 1969 C/AA C/FF   **From 260 UNC**

De La Rue Specimen 1 Nov 1968 C/V
                        1 Sep 1969 C/AA C/FF   **From 220 UNC**

CL 31b Final date

CL 32	£10	Brown University of Glasgow reverse 150 x 94mm				VF	EF	UNC
		Robert D Fairbairn General Manager						
		20 Apr 1964	C/A - C/B	200,000				
		1 Dec 1967	C/C - C/D	200,000		75	300	550

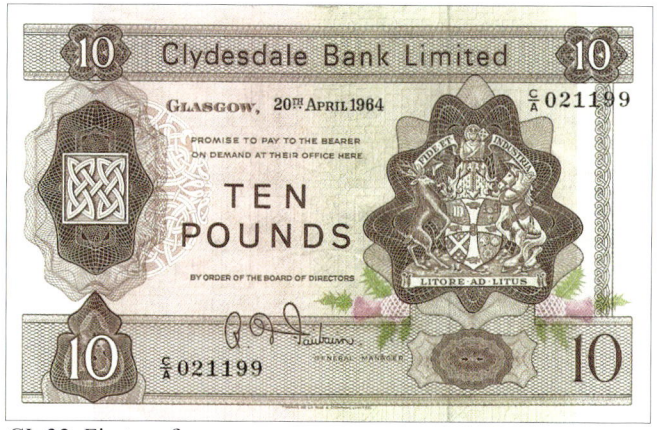

CL 32 First prefix

De La Rue Colour Trial Olive/Green 20 Apr 1964 C/A **From 500 UNC**

Specimen 20 Apr 1964 C/A 1 Dec 1967 C/C **From 350 UNC**

De La Rue Specimen 20 Apr 1964 C/A 1 Dec 1967 C/C **From 280 UNC**

CL 33	£20	Red George Square Glasgow reverse 162 x 94mm						
		Robert D Fairbairn General Manager						
		19 Nov 1964	C/A - C/D	200,000				
		1 Dec 1967	C/E - C/H	200,000		60	220	450

CL 33 First prefix

Specimen 19 Nov 1964 C/A 1 Dec 1967 C/E **From 380 UNC**

De La Rue Specimen 19 Nov 1964 C/A 1 Dec 1967 C/E **From 320 UNC**

£100 Essay 1964

						VF	EF	UNC
CL 34	£100	Purple River Dee and Invercauld Bridge		162 x 94mm				
		Robert D Fairbairn General Manager						
	29 Apr 1965	C/A 000001	-	010000	10,000			
	1 Feb 1968	C/B 000001	-	002000	2,000	1150	2400	-

CL 34 First date 1965

CL 34 Reverse

Specimen 29 Apr 1965 C/A 1 Feb 1968 C/B   **From 600 UNC**

De La Rue Specimen 29 Apr 1965 C/A 1 Feb 1968 C/B   **From 350 UNC**

EIGHTH ISSUE – 1971 to 2009

FAMOUS SCOTS series

PART A 1971 to 1981

Heading: CLYDESDALE BANK LIMITED

This long lasting series was designed by Louis Woudhuysen and, as with the series it replaced, the notes were engraved and printed by **Thomas De La Rue & Co Limited**. Each denomination featured a historical figure on the obverse and scenes related to their lives on the reverse. The watermark on all notes is a three-masted sailing ship motif. This series remained in issue until 2009 but has been sub-divided here, firstly to reflect the bank's name change and secondly further size reductions.

The bank took the decision, possibly prompted by the move made by the British Linen Bank to put a portrait of Sir Walter Scott on their notes in 1968, to introduce a range of notes featuring portraits of Scottish historical figures. Some were better known than others and new figures were introduced during the long life of this series.

The **£1** note featured Robert the Bruce from 1971 to 1988 when it was discontinued. Robert the Bruce was then promoted to the £20 note where he replaced Lord Kelvin. The reverse depicts the Bannockburn battle scene.

The **£5** note featured Robert Burns throughout the series from 1971 to 2002. The reverse shows a mouse and a wild rose, both featured in Burns's poems.

The **£10** note featured David Livingstone from 1972 to 1997 when he was replaced by Mary Slessor. The first Livingstone reverse has an African scene with three tribesmen, a palm tree, a mounted camel and a dhow. In 1988 the reverse was redesigned to depict his birthplace in Blantyre, Lanarkshire.

The **£20** note featured Lord Kelvin from 1971 to 1990 when he was replaced by Robert the Bruce. The reverse depicts Lord Kelvin's lecture theatre in Glasgow University.

The **£50** note, introduced in 1981, featured Adam Smith throughout while the reverse depicts a range of early agricultural and industrial implements.

The **£100** note also featured Lord Kelvin throughout and from 1972 to 1991 was the exact same design as the £20 note. The later issues from 1996 re-introduced on the reverse the view of Glasgow University first seen on the 1964 £10 note.

As before, £1,000,000 worth of notes per prefix were printed, i.e. 1,000,000 £1 notes, 200,000 £5 notes, 100,000 £10 notes, 50,000 £20 notes and 10,000 £100 notes. When the £50 note was introduced this pattern continued with 20,000 notes per prefix. Some interesting stage proofs, essays and other artwork have been released from the De La Rue archives but are not comprehensively covered here. Many of the individual pieces are unique.

Rapidly rising issue volumes resulted in an increasing number of prefixes being used. Prefix letters I and O are not used. Unfortunately there are gaps in the note registers covering this long series. While the £1 records are complete right through to 1988, the £5 and £10 records are incomplete from 1980 onwards and the £20, £50 and £100 notes from 1971 onwards. We have however been assisted by De La Rue whose internal archival specimen notes confirm the first prefix used on each date. There is however no confirmation of the last prefix of each date and many £10 notes have split prefixes at either 025000 or 075000. Issue details of post-2000 notes have been collated from information provided by the bank but rely in places on firm sightings as reported by collectors. Areas of uncertainty are indicated by *italics*. All specimens have 000000 serials unless indicated.

CL 35a £1 Green Robert the Bruce Bannockburn battle scene reverse   VF   EF   UNC
            Magnetic Sorting Codes on reverse
            Robert D Fairbairn General Manager 135 x 67mm
            1 Mar 1971   D/A   -   D/F   6,000,000   5   15   35

CL 35a First prefix

Specimen 1 Mar 1971 D/A   From **220** UNC

De La Rue Specimen 1 Mar 1971 D/A   From **180** UNC

CL 35b	£1	**Alexander Ross Macmillan** General Manager				VF	EF	UNC
		1 May 1972	D/G	- D/M	6,000,000			
		1 Aug 1973	D/N	- D/Q	3,000,000	5	15	30

CL 35b First prefix 1972 low serial

Specimen 1 May 1972 D/G   From 200 UNC

De La Rue Specimen First prefix of both dates   From 160 UNC

CL 35c	£1	**Alexander Ross Macmillan** Chief General Manager				VF	EF	UNC
		1 Mar 1974	D/R	- D/X	7,000,000			
		6 Jan 1975	D/Y	- D/Z	2,000,000			
			D/AA	- D/AF 500000	5,500,000			
		2 Feb 1976	D/AF 500001	- D/AJ 500000	3,000,000			
		1 Mar 1977	D/AJ 500001	- D/AN	4,500,000			
		1 Feb 1978	D/AP	- D/AU	6,000,000			
		31 Jan 1979	D/AV	- D/BC	8,000,000			
		1 Feb 1980	D/BD	- D/BN	10,000,000			
		27 Feb 1981	D/BP	- D/BT	5,000,000	5	12	20

CL 35c 1975

Specimen 1 Mar 1974 D/R 6 Jan 1975 D/Y 2 Feb 1976 D/AF
1 Feb 1978 D/AP 31 Jan 1979 D/AV
1 Feb 1980 D/BD 27 Feb 1981 D/BP   From 180 UNC

De La Rue Specimen First prefix of each date   From 140 UNC

CL 35 Reverse

CL 36a	£5	Blue Robert Burns Wild rose & field mouse reverse **Magnetic Sorting Codes on reverse** **Robert D Fairbairn** General Manager 146 x 78mm				VF	EF	UNC
		1 Mar 1971	D/A	-	D/K 2,000,000	20	50	130

CL 36a 1971 First prefix low serial

CL 36 Encoded reverse

Specimen 1 Mar 1971 D/A   From 250 UNC

De La Rue Specimen 1 Mar 1971 D/A   From 220 UNC

CL 36b	£5	**Alexander Ross Macmillan** General Manager				VF	EF	UNC
		1 May 1972	D/L	- D/V	2,000,000			
		1 Aug 1973	D/W	- D/AA	1,000,000	20	50	120

CL 36b Solid serial

Specimen 1 May 1972 D/L   **From 230 UNC**

De La Rue Specimen 1 May 1972 D/L   **From 180 UNC**

CL 36c	£5	**Alexander Ross Macmillan** Chief General Manager				VF	EF	UNC
		1 Mar 1974	D/AB	- D/AJ	1,600,000			
		6 Jan 1975	D/AK	- D/BB 100000	3,300,000			
		2 Feb 1976	D/BB 100001	- D/BZ	4,500,000			
		31 Jan 1979	D/CA	- D/CF	1,200,000			
		1 Feb 1980	D/CG	- D/DB	4,000,000			
		27 Feb 1981	D/DC	- D/DX	4,000,000	15	45	85

CL 36c 1975

Specimen 1 Mar 1974 D/AB 6 Jan 1975 D/AK
          31 Jan 1979 D/CA 1 Feb 1980 D/CG
          27 Feb 1981 D/DC   **From 200 UNC**

De La Rue Specimen First prefix of each date   **From 160 UNC**

£10 note issuance features a large number of split prefixes.

CL 37a   **£10**   **Brown David Livingstone African scene reverse**   VF   EF   UNC
                     Alexander Ross Macmillan General Manager 150 x 85mm
                        1 Mar 1972   D/A   -   D/D 087000   387,000
                        1 Aug 1973   D/D 087001   -   D/F   213,000   50   160   360

CL 37a First prefix

Specimen 1 Mar 1972 D/A   From 300 UNC

De La Rue Specimen 1 Mar 1972 D/A   From 250 UNC

CL 37b   **£10**   **Alexander Ross Macmillan** Chief General Manager
                     1 Mar 1974   D/G   -   D/H   200,000
                     6 Jan 1975   D/J   -   D/K   200,000
                     2 Feb 1976   D/L   -   D/S 075000   675,000
                     1 Mar 1977   D/S 075001   -   D/AC 075000   1,100,000
                     1 Feb 1978   D/AC 075001 -   D/AT 075000   1,500,000
                     31 Jan 1979   D/AT 075001 -   D/BP 075000   2,000,000
                     1 Feb 1980   D/BP 075001 -   D/CQ 075000   2,500,000
                     27 Feb 1981   D/CQ 075001 -   D/EG 075000   4,000,000   40   140   300

CL 37b 1977

Specimen 1 Mar 1974 D/G   From 280 UNC

De La Rue Specimen First prefix of each date
                        and 27 Feb 1981 D/DW   From 240 UNC

							VF	EF	UNC
CL 38a	£20	Purple Lord Kelvin Glasgow University lecture room reverse							
		Alexander Ross Macmillan General Manager 160 x 92mm							
		1 Mar 1972	D/A	-	D/D	200,000			
		1 Aug 1973	D/E	-	D/F	100,000	120	250	450

CL 38a Second prefix

CL 38 Reverse

Specimen 1 Mar 1972 D/A From 350 UNC

De La Rue Specimen 1 Mar 1972 D/A From 300 UNC

CL 38a Specimen

CL 38b	£20	Alexander Ross Macmillan Chief General Manager					VF	EF	UNC
		1 Mar 1974	D/G	-	D/H	100,000			
		2 Feb 1976	D/J	-	D/L	150,000			
		1 Feb 1978	D/M	-	D/P	150,000			
		31 Jan 1979	D/Q	-	D/U	250,000			
		1 Feb 1980	D/V	-	D/AE	500,000			
		27 Feb 1981	D/AF	-	D/AV	750,000	100	225	400

CL 38b 1978

Specimen 1 Mar 1974 D/G 1 Feb 1980 D/V　　　　　　　　From 320 UNC

De La Rue Specimen First prefix of each date　　　　　　From 280 UNC

CL 39	£50	Olive Adam Smith Agricultural & Industrial implements reverse							
		Alexander Ross Macmillan Chief General Manager							
		170 x 95mm							
		1 Sep 1981	D/A	-	D/Q	300,000	100	250	550

CL 39 First prefix

CL 39 Reverse

Specimen 1 Sep 1981 D/A **From 400 UNC**

£100 Essay 1970

CL 40a   **£100 Red Lord Kelvin Glasgow University lecture room reverse**   VF   EF   UNC
Alexander Ross Macmillan General Manager   160 x 90mm
     1 Mar 1972   D/A   -   D/C *002500*   *22,500*   **250   600   1300**

     Specimen   1 Mar 1972 D/A   **From 480 UNC**

     De La Rue Specimen   1 Mar 1972 D/A   **From 420 UNC**

CL 40a   1972

CL 40b   **£100 Alexander Ross Macmillan** Chief General Manager
     6 Jan 1975   D/C *002501*   -   D/D   *17,500*
     2 Feb 1976   D/E   -   D/F   20,000   **225   550   1250**

     De La Rue Specimen   First prefix of both dates   **From 400 UNC**

CL 40b   Last prefix

CL 40 Reverse

EIGHTH ISSUE – 1971 *to* 2009

FAMOUS SCOTS series

PART B 1981 *to* 1992

Heading: CLYDESDALE BANK PLC

The change of heading came about as a result of the bank's amended legal status following a new Companies Act. The only amendment to the design was the addition of a £ symbol in the value panels. £1,000,000 worth of notes per prefix were printed as before, i.e. 1,000,000 £1 notes, 200,000 £5 notes, 100,000 £10 notes, 50,000 £20 notes, 20,000 £50 notes and 10,000 £100 notes per prefix. From 1985 onwards the electronic sorting codes on the back of the £1 and £5 notes were discontinued following the introduction of more sophisticated note sorting equipment.

The first replacement notes are seen during this series, appearing from 1985 onwards. First used in Scotland in 1970, De La Rue did not introduce them earlier at the request of the bank. No £50 and £100 replacement notes have been recorded to date though they may have been issued. As before gaps in the official note registers have left areas of uncertainty which are indicated by *italics*. All specimens have 000000 serials unless indicated. Some of the final run of £1 notes were encapsulated.

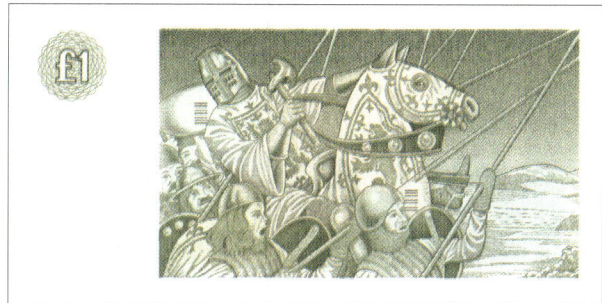

CL 41a/b Magnetic Sorting Codes reverse

CL 41a £1 **Alexander Ross Macmillan** Chief General Manager   **VF EF UNC**
Magnetic Sorting Codes on reverse
29 Mar 1982   D/BU   -   D/CD   10,000,000   5   10   16

CL 41a First prefix

Specimen 29 Mar 1982 D/BU A/A   From 200 UNC

De La Rue Specimen 29 Mar 1982 D/BU   From 160 UNC

CL 41b £1 **Arthur Richard Cole Hamilton** Chief General Manager
5 Jan 1983   D/CE   -   D/CR   12,000,000   4   8   15

CL 41b Last prefix

Specimen 5 Jan 1983 D/CE   From 200 UNC

De La Rue Specimen 5 Jan 1983 D/CE   From 160 UNC

CL 41c £1 **Arthur Richard Cole Hamilton** Chief General Manager
No sorting codes
 8 Apr 1985   D/CS   -   D/CX   6,000,000
25 Nov 1985   D/CY   -   D/DK   12,000,000   4   8   15

Specimen 8 Apr 1985 D/CS   From 180 UNC

De La Rue Specimen First prefix of both dates   From 140 UNC

CL 41cr	£1	**Replacement**				VF	EF	UNC
		8 Apr 1985	D/ZZ 005401	-	038538	12	30	60
		25 Nov 1985	D/ZZ 045228	-	117932	15	40	80

CL 41cr Replacement

CL 41d	£1	**Arthur Richard Cole Hamilton** Chief Executive						
		18 Sep 1987	D/DL	-	D/DR	6,000,000		
		9 Nov 1988	D/DS	-	D/DW	5,000,000	3	5	10

CL 41d Final prefix high serial

De La Rue Specimen First prefix of both dates   **From 180 UNC**

CL 41dr	£1	**Replacement**						
		18 Sep 1987	D/ZZ 122860	-	136328			
		9 Nov 1988	D/ZZ 146387	-	163759	12	30	60

CL 41dr Replacement

These were the very last issues of the £1 note which was discontinued in 1988 and withdrawn.

							VF	EF	UNC
CL 42a	£5	**Alexander Ross Macmillan** Chief General Manager **Magnetic Sorting Codes on reverse** 29 Mar 1982 D/DY - D/FP 8,000,000					15	35	80

CL 42a 1982

Specimen 29 Mar 1982 D/DY A/A   **From 250 UNC**

De La Rue Specimen 29 Mar 1982 D/DY   **From 220 UNC**

							VF	EF	UNC
CL 42b	£5	**Arthur Richard Cole Hamilton** Chief General Manager 5 Jan 1983 D/FQ - D/HL 9,000,000					15	35	70

CL 42b 1983

Specimen 5 Jan 1983 D/FQ   **From 250 UNC**

De La Rue Specimen 5 Jan 1983 D/FQ   **From 220 UNC**

							VF	EF	UNC
CL 42c	£5	**Arthur Richard Cole Hamilton** Chief General Manager **No sorting codes**							
		18 Sep 1986	D/HM	-	D/JG	4,000,000	15	35	65
		De La Rue Specimen 18 Sep 1986 D/HM						From 180 UNC	

CL 42cr	£5	Replacement	
		18 Sep 1986	*none traced to date*

CL 42c/d Reverse

CL 42d	£5	**Arthur Richard Cole Hamilton** Chief Executive							
		18 Sep 1987	D/JH	-	D/JS	2,000,000			
		2 Aug 1988	D/JT	-	D/KY	6,000,000			
		28 Jun 1989	D/KZ	-	D/LU	4,000,000	12	25	50

CL 42d Last date / prefix

Specimen 28 Jun 1989 A/A   From 230 UNC

De La Rue Specimen First prefix of each date   From 180 UNC

CL 42dr	£5	Replacement	
		18 Sep 1987	*none traced to date*
		2 Aug 1988	*none traced to date*
		28 Jun 1989	*none traced to date*

Unravelling £10 note issuance remains difficult even though first prefixes are confirmed for each date. It seems probable that every date and type change has a prefix split firstly at 075000 and later at 025000. Exactly where the split changes is still unclear. *Italics* indicate areas of uncertainty.

CL 43a £10 **Alexander Ross Macmillan** Chief General Manager   **VF EF UNC**
               29 Mar 1982   D/EG 075001 - D/GW 025000   6,150,000   **40 100 240**

CL 43a Last Split Prefix

Specimen 29 Mar 1982 A/A   **From 350 UNC**

De La Rue Specimen 29 Mar 1982 D/EG D/EX D/FS   **From 280 UNC**

CL 43 Reverse

CL 43b	£10	**Arthur Richard Cole Hamilton** Chief General Manager				VF	EF	UNC
		5 Jan 1983	D/GW 025001 - D/KU 025000	7,000,000				
		8 Apr 1985	D/KU 025001 - D/NG 025000	6,000,000				
		18 Sep 1986	D/NG 025001 - D/PY 025000	4,000,000		35	80	200

Specimen 5 Jan 1983 D/GW From 350 UNC

De La Rue Specimen First prefix of each date From 250 UNC

CL 43b Last Split Prefix

CL 43br	£10	**Replacement**					
		5 Jan 1983	*believed not to exist*				
		8 Apr 1985	D/ZZ 005012 - 012337				
		18 Sep 1986	D/ZZ 037797		120	200	450

CL 43br Replacement 1985

CL 43c £10 **Arthur Richard Cole Hamilton** Chief Executive   VF EF UNC
18 Sep 1987   D/PY 025001 - D/SW 025000   7,000,000   35 80 180

CL 43c Last Split prefix

De La Rue Specimen 18 Sep 1987 D/PY   From 200 UNC

CL 43cr £10 **Replacement**
18 Sep 1987   D/ZZ 052046 - 065093   120 200 450

In 1988 the £10 note was redesigned. David Livingstone's portrait was re-engraved with a map of his Zambezi expedition as background. An entirely new reverse was designed, featuring his birthplace in Blantyre, near Hamilton in the Clyde Valley.

CL 44 £10 **David Livingstone Blantyre reverse**
Arthur Richard Cole Hamilton Chief Executive
7 May 1988   D/SW 025001 - D/WE 025000   8,000,000
3 Sep 1989   D/WE 025001 - D/YD *025000*   *4,500,000*
1 Mar 1990   D/YD *025001* - D/ZY *100000* total for both prefixes
             E/AA 000001 - E/CM *025000*   *10,500,000*
9 Nov 1990   E/CM *025001* - E/GR 025000   *10,000,000*   25 45 80

CL 44 First prefix first serial

CL 44 Last Split Prefix high serial

CL 44 Reverse

Specimen 7 May 1988 D/SW
9 Nov 1990 E/CM no prefix/serials   **From 250 UNC**

De La Rue Specimen First prefix of each date   **From 180 UNC**

CL 44r	£10	Replacement		VF	EF	UNC
		7 May 1988 D/ZZ 090087				
		3 Sep 1989 D/ZZ 104001 - 123599				
		1 Mar 1990 D/ZZ 147112		75	150	350
		9 Nov 1990 *none traced to date*				

CL 44r Replacement

CL 45a   £20   **Alexander Ross Macmillan** Chief General Manager   **VF   EF   UNC**
              29 Mar 1982   D/AW   -   D/BR   1,000,000   **75   150   340**

CL 45a 1982

CL 45 Reverse

Specimen 29 Mar 1982 D/AW A/A   From 400 UNC

De La Rue Specimen 29 Mar 1982 D/AW   From 350 UNC

Clydesdale Bank

							VF	EF	UNC
CL 45b	**£20**	**Arthur Richard Cole Hamilton** Chief General Manager							
		5 Jan 1983	D/BS	-	D/CX	1,500,000			
		8 Apr 1985	D/CY	-	D/ED	1,500,000	70	125	300

CL 45b 1985

Specimen 5 Jan 1983 D/BS   From 400 UNC

De La Rue Specimen First prefix of both dates   From 350 UNC

CL 45br	**£20**	**Replacement**			
		5 Jan 1983	*believed not to exist*		
		8 Apr 1985	D/ZZ 014289		**RARE**

CL 45br Replacement

							VF	EF	UNC
CL 45c	**£20**	**Arthur Richard Cole Hamilton** Chief Executive							
		18 Sep 1987	D/EE	-	D/EZ	1,000,000			
		2 Aug 1990	D/FA	-	D/FV	1,000,000	70	125	300

CL 45c Final prefix

      Specimen 2 Aug 1990 D/FA   From 400 UNC

      De La Rue Specimen First prefix of both dates   From 350 UNC

CL 45cr £20 **Replacement**
                      18 Sep 1987   *none traced to date*
                      2 Aug 1990   *none traced to date*

The final prefix of the £50 notes is unconfirmed but there are firm sightings of D/AV.

CL 46	**£50**	**Arthur Richard Cole Hamilton** Chief Executive				**VF**	**EF**	**UNC**
		3 Sep 1989	D/R	-	D/AF	300,000		
		30 Apr 1992	D/AG	-	*D/AW*	*300,000*	80	230	500

CL 46 1992

      Specimen 3 Sep 1989 D/R 30 Apr 1992 D/AG   From 380 UNC

      De La Rue Specimen First prefix of both dates   From 320 UNC

Clydesdale Bank

CL 46r   **£50**   **Replacement**
       3 Sep 1989   *none traced to date*
       30 Apr 1992   *none traced to date*

								VF	EF	UNC
CL 47a	**£100**	**Arthur Richard Cole Hamilton** Chief General Manager								
		8 Apr 1985	D/G	-	D/L		50,000	**200**	**500**	**1100**

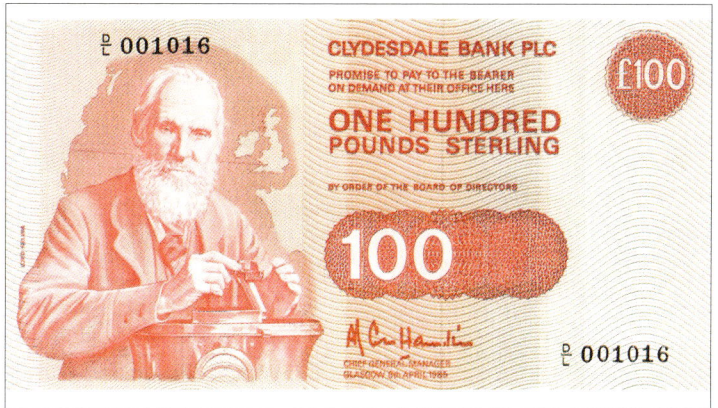

CL 47a Last prefix

CL 47 Reverse

       De La Rue Specimen   8 Sep 1985 D/G   **From 460 UNC**

CL 47ar   **£100**   **Replacement**
       8 Apr 1985   *none traced to date*

CL 47b	**£100**	**Arthur Richard Cole Hamilton** Chief Executive								
		9 Nov 1991	D/M	-	D/U		80,000	**180**	**475**	**950**

       De La Rue Specimen   9 Nov 1991 D/M   **From 440 UNC**

CL 47br   **£100**   **Replacement**
       9 Nov 1991   *none traced to date*

EIGHTH ISSUE – 1971 *to* 2009

FAMOUS SCOTS series

PART C 1990 *to* 2009 reduced size

Heading: CLYDESDALE BANK PLC

The introduction of reduced size notes for all denominations except the £100 note prompted adjustments to the designs of all the notes. As indicated in the listings, numbers per prefix increased to 1,000,000 at different stages on most of the denominations. From 1996 onwards the bank started to issue commemorative notes, most of which went into general circulation. For the sake of continuity each denomination is listed chronologically from 1990 to the end of the series despite the design changes. With the exception of the £10 note, prefixes are re-set from the outset, the £10 following suit only when the design was changed in 1997. Prefix letters I and O not used. This series is characterised by frequent changes of signatory, several only appearing on a few of the denominations. As before areas of uncertainty are indicated by *italics*. All specimens have 000000 serials unless indicated.

In a charity auction in September 2009 the final ten notes of the last date of each denomination were sold by the bank in matching number sets.

						VF	EF	UNC
CL 48a	£5	**Robert Burns Minor modifications to design** 135 x 70mm						
		Arthur Richard Cole Hamilton Chief Executive						
		2 Apr 1990	E/AA	–	E/CM	12,000,000	6	15	30

CL 48a First prefix serial 7

CL 48 Reverse

Specimen 2 Apr 1990 E/AA   From 220 UNC

De La Rue Specimen 2 Apr 1990 E/AA   From 170 UNC

CL 48ar   £5   **Replacement**
              2 Apr 1990   E/ZZ 002417   **RARE**

CL 48ar Replacement

CL 48b   £5   **Frank Cicutto** Chief Executive   VF   EF   UNC
              1 Sep 1994   E/CN   -   E/DN   5,000,000   6   12   22

CL 48b First

    Specimen 1 Sep 1994 E/CN   From 220 UNC

    De La Rue Specimen 1 Sep 1994 E/CN   From 170 UNC

CL 48br £5   **Replacement**
              1 Sep 1994   E/ZZ 020714   -   028726   80   180   350

						VF	EF	UNC
CL 48c	£5	**Fred Goodwin** Chief Executive **1,000,000 notes per prefix**						
		21 Jul 1996	E/DP	-	E/DT	5,000,000		
		1 Dec 1997	E/DU	-	E/DY	5,000,000	6	9	16

CL 48c

De La Rue Specimen First prefix of both dates   **From 200 UNC**

CL 48cr	£5	**Replacement**						
		21 Jul 1996	*none traced to date*					
		1 Dec 1997	*none traced to date*					

						VF	EF	UNC
CL 48d	£5	**Grahame Savage** Chief Executive						
		19 Jun 2002	E/DZ	-	E/ED	5,000,000	6	8	14

CL 48d First Prefix low serial

De La Rue Specimen 19 Jun 2002 E/DZ   **From 150 UNC**

CL 48dr	**£5**	*Replacement*			**VF**	**EF**	**UNC**
		19 Jun 2002 E/ZZ 054409 - 056776			**80**	**180**	**350**

The Clydesdale's first commemorative notes were issued in October 1996 to mark the 200th anniversary of the national's poet's death at the age of 38. Each note of the four note set carries the opening lines of one of Burns' best-loved poems. The design is otherwise unchanged although a special R/B prefix was adopted. An unspecified number of sets with matching final numbers were sold by the bank in special folders at £40 per set. The great majority of the balance of the notes ended up in circulation, however. Some laminated sets were issued but the process damaged the notes.

CL 49a   **£5**   **Burns Commemorative** Special prefix
"Then let us pray that come it may, …"
21 Jul 1996   R/B 0000001 - 1000000   1,000,000   -   **12**   **30**

CL 49a Commemorative Special prefix

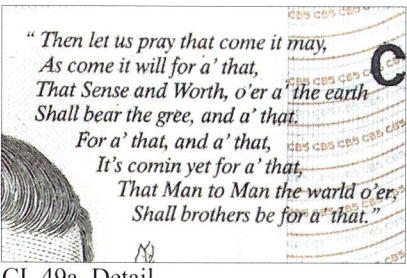

CL 49a Detail

					VF	EF	UNC
CL 49b	£5	**Burns Commemorative** Special prefix "Now wha this tale o' truth shall read, …" 21 Jul 1996 R/B 1000001 - 2000000 1,000,000			-	12	30

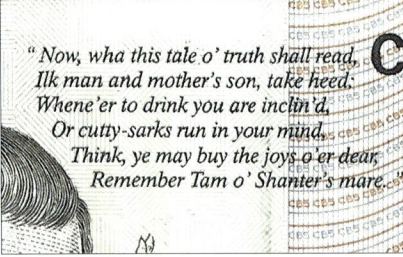

CL 49b Detail

					VF	EF	UNC
CL 49c	£5	**Burns Commemorative** Special prefix "But to see her was to love her, …" 21 Jul 1996 R/B 2000001 - 3000000 1,000,000			-	12	30

CL 49c Detail

					VF	EF	UNC
CL 49d	£5	**Burns Commemorative** Special prefix "By Oppression's woes and pains! …" 21 Jul 1996 R/B 3000001 - 4000000 1,000,000			-	12	30

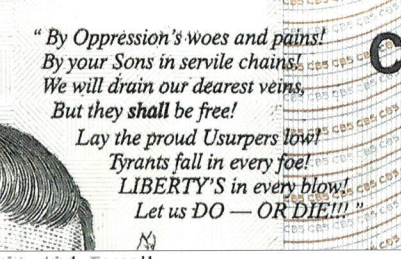

CL 49d Detail

Set of Four Matching Low serials 21 Jul 1996 R/B   **170 UNC**

Specimen Set of four 21 Jul 1996 R/B   **800 UNC**

One or two unclear issues remain regarding £10 notes from 1992 to 1997. These are shown in *italics*. It is possible the final prefix of CL 50c goes beyond E/WX.

			VF	EF	UNC
CL 50a	**£10**	David Livingstone Minor modifications to design			
		Arthur Richard Cole Hamilton Chief Executive 142 x 75mm			
		3 Sep 1992 E/GR 025001 - E/QZ 025000 20,000,000	18	45	90

CL 50a First Split Prefix serial 4 (after split)

CL 50 Reverse

Specimen 3 Sep 1992 E/GR	**From 250 UNC**
De La Rue Specimen 3 Sep 1992 E/GR	**From 220 UNC**

CL 50ar	**£10**	Replacement			
		3 Sep 1992 E/ZZ 027960 - 031417	110	250	-

CL 50b	£10	Charles M Love Chief Executive			VF	EF	UNC
		5 Jan 1993 E/QZ 025001 - E/VD 025000 10,000,000			15	35	80

CL 50b First Split Prefix low serial

Specimen 5 Jan 1993 E/QZ   From 250 UNC

De La Rue Specimen 5 Jan 1993 E/QZ   From 220 UNC

CL 50br	£10	Replacement				
		5 Jan 1993 E/ZZ 052648 - 064998		110	250	-

CL 50c	£10	Fred Goodwin Chief Executive					
		100,000 notes per prefix					
		22 Mar 1996 E/VD 025001 - *E/WV 025000* 4,000,000					
		1,000,000 notes per prefix					
		27 Feb 1997 E/WW - *E/WX* 2,000,000			15	30	60

CL 50c Last recorded perfix

De La Rue Specimen First prefix of both dates   From 180 UNC

CL 50cr	£10	Replacement				VF	EF	UNC
		22 Mar 1996	E/ZZ 074325	-	086284	100	220	250
		27 Feb 1997	*none traced to date*					

CL 50cr Replacement

In 1997 a new design was prepared featuring the missionary Mary Slessor (1848-1915), the first time a non-royal female figure had been chosen to appear on a Scottish banknote. The reverse design draws on a stained glass window in the McManus Gallery, Dundee created by William Aikman (1868-1959) and includes features such as the girl at a loom, Mary Slessor with African children and a map of the Calabar region of Nigeria.

Additional security features were introduced including a metallic diamond over the value panel upper right and a windowed thread. The CB logo appears on the right of the central value panel. One set of serial numbers now features rising digit sizes while the other is in vertical format. The prefixes of both regular and replacement notes were re-set and the bank also issued a number of commemoratives notes with the prefix NAB to mark the ten years that the bank had been part of the National Australia Bank. Total issuance of this commemorative note is uncertain as indicated in *italics*.

CL 51a	£10	Mary Slessor Map & scenes from Nigeria reverse						
		Fred Goodwin Chief Executive						
		1 May 1997	A/AA	-	A/AK 300000	9,300,000	**15**	**25**	**50**

CL 51a First prefix

CL 51 Reverse

Specimen 1 May 1997 A/AA From 230 UNC

De La Rue Specimen 1 May 1997 A/AA From 170 UNC

				VF	EF	UNC
CL 51ar	£10	Replacement		60	120	200
		1 May 1997 E/ZZ 017035 - 042134				

CL 51ar Replacement

					VF	EF	UNC
CL 51b	£10	**National Australia Bank Commemorative** Special prefix					
		Encapsulated in acrylic for issue to staff					
		1 May 1997 NAB 000001 - 006000	6,000		-	50	
		Issued to the public					
		1 May 1997 NAB 006001 - *700000*	694,000		20	40	100

CL 51b First commemorative £10 Special prefix

					VF	EF	UNC
CL 51c	£10	**John Robertson Wright** Chief Executive					
		5 Nov 1998	A/AK 300001 - A/BF 300000	20,000,000			
		12 Oct 1999	A/BF 300001 - A/CA 800000	19,500,000	-	15	35

CL 51c First Split prefix

Specimen 12 Oct 1999 A/BF	From 230 UNC
De La Rue Specimen First prefix of both dates	From 170 UNC

					VF	EF	UNC
CL 51cr	£10	**Replacement**					
		5 Nov 1998	E/ZZ 047127 - 056014				
		12 Oct 1999	E/ZZ 061313 - 101533		45	85	160

					VF	EF	UNC
CL 51d	£10	**Year 2000 Commemorative** Special prefix					
		John Robertson Wright Chief Executive					
		1 Jan 2000	MM 000001 - 500000	500,000	15	25	60

CL 51d Year 2000 Commemorative Special prefix

Specimen 1 Jan 2000 MM	From 280 UNC
De La Rue Specimen 1 Jan 2000 MM	From 220 UNC

					VF	EF	UNC
CL 51e	£10	**Steve Targett** Chief Executive					
		26 Jan 2003 A/CA 800001 - A/CL 800000 10,000,000			-	15	30

CL 51e   First Split Prefix

CL 51er	£10	**Replacement**					
		26 Jan 2003 E/ZZ 103347 - 119189			30	70	140

CL 51f	£10	**Ross Pinney** Chief Executive					
		25 Apr 2003 A/CL 800001 - A/CZ 300000 12,500,000			-	15	25

CL 51f   First Split Prefix

CL 51fr	£10	**Replacement**					
		25 Apr 2003 E/ZZ 121008 - 128261			30	70	140

CL 51fr   Replacement

					VF	EF	UNC
CL 51g	£10	**David Thorburn** Chief Operating Officer					
		21 Nov 2004 A/CZ 300001 - A/DS 800000 17,500,000			-	15	25

CL 51g First Split Prefix low serial

CL 51gr	£10	Replacement					
		21 Nov 2004 E/ZZ 131203 - 174826			30	70	140

CL 51h	£10	**Modified CB logo David Thorburn** Chief Operating Officer					
		14 Mar 2006 A/DS 800001 - A/EH 800000 15,000,000					
		16 Apr 2007 A/EH 800001 - A/FP 800000 30,000,000			-	12	20

CL 51h First Split Prefix Modified logo

Specimen 14 Mar 2006 A/DS   From **230** UNC

CL 51hr	£10	Replacement					
		14 Mar 2006 E/ZZ 179205 - 195101					
		16 Apr 2007 E/ZZ 197023 - 204188			30	60	120

The final appearance of Mary Slessor was on a Commonwealth Games commemorative note issued to coincide with the opening of the 18th Games in Melbourne, Australia. The notes are dated the day the Games opened. A specially designed reverse was created featuring a number of sports in a stylistic departure from the more traditional obverse of the note. A special prefix was used.

CL 52	£10	Commonwealth Games Commemorative Special prefix		VF	EF	UNC
		David Thorburn Chief Operating Officer				
		15 Mar 2006 CG/1 - CG/5	5,000,000	12	25	40

CL 52 First prefix

CL 52 Reverse

Specimen 15 Mar 2006 CG/1   From 150 UNC

The £20 note went through more design changes than any of the other denominations in this series and these are listed in chronological order to the extent possible. The reduced size note now features Robert the Bruce who was promoted from the discontinued £1 note. The reverse shows him on horseback with the Monymusk Reliquary. Stirling Castle is in the background. The colours are now in more vivid shades of purple and red. While the regular prefixes are re-set it appears that replacement note serial numbers continued from the previous issue.

CL 53a	£20	Robert the Bruce Stirling Castle reverse 150 x 80mm			VF	EF	UNC
		Arthur Richard Cole Hamilton Chief Executive					
		30 Nov 1990	E/AA - E/DH	4,000,000			
		2 Aug 1991	E/DJ - E/JH	6,000,000			
		3 Sep 1992	E/JJ - E/NM	5,000,000	40	90	180

CL 53a First prefix serial 11

CL 53 Reverse

Specimen 30 Nov 1990 E/AA 2 Aug 1991 E/DJ		From 300 UNC
De La Rue Specimen First prefix of each date		From 250 UNC

CL 53ar	£20	Replacement					
		30 Nov 1990	*none traced to date*				
		2 Aug 1991	E/ZZ 018675	-	022610		
		3 Sep 1992	E/ZZ 032090		038728	130	280	-

					VF	EF	UNC
CL 53b	£20	**Charles M Love** Chief Executive					
		5 Jan 1993 E/NN - E/SR		5,000,000	50	140	220

CL 53b First prefix serial 7

Specimen 5 Jan 1993 E/NN		From 280 UNC
De La Rue Specimen 5 Jan 1993 E/NN		From 240 UNC

CL 53br	£20	Replacement					
		5 Jan 1993 E/ZZ 042680 - 043748			150	300	-

In 1994 the design was amended and enhanced security features added, including even more vivid colours. The left hand serial numbers now have rising digit sizes while those on the right are in vertical format. It is believed there were 50,000 notes per prefix up to and including prefix F/AX but this has not been confirmed, hence the issue total is in *italics*.

CL 54a	£20	**Frank Cicutto** Chief Executive				
		50,000 notes per prefix				
		1 Sep 1994 E/SS - E/ZY F/AA - F/AX	*9,850,000*	30	60	120

CL 54a E/SS Number 1 note

CL 54 Reverse

Specimen 1 Sep 1994 E/SS From 260 UNC

De La Rue Specimen 1 Sep 1994 E/SS From 220 UNC

			VF	EF	UNC
CL 54ar	£20	Replacement 1 Sep 1994 E/ZZ 060369 - 074243	120	250	450

CL 54ar Replacement

CL 54b	£20	**Fred Goodwin** Chief Executive **1,000,000 notes per prefix** 2 Dec 1996 F/AY - F/BC	5,000,000	-	45	90

Specimen 2 Dec 1996 F/AY From 260 UNC

De La Rue Specimen 2 Dec 1996 F/AY From 220 UNC

CL 54br	£20	Replacement 2 Dec 1996 E/ZZ 081172 - 094246	120	250	450

The bank's first commemorative £20 note was issued to mark the holding of the Commonwealth Heads of Government Meeting in Edinburgh in October 1997. The obverse was unchanged apart from the conference's emblem but a new reverse was prepared featuring the Clydesdale Bank Plaza and the Edinburgh International Conference Centre. A run of notes with a special prefix preceded the issue of notes with regular prefixes. It is probable but not confirmed that the full print run totalled 5,000,000 notes.

				VF	EF	UNC
CL 55a	**£20**	**Commonwealth Heads of Government Commemorative**				
		Fred Goodwin Chief Executive Special prefix				
		Clydesdale Bank Plaza &				
		Edinburgh International Conference Centre reverse				
		30 Sep 1997 C/HG 000001 - 050000	50,000	**35**	**60**	**120**

CL 55a Commemorative Special prefix

CL 55 Reverse

Specimen 30 Sep 1997 C/HG   From **320** UNC

De La Rue Specimen 30 Sep 1997 C/HG   From **260** UNC

						VF	EF	UNC
CL 55b	£20	Robert the Bruce Regular prefix **Fred Goodwin** Chief Executive						
		30 Sep 1997 F/BD - F/BH			*4,950,000*	-	**40**	**80**

CL55br	£20	Replacement						
		30 Sep 1997 E/ZZ 097821 - 114633				**100**	**180**	**360**

The design reverts to the 1996 version but now includes a windowed thread and a square gold foil element over the upper right value panel. The CB logo appears on the right of the central value panel. The prefixes of both regular issues and replacements are re-set.

CL 56	£20	Robert the Bruce Further security enhancements **Fred Goodwin** Chief Executive **Stirling Castle reverse**						
		1 Nov 1997 A/AA - A/AK			10,000,000	-	**35**	**75**

CL 56 First prefix

Specimen 1 Nov 1997 A/AA — From **260 UNC**

De La Rue Specimen 1 Nov 1997 A/AA — From **220 UNC**

CL 56r	£20	Replacement						
		1 Nov 1997 E/ZZ 000737 - 022571				**70**	**150**	**300**

In 1999 another commemorative note was issued to mark Glasgow's award as 1999 UK City of Architecture and Design. A new obverse was designed featuring the renowned architect, Alexander 'Greek' Thomson (1817-1875). The reverse was also redesigned and featured an interior view of the dome of Holmwood House, designed by Thomson, and an outline of the side elevation of the Lighthouse building in Glasgow designed by Charles Rennie Mackintosh (1868-1928) and now occupied by the Glasgow School of Art. The building was badly damaged by fire in May 2014 but is being restored.

				VF	EF	UNC
CL 57a	£20	Alexander Greek Thomson Commemorative **John Robertson Wright** Chief Executive Special prefix				
		9 Apr 1999 G/AD 000001 - 050000	50,000	35	60	120

CL 57a Commemorative Special prefix

CL 57 Reverse

CL 57b	£20	Alexander Greek Thomson Commemorative **John Robertson Wright** Chief Executive Regular prefix				
		9 Apr 1999 A/AL - A/AQ 950000	4,950,000	-	40	80
		Specimen 9 Apr 1999 A/AL			From 320	UNC
		De La Rue Specimen 9 Apr 1999 A/AL			From 260	UNC

						VF	EF	UNC
CL 57br	£20	Replacement						
		9 Apr 1999	E/ZZ 025022	-	035955	70	150	300

CL 57br Replacement Commemorative

The notes now revert to the modified 1997 version of the Robert the Bruce design.

CL 58a	£20	**John Robertson Wright** Chief Executive						
		12 Oct 1999	A/AQ 950001 - A/BL 450000	19,500,000	-	35	65

CL 58a First Split Prefix

Specimen 12 Oct 1999 A/AQ		From 260 UNC
De La Rue Specimen 12 Oct 1999 A/AQ		From 220 UNC

CL 58ar	£20	Replacement						
		12 Oct 1999	E/ZZ 038358	-	085155	70	150	300

As with the £10 note, a £20 note was prepared to commemorate the Millennium, with a special prefix. Apart from a special Year 2000 motif the note is unchanged from the regular issues. Matched serial pairs can be found.

				VF	EF	UNC
CL 58b	**£20**	**Year 2000 Commemorative** Special prefix **John Robertson Wright** Chief Executive				
		1 Jan 2000 MM 000001 - 500000 500,000		25	50	100

CL 58b Year 2000 Commemorative Special prefix

Specimen 1 Jan 2000 MM		From 320 UNC
De La Rue Specimen 1 Jan 2000 MM		From 260 UNC

CL 58c	**£20**	**Grahame Savage** Chief Executive				
		19 Jun 2002 A/BL 450001 - A/BP 3,550,000		-	35	65

CL 58c First Split Prefix

CL 58cr	**£20**	**Replacement**				
		19 Jun 2002 E/ZZ 088173 - 094923		70	150	300

							VF	EF	UNC
CL 58d	£20	**Steve Targett** Chief Executive							
		26 Jan 2003	A/BQ	-	A/BW 450000	6,450,000	-	**35**	**65**

CL 58d   First prefix low serial

CL 58dr	£20	**Replacement**							
		26 Jan 2003	E/ZZ 104181	-	106715		**70**	**150**	**300**

CL 58e	£20	**Ross Pinney** Chief Executive							
		25 Apr 2003	A/BW 450001	-	A/CS 450000	20,000,000	-	**35**	**65**

CL 58e   First Split Prefix low serial (after split)

CL 58er	£20	**Replacement**							
		25 Apr 2003	E/ZZ 110317	-	128261		**70**	**150**	**300**

					VF	EF	UNC
CL 58f	**£20**	**David Thorburn** Chief Operating Officer					
		21 Nov 2004 A/CS 450001 - A/DK 950000 17,500,000			-	30	65

CL 58f First Split Prefix

CL 58fr	**£20**	**Replacement**					
		21 Nov 2004 E/ZZ 131160 - 144962			70	150	300

In 2005 another commemorative note was issued to mark the opening of the Clydesdale Bank Exchange Building in Glasgow. A new reverse was prepared depicting this building. The note is dated the day of the opening ceremony. The obverse was unchanged apart from the modified CB logo. No special prefix was allocated.

CL 59	**£20**	**Robert the Bruce obverse Modified CB logo Commemorative**					
		David Thorburn Chief Operating Officer					
		Clydesdale Bank Exchange Building reverse					
		6 Jun 2005 A/DK 950001 - A/EJ 450000	22,500,000		25	50	100

CL 59 Modified CB logo First Split prefix

CL 59 Reverse

CL 59r £20 Replacement   VF   EF   UNC
              6 Jun 2005   E/ZZ 146012   -   178529   70   150   300

CL 59ar Replacement

A final commemorative £20 note was issued in 2006, to mark the 700th anniversary of the enthronement of Robert the Bruce as King of Scots at Scone Palace on 25th March 1306. A special prefix was again used.

CL 60 £20 **Robert the Bruce 700th Anniversary Commemorative**
              David Thorburn Chief Operating Officer Special prefix
              25 Mar 2006   RB/1   -   RB/2   2,000,000   **25**   **60**   **100**

CL 60 First prefix

CL 60 Reverse

The notes now revert to the 1997 version of the Robert the Bruce design retaining the modified CB logo.

CL 61	£20	**David Thorburn** Chief Operating Officer			VF	EF	UNC
		24 Jun 2006 A/EJ 450001 - A/FH 450000	23,000,000		-	30	60

CL 61 Final prefix, high serial

Specimen 24 Jun 2006 A/EJ   From 260 UNC

					VF	EF	UNC
CL 61r	**£20**	Replacement 24 Jun 2006 E/ZZ 180028 - 200622			70	150	300

The £50 note was redesigned in 1996 when it was reduced in size. The overall design is similar but there are enhanced security features including a windowed thread and more vivid colours. The left hand serial numbers now have rising digit sizes while those on the right are in vertical format. Up to and including prefix A/CB there are 20,000 notes per prefix. Although none has been observed it is possible replacement £50 notes were issued.

CL 62a	**£50**	Green/Multi-Coloured Adam Smith 155 x 85mm **Fred Goodwin** Chief Executive 22 Mar 1996 A/AA - A/CB			1,000,000	70	130	250

CL 62a 1996

CL 62 Reverse

Specimen 22 Mar 1996 A/AA   From 350 UNC

De La Rue Specimen 22 Mar 1996 A/AA   From 320 UNC

CL 62ar	**£50**	Replacement 22 Mar 1996 *none traced to date*

A commemorative pair of £50 and £100 notes was issued to mark the 550th anniversary of the foundation of Glasgow University. An emblem is added to the front of the notes which are otherwise unchanged apart from the special prefix. These are the only Clydesdale notes to carry the signature of Stuart Grimshaw. Some were made available in pairs with matching serials.

				VF	EF	UNC
CL 62b	£50	**Glasgow University Commemorative** Special prefix **Stuart Grimshaw** Chief Executive 6 Jan 2001 GU 000001 - 100000 100,000		80	150	300

CL 62b Glasgow University Commemorative Special prefix

The notes now revert to the 1996 design.

CL 62c	£50	**Ross Pinney** Chief Executive 25 Apr 2003 A/CC 000001 - 500000 500,000	70	120	200

CL 62c First prefix low serial

Specimen 25 Apr 2003 A/CC   From 350 UNC

CL 62cr £50 Replacement
25 Apr 2003 *none traced to date*

CL 62d £50 **David Thorburn** Chief Operating Officer **CB logo added** VF EF UNC
9 Jan 2006 A/CC 500001 - 750000 250,000 **70** **120** **200**

CL 62d CB logo added High serial

CL 62dr £50 Replacement
9 Jan 2006 *none traced to date*

The £100 note was also redesigned in 1996 and given a new reverse featuring the main Glasgow University building using a view reminiscent of that found on the reverse of the 1964 £10 note. A composite essay of the reverse design has been recorded. There are enhanced security features including a windowed thread and more vivid shades of red and purple. 10,000 notes per prefix, as before. The left hand serial numbers now have rising digit sizes while those on the right are in vertical format. Although none has been observed it is possible replacement £100 notes were issued.

CL 63a	**£100**	**Fred Goodwin** Chief Executive				**VF**	**EF**	**UNC**
		2 Oct 1996 A/AA - A/BA 010000			250,000	**140**	**220**	**360**

CL 63a First prefix

CL 63 Reverse

Specimen 2 Oct 1996 A/AA   From 450 UNC

De La Rue Specimen 2 Oct 1996 A/AA   From 400 UNC

CL 63ar   **£100 Replacement**
               2 Oct 1996   *none traced to date*

CL 63b   **£100 Glasgow University Commemorative** Special prefix   **VF EF UNC**
                  Stuart Grimshaw Chief Executive
                  6 Jan 2001   GU 000001 - 050000   50,000   **140 250 400**

CL 63b Glasgow University Commemorative Special prefix

SIGNATORY CHART – FAMOUS SCOTS SERIES

Signatory	Date	£1	£5	£10	£20	£50	£100
Fairbairn	1971	X	X	-	-	-	-
Macmillan	1972 to 1982	X	X	X	X	X	X
Cole Hamilton	1983 to 1992	X	X	X	X	X	X
Love	1993	-	-	X	X	-	-
Cicutto	1994	-	X	-	X	-	-
Goodwin	1996 to 1997	-	X	X	X	X	X
Wright	1998 to 2000	-	-	X	X	-	-
Grimshaw	2001	-	-	-	-	X	X
Savage	2002	-	X	-	X	-	-
Targett	2003	-	-	X	X	-	-
Pinney	2003 to 2004	-	-	X	X	X	-
Thorburn	2004 to 2007	-	-	X	X	X	-

X = Issued
 - = Not issued

NINTH ISSUE – 2009 *to* date

WORLD HERITAGE SITE series

This new series of notes, issued to mark the Scottish Homecoming project in 2009, features a new selection of prominent and innovative Scots on the obverse and Scottish World Heritage sites on the reverse. The notes employ the latest security enhancements such as the 'Depth Image' hologram and have been engraved using computer-aided techniques which have largely replaced traditional human engraving work.

The **£5** note features Sir Alexander Fleming (6th August 1881 – 11th March 1955) on the obverse. Fleming, the son of an Ayrshire farmer, was the Scottish biologist who discovered penicillin in 1928. The reverse features St Kilda, the island group off the Outer Hebrides which had been populated for over 5,000 years and was home to a small Gaelic-speaking community until 1930 when it was evacuated. It is world famous also for its seabird colonies.

The **£10** note features Robert Burns (25th January 1759 – 21st July 1796), the Scottish national poet whose face has been on Clydesdale notes since 1971. The reverse features the Old and New Towns of Edinburgh.

The **£20** note features Robert the Bruce (11th July 1274 – 7th June 1329), the King of the Scots during the Scottish independence wars against the English. He too has featured on Clydesdale notes since 1971. The reverse depicts New Lanark, the 18th century model industrial community developed by the philanthropist Robert Owen, with not a little support from his father-in-law David Dale who happened to be the Royal Bank of Scotland's highly successful Glasgow agent.

The **£50** note features Elsie Inglis (16th August 1864 – 26th November 1916), a Scottish doctor and suffragette who devoted her life to women's care and founded the Scottish Women's Hospitals network. The reverse depicts the Antonine Wall, constructed by the Romans in 142AD as the northernmost bulwark of the Roman Empire in Britain.

The **£100** note features Charles Rennie Mackintosh (7th June 1868 – 10th December 1928), the world-renowned Scottish architect and designer. The reverse features the Heart of Neolithic Orkney, one of the most extensive groups of Neolithic monuments in the world.

The dates on each note reflect the birthday of the individual featured. Initial prefixes reflect the World Heritage Site theme but progress rapidly through the alphabet. 1,000,000 notes per prefix on all denominations. Prefix letters I and O not used. Replacement serial numbers run on from the previous series in the case of the £5, £10 and £20 notes while those for the £50 and £100 notes may be the first for these denominations. Many notes with low and 'special' numbers were sold in a charity auction when the series was first launched. One uncut sheet of specimen notes of each denomination was also auctioned off, the sheets comprising 45 £5 notes, 40 £10 notes, 40 £20 notes, 35 £50 notes and 35 £100 notes. The notes each carried the prefix/serials W/HS 000000 and most have been cut up for individual sale. They differ from regular specimens by lacking the diagonal SPECIMEN stamp.

In a few cases replacement note serial numbers of adjacent dates overlap and this may reflect changes in De La Rue production processes. Also, two replacement notes with identical serial numbers have been recorded on different dates. This is believed to be an error rather than an indication that overlapping or duplicate runs of serial numbers were printed.

					EF	UNC
CL 64a	£5	**Sir Alexander Fleming St Kilda reverse**				
		David Thorburn Chief Operating Officer				
		6 Aug 2009 W/HS - W/JG		15,000,000	6	15

CL 64a First prefix serial 7

CL 64 Reverse

Specimen 6 Aug 2009 W/HS   From 120 UNC

CL 64ar	£5	**Replacement**		
		6 Aug 2009 E/ZZ 076309 - 107135	12	30

CL 64ar Replacement

CL 65a	**£10**	**Robert Burns Edinburgh Old & New Towns reverse**		**EF**	**UNC**
		David Thorburn Chief Operating Officer			
		25 Jan 2009 W/HS - W/KN 45,000,000		12	25

CL 65a First prefix serial 7

CL 65 Reverse

Specimen 25 Jan 2009 W/HS W/JC		From 120 UNC

CL 65ar	**£10**	**Replacement**			
		25 Jan 2009 E/ZZ 206059 - 259134		30	50

CL 65ar Replacement

CL 65b	£10	**David Thorburn** Chief Executive			EF	UNC
		25 Jan 2013	W/KP - W/LB 500000	12,500,000		
		25 Jan 2014	W/LB 500001 - W/LS 500000	15,000,000	12	22

CL 65b 2013 First prefix low serial

CL 65b 2014 First Split Prefix

CL 65br	£10	Replacement					
		25 Jan 2013	E/ZZ 261269	-	310875	overlap with 2014	
		25 Jan 2014	E/ZZ 284213	-	314750	overlap with polymer	30	50

					EF	UNC
CL 66a	£20	**Robert the Bruce New Lanark reverse**				
		David Thorburn Chief Operating Officer				
		11 Jul 2009 W/HS - W/KN		45,000,000	25	50

CL 66a First prefix serial 7

Specimen 11 Jul 2009 W/HS   From 130 UNC

CL 66ar	£20	**Replacement**			35	80
		11 Jul 2009 E/ZZ 202018 - 346935				

CL 66ar Replacement

CL 66 Reverse

The final 2014 print run of the £20 note was cut short apparently due to paper supply difficulties at De La Rue.

						EF	UNC
CL 66b	£20	**David Thorburn** Chief Executive					
		11 Jul 2013	W/KP - W/LU		30,000,000		
		11 Jul 2014	W/LV - W/MK 850000		14,850,000	25	40

CL 66b First prefix low serial

CL 66br	£20	Replacement					
		11 Jul 2013	E/ZZ 348080	-	394175		
		11 Jul 2014	E/ZZ 409077	-	554222	35	70

When Deborah Crosbie's printed signature appeared on the 2015 £20 note the Clydesdale stated that these were the first ever Scottish banknotes to be signed by a woman. This was not quite true as some National Bank of Scotland notes had been hand signed by female 'clerkesses' during the First World War.

CL 66c	£20	**Deborah Crosbie** Chief Operating Officer					
		11 Jul 2015	W/ML - W/NR		30,000,000	25	35
			continuing				

CL 66cr	£20	Replacement					
		11 Jul 2015	E/ZZ 560197	-	576958	25	50

CL 66c Deborah Crosbie signature

					EF	UNC
CL 67a	£50	Elsie Inglis Antonine Wall reverse **David Thorburn** Chief Operating Officer 16 Aug 2009 W/HS - W/HT		2,000,000	60	110

CL 67a First prefix serial 7

	Specimen 16 Aug 2009 W/HS		From 160 UNC

CL 67ar	£50	Replacement 16 Aug 2009 E/ZZ 000232 - 014294		70	150

CL 67ar Replacement

CL 67b	£50	**David J Duffy** Chief Executive Officer 16 Aug 2015 W/HU to 500000	500,000	60	95

CL 67b First prefix low serial

CL 67br	£50	Replacement			EF	UNC
		16 Aug 2015	E/ZZ 016322 - 018852		70	150

CL 67br Replacement

CL 67 Reverse

						EF	UNC
CL 68	£100	Charles Rennie Mackintosh Heart of Neolithic Orkney reverse					
		David Thorburn Chief Operating Officer					
		7 Jun 2009	W/HS to 200000		200,000	130	250

CL 68 First prefix serial 7

CL 68 Reverse

Specimen 7 Jun 2009 W/HS   From 180 UNC

CL 68r	£100	**Replacement**					
		7 Jun 2009	E/ZZ 000309	-	003509	140	320

CL 68r Replacement

POLYMER ISSUE – 2015 *to* date

Reduced Size

A new era began on 23rd March 2015 when the Clydesdale became the first Scottish bank to issue a polymer note. Their new £5 note was also the first polymer note in Great Britain, though not in the UK as a whole (Belfast's Northern Bank issued one in 1999), nor in the British Isles (a polymer £1 note was issued in the Isle of Man in 1983 using Bradvek, a variant of Tyvek). The notes were manufactured by De La Rue using their Safeguard ® substrate.

The new £5 note features Sir William Arrol (13th February 1839 – 20th February 1913), a leading Scottish engineering entrepreneur responsible for designing and building not only the Forth Bridge but also London's Tower Bridge and many other famous structures. The caption on the reverse reads 'UNESCO World Heritage Site nomination'. A notable security feature of the new note is the clear window made possible by the polymer substrate. This issue should be regarded as a commemorative as it was a limited edition of 2,000,000 notes with a special prefix, although nearly all the notes went into general circulation.

CL 69	£5	Blue David Thorburn Chief Executive 125 x 65mm		EF	UNC
		13 Feb 2015 FB/1 - FB/2	2,000,000	6	15

Specimen 13 Feb 2015 FB/1   From 200 UNC

CL 69 First prefix serial 7

CL 69 Reverse

CL 70 Reverse with revised text

CL 69r	£5	Replacement				EF	UNC
		13 Feb 2015 ZZ/1 000007 - 030765				20	55

CL 69r Replacement

On 8th July 2015 the bank celebrated confirmation of the Forth Bridge's new UNESCO World Heritage List status by announcing plans to begin full production of its new polymer £5 notes. The new notes were first issued on 27th September 2016 and were unchanged apart from a new signatory and revisions to the captions on the front and reverse confirming the Bridge's new status. The first prefix reverts to W/HS. Replacement note serials appear to run on from the commemorative polymer issue.

CL 70a	£5	**Blue David J Duffy** Chief Executive Officer					
		13 Feb 2016 W/HS - W/JG			15,000,000	6	12
		continuing					

CL 70 First prefix low serial

CL 70ar	£5	Replacement					
		13 Feb 2016 ZZ/1 033001 - 110861				15	45

CL 70r Replacement

£10 notes featuring a portrait of Robert Burns on the front and views of Edinburgh and its castle on the reverse were issued in September 2017. Polymer £20 notes are expected to be issued by 2020. No decision has been taken on issuing polymer £50 and £100 notes but it is not thought likely to happen unless the Bank of England decides to proceed with a polymer £50 note. One uncut sheet of 45 polymer £10 notes was sold in a charity auction. The sheet comprised 5 notes each of the 9 prefixes from W/HS to W/JA. None had the usual SPECIMEN overprint and all notes had 000000 serials.

						EF	UNC
CL 71a	**£10**	**Brown/Orange Robert Burns** 132 x 69mm					
		David J Duffy Chief Executive Officer					
		25 Jul 2017 W/HS - W/KN			45,000,000	12	16
		continuing					

CL 71a First prefix

CL 71a Reverse

CL 71ar	**£10**	**Replacement** overlaps with final paper £10 CL 65br					
		25 Jul 2017 E/ZZ 293250 - 476471				14	35

CL 71ar Replacement

INDEX

Issuer	Catalogue Abbreviation	page
Abbey Bank of Industry	PR	1083
Aberdeen, Banking Company **in** (see Banking Company **in** Aberdeen)	BC	407
Aberdeen, Banking Company **of** (see Banking Company **of** Aberdeen)	AB	976
Aberdeen Banking Company (1) (see Banking Company **of** Aberdeen)	AB	976
Aberdeen Banking Company (2) (see Banking Company **in** Aberdeen)	BC	407
Aberdeen Commercial Banking Company	AC	958
Aberdeen, Company of the Bank of (see Company of the Bank of Aberdeen)	PR	1096
Aberdeen Exchange & Deposit Bank (see Stephen Maberly & Company)	PR	1114
Aberdeen, Montrose, Dundee, Edinburgh & Glasgow Exchange & Deposit Banks (see John Maberly & Company)	PR	1111
Aberdeen Town & County Bank (see Town & County Bank)	TC	655
Air (Ayr) Bank (see Douglas Heron & Company)	DH	1001
William Alexander of Menstrie	PR	1084
Alloa Glass Works Company	PR	1085
Arbroath Banking Company	AR	959
Ayrshire Banking Company	AY	978
David Bain, Glasgow	PR	1085
Balgonie Iron Works	PR	1086
Ballindalloch Works	PR	1087
Bank of Dundreary	PR	1088
Bank of Economy	PR	1088
Bank of Elegance	PR	1089
Bank of Mona (see City of Glasgow Bank)	BM	998
Bank of Poyais	PR	1090
Bank of Scotland	**BA**	**38**
Banking Company **in** Aberdeen	BC	407
Banking Company **of** Aberdeen	AB	976
Bannockburn (see Gibson, Balfour & Aitken)	GI	1023
Batson, Berry, Bailey & Langhorn (see Tweed Bank)	TW	1071
Batson, Berry, Langhorn & Wilson (see Tweed Bank)	TW	1071
Batson, Berry & Langhorn (see Tweed Bank)	TW	1071
Batson, Reed & Company (see Northumberland Bank)	NO	1056
John Belch & Company	JB	980
Berwick Bank (1): Surtees, Burdon & Company	BS	980
Berwick Bank (2): Mowbray, Hollingworth & Company	BB	983
Berwick & Kelso Bank: Mowbray, Hollingworth & Company	BK	984
British Linen Bank	**BL**	**235**
John Bruce (see Perth United Company)	PE	455
Caithness Banking Company	CN	962
Caledonian Bank	**CA**	**322**
Campbell Richmond & Company	PR	1090
Campbell Thomson & Company	CT	985
Cargill MacDuff & Company	PR	1091
Carrick, Brown & Company (see Ship Bank)	SH	457
Carron Company	PR	1091
Catrine Works	PR	1093
Central Bank of Scotland	CE	414
Chapel Hill Bank	PR	1093
City Banking Company of Glasgow	CB	985
City of Glasgow Bank	CG	987

Issuer	Catalogue Abbreviation	page
Clackmannan Colliery	PR	1094
Clydesdale Bank (*including* Clydesdale & North of Scotland Bank 506)	**CL**	**467**
Cochrane, Murdoch & Company (*see* Glasgow Arms Bank)	GA	1024
Commercial Bank of New Mill Moor	PR	1095
Commercial Bank of Scotland	**CO**	**826**
Company of the Bank of Aberdeen	PR	1096
Company of Scotland trading to Africa and the Indies (*see* Darien Company)	PR	1099
Craig & Simpson	PR	1096
Craigie Banking Company (John Ramsay & Company) (*see* Perth United Company)	PE	455
John, James & George Lindsay Craufurd	PR	1098
John Craw & Company	PR	1099
Cupar Banking Company	CU	1001
Darien Company	PR	1099
Deanston Cotton Mill	PR	1100
George Dempster & Company (*see* Dundee Banking Company)	DB	963
Dennistoun, Nicholson Inglis & Company (*see* Glasgow Bank Company)	GB	428
Douglas Heron & Company	DH	1001
Sir William Douglas, John Napier & Company (*see* Galloway Banking Company)	GL	1020
Dumfries (*see* William Duncan)	PR	1101
Dumfries Bank (Alexander Johnston, Hugh Lawson & Company)	DM	1003
Dumfries Banking Company	DS	1003
Dumfries Commercial Bank	DF	1004
Dunbar (*see* Middlesmass, Hay & Company)	MH	1051
William Duncan (*see* Dumfries)	PR	1101
Dundee Banking Company	DB	963
Dundee Commercial Bank (1)	DD	1007
Dundee Commercial Bank (2)	DC	672
Dundee New Bank	DN	973
Dundee Union Bank	DU	1008
Dunlop, Houston & Company (*see* Ship Bank)	SH	457
Dunlop, Houston, Gammell & Company (*see* Greenock Bank Company)	GN	1028
East Lothian Banking Company	EA	1011
Eastern Bank of Scotland	EB	675
Edinburgh & Glasgow Bank	EG	681
Edinburgh & Leith Bank	EL	684
Ekopia Resource Exchange, Findhorn	PR	1101
Falkirk	PR	1105
Falkirk Banking Company	FB	1014
Falkirk Union Banking Company	FU	1015
Farming Banking Company at Kincardine	FA	1017
Fife Banking Company	FI	1018
Alexander Fleming & Company	PR	1106
Sir William Forbes, James Hunter & Company	FH	419
Galloway Banking Company	GL	1020
Gartmore Banking Company	GM	1022
Gibson, Balfour, Aitken & Company	GI	1023
Glasgow Arms Bank	GA	1024
Glasgow Bank Company	GB	428
Glasgow Banking Company (Glasgow Bank / Bank of Glasgow)	GC	1027
Glasgow City Bank (*see* City Banking Company of Glasgow)	CB	985
Glasgow Joint Stock Banking Company	GJ	687

Issuer	Catalogue Abbreviation	page
Glasgow Merchant Bank (see Merchant Banking Company of Glasgow)	MB	1050
Glasgow & Ship Bank Company	GS	431
Glasgow Union Bank	PR	1106
Glasgow Union Banking Company	GU	432
James Gracie & Company (see Dumfries Commercial Bank)	DF	1004
Greenock Bank Company	GN	1028
Greenock Commercial Banking Company	GK	1033
Greenock Union Bank	GR	688
Hawick Pound	PR	1107
Hay & Ogilvie (see Shetland Bank)	SL	1064
Alexander Humphrys (see William Alexander of Menstrie)	PR	1084
Hunters & Company	HU	434
Inglis Borthwick Gilchrist & Company	IB	1034
James Inglis & Company (see Inglis Borthwick Gilchrist & Company)	IB	1034
Alexander Johnston, Hugh Lawson & Company (see Dumfries Bank)	DM	1003
George Keller & Company	PR	1108
Kilmarnock Banking Company	KB	437
Kirkliston (see Alexander Fleming & Company)	PR	1106
William Kirkwood & Company	PR	1109
Leith Banking Company	LB	1035
Lipton's	PR	1110
John Maberly & Company	PR	1111
Stephen Maberly	PR	1114
J Stewart Mackenzie (Stornaway)	PR	1114
Malachi Malagrowther	PR	1115
Mansfield, Bonars & Company (see Ramsays Bonars & Company)	RA	1059
Mansfield, Hunter & Company (see Ramsays Bonars & Company)	RA	1059
Mansfield, Ramsay & Company (see Ramsays Bonars & Company)	RA	1059
Mason Barrowman Company	PR	1117
Maxwell, Ritchie & Company (see Thistle Bank)	TH	463
John McAdam & Company	JM	1049
McKeith Rintoul & Co (see Perth United Company)	PE	455
Menstrie, William Alexander of (see William Alexander of Menstrie)	PR	1084
Merchant Banking Company of Glasgow	MB	1050
Metropolitan Bank of Scotland	ME	1051
Daniel M'Funn, Duncan Buchanan & Company	PR	1116
Middlemass, Hay & Company	MH	1051
Montrose	PR	1118
Montrose Banking Company	MO	1052
Moores, Carrick & Company (see Ship Bank)	SH	457
Morris & Company	PR	1118
Morris, Kirkwood, Bland & Company	PR	1119
Mowbray, Hollingworth & Company (see Berwick Bank [2])	BB	983
Mowbray, Hollingworth & Company (see Berwick & Kelso Bank)	BK	984
Murdoch, Robertson & Company (see Glasgow Arms Bank)	GA	1024
Mutual Exchange Deposit, Discount & Loan Company	PR	1119
Sir William Napier & Company (see Renfrewshire Banking Company)	RE	1061
National Bank of Scotland	**NA**	**899**
National Commercial Bank of Scotland	**NC**	**949**
New Lanark Mills	PR	1120
Newcastle Exchange Bank (see Berwick Bank [1])	BS	980

Issuer	Catalogue Abbreviation	page
North British Bank	NB	1055
North of Scotland Bank (*including* North of Scotland & Town & County Bank 623)	**NS**	**601**
Northumberland Bank	NO	1056
Paisley Banking Company	PA	439
Paisley Commercial Banking Company	PC	1057
Paisley Union Banking Company	PU	443
Perth Banking Company	PB	446
Perth Banking Company (John Stewart & Company) (*see* Perth United Company)	PE	446
Perth General Bank	PG	1058
Perth Union Bank	PH	975
Perth United Banking Company	PE	455
Perth United Company	PE	455
Prisoners of War Camps (*see* War Department)	PR	1127
John Ramsay & Company (Craigie Banking Company) (*see* Perth United Company)	PE	455
Ramsays, Bonars & Company	RA	1059
Renfrewshire Banking Company	RE	1061
John Richmond & Sons, Glasgow	PR	1120
Douglas Robertson & Company	PR	1121
R Robertson Junior & Company	PR	1122
Royal Bank of Fashion, Dundee	PR	1123
Royal Bank of Scotland	**RB**	**691**
Scottish Banking Company	PR	1123
Shadforth, Batson & Company (*see* Northumberland Bank)	NO	1056
Shetland Bank	SL	1064
Ship Bank	SH	457
Shortbridge, Scot & Company	PR	1125
James Smiton	PR	1125
Southern Bank of Scotland	SO	689
Speirs, Murdoch & Company (*see* Glasgow Arms Bank)	GA	1024
Stewart Buchanan & Company (Tannerie Banking Company) (*see* Perth United Company)	PE	455
John Stewart & Company (Perth Banking Company) (*see* Perth United Company)	PE	455
Stirling Banking Company	ST	1065
Stirling Merchant Banking Company	SM	1067
Stirlingshire Banking Company	SB	1069
Stornaway (*see* J Stewart Mackenzie)	PR	1114
Prince Charles Edward Stuart	PR	1126
Surtees, Burdon & Company (*see* Berwick Bank [1])	BS	980
Tannerie Banking Company (Stewart Buchanan & Company) (*see* Perth United Company)	PE	455
Thistle Bank	TH	463
Andrew, George & Andrew Thomson	AT	1070
Town & County Bank	**TC**	**655**
Tweed Bank	TW	1071
Union Bank Company (*see* Paisley Union Banking Company)	PU	443
Union Bank of Scotland	**UB**	**339**
War Department / Prisoners of War Camps	PR	1127
Wedderspoon & Company (*see* Perth United Company)	PE	455
Western Bank of Scotland	WE	1075
Andrew Whitecock, Duncan Dick & Company	PR	1129

Non-Issuers (pre 1844 only)   **1079**

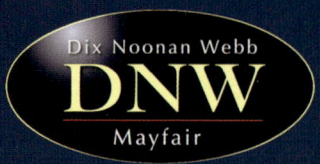

The Collectors' Auctioneer

Specialists in the sale by auction
of all types of coins, tokens, historical and art medals,
numismatic books and paper money,
orders, decorations, war medals, militaria and Jewellery
Dix Noonan Webb regularly sell Scottish Banknotes by auction
For more information, please contact Chris Webb

16 Bolton Street   Mayfair   London   England   W1J 8BQ
Telephone 020 7016 1700   Email auctions@dnw.co.uk

www.dnw.co.uk

SPINK

LONDON
1666

THE NO. 1 CHOICE
FOR BANKNOTE COLLECTORS

SALES IN APRIL, JULY, OCTOBER & DECEMBER

For more information please contact Barnaby Faull:
Tel: + 44 020 7563 4031 | Fax: +44 020 7563 4066 | Email: bfaull@spink.com
SPINK LONDON | 69 Southampton Row | Bloomsbury | London | WC1B 4ET

#SPINK_AUCTIONS | WWW.SPINK.COM

Colin Narbeth & Son Ltd.

Banknote Specialists
20 Cecil Court, London WC2N 4HE

Monday - Saturday
10.30am - 5.30pm
Tel: +44 (0)207 379 6975
narbeth@btconnect.com
Paper money bought & sold.
Buy online or visit our London shop.

colin-narbeth.com

WWW.SCOTMINT.COM

Scotland's Leading Scottish Banknote Dealers

Buying & Selling all types of Scottish Banknotes.

Retail shop: 68 Sandgate, Ayr Scotland KA7 1BX
Tel: 01292 268244   Email: rob@scotmint.com

Coincraft

Helping Collectors For Over 60 Years

'Nice People to do Business with'
WE NEED TO BUY
GIVE US A TRY - YOU'LL LIKE OUR OFFER

Visit our shop opposite the British Museum
45 Great Russell Street, London WC1B 3JL

Open weekdays: 9.30am – 5pm, Saturdays by appointment

Check out our website for a vast range of British and ancient coins, British and world banknotes, medals, antiquities and numismatic books, special offers and much more

www.coincraft.com

Contact us for a complimentary copy of our monthly newspaper/catalogue: *The Phoenix*

Tel: 020 7636 1188
Fax: 020 7323 2860
Email: info@coincraft.com

Follow us at: